The Story of
EDUCATION

The Story of

EDUCATION

CARROLL ATKINSON
and
EUGENE T. MALESKA

CHILTON COMPANY · BOOK DIVISION
Publishers
PHILADELPHIA AND NEW YORK

Dedicated
to Two Educational Leaders

W. BARNIE CATON

Superintendent of Schools
Gallup, New Mexico

and

HEROLD C. HUNT

Charles William Eliot Professor of Education
Harvard University

Preface

This is admittedly an ambitious book. Primarily it attempts to relate the major events and forces that have affected American education since colonial days. But it goes farther than that. Reaching as far back as primitive times, it traces the course of man's endeavors to enlighten each new generation in various types of societies and states.

The reader is asked to think of modern American education as a great river fed by many streams. The training of youth in bygone Oriental periods is one of those streams. Ancient Hebrew culture is another. The golden ages of the Greeks and the Romans, the dark medieval period, the shining Renaissance—all these, and others, have poured down through the centuries to swell the tide and broaden the banks. True, the currents have criss-crossed at times, and the waters from one source have merged inextricably with those of another. But, in the final analysis, education today is a product of the many springs and rivulets that flowed in other epochs. This book seeks to explore those sources and to follow their progress into the mainstream.

But it would be naive and erroneous to assume that education has been funneled into one channel today. Schools in the various European countries have moved in their own directions, each reflecting the cultural patterns of the respective nations. For contrast and comparison, a brief description of the present status and progress of education in a few of these lands is presented in a single chapter.

Psychology, too, is given a special place in this book. Although the ancient Greeks studied man's *psyche,* many centuries elapsed before the subject really broke through the dikes of education. The trickle that flowed in during the seventeenth century has now grown to the size of a deluge. Esteem for psychology has recently affected schools all over the world, but especially those in the United States. Therefore, the subject is treated separately in Part Five. Detailed attention is given to facets of educational psychology involving the stages of children's growth.

Since the core of all education is the work of the individual teacher, a section of the book is devoted to the teaching profession. Emphasis is placed on the preparation, the problems, the intrinsic rewards, the salaries, and the responsibilities of American teachers. In brief, it is hoped that the facts related in this area will serve as a guide for students considering the profession and will help other Americans to evaluate the job teachers do and the obstacles they face.

But even the best teachers cannot function properly without sound leadership. Most critics claim that this is the area in which our schools are most desperately in need of improvement. They cite boards of education that are politically oriented, ignorant of the needs of children, or openly hostile to public schools. They disparage the selection and preparation not only of board members but also of school principals and superintendents. From the local level all the way to the federal government, they maintain, education suffers from a lack of direction.

There is some truth in the above accusations; but much progress has been made in educational leadership, especially in the twentieth century. To acquaint the reader with many aspects of this important topic, a special chapter in the book delves into the history and problems of the administration of schools in the United States. Under this general heading several different topics are considered, ranging from the necessity for responsible leadership in the erection and use of the school plant all the way to the field of public relations. Parents and teachers should be particularly interested in the discussion of guidance and discipline as part of the process of leadership.

The heart of the book lies in Part Two—Evolution of Education in America. Here the reader will find various approaches to the subject. One is the chronological pattern, starting with colonial America and proceeding to current times. Another is a description of the separate rungs on the "educational ladder" that has developed in the United States, from elementary school through college. An analysis of pre-school education, as well as adult education, is included. Moreover, such controversial matters as the place of religion, morality, and academic freedom in American public schools are discussed so that the reader may be better equipped to assess the pros and cons. In these instances, as in all other cases throughout the book, the authors have tried assiduously to avoid partiality.

This effort to give fair treatment to both sides of a problem is followed through in the last chapter which deals with the delicate and timely topic of "Current Trends and Issues." Here the authors have selected the innovations and problems that are being thrashed out in educational journals or are hitting the headlines of newspapers. The list extends from the debate on teaching machines and educational television to the questions of integration of schools and federal aid to education.

Naturally, in the writing of so comprehensive a book, certain dilemmas were encountered. In describing the accomplishments of those people who have had a great effect, directly or indirectly, on the path of education, the authors were forced to select those that they considered most pertinent to the story they had to tell. No claim to infallibility in these choices is made. Here and there a reader will search in vain for a discussion of an educator whom he considers to be important. However, it is believed that, for the specific purpose of this book, the contributions of most of the influential leaders have been covered adequately.

Another problem that emerged for the authors was repetition. The very plan of this project caused certain educational leaders, movements, and procedures to appear under various headings. But no apology is offered for this feature of the book. In fact, it is felt that the presentation of similar facts in different settings will enhance and intensify the reader's concepts. In this connection, cross-references have been supplied in many instances as a guide for those who wish to make comparisons.

This leads to the question of what types of readers the authors had in mind when writing the book. *The Story of Education* is chiefly intended for interested laymen and for students who are preparing to be teachers. Among those who may derive information and pleasure from these pages are parents, members of boards of education, school administrators, teachers, librarians, counselors, attendance officers, psychologists, and other citizens who wish to know the status and history of education—especially in the United States. Therefore, an attempt has been made to avoid the approach of the professor lecturing from his chair in perfect "pedagese." Although much research and care have gone into the gathering of the facts herein, the aim in the presentation is to be more appealing than appalling. What follows is not a documented thesis but a new unraveling of the tale of man's adventures in the acquisition of knowledge and culture.

The authors conceive of several ways in which the readers will use this book. The great majority, it is hoped, will want to peruse it sequentially from beginning to end with or without professional guidance. Others may prefer to browse through, choosing only those areas in which their greatest interests lie. A third group may wish to have the book in their personal libraries as a ready reference when questions on education arise.

Whatever the motives of the reader, the authors send this book forth with the profound hope that it will shed some light on one of the most important aspects of civilization—the education of our youth. The past is not the "bucket of ashes" that Carl Sandburg called it in an ironic poem. It is a living flame that lights up the present and the future. Given the chance to see his past mistakes, man can make intelligent decisions today.

This is indeed a time for decision in education; just as there were many other moments in history when schools might have taken one direction or another. At the present writing, Americans are confronted with a complex set of dilemmas. The launching of Sputnik I triggered critical salvos aimed at the schools in our country. Progressive education, it was claimed, had gone too far in "sugar-coating the pill" for children. There was a need for a return to old-fashioned discipline and methods. The schools, these observers said, were extending themselves beyond their proper sphere. Let the home take care of the social and emotional growth of the child—let the schools concentrate on imparting knowledge. The attempt to consider the "whole child" had resulted in the dissipation of teachers' energies. Let the teachers teach. Period.

So went the claims of outraged citizens when the combination of Russian achievements and a rise in juvenile delinquency in America shocked the nation into a re-appraisal of education. The criticisms were not new. They had been voiced for many years by enemies of public education, by elder statesmen who looked with nostalgia on the "old school," and, most important, by some well-intentioned and well-informed laymen and educators who felt that the schools had recently gone up the wrong road in America.

Meanwhile, others have stood firm in favor of the "experiential program" and, while deploring the excesses of some Progressives, have pointed out that the fault lies not so much in the curriculum or the methods as in the fact that Americans have not given education the support it deserves. Today these defenders of the modern schools observe that our expenditures for the prevention of crime exceed by several billion dollars the outlay for schools. They cite Americans' large whiskey and cigarette bills in contrast to the taxes paid for education. They note the low salaries of teachers, the paucity of schoolrooms in relation to the rising pupil population, and the density or hostility of some school board members. Their argument is: "Don't blame the schools. We have the answers; but we must be given the personnel, the tools, and the support in order to do a good job. To return whole-hog now to traditional education would be a grave mistake."

The above problem, as has been noted, is only a part of a network of dilemmas facing American citizens today. And let it be understood that it is the people, not the educators, who will make the decisions. On the whole, schools reflect the society in which they exist. Whether this situation is good or bad is debatable. But it is a fact, especially in a democracy, that educators must, in the end, follow the dictates of the parents and other taxpayers.

Therefore, the essential purpose of this book is to give citizens a sound basis for the important decisions that they will be making in the next few years. The course that American education takes in the future should be guided not by reckless trial and error, not by emotionalism, and not by the persuasive arguments of a few proponents or critics of modern schools. It should stem from the sober judgment of the people who have looked at all the facts. These facts, it must be reiterated, are found in more than a mere survey of present conditions. The panorama of the past must be observed in order to gain the proper perspective. Janus-eyed, we must look backward as well as forward to new frontiers.

CARROLL ATKINSON
EUGENE T. MALESKA

Contents

The Story of
EDUCATION

PART ONE

History

History

History is the account of past facts affecting one or more nations or peoples. The occurrences are arranged in due order, usually with comments and explanations. When teacher-training programs began in the United States about 1820, the first professional study ever offered was a history of education course. The intent was to give neophytes a perspective on the profession they were about to enter, as well as an understanding of its problems throughout the previous centuries. It still is a vitally essential teacher-training course in the colleges of today.

Philosophy (literally "love of knowledge") is the study of principles that cause, control, or explain facts and events. It is a system of general beliefs or views regarding God, existence, and similarly serious subjects. Philosophies are men's attempts to reason things out while religions represent their emotional responses to power and wisdom greater than their own.

History, philosophy, and education have been closely related through the ages. Quite early in his development the human being began to inquire into the truth, and to teach what he had found. The Old Testament contains the traditions, customs, history, religion, laws, health rules, short stories, poetry, and basic philosophy of the ancient Hebrews. So it has been with all peoples; eventually a philosophy evolves from their experiences that thereafter serves as a guide for future actions, thus shaping the history of the future. In the following presentations we shall see how the fields of history, philosophy, and education are interwoven.

Primitive Education

Prehistoric man's first problems as he wandered over the earth chiefly centered on food, clothing, shelter, and safety. Rarely did there appear those personal and economic maladjustments so familiar in modern-day society. To be sure, individual differences in strength, skill, or luck resulted in relative degrees of success in the providing of essentials for daily living. But once a savage had made for himself hunting, fishing, and farming equipment he was virtually on a par with his neighbors. The forest, soil, and sea were free to him for use to the limit of his capacity. Since he was his own master, producing goods for consumption rather than for sale, he did not need to fear the vicissitudes of unemployment. Only his own lack of ability or ambition could prevent his gaining as good a living as anyone else in the group.

This does not mean that primitive man in all respects was economically secure. If he escaped the disabling effects of accidents and diseases, he inevitably had to face the lowered efficiency of old age. To sustain life then as now food was necessary. The perishable nature of nourishing items prevented their accumulation during that period of life when working efficiency is greatest, no matter how much thrift was practiced.

It is no wonder that the elders in primitive societies tried to keep a firm hand on youth because, where no provision had been made for the care and respect of the aged, their acute suffering was inevitable. Doubtless in all stages of civilization a definite, though invariably camouflaged, purpose of education has been to hold youth sufficiently under control as the most effective means of protecting the declining years of those now strong and healthy but soon to pass out of the prime of life. Thus education from its very beginning has been a defense against the self-centered aggressiveness of youth. For that reason alone it may be surmised that conservatism will always be the favorite philosophy of senior citizens.

In the dawn of mankind this conservatism was buttressed by fear of the unknown. To primitive peoples, religion and education were inextricable. Youths were taught that all objects were animate. Trees, rivers, rocks, and other objects of nature were spirits possessing human-like characteristics. They could be angry or pleased; they had the power to destroy or help man, or to ignore him completely. This belief is called animism, the earliest known form of religion. In our twentieth-century world there still remain out-of-the-way spots where life is just as pristine. In such a society the present is always important, the future neither understood nor anticipated. Today scientists can study educational processes similar to those of our earliest ancestors by seeking out jungle people who, because of their environment, still maintain a primitive way of living.

The conduct of primitives, ancient or modern, has always been controlled by fixed folkways. Within a single tribe these remain relatively stable over long periods of time although a wide variety of practices may appear in different parts of the world. However, customs do change when tribes come into contact with each other and exchange ideas, or when living conditions reach a point where survival makes change inevitable. Notwithstanding, the intent of primitive education has ever been to transmit the folkways intact and unchanged. To do this, explicit rules cover the important though simple lifetime activities: duties of children toward parents, respect for elders and leaders, sexual relationships, attitudes toward property, division of spoils from the hunt, rules of the game in warfare, taboos, accepted interpretations of natural phenomena, and religious rites and ceremonies.

Primitive man eventually developed new arts, discovered and elaborated new bodies of knowledge, and invented stories, songs, implements and institutions. But his educational activities were directed to the transmission of knowledge and skills and to the testing and control of the learner rather than to the development of creativity. No serious thought was given to the passing on of cultural traditions for the purpose of improving society. The assumption was that the social order is the work of the gods and therefore not to be tampered with.

Any organized attempt to alter the beliefs received from previous generations was considered an act of impiety. The thought was that prosperity and security must depend upon retention of the existing social order, and those who dared to challenge the *status quo* were dealt with summarily. Practical problems were to get a living; to provide protection from the forces of nature, real or imagined; and from enemies, animal or human. Thus, security had to be the basic aim of primitive education.

To insure security, there must be conformity, the second basic aim of primitive education. That was the real purpose of tribal taboos, ceremonies, and customs imposed by the elders upon the younger generation. History shows that in any society where changes are frequent and unpredictable, there invariably exists a sense of insecurity. Consequently, leadership on the subsistence level has habitually been harsh in order to restrain the natural impulse of youth to strike out in new and strange directions that may possibly lead to chaos and cataclysm.

Primitive education was considered completed when the individual finally reached the group standard. The training itself included ways and means of satisfying basic physical needs. Hunting, fishing, and fighting were the educational pursuits of the boys. Girls were taught to cook, make clothes, care for children, and perform similar domestic tasks.

A ceremonial marked the passage of youth into adulthood—quite often the young females were merely distributed among the men as wives. This initiation occurred at about the period of adolescence and signified the beginning of adult responsibilites. The ceremonial itself might take several days or even weeks. Regardless of the time spent the youth was made to see the entire experience as an introduction into adult rights and obligations.

In primitive societies the education of children within the family was of relatively low order. Children often did not enjoy the dignity of being regarded as persons; frequently they were treated as chattels to be given away or even killed whenever the father so decided. Since the mother was often treated as just another piece of property, her stature as a teacher in the home was quite unimpressive. It is true that the family did serve to familiarize the children with the mores of the tribe; but organized education did not begin until puberty when the boys were taken from the home and made into men through the educational experiences of the ceremonial initiation.

At first the family imparted some aspects of practical and religious education, but a by-product of any advancing civilization is specialization. So, with the beginning of community life, there developed a greater organization in living. It was the religious ceremonies that led to the earliest type of formal education because myths, chants, and dances that had to be learned by young and old alike required group activity rather than individual instruction. Thus the first of all professional teachers was the priest or similar tribal official, such as a medicine man or witch doctor. It was his responsibility to attend to spiritual needs. As an educational figure he was important in the developing of weird rituals, ceremonials, dances, and other bewildering forms of worship so typical of primitive tribes. His specialized job was to keep the spirits contented, especially the evil and temperamental ones.

Freudian psychoanalysis holds that the concept of dualism of body and spirit within man came originally to primitive peoples through their dream experiences. Whether or not this is a valid explanation, the human being did acquire a vast variety of superstitions and beliefs in magic, which are still part and parcel of our background. Many of these ideas, rooted in antiquity, we still prize and refuse to give up even in the face of modern scientific findings.

This process of acquiring superstition has been a continuous one: primitive beliefs still persist in the modern world and new ones are constantly being created. Most of them have no logical explanation; others are explained so as to fit historical events: for example, the alleged unluckiness of the figure 13 referring to the tragic deaths of

Jesus Christ (c. 4 B.C.–29 A.D.) and the Twelve Apostles. Testifying to the strength of that particular superstition, many of our skyscrapers do not have a thirteenth floor—a good example of the failure of modern education to eliminate superstition.

If we consider the term in its broadest sense, education in today's society has elements in common with that of primitive society. Civilized man is still concerned with making the most of his material environment. Like his prehistoric ancestors, he has economic and social problems along with religions and philosophies. But the basic emphasis has shifted from the group to the individual. Survival under the hard conditions of primitive life was accomplished only by subordinating interests of the individual to interests of the group. Although the group is still regarded as important today, the individual is encouraged to open new vistas for himself and society. Indeed there are some who complain that we have gone too far in this direction.

Oriental Education

From its beginning, Oriental education dictated all thinking, feeling, and action. External authority dominated its aims and processes— the individual was entirely submerged. Learning was but a recapitulation of the past, a summing up within man of his ancestral background, and a sort of "fencing in" of mental boundaries beyond which he might not advance. Details of just how this worked out varied from nationality to nationality, but in each the omnipotent authority of tradition determined the character of man's education and thus controlled his destiny. Ancestral tradition formed this authority in China and traditions of caste in India; in ancient Persia it stemmed from a belief in national destiny as dictated by military traditions.

Oriental education was not set up to build the ideal man but rather to prepare him to fit into his proper place in the established order of things. Individual development was sacrificed to the fixing of existing standards and the perpetuation of national ideals. That these objectives have been obtained is clearly shown in the 5000-year national culture of the Chinese and the 4000-year history of the Hindus. It can be said that those philosophies of complacency among Asiatic peoples were the world's first educational systems based upon specific theories and practices. Oriental education was definitely an advance over the primitive to the degree and extent of its organization. The broad general principles that govern all education in the East are clearly illustrated through the history of the Chinese.

Confucius (c. 551–478 B.C.) stands out as one of the world's greatest thinkers. Unquestionably his voluminous writings were not all original but represented the accumulated wisdom of the preceding centuries. They became the guide of centuries to follow, the standard and inspiration for the great bulk of all ensuing Chinese literature. It is said that through his *Wu Ching* collection and his epigrams Confucius influenced more human lives than any other man in history. His thinking came to be regarded as the rule for living and the definition of culture for the Chinese, Koreans, Japanese, and other Oriental peoples. But in the truest sense of the word it is incorrect to call Confucianism a religion. As it was originally conceived there were no deities, theological creeds, or ritualistic worship. Rather it was a system of utilitarian morality to be implanted within each individual through authoritarian sanction of family and state.

Moral training is the type of education emphasized by the Chinese. Confucianism centers upon the idea of noble living. Human relationships, duty, order, and morality are the matters of prime importance. All these are based upon the doctrine of personal submission: a subject must submit to the ruler, son to father, wife to husband, brother to brother, friend to friend. Under such a philosophy the home naturally becomes the center for most of the training. Even today, school is regarded only as an adjunct in the educational process. The child's practical training, as in primitive civilizations, remains a family responsibility and one that is taken very seriously.

Confucius was a master teacher. Like Socrates (470?–399 B.C.) in Greece it was his habit to walk from place to place with a number of followers who were intensely absorbing his viewpoints on life. In his writings can be found numerous examples of how he adjusted himself to the individual differences of those about him—an adjustment that some pedagogues even in this century fail to make!

Like all other great teachers Confucius maintained close personal relationships with his pupils; he stimulated thought among those whose lives he touched. But as invariably is the case the followers of Confucius soon after his death departed in their own teaching from the example that had been set by the master. As a result the Chinese schools grew formalized and learning took on a meaningless character.

At the lower levels it became customary for a teacher to read a line from the traditional texts and have the pupils repeat it after him. The children then returned to their seats and committed the line to memory by continuing to repeat it aloud. When the line was committed to memory each pupil was expected to "back his book," that is, turn his back on the book and recite the entire lesson. It can be understood why ancient Chinese schools had the reputation of having been such noisy places. In the upper levels of instruction entire sacred books were committed to memory. Since real motivation was lacking, discipline necessarily was severe.

The Chinese have been noted for their independence of spirit. Despite invasions and defeats it has always been their conquerors who eventually lose identity by being swallowed into the great masses that today represent the oldest existing civilization. Thousands of years passed before the Chinese built a single large city. Then came a young half-Chinese, half-Mongolian conqueror who named himself Shih Huang-ti (259–210 B.C.), or "First Emperor." He not only welded the people into a strong nation but also speeded up the building of the famous Great Wall, stretching 1500 miles from the Yellow Sea to the deserts of Central Asia. Much of this wall was made of stone and brick, about 30 feet high, and wide enough on top for carts to be driven over it.

It is said that a bitter disagreement arose between Emperor Shih Huang-ti and the scholars and writers of China, who refused to admit anyone's right to rule by force. They quoted the classics against him, an act that stirred up a tremendous revolt. In retaliation the ruler put many intellectuals to work on the wall. The quarrel ended by his burying some of them alive in the structure and very nearly destroying their literature. If the tale is true that probably was the first struggle for academic freedom on record.*

Characteristically the Chinese have since hated Shih Huang-ti more for the burning of the classics than for his torturing of human beings, and as a memento to this hatred the site supposed to be his tomb has been kept a dung heap. After Shih Huang-ti's son was overthrown, the new emperor offered a huge reward for recovery of the classics. A partly preserved set of precious bamboo slabs (used at that time for recording) was discovered buried in the home of the great-grandson of Confucius, and a very old man was found who had memorized them in his youth and thus was able to fill in the rotted portions. Chinese scholars were determined never again to come that close to losing Confucius' writings; so to make them imperishable they were engraved on stone. Those classics have continued to influence Chinese thinking down to the present day. A study of Confucius' writings shows him generally to be bright and humorous, interested in common things of life, and scarcely concerned with what comes after life.

* It should be noted that many historians consider this story, though widely accepted, a hoax.

China introduced to the world the first great civil service system, designed for selection of public officials by examination. As to be expected from the kind of preparation Chinese schools had given their scholars, the highest marks were awarded to those candidates with the greatest powers of retention. Their statements were marked for literary excellence as well as factual content, but success was not attained through originality; what counted was ability to conform to the style of the ancient and acknowledged master of literary classics. How this civil service system helped to keep Chinese education unprogressive was shown by the fact that those aspiring to become officials were still being tested on combative archery even after wars were fought with firearms.

However, every ambitious boy lived in hopes of taking these literary tests, for, if he passed them, he became a member of the privileged ruling class known as mandarins. Those officials in the centuries before the Chinese Revolution formed the liaison between the self-governing communities and the emperor. Now a thing of the past is the mandarin dressed in beautifully embroidered robes and living a life of luxurious ease. But that official did make an indelible impression upon Chinese civilization because of his emphasis on academic attainment rather than the force of military power.

The Chinese pioneered in the mechanical process of recording thoughts centuries before the western world got around to this aspect of the advancement of culture. During Shih Huang-ti's time ink made of lampblack and the writing brush were invented. Five centuries later (about 300 A.D.) the Chinese discovered how to make paper; the same fundamental process (much improved, of course) is used in modern-day manufacture. Another five hundred years were to pass before the Chinese invented printing by the block method. Their oldest document now in existence was dated 868, as compared with the invention of the printing press in Germany just prior to 1450, supposedly by Johannes Gutenberg (1397–1468).

The Industrial Revolution in the western world led to the struggle for control of undeveloped countries and markets, and, after 1880, China was divided into spheres of influence. The Boxer Rebellion, an anti-foreigner movement, culminated in the beheading of the foreign legations in Peking. British, French, German, Russian, and American troops stormed the ancient capital and held it until a favorable treaty was made. Huge indemnities were assessed. The United States, after repaying its citizens who had suffered injury or loss, returned the remainder of its indemnity to China for a university to prepare Chinese students for study in America.

Only 32,000 of pre-war China's 450,000,000 people were college graduates, but their importance was far out of proportion to their number as they practically monopolized the key positions in public life. In 1847 three Chinese youths ventured 12,000 miles to enroll in the Monson (Massachusetts) Academy. In the years that followed before Communism took over, more than 10,000 Chinese students came to this country for an education. World War II interrupted this flow, and 1700 war-stranded students remained in the United States. At the time the new Communist government came into power, China had more than 30 universities and colleges that may be said to be of American origin.

These halls of learning were widely recognized for their services by Chinese educators, writers, and statesmen. In facing the problem of the rural people who constitute the largest portion of the population, the institutions pioneered the introduction of improved seeds, livestock, implements, methods of sanitation, and training of rural leaders. In medicine, doctors and nurses were trained and public health programs promoted. Thousands of teachers went from these institutions into schools of all instructional levels scattered throughout China. Little is as yet known about the changes in educational procedures of recent years.

Hebraic Education

Hebraic education marked the transition point between Oriental and western systems for training of youth. Adherence to strict religious and moral ideals during a 3500-year cultural development has preserved for the Jews a remarkable unity even though they have been widely dispersed over the face of the earth. Of all the ancient peoples in the western world the Jews were the most literate—they were the only people of antiquity to attempt to teach everyone to read. A moral discipline maintained almost entirely by education has permitted the Jews alone of all ancients to preserve their identity.

During Biblical times, and to a lesser extent even now, Jewish children were trained to be loyal to the group. Under domination throughout most of their history, the Jews constantly faced the danger of becoming an extinct group. Such a fate was escaped even during periods of captivity when there was no place to call their own, almost entirely because they used education to bind themselves together. Fealty was definitely planned as a product of their educational system and was strengthened by a common language and a common religion.

The monotheistic religious concept has been fortified down through the centuries by Hebraic education. The Jews have always held a firm conviction that they are a "chosen people" to whom someday a Messiah is to come for the purpose of restoring them to God's favor, a position they believe they lost through their own faithlessness. The primary condition for this restoration is holiness on their part. Thus the immediate purpose of all Hebraic education is to teach the Jews to make holiness before the Lord the aim of daily life. Under the influence of Moses (c. 1500 B.C.) and later prophets, first orally and then in written form, rules and regulations for everyday living were developed and transmitted to the people as the Torah (Laws) and Talmud (Interpretations). Thus ever since the time of Moses it has been the purpose of Hebraic education to train faithful and obedient servants to a personal and living God, both as an immediate means of assuring harmony in everyday civic life and as the path leading to a glorious future for the chosen people.

As in Oriental religions the individual is still subject to external authority, but with the Jews it is the authority of Jehovah and not of ancestor, caste, or state. Education is democratic—it is meant for everyone regardless of class, since all Jews must be educated if the group is to survive. The practice is to ostracize the ignorant man, and thus, by having him suffer civil disfranchisement, make it highly undesirable for others to remain ignorant. The reasoning is equally logical: if a man is ignorant he cannot be truly religious, and to be otherwise is a detriment to the group. Ancient Jews felt that education was deficient if it did not include the training of both the home and the school. As far back as Biblical times they had made the formal education of words parallel the informal education of deeds. Analyses made of Hebraic education indicate that more importance was placed on the home than on the school.

The prime example of an aristocracy of learning was found in ancient Egypt where the priestly class jealously kept to itself the privilege of investigation and study. The common people were forbidden to learn to read the complicated Egyptian picture language, which was regarded as sacred. However, a slave boy of exceptional ability managed to find aristocratic patrons who educated him, as is shown in the Bible story of Joseph (c. 1900 B.C.). His people were Mesopotamians whom the Egyptians had held in slavery for several hundred years. Doubtless it was because of their appreciation of the long-denied privilege of an education that when these Hebrews obtained their freedom they became the earliest of the Mediterranean peoples to establish a system of universal education—that is, one for all the boys.

One of the greatest Hebraic contributions to civilization was their giving to women a much higher position in society than females had ever held before; in the family they were considered "junior partners" and not slaves as in Oriental countries. Still, in educational matters the Jewish women were not permitted to go beyond the informal training for domestic life as carried on in the home.

Throughout all Jewish history the mother has remained important in the training of daughters. Within a family circle the father serves not only as the patriarchal ruler but also as teacher, with the wife sharing the burden of instruction. That this Jewish family education has definitely been of high order doubtless is due to the fact that the father possesses such great powers and responsibilities in the training of his children, and those duties have always been shared by the mother. Importance of parents is indicated in the injunction of the Book of Proverbs: "My son, hear the instruction of thy father and forsake not the teaching of thy mother." The entire family is held responsible for the behavior and training of each of its members—a well-bred child is considered a credit to his parents, and the badly reared a source of shame.

Formal education for the ancient Jewish boy began in a school attached to the synagogue when he was about six years of age. Isaiah (c. 760 B.C.) had recommended that it begin at the time a child is weaned. The first objective was to achieve literacy and then to learn the Pentateuch, which set forth the basic customs of the people. As in China the pupils shouted their lessons aloud. Schools lasted from dawn to dark and continued all year round except for religious holidays. Since papyrus and parchment were far too expensive for anything except finished writing, pupils scratched notes and compositions on tablets of white wax.

The more brilliant older students were encouraged to search out the meanings of what they had learned, provided they did not venture too far from the traditional beliefs of their fathers. Classes in Hebrew law and religious duties were conducted by priests called scribes (penmen). It was quite common to see students clustered around famous priests and sages, under trees and on the porches of public buildings, asking and answering questions that centered chiefly about philosophy and religion.

The gentle but firm discipline typically found in the Jewish home, past and present, usually creates a deep respect and habitual obedience to elders at all age levels. As noted before, it has been this family discipline that largely accounts for the success of the Jews in surviving the many hardships and cruelties they have had to face. But in early Jewish history the discipline in schools was quite severe. As it had been with their early oppressors, the Egyptians, the rod was a symbol of instruction. Throughout the Old Testament are admonishments: "He that spareth his rod hateth his son; but he that loveth him chasteneth him betimes"; also, "The rod and reproof give wisdom: but a child left to himself bringeth his mother to shame."

However, later Hebraic methods became more temperate as, for example, when the Talmud recommended that older pupils should not be compelled to undergo corporal punishment for fear of instilling a rebellious spirit within them. In similar vein the limitations set up by congenital dullness were recognized in the admonition not to punish such children because of their lack of capacity for learning inasmuch as punishment would have but little effect. A modern progressive education thought seems to have crept into the Talmud when it was directed that children be punished with one hand and caressed with two.

Hebraic education had some very practical aspects, especially its emphasis upon vocational training. The duty of every father was to teach his son a trade; manual labor is honorable, and one should be an artisan as well as a scholar. Thus it can perhaps be better understood why Jesus in his youth learned the carpentry trade—that was the customary educational practice of the time in all Jewish homes. However, the Jews made little provision for physical training although Mosaic law included some rules of hygiene and fathers were urged to teach their children to swim.

Passing the age of adolescence among the Jews was celebrated by the ritual of making the boy a "son of the law." This transformation indicated that the youth's father was no longer responsible for his conduct, that according to the law he now stood upon his own feet and thereafter was answerable for his own acts.

Before elementary schools of the synagogue were started, higher education had already reached an organized basis for the purpose of training priests and scribes. Most important in that Hebraic curriculum was the learning of the Mosaic law, but it became largely a matter of rote memory as schooling degenerated into a training in ritualistic observances. Tending to stifle spontaneity and initiative of Jewish students was the Biblical injunction of Jehovah: "What thing soever I command you, observe to do it." Under such a restriction teaching methods became as barren in their formality as in Oriental education. Understanding and appreciation of meanings were definitely subordinated to memorizing of the exact word.

Then came reformers who saw the superficiality of such a system; the best known, of course, was Jesus. Those later prophets set up as a new goal for educational endeavor the deepening of religious insight and fervor. However, in the ensuing Hebraic education this new and enlightened aim was seldom realized. Attention of most of the scribes continued to be devoted to observances of formalized religious rites.

Jews in America today, as throughout their entire history, are notably education-conscious. As a group they seem far more anxious than the average to take advantage of every opportunity to make the most possible out of their lives. A 1946 census of Jewish college students showed 200,000 in the United States and Canada. That number represented 9 per cent of the total enrollment of all students at that time even though several institutions had quota systems drastically limiting Jewish enrollments. A traditional drive for learning in the Jewish home in which college is regarded as a natural educational goal of sons and daughters is regarded as one cause of this phenomenon. It is quite common for a New York City Jewish youth to rush from a public school to his home or synagogue in order to get additional daily instruction in matters pertaining to his religious life. He is simply following the traditions of his people. No one can deny the effectiveness of Hebraic education!

Education in Ancient Greece

In the late nineteenth century the excavations of archaeologists led to some important discoveries about the culture of pre-Hellenic Greece. It was learned that Aegean civilization had progressed rapidly from the Stone Age to the Bronze Age. Two remarkable examples are the Minoan people of Crete and the Mycenaean Greeks on the mainland. Both groups date from 3000 B.C., and both can be considered as chief among the forerunners of Hellenic culture.

Pictographs were used in the early period of Minoan civilization. Around 2000 B.C. these gave way to linear writing in pen and ink! Less than a century later the culture of these extraordinary people had passed to Troy and to the Greek mainland. Minoan Crete, after flourishing for only a few thousand years, was buried in the sands of history —but its culture had already made an indelible mark upon the world.

Mycenae apparently imitated the Minoan people in most of the arts, but developed its own culture in such diverse fields as architecture and politics. The amazing thing about the Mycenaean Greeks is that they were illiterate. Moreover, their period of greatness lasted only about three centuries, from 1600 to 1300 B.C. under the Achaeans. But when the invaders from northern Greece put the quietus on

Mycenae, they took away more than gold and trinkets. They took a knowledge of a way of life that was new to them. Thus, some of the groundwork was laid for the type of culture that flourished centuries later in Sparta and Athens.

The first great European poet was a blind Greek genius named Homer (c. 800 B.C.) who developed two epics—the *Iliad* and the *Odyssey*—from legendary material handed down from generation to generation ever since the Achaeans had ruled at Mycenae. From his works an insight into the culture from 1200 B.C. to his own century can be obtained.

No formal educational institution existed in Homeric times. Informal teaching was done through the family or clan. The twofold ideals to be imitated were Odysseus and Achilles. The former typified the shrewd and eloquent leader, invaluable in the councils of peace. Achilles, the hero of the *Iliad*, was an example of courage, strength, and endurance.

Homeric education was primarily practical and social. It trained men in the arts of peace and war and women in domestic efficiency. The purpose was to acquire those qualities and skills needed for group living.

An important historical characteristic of ancient Hellas was the development of city-states as a result of the mountainous topography separating one tribe from another. Each a center of a relatively small unit of surrounding territory inhabited by farmers and herdsmen, these areas were originally ruled by kings or aristocratic families. Such rulers were usually "strong men" who had gained their power by physical and mental prowess and wealth. Later, some city-states developed into democracies of a sort; others became oligarchies.

In all, there were about twenty city-states on the mainland. Two of the most important were Laconia (inhabited by Dorian Greeks) and Attica (inhabited by Ionic Greeks). Their chief cities were respectively Sparta and Athens. It is to these centers of ancient culture that we now turn our attention.

Spartan Education

It should be noted that the political foundations of Greek culture had a much more democratic basis than those of either the Orient or the Near East. However, Greek education was far from democratic in the sense we understand this term today. The people were divided into distinct classes with such different purposes in life that divergent types of training were required. The largest element in each city-state population was the slave class, and for them there was no formal education. Also, foreigners in Sparta were not eligible for the educational facilities available to the citizen class. But among members of the favored Spartan minority there were no such distinctions as developed in Athens where family wealth eventually played a major role in determining the nature and extent of formal training.

Like the primitive and Oriental leaders, Spartan authorities considered the preservation of folkways the basic aim of education. Social survival depended primarily on the military prowess of the soldiers who dominated the subject populations surrounding and outnumbering them. Of special interest today is the fact that Nazi Germany, Fascist Italy, and Imperial Japan all used the Spartan educational system as their model before catapulting mankind into World War II. All three, like Sparta, carefully controlled the thoughts and actions of growing youth as the most effective means of building the glory and efficiency of the state. Each used a rigid doctrine of devotion to a single purpose, the training of a powerful body of warriors for the purpose of protecting themselves from outside attack and of keeping neighbors in subjection.

Beset by their enemies the Spartans had called upon Lycurgus (c. 800 B.C.) to draw up a constitution and to develop a new set of laws. It was those laws of Lycurgus that formed the basis of the Spartan educational system, with the aim of giving to each individual physical perfection and habits of complete obedience so as to make him an ideal soldier. Not only were the finer sentiments of generosity, sympathy, and mercy neglected as educational aims, but their destruction was deliberately sought. The Spartan ideal of good citizenship was to develop strength, endurance, courage, patriotism, military efficiency, and cunningness. Physical training and military sciences were given great importance; the former was supplemented by music and dancing. Intellectual development was practically limited to the memorizing of the laws of Lycurgus and small portions of the Homeric epics that glorified warfare.

Thus in Sparta (after 600 B.C.) the state became the one dominant agency that controlled the life of the individual from birth to death. The citizen so identified himself with the state that probably it never occurred to him he might have interests separate from and antagonistic to it. Education consisted of rigid transmission of established customs and folkways. Civic character was achieved by following closely aristocratic or noble example.

The state dictated all aspects of family life; marriage, for instance, was controlled and made compulsory. A child was considered as belonging to the state, and it was the state council that decided at birth whether the infant seemed sufficiently healthy to become a strong warrior and citizen, or the future mother of one. An infant judged weak or defective was ordered exposed to the elements. Many died on the mountainside, some being devoured by wild beasts. Others were taken by helots (bondsmen of the lowest class of serfs) to be brought up as slaves, tradesmen, or laborers. Female infants were rescued with the purpose in mind of eventually turning them into prostitutes.

If a child passed inspection, he was taken home to be raised by his parents until he reached the age of seven. During those first years the mother had general charge of his upbringing; the father was responsible for gradually inducting him into the ways of adult society by teaching those moral characteristics deemed necessary. Lessons in self-control began from the day of birth. Frequently a child was left alone in the dark and then punished if he cried. A boy was made hardy by fasting; the foods he ate were simple and coarse. The young Spartan had plenty of sleep and outdoor exercise, and by the time he was ready to leave his mother he had learned well the habits of obedience, silence, and respect for elders.

At seven the boy was placed in a boarding-school type of barracks where until 18 he remained under the supervision of older boys and a state official called the *paidonmous*. There he was under strict discipline in a semi-military organization of bands or packs under the leadership of young adults. He had a bed of straw or hay, no blankets, no shoes, and scanty clothing. The food was unusually plain and limited in quantity.

Boys were encouraged to steal, but were severely punished for their lack of skill when caught. Intended solely to develop qualities serviceable in war, this training was made as rigorous as possible through games, exercises, drills, and participation in jumping, running, wrestling, spear throwing, and quoits. Trainees were constantly instructed in moral and civic virtues, and in affairs of state through discussions at the public mess tables. In all fairness to Spartan education, it must be said that the young men learned to converse in an intelligent and agreeable manner and acquired a dignity of bearing and a practical wisdom far beyond their actual years.

At 18 the youths began two years of intensive military training in which they operated under the close supervision of the army. Some of those who had demonstrated qualities of leadership remained in the barracks to supervise the younger boys. At the age of 20 all youths took the oath of allegiance to the state, and then there followed 10 years in which they served as active members of the armed forces, engaging in the defensive and offensive wars of the country. When a man reached 30 he became a full-fledged citizen, was compelled to marry, and took his seat in the public assembly or council. Thereafter each citizen at certain times had to return to the public barracks to act as mentor and example to the boys going through the process of training. Thus a characteristic of Spartan education was that every citizen assumed the civic responsibility of being a teacher.

The home was the school for girls. There they remained with their brothers until the age of seven. Then when the boys left for the public barracks, the girls continued to live at home but went through strenuous physical exercises after being organized into packs similar to those of the boys. In fact, the typical Spartan girl resembled somewhat our modern "tomboy"—the purpose of her training was to build a physical body that would prepare her to bring into the world and rear sturdy and patriotic sons capable of carrying on Spartan traditions. Girls were also given training in household duties, designed not only for intelligent rearing of children but also for the control of domestic slaves. Spartans, somewhat like the Jews, gave women a relatively high social position. In this area of ethos, they were far more advanced than the Orientals or the neighboring Athenians.

Sparta laid educational responsibilities upon all classes. Teachers of military and physical training held the status of public officials and possessed the rights and privileges of that position. Discipline was severe and cruel; corporal punishment was used for lack of alertness as well as for moral delinquencies. Flogging was practiced not only to promote obedience but also to harden the body. Each adult citizen was duty-bound to punish any boy caught in the act of violating a rule of proper conduct. Sparta used fear of public disapproval effectively to maintain the unique standards of morality established by the state for old and young alike.

Spartan education has been called the military-dictatorship ideal. It aimed to train the warrior-citizen to take his place in a military state. Everything was subordinated to the end that youth be molded into the exact adult pattern deemed necessary to perpetuate the state as it was. Barracks life for boys of seven to eighteen contributed greatly to the aim of building strong bodies that could take punishment, and minds disciplined to obey without question.

When youths of 18 went into military service, they organized blitzkrieg bands that roamed the countryside. These groups practiced caring for themselves in simulated warfare, foraging for food, and attacking the enemy. But in this case the "enemy" consisted of poor farmers and harassed helots. Thus the youths not only were learning the methods of Spartan warfare but also were helping to police the subject populations in the interest of the state—or so it was rationalized. It is easy to understand why Sparta produced very little lasting art, literature, philosophy, or science—just as has been the case in modern dictatorships.

Athenian Education

There was no truly religious aim in the educational system of the Greeks, either Spartan or Athenian. Their gods were but magnified men, possessing both good and evil qualities. They were useful in that they set an example of justice, forbearance, and hospitality; but they also taught men to lie, steal, and even to kill.

In the Greek thinking there existed no promise of a glorious reward in the hereafter, as used so effectively by the Hebrews and later by the Christians to furnish a motive for right living. The Greek Hades was pictured as dark, cold, and lifeless—the fun was in living, not in dying. However, far more than any other of the ancient peoples, the Athenians made invaluable contributions to the development of modern culture in their art, literature, philosophy, politics, and science. It was they who gave the world the first "working model" of a democracy in action.

Athenian education is divided into two periods: the early one continued from the first Olympiad until the close of the Persian wars in 480 B.C.; the later period ended in the Macedonian conquest in 338 B.C.

In early Athens as in Sparta the aim of education was to develop citizens. But Athenians believed education must be well-rounded and that the citizens should have a trained mind in a trained body. Individual excellence for public usefulness was continually drummed into youths—in other words, training was conceived as a protection for the state. Thus civic instruction dominated the early Athenian schooling; everything else was subordinated to this end. Prerequisite to citizenship was broad culture in which the individual strove for the development of beauty and grace in body, mind, and spirit. The entire purpose of this education was to develop virtues, always of a civic nature. Education of a son was regarded a duty of the father, and if he failed to carry out his responsibility the son was not obligated to assist his father in old age. A rigid public opinion was depended upon to uphold the traditional ideals of morality, and in the earlier Athenian period that censorship was quite puritanical.

Reforms in government creating for the free citizens of Athens a "pure" though highly restricted democracy were instituted by Solon (c. 639–559 B.C.). This famous lawgiver established a code that solved many distressing economic and social problems. Athenian prosperity dated from Solon's time. The educational system was largely a result of his influence with the emphasis placed upon the individual and the development of his personality. To this end dancing, music, and poetry were taught—not as a means of pleasure and amusement but as an elevating influence on intellect and morals.

Although highly organized, physical training did not have for its primary purpose the building of stronger men or better warriors, but rather the development of grace and harmony. Intellectual training was recognized as essential for those activities going on continuously in market places, agorae, and assembly meetings. For the first time in history we find the scholar in politics. In contrast, Spartan politicians were ex-soldiers whose minimum age was 60.

Vocational training for boys and domestic arts for girls were badly neglected—and for logical reasons. Approximately one-fifth of the Athenian population were free citizens; most of the other 80 per cent were slaves performing the menial duties. Thus manual work became despised by the privileged minority.

In social position the teacher ranked very low. Parents placed young boys in charge of a *pedagogue,* usually an aged and trusted slave who often was no good for any other purpose. Like the modern governess this *pedagogue* served as a combination guardian-counselor-servant, responsible for the intellectual and moral development of his young charge. He took him to the music school and the gymnasium (a place for athletic exercises, with baths, and also with rooms for learned discussions). He supervised the young citizen's activities, instructed him in honesty and patriotism, and had authority to use corporal punishment when necessary. In his later training, however, a youth came under the supervision of state officials who served as his drillmasters and moral censors.

The early Athenian educational system developed largely into one of learning from teachers rather than books. The pupil first acquired skill in reading by the alphabet method; for writing he used a waxed tablet and stylus. Only as much arithmetic was learned as might be needed in reckonings in the market place. Selections from Homer, Solon, and Aesop (c. 500 B.C.) were dictated, then memorized and chanted. Musical instruction on the lyre and flute was also given. Gymnastic drills, sports, and games became popular but little importance was attached to winning. As previously noted, military science and practice of civic virtues completed this education designed as preparation for active participation of a free citizen in a democratic city-state.

As in Sparta the early Athenian educational method was one of rigid training rather than instruction, and close imitation was an essential virtue. But most of the vitalizing experiences came from actual participation in the activities of life. Older boys learned civic lessons not from books but through watching civic life in action and eventually taking part in it. Discipline was exceedingly severe; seldom did there exist any bond of affection between teacher and pupil even though classes were small enough to invite intellectual comradeship. As Plato (427?–347 B.C.) said in *Protagoras:* "And if the boy obeys willingly, it is well, but if not, like a tree twisted and bent, they make him straight by threats and blows."

Athenians believed that "woman's place is in the home," that she needed no schooling to perform her duties there—formal education was a privilege for men only. There was, in fact, very little real family life in Athens, and usually the home did not amount to much as an educational agency. Women were not held in high esteem as among the Spartiates or Jews. Not infrequently the wives of the more prominent Athenians were so ignorant that they could play only an insignificant role in the rearing of their children. Some mothers did give that training normally required by girls, but usually even this task remained a responsibility of slave nurses.

In the later Athenian period the prosperity resulting from the successful outcome of the Persian wars brought with it a more cosmopolitan type of education. Wealth amassed from trade led to opportunities for the pursuits of leisure and the patronage of cultural arts. The civic ideal of devotion to the public welfare began to die out as the old democratic and moral ideals were being rejected because of the rise of a new spirit of sophistication. Desire for fame and fortune made its influence felt in the demands on education. Personal advancement formed an important goal for this age. As in later centuries in the western world, "rugged individualism" with all its selfish self-centeredness largely dominated the picture.

About 500 B.C. a new type of educator came on the scene. The Sophists provided a purely intellectual training that reflected the political, economic, and philosophical changes that were taking place. Those men, mainly itinerant teachers from Asia Minor and the Aegean Islands, were attracted to Athens by its activities and opportunities to profit therefrom. They charged fees for services rendered which, considering the traditional admiration for amateurism, shocked many a conservative Athenian. Intellectual leaders like Plato never forgave the Sophists for their mercenary attitude.

This new type of teaching was highly informal. Sophists came and went as they pleased, talked on street corners, sometimes rented rooms for classwork, and gathered students any way they could. Some were *bona fide* educators specializing in certain fields of knowledge, but others were mere opportunists pandering to the popular intellectual interests of the time.* However, this much can be said of the Sophists: they taught their followers not to accept the *status quo* merely because it existed, but to question everything—even the accepted conventions and foundations of Athenian Society. Moreover, they were practical men, who did try to adjust their methods to meet the individual differences of their students. Their guiding principle was best expressed by the famous Sophist named Protagoras (c. 480–410 B.C.) when he said: "Man is the measure of all things."

Even though thinking as developed by the Sophists was superficial, it represented considerable cleverness in meeting such practical problems as discrimination in the use of words. The Sophists trained public speakers at a time when ability to talk persuasively was a direct path to prominence in civic life. Also, they encouraged the study of literature for grammatical and rhetorical analysis and for sheer pleasure.

This new conception of education for personal enjoyment resulted in the utilization of games and sports for amusement purposes. New musical instruments and literary forms were also invented. And so, a type of political instruction that was almost purely intellectual began to supplant physical and military training for those of age 16 and above.

The Sophists in due time faced caustic charges of being "quacks," shallow sellers of "tricks of the trade," rather than seekers after the truth. So long as Athens remained prosperous and powerful prior to the struggle with Sparta known as the Peloponnesian Wars, these teachers were not only tolerated but greeted with enthusiasm, especially by the younger men. But simultaneously with the dimming of Athenian power they began to lose their influence. Many of them found it wise to leave Athens for "reasons of health."

However, the Sophists did give a powerful impetus to advancing

---

* Originally, the word *Sophist* meant "a wise, skillful man." But after these teachers had gained popularity, their critics began to use the term in such a deprecatory way that it soon took on unfavorable connotations. Thus a sophist of today is one who deliberately uses fallacious or specious arguments.

education of an intellectual type; they contributed a great deal to the world by starting to organize large bodies of knowledge into teachable form. The way for Plato and Aristotle (c. 384–322 B.C.) was also prepared. It was in Athens that these two philosophical explorers and organizers of thought set up their informal academies—early universities of a sort where students met with famous teachers under the shade of trees. Instruction was carried on in the form of questions and answers called dialogues, and much of the discussion concerned the practical problems of teaching.

Before considering the Greek philosophers in greater detail, let us briefly review the status of Athenian education in the fourth century B.C. and conclude this section with a few comments on the contributions of ancient Greek schools to civilization.

Lower education in that era did not undergo the marked changes that occurred in higher education, but foundations were being laid for more systematic institutionalizing of schools and for greater state control. The main objective was to achieve literacy. After the rudiments of reading and writing had been mastered, the pupil started immediately on the best of Greek literature including Homer. Out of this reading and writing some elementary instruction in grammar and numbers was developed. Thus education had lost its primitive character and had set a broad pattern on which future schools could be organized. During the next few centuries the school as a separate institution began to take the forms we know today—elementary, secondary, and higher education.

It was in the realm of higher education that the Greek influence was most greatly felt. Long after Athens ceased to be a political power, its various philosophical and rhetorical schools (known collectively as the University of Athens) served as a mecca for students from other parts of the civilized world, and the Greek tongue became the universal language of culture.

The conquests of Alexander the Great helped to spread the knowledge and mores of the Athenians far and wide. Wherever his armies went, there soon followed the Greek teachers, philosophers, and other thought leaders. Soon Greek universities were flourishing on the island of Rhodes, at Tarsus and Pergamum in Asia Minor, and at Alexandria in Egypt. The last of these—an immense library and museum—became the new center of world culture. Later, it was superseded in stature by a center at Constantinople. For a thousand years thereafter, Greek culture was saved at Constantinople until the world was ready to embrace it again in the Renaissance.

Greek Origins of Modern Philosophy

Since the days of prehistoric man all groups of people have developed in more or less definite form their own peculiar philosophies, but the Athenians were the first to make an organized study of theirs. They felt a definite need for a more comprehensive understanding of the world that would include within it a sound philosophy of education. In this the three greatest of the Greek philosophers differed in their theories.

Socrates (c. 470?–399 B.C.) considered the first step to be making the student aware of his own ignorance by asking him questions, and then by further questioning to help him find the truth for himself. Plato doubted the capability of all men to learn in this way and suggested that philosophers who understand the truth be given the task of imparting it to others. The philosophers, he also said, should attempt to educate each person only so far as his particular nature permits. Aristotle believed the purpose of education was to make men rational, so that they could decide by correct reasoning the proper course of their private and public conduct. In essence his theory was that when a man knows how to govern himself he will be a good citizen.

This theory of Aristotle's really had its roots in the life and precepts of Socrates. Aristotle's teacher was Plato; and that philosopher, in turn, studied under Socrates. Indeed it is largely through Plato's works that we know so much about the great independent thinker who constantly irritated the conservatives of his day. Socrates himself never wrote a book nor did he ever organize a formal school of philosophy; but his influence on mankind's thinking and educational practices is immense and astounding. His ideas have lived not only through the prolific writings and influence of Plato and Aristotle but also through several schools started by other followers of his.

Contrary to popular belief, Socrates was not a Sophist. In fact, he often needled those teachers for their skepticism. His chief aim was to arouse in mankind a love of truth and virtue. Knowledge, he claimed, is virtue. No man purposely does wrong; it is ignorance that leads him astray. Thus Socrates implied that universal education would make the world a better place in which to live.

Plato's *Republic* has been one of the most influential books of all time. The imaginary society he conceived consisted of artisans, warriors, and philosophers. He paid but little attention to education for the great masses of people who labored. The schooling of his warriors ended at 20, but those destined to become philosopher-kings would continue for 10 more years in a course of higher study made up primarily of mathematics and science. At the age of 30 the less brilliant of this ruling class would go into the lower civil offices of the state while the more brilliant continued their studies, principally philosophy, for five more years. Then after 15 years of experience of working in the world of philosophers, at 50, this group would be ready to take over the reins of government as the chief policy-making officials. Plato's conception of intellectual training was democratic in that it allowed for the continual advancement of men with outstanding ability; it was undemocratic in that it trained for leadership in an aristocratic society.

Aristotle looked upon education as a branch of politics in the sense that it is essential for the building of a cohesive community life and public morale. He held that education should be under state control and approximately the same for rich and poor alike, so that among free citizens (as distinguished from slaves who made up four-fifths of the Athenian population) there would not develop disparities and class inequalities. Aristotle's education can be called liberal since it was for free men, but it lacked practical and vocational aspects so essential in training for a democracy. He disparaged the "lower occupations" of artisanship, trade, or farming because they distort the body, destroy harmonious development, and do not allow time for pursuits of citizenship and intellectual investigation.

Before leaving Aristotle, it should be noted that he placed great store in the study of science. He was among the first to see the importance of learning by direct experience and to recommend inductive experiential work as part of the curriculum. Moreover, he advocated that education should follow the growth pattern of a child—a concept that many people now consider to be quite modern.

In the development of philosophical thought the informal teaching of the Sophists gave way in the fourth century B.C. to institutionalized schools. Plato founded the Academy, and Aristotle the Lyceum. Antisthenes (c. 444?–371 B.C.) in his School of the Cynics taught that virtue is the only good and that material pleasure, if sought for its own sake, is an evil. Thus Antisthenes reflected the philosophy of Socrates, who had been his teacher.

Regarded by many as the greatest of all Greek teachers, Isocrates (c. 436–338 B.C.) founded a rhetorical school in which he insisted that the power of speech should be used for democratic purposes. Isocrates rose above the level of the Sophists because he gave importance to morality and truth in essays and speeches, rather than shrewd reasoning merely to win an argument. It is interesting to note that he, too, had been a pupil of Socrates—a man whose tenets really took root and flourished in many directions. Isocrates, in turn, had more influence on young orators than any other man of his time.

The schools of those days somewhat resembled college fraternities in their emphasis upon careful selection of members. Many lived together, like monastics, under regulations accepted by all. Recruits were chosen from the students then being attracted to Athens by its fame as a cultural center. Each school developed its own distinctive philosophy of education, and debates on nuances of thinking resounded through the city.

After Athens had become a conquered state the educational emphasis shifted somewhat, with the philosophical schools turning to knowledge for its own sake and becoming semi-religious. New philosophical religions arose to satisfy men's desires to explore their fate and to describe the nature of things.

Zeno of Citium (c. 336–c. 264 B.C.) set up his school, known as *Stoa*,* which followed generally the educational traditions of Socrates. Zeno had been exposed to the tenets of Antisthenes and other Cynics like Diogenes (c. 412–323 B.C.) whose quest with a lantern is well known. Naturally, therefore, his own doctrines had their foundations in the Socratic ideals of self-sufficiency, endurance, and virtue. The Stoics preached that nature is inherently reasonable, and hence conformity to the natural order of things is living according to the dictates of reason. They taught that calm indifference to painful circumstances and tranquil acceptance of what life brings are the highest values. Moral life consists of finding reason in nature and living resolutely in the light of these findings. Thus Stoicism came to imply an imperturbable acceptance of life's difficulties.

The doctrines of the Stoics helped to shape the characteristics of later Christian thought and practice. This happened partly because the Roman leaders accepted Stoicism more than any other Greek philosophy and partly because some of the early Christians felt a kinship with its basic ideas. In this connection it should be remembered that the Stoics considered virtue as the highest good of life.

Quite different was the school set up by Epicurus (c. 341–270 B.C.) which held matter to be eternal, indestructible, and uncreated; the universe to be merely infinite space filled with material atoms, operated by chance rather than by creative intelligence or reason. To Epicurus our universe was mechanistic, not divinely related—he

---

* Zeno's group assembled in the Stoa Poecile (literally, "painted porch"). It was one of the many stoae surrounding the agora. These colonnades were the favorite places for intellectuals to meet.

claimed happiness to consist of avoiding pain and seeking pleasure. He taught that through *ataraxia* (serenity) man could triumph over the evils of pain, useless desires, and obstructing fears. This *ataraxia* could be sought because man had freedom to pursue his own course. To him the highest good was the pleasure of intellectual pursuits. It is ironic that Epicurus' stress on intellectual pursuits was later forgotten, and Epicureanism popularly came to mean: "Eat, drink, and be merry, for tomorrow we die"—an idea which is a gross distortion of his actual philosophy.

We have glanced briefly at some of the major philosophical schools of the Greeks, each with its own educational implications. They represent an invaluable heritage to ensuing history and mark the starting point of educational philosophy. Throughout the centuries of formal education the great and near-great teachers have been those who, over and above the ability to impart knowledge and skills, influence their students toward a positive philosophy of life. That is why some scholars claim that every teacher should study Plato, Aristotle, and their contemporaries. Whether one agrees or not, the tremendous influence of the Greek philosophers on Western education cannot be denied.

Roman Education

According to the mythical story of the twin boys nursed by a wolf, one of them (Romulus) founded Rome on the spot where the beast had discovered and adopted them in the year now reckoned as 753 B.C. For more than a thousand years before that date Indo-Europeans and other tribesmen had gradually been settling the Italian peninsula. From the eighth to the sixth centuries B.C. the city-states were ruled by kings. Throughout that period there had apparently existed a senate serving as an advisory council to the rulers. Descendants of the noble families formed a hereditary aristocratic class know as patricians as distinguished from the plebeians, or common people. The founding of the Roman Empire when the kings were overthrown is usually given as 509 B.C. However, the patricians continued thereafter to be the dominant political power, maintaining their control through the senate which annually chose two consuls to serve as joint chief executives. But as plebeians increased in number, they challenged the patrician rule more and more.

It was during the third and second centuries B.C. that the center of political and economic gravity shifted from the eastern Mediterranean to Rome. In affairs of government Romans proved themselves more adept than any other people before them. Their greatest contribution to the Western world was the establishment of a substantial foundation for the social order. They were practical people who built institutions through which the ideals of more imaginative peoples might be realized. Their body of civil laws remains today the foundation for most of the legal systems in the Western world. It can be said that our modern ideals have been taken from Hebraic and Greek sources, but our institutions came from Rome.

Roman genius for adaptation and application was far greater than any gift for originality. That is shown by the relative shallowness of contributions to art and literature, although Cicero (106–43 B.C.), Virgil (70–19 B.C.), and Horace (65–8 B.C.) did leave lasting impressions upon literature, as any schoolboy studying Latin can well testify. Romans made their greatest contributions in the fields of applied rather than pure science; they took the speculations of the Greek philosophers and applied them to the building of roads and bridges and to the development of agriculture. Great genius for organization was particularly shown in Roman military and political institutions through which there was gained and held for more than four centuries the world's greatest empire up to that time.

They made an important contribution even in religion, when they turned their attention to it—a despised and persecuted sect was transformed into the beginnings of the great Roman Catholic Church with its highly complicated worldwide organization. In education the Romans have been called "ferrymen," because they carried the Greek and Hebraic ideas across a long span of time, thus preserving them for posterity.

Rome's earliest education was directed entirely toward making the boy a *vir bonus* (good man), which meant a good citizen and a good soldier. Duties of Roman citizenship were taught by parents to both boys and girls. Those civic responsibilities were expressed in the laws of the Twelve Tables, in poems and songs telling of Roman heroes of the past, and in the accepted religious beliefs and practices. There were no formal schools in early Rome. A boy of the citizen class became acquainted with government as he accompanied his father about the city. When the age of 16 was reached, the youth was given the *toga virilis,* or man's costume, indicating that now he was a citizen. Also at 16 each young Roman was sent to an army camp for active military service, which completed his formal education. The new citizen thenceforth was expected to continue his learning by participation in civic life.

Prior to the third century B.C. the Romans had been largely untouched by Greek culture and had developed their own peculiar qualities of character and intellect. They idolized traits of mind appropriate to rugged, agricultural, and warlike primitive tribes, such as filial duty, honesty, courage, integrity, and dignity. But after the Roman conquest of Greece in the second century B.C., educated Greek slaves were brought to Rome as pedagogues, and with them came Greek learning and school methods.

Then characteristically the Romans took the educational ideas of the Greeks and developed them into the most formal school system up to that time. Unfortunately these schools were planned only for children of the wealthy. Until the age of seven the boys and girls of the upper classes were educated at home by tutors, usually Greek slaves. Then until 10 they attended a primary school, called the "school of the teacher of letters," in which they learned reading, writing, and the rudiments of arithmetic. Here formal education ended for the girls. Boys went on to the "school of the teacher of grammar" where they learned not only grammar but also the literature of Greece and Rome, some mythology, geography, and history.

But training did not stop there. A modest forerunner of our present college education came next. At 16, boys attended the "school of the teacher of rhetoric" where for two or three years they studied declamation and extemporaneous speaking. In harmony with the Roman belief that one of the chief marks of an educated man is to know the duties of a citizen and to be able to speak on them in a convincing way, debates on the subject of Roman law and the proper conduct of the citizen formed an important part of this final stage of the youth's formal education. Although this system produced some famous orators and authors, it was unfortunate that only the sons of the wealthy were able to get a complete education, such as it was. This tended to produce a social structure in which a small group of rich, educated men largely controlled the government while most of the people had little knowledge or interest in problems of public life.

Early Roman education repressed the freedom of the individual in the interest of the state; definitely it was a training intended to prepare for practical life. Whereas the Athenians had been highly theoretical and subjective, the Romans were objective in striving always for the achievement of some concrete purpose possessing material values. Just as in Sparta, emphasis was placed upon physical, military, and civic training. Vocational education, disdained so patronizingly by the free citizens of Athens, gained a highly respected place in early Rome.

A large part of the content was centered in the laws of the Twelve

Tables, which defined public and private relationships and stated clearly the property rights of individuals living under Roman control and protection. These were memorized, presumably for the purpose of practical guidance in later life. The Twelve Tables were not studied critically—in fact, there was but little of the intellectual in early Roman education. Direct imitation was the method generally used, and great importance was attached to habit formation. Discipline was strict and harsh.

The family became a significant institution in early Roman life, one that was largely responsible for Rome's maintaining so long its world-power position. Under what was known as *patricia potestas*, corporal punishment, and even death, could be inflicted by the father on other members of the family at his own discretion. Thus he was the unquestioned head of the household, but the mother also was held in high esteem. While this earlier custom did place the wife under the absolute power of her husband to do with what he pleased, in actual practice she went freely into society, taught the children, and sometimes even aided her husband in his career.

In those days of ancient Rome both state and society honored womanhood, and parents cooperated in training children in stern, simple virtues. The girl was taught by her mother the essential moral values and domestic arts such as spinning, weaving, and care of the home. At first there was but little practical need for women to know reading and writing, and so they were seldom taught those subjects. This omission was somewhat rectified when the Greek elementary schools were set up by private teachers after 200 B.C.

Educational ideals and practices in the early period were purely Roman. But as Greece was being conquered bit by bit, the influence of the vanquished began to take root and education became composite and cosmopolitan. This change from early to late attitudes came more gradually to the conservative Romans than it had to the Athenians. Cato the Elder (234–149 B.C.) bitterly opposed the growth of Greek ideas and customs because he thought they were decadent. Upon his eloquent insistence the senate, in 161 B.C., decreed the expulsion of all philosophers and rhetoricians from Rome. However, after Cato's death and the final conquest of Greece through the destruction of Corinth in 146 B.C., foreign influences found easy access. Cicero's *De Oratore*, in 55 B.C., marked the final triumph of Greek influences upon Roman education; it was the first as well as the best formulation by a Roman of the Greek educational ideal.

In the days of the Republic, when the basis for economic and political life was rather broad, education was a common expectation for relatively large numbers of Romans. But as conditions became more restricted in the later days of the Empire, schooling became virtually limited to the aristocratic, senatorial, and knightly classes. Some of the emperors were noted for their support and patronage of educational institutions. Antonius Pius (86–161) laid upon towns the obligation of paying the salaries of teachers and of giving them exemptions. This decree stimulated the already established custom of municipal control and support of education. Emperor Pius planned for the cities to pay the teachers' salaries at public expense, and he said he would supply funds from the imperial treasury if the cities were unable to do so. However, this imperial patronage was more or less haphazard, depending as it did upon the personal interests of the individual emperors in promoting learning or upon their efforts to gain personal support from certain sections of the population.

Later Roman education moved mainly in the direction of intellectual development. To become an accomplished speaker and debater was the main purpose of formal training, and language ability was given significance. Emphasis upon moral character was retained for some time; but as the Roman Empire became more corrupt, and the people as a whole showed interest only in material things for their own selfish and sensuous satisfactions, morality went into decline. Gone also were the ideals of the Republic and early Empire that had promoted training for service to society. In the later imperial period rhetorical training was taken by the student merely for affectation and personal display.

Christian Education

Of the many influences shaping modern educational thought, doubtless the greatest has been Christianity. The birth of Jesus Christ (c. 4 B.C.–29) during the reign of Emperor Octavius Augustus (63 B.C.–14) came at the height of Roman military and political power, when the Jews in Palestine were groaning under the oppression of their Roman overlords. In their years of struggle the Jews hopefully had looked forward to a long-promised Messiah whose coming would usher in a new and glorious day for the chosen children of Israel.

But the Jews were not united either on political or religious matters. The Pharisees, who formed the majority, wanted to resist all foreign influences so as not to undermine the sacred precepts of their ancestors. A minority group, called the Sadducees, was locked in a struggle with the Pharisees when Christ came on the scene.

Jesus, as is well known, reproached the Pharisees time and again. But the Sadducees received no consolation. Jesus claimed to be the Messiah, gathered disciples, and formed what amounted to a new sect. He embraced the poor and the outcasts and gave them stature and new hope—a rare thing for the downtrodden in that era or in any other era.

Excitement reigned in Jerusalem when Jesus arrived before the Passover. By that time the Roman officials and the coterie that held religious power among the Jews were uneasy about this "Messiah" who could stir up such enthusiasm among the people. And so, when Jesus scourged the money-changers in the temple, the leaders took action. His strange preaching on the mountain, along with reports of miraculous deeds, were disturbing but did not seem to pose an immediate threat. However, the attempt to conduct a stormy reform in the heart of the city was too much for the authorities to bear. A betrayer was found, an arrest was made at Gethsemane, a trial was held before the ecclesiastical court of the Sanhedrin, and a conviction of blasphemy was handed down. In Jewish law this crime was punishable by death; the only man empowered to carry out the sentence was the Roman governor. Pontius Pilate's attempts at evasion and his eventual capitulation to the blood lust of the mob have often been recounted.

But if the Roman and Jewish leaders thought that they would have some respite after Jesus was crucified, they were grievously mistaken. The new religion that sprang up had the same immortal quality as its founder.

The early problem of Christianity was to harmonize individual freedom with social stability, the same enigma that had faced the various pagan philosophies. Socrates, Plato, Aristotle, had all based their solutions on the intellectual nature of man. But mankind, judged as a whole, is far more emotionally than intellectually endowed, with the result that such a philosophy reaches only a small minority. Stoicism also had made reason the proper rule of life, stressing virtue as being its own reward. That philosophy attracted many of the educated class in Rome but was too intellectual ever to have any mass appeal. It remained for Christianity to offer an ethical system based upon the emotional and moral nature of man, one possessing a universal appeal to inspire goodness and virtues as objectives in life.

Historians are quite unanimous in considering Jesus the greatest of all teachers. His personality was magnetic, preparation complete, and methods effective. Stressing human relationships, he prepared his listeners for the truths to be taught by use of concrete examples applied to life situations. The 53 parables as recorded in the Gospels express meanings in such a simple and obvious manner that the intended significance can hardly be missed. Jesus knew human characteristics, recognizing that the average individual can be reached much better through his feelings than his intellect. However, he made no use of competition, acquisition, or other instinctive motives. It was not a part of Jesus' philosophy to have a system of rewards in heaven and punishments in an eternal hell as a commanding motive for righteousness. The early church leaders later borrowed that idea from Zoroastrianism, which was the state religion of the Persians before most of them were converted to Mohammedanism.

Jesus himself tried to reach his followers by the simple creed of unselfish love for both God and man. In so doing his methods were objective, direct, and personal. He emphasized moral training, and the concept of brotherly love under the Fatherhood of God. Although the content of his teaching was concerned with human behavior, Jesus was not interested in the formation of specific habits and skills. As shown by his utterances against the Pharisees, he strenuously opposed the memorizing of rules and regulations.

It is noteworthy that Jesus seemed to concentrate all his efforts on the teaching of essentials; fundamental universal truths were the only ones with which he dealt. He prescribed neither literary studies nor courses in theology. Yet as a product of his educational leadership came the most efficient religious and social workers the world has ever known.

Jesus encouraged questions but often anticipated them in the minds of his listeners. Finally, as the mark of a truly great teacher, he loved children as is so aptly shown in one of his most frequently quoted passages: "Suffer little children to come unto me and forbid them not; for of such is the kingdom of God."

Since early Christian education was based on feeling rather than reason, at first there was no intellectual content, not even for the clergy. Sports and amusements were looked upon as sinful, with the result that recreational activities and physical training were barred. The only types of music instruction tolerated were the writing and singing of psalms and hymns to be used in church worship. Generally speaking, those first-century Christians looked with suspicion on all intellectual learning because of their bitter opposition to the subjects being taught in the pagan schools.

However, in the second century, pagan teachers had been converted to Christianity and some of these began opening schools for the purpose of giving elementary training in Christian doctrines to prospective church leaders and workers. Thus, under the guise of "handmaids to the Scriptures," there were introduced grammar, rhetoric, literature, and even philosophy. Especially in the Near East, where it first took hold, this new type of curriculum spread. The Church in western Europe continued to be opposed to all pagan learning. Occasionally, however, a few leaders contended that, with proper selection, pagan culture could be made to contribute to a better understanding of the Scriptures.

It was not until the beginning of the fifth century, after a long bitter controversy concerning the nature of the deity of Jesus, that the structure of orthodox belief was finally completed by Saint Augustine (354–430). Up to that time Christian education had been largely limited to the training of clergy, converts, and children in the fundamentals and commonly accepted doctrines of the early Roman Catholic Church. Conformity had been achieved by a catechetical form of instruction similar to the Socratic method, yet markedly different because the answers were fixed in advance.

The methods employed in early church education were ascetic and disciplinary—they were intended to train the body as well as the mind. However, with an ever-increasing number of converts coming from the better educated classes, more conventional methods of instruction began to prevail among Christian educators. This tendency was not entirely a blessing due to the fact that toward the end of the Roman Empire school methods were rapidly becoming formalized and lifeless.

Too much emphasis was eventually placed on the letter and too little on the spirit of instruction, with the result that early Christian education in adopting pagan methodology lost much of its spiritual value. Among those protesting most vigorously was Saint Augustine. He advocated putting more emphasis on deeds and less on words. Grammar, he said, should be taught not by rules but by association with men who habitually used correct speech. In teaching rhetoric he would emphasize not so much a study of the rules as an appreciation of great orations. Saint Augustine opposed the compulsory study of any subject, insisting that no one does his best against his own will even when what he does is good. This famous church father encouraged questions from students, in the belief that such a procedure helped the teacher to judge the degree of comprehension and to shape the further direction of the discourse. In this practice St. Augustine was far ahead of his time; it was not a propitious moment for such a reform movement.

The initial agency of Christian education was the Church itself. Small groups got together at stated times to read, study, and take Communion. The Christian home with its position of honor for motherhood also proved an effective medium for training its members in morals and religious doctrines. The catechumenal school made an early appearance through the church organization. At first the only purpose of its instruction was to prepare candidates for baptism and church membership. This brief course of training for Hebraic and pagan converts as well as for children of believers consisted of simple elements of church doctrine and ritual with emphasis upon the moral virtues of Christ-like living.

For instruction in religious discipline and psalmody, meetings were held at stated intervals in some part of the church. Both sexes received this instruction, lasting for about two years and later extending to four. No one was received into full Communion or allowed to be baptized until the course of training was completed. These catechumenal schools continued for many centuries as the elementary schools of the Church.

When pagan teachers, converted to Christianity, attempted to reconcile their new religious beliefs with Greek philosophies, there sprang up a new type of school called "catechetical" because of its use of the question-and-answer method. This was a form of secondary education used largely for the training of church leaders although finally it came to include almost all the pagan studies. After the Church had begun to perfect its organization and bishoprics were established, theological training or cathedral schools were organized in each bishopric. Those usually were under the direction of the bishop himself. After Christianity had won its ultimate victory over paganism in western Europe, the catechetical schools began disappearing and it was the cathedral schools that remained as the Christian institutions of secondary or higher education.

Christian educational theory as represented by the leading early church fathers denied the values of the material and practical affairs of life and discounted those of the Greek intellectual pursuits. This left only the values of strictly moral and disciplined mental life to contribute to spiritual salvation. Secular learning was shunned because it improperly elevated human reason above religious faith. The child was subject to evil and, therefore, needed constant supervision. If necessary, even severe discipline was used in order to achieve the proper measure of obedience and submissiveness. Girls especially needed careful supervision, so retirement and seclusion were the desired ends in their education. Thus, the discipline of the nunnery was admired, and the life of perpetual virginity glorified.

Medieval Education

Tradition dates the fall of the Roman Empire as 476, when invading Germans deposed the youthful Romulus Augustulus (461–476). The medieval period covers roughly from then until the beginning of the fifteenth century. Those years marked the transition from ancient to modern civilization during which time political, economic, and religious institutions were gradually paving the way for our present scientific age. Within five centuries, five educational systems were developed: monasticism, chivalry, guilds, Scholasticism, and universities.

Monasticism as a way of life did not originate with Christianity, since it is found in earlier religions where ascetics devoted themselves to a solitary and contemplative life apart from the busy affairs of the world. Very early in Church history believers had fled into the desert to live entirely alone as hermits. But social instincts could not be quelled entirely. About 330, Saint Pachomius (c. 292–346), a hermit, organized a community form of monasticism on an island in the Nile River. There the monks lived apart in separate cells for meditation but came together for prayers and meals. At first each monastery was organized under its own system of rules, and these varied considerably. But in 528 Saint Benedict (480–543) formulated a code of 73 articles covering in detail the daily life of members of his particular monastery. Eventually, this "Rule of Benedict" was adopted by all monastic orders in western Europe.

Monasticism denied all desires of the body. Frequently a monk's virtues were measured by his ingenuity in physically punishing himself. This discipline sought to provide spiritual growth and moral improvement of the penitent. The Rule of Benedict imposed upon a monk the three vows of chastity, poverty, and obedience. Logically that meant a restriction to literary and vocational training, both of which were looked upon as phases of religious and moral education. Monastic training prepared not for this world but for the next.

In convents for nuns, operating under similar rules, weaving and embroidering church vestments, hangings, and altar cloths took the place of agricultural chores that were so much a part of the life of a monk.

Monastic reading requirements resulted in collections of manuscripts in libraries. This made necessary continuous copying to provide duplicates not only for local use but for exchange with other monasteries. Contrary to common belief, there was more than mere copying—medieval monks produced many original, though usually rather mediocre, writings of a historical as well as a religious and moral nature. But they can be excused for the pedestrian quality of their prose. There was little inspiration for originality.

Monasteries at first educated only their own monks but later opened their schools to boys who did not intend to enter the order. Pupils, starting at the age of 10 and usually remaining eight years, studied the seven liberal arts that had been handed down from the Greeks and Romans: the trivium (grammar, logic, rhetoric) and the quadrivium (arithmetic, astronomy, geometry, music). These monastic subjects had somewhat different meanings from what they have today. Grammar, the subject most emphasized, was really an introduction to literature; logic resembled that in universities of today; rhetoric was largely written composition but also included some church history and canonical law. All instruction was in Latin. The chief characteristic of monastic education was meditation, since it was believed that the highest knowledge and deepest experiences in life are to be gained only through divine inspiration and intuition. Because of the general ascetic nature of monasticism its school discipline was severe, and the rod seldom spared.

In the earlier medieval period the people, even kings and lords, remained largely illiterate. There were prominent exceptions, of course. Under Charlemagne (742–814), an ardent Christian with tremendous zeal for education, the monastic school reached its peak efficiency. This Frankish-German warrior brought about an educational revival throughout his vast empire. To develop more intelligent leaders for church and state Charlemagne established at court a "palace school" for the sons of nobility; to achieve educational reforms he reached into England and imported Alcuin (735–804), the greatest schoolmaster of that day. A century later King Alfred the Great (849–901) raised the standards of the English monastic schools, and he himself began the writing of the *Anglo-Saxon Chronicle*. But it must be remembered that such men were exceptional in an age when ignorance prevailed.

Feudalism has been called a complete organization of society through the medium of land tenure in which, from king down to the lowest peasant, all were bound together by obligations of service and defense. The lord protected his vassal and the vassal served the lord;

the lord judged as well as defended his vassal, the vassal gave homage as well as service to his lord. Under such a political-economic system the education of the serfs, or semi-slave class, was primarily vocational training in agricultural pursuits as learned by direct imitation. Parish school priests gave the simple religious instruction needed for participation in the rites and ceremonies of the Church.

However, there developed a system of training for the nobility known as chivalry that lasted from the ninth through the sixteenth century. It was a direct outgrowth of barbarian feudalism and continued until that system began to disintegrate as the movement toward strong central governments gained momentum. The word "chivalry" is derived from the French *cheval,* or horse, since horsemanship was a basic accomplishment. The aim was to teach high morals and social ideals, and it proved an effective method of putting Christian principles into action in a way that could be easily understood by the converted Teutonic tribes. Chivalry attempted to take what good there was in an ignorant, brutal, unprincipled society, and bring it into some accord with the standards of Christianity.

Sometimes sons and daughters of noble families were educated in the courts of fellow nobles, usually those of higher rank, as a means of getting the offspring away from parental softheartedness. Up to seven a boy's training was in the home. The next seven years he served as a page to some noble lady who taught him manners, ideals of chivalry, and music. At 14 he became a squire (attendant to a knight), caring for horses and armor, and aiding in battle. At 21 his education was complete; he was ready for knighthood.

Lessons in jousting, horsemanship, falconry, boxing, singing, swimming, and chess—the so-called "seven free arts"—had been given to the candidate for knighthood before his twenty-first year. Confessing, fasting, keeping vigil all night in his armament now formed the traditional preparation for the initiation ceremony in which elaborate religious rites were performed. After promising to be faithful, to protect women and orphans, never to lie or slander, to live in harmony with his equals, and to protect the Church, he received the accolade, a slight blow on the neck or shoulder with the flat of a sword. Then a sword and spurs were buckled on him and he was dubbed a knight.

Girls became maids-in-waiting to the ladies of the court who taught them the polite manners of society and the feminine arts of sewing, weaving, and embroidering. All education in chivalry was largely aimed at the acquisition of skills, so the methods most commonly used were example and practice—definitely a learn-by-doing procedure. The individual was motivated by high ideals and controlled by a strict adherence to recognized social standards. Unfortunately chivalry emphasized manners almost to the point of excluding morals. There was much affectation and superficiality about it all. Moreover, it was strictly limited to the upper classes.

The guild system began developing in the twelfth century. It was a by-product of the Crusades which originally had been a religious movement. It so happened that the Crusades were among the factors that had given a decided impetus to increased trade and commerce, rapid growth of free prosperous cities, and the emergence of a new middle class called bourgeoise. Guilds were organizations or associations of men engaged in commerce and industry, each usually having a monopoly in the local retail trade of its product with the privilege of taxing goods brought in by outsiders. Eventually, because of divergence of interests, these craft guilds split into two groups: skilled workers, forerunners of modern trade unions; and owners of businesses, predecessors of modern trade associations.

Naturally from such people there was a demand for a different kind of education that would fit better the needs of a burgeoning industrial society. Since schooling of a practical nature was desired, the demand arose for vocational training as the best preparation for commercial and industrial activities. But the burghers (city fathers) saw the danger of too narrow a type of vocational or trade training. They saw to it that elementary instruction included the rudiments of reading, writing, and, of course, arithmetic with its values in calculating business transactions. Masters obligated themselves to give this kind of broad instruction to their apprentices and were required to see that religious training was not neglected. As a matter of fact, most guild schools were taught by parish priests.

A distinct step toward modern education was made when studies were conducted in the vernacular languages instead of Latin. This brought about two new types of educational organization: chantry schools were founded out of bequests made by wealthy merchants or traders; burgher schools were supported and controlled by public authorities. Each had as its purpose the spreading of practical knowledge and religious training. However, the methods still resembled those used in monastic and parish schools with emphasis on example, imitation, and practice. In discipline masters usually were very harsh in their treatment of apprentices, thus continuing the monastic idea that the rod is the best teacher.

Medieval education in the types of schools described above represented the heyday of reliance on the textbook; in fact, most teachers probably knew little more than what the book contained. Especially in the early Middle Ages books were so scarce that it was only natural they should be regarded with great respect and even reverence. There was no encouragement for critical analysis, initiative, and originality. Memorization of whatever book happened to be available was the extent of the usual schooling.

Scholastic Education

At about the twelfth century, the first great intellectual revival took place—namely, Scholasticism. The term sometimes refers to the whole body of thought and writings of the schools and schoolmen in the Middle Ages. It is derived from *scholasticus,* one who becomes a teacher or student in the cathedral schools and universities. Some historians have identified Scholasticism with the deductive logic of Aristotle as he was interpreted by scholars in the later medieval period. Most commonly, however, Scholasticism is known as the method of selecting and classifying general principles or statements taken from religious or classical authorities, using a systematic order of commenting upon those statements, examining arguments on both sides, refuting arguments on the opposite side, and drawing conclusions.

The range of knowledge within which the Scholastic mind might work was limited; scholars defended only such things as the Church held to be orthodox. Mainly, deductions which could be drawn from generally accepted principles were sought. Two distinct methods were used. In his lecture a teacher read the text together with its glossaries and annotations. This proved largely a process of slow dictation to permit students to make authentic copies of authoritative works.

Then came the disputation, or debate, where individuals or groups of students opposed each other. The usual procedure was to propose a thesis, offer the proof, raise and refute objections, and treat the entire proposition in a minutely logical manner. Under such a teaching system it was necessary to work intensely on a very few subjects or questions. Sometimes this reached ridiculous extremes. The classic example concerns a disputation that required three days of time and effort on the part of Europe's leading scholars to determine just how many angels could dance on the point of a needle.

An important influence during the latter part of this movement was the infiltration into Christian Europe of Aristotelian science from Spain, then controlled by the Saracens. Moorish Spain had attained its most advanced intellectual heights at the time when the church fathers were still frowning upon new knowledge and doing everything possible to keep it from being developed in the Western Christian world. These Saracens not only preserved learning but they were improving upon it during the time Christian scholars were frittering away their intellectual efforts in fruitless arguments over inconsequential matters. So to the Saracens, along with the early monks, fell the honor of conserving ancient learning both in content and spirit. It was these Mohammedans who eventually gave to Christian scholars the impetus needed to take up the humanities in the period which came to be known as the Renaissance.

Another influence at that time was the growing skepticism about the unchallenged values of faith on the part of disillusioned returning Crusaders. After their long sojourn among the Greeks and Arabs of the Near East, these wayfaring men had seen enough to make them dissatisfied with the conditions they found upon reaching their homes. So it was in the thirteenth century that, in a slightly modified form and after a long bitter struggle, Scholasticism reached its highest point. Then a compromise and union of Aristotelian philosophy and Christian theology within a highly organized logical system was set forth in one of the world's greatest books, *Summa Theologica,* written by St. Thomas Aquinas (c. 1225–1274). It remains today the authoritative exposition of Roman Catholic theology.

Earlier representatives of Scholasticism, associated with monastic and cathedral schools, presented their ideas both by writing and by teaching. Widely read and copied, some of their manuscripts were frequently used as textbooks in schools. Students began traveling long distances in order to listen to lectures of the more eminent of these Scholastics. In due time the reputation of certain schoolmen spread so far and attracted so many mature students that there came into existence the medieval university.

Originally the university was a guild chartered by king, emperor, or Pope. Such high-ranking support made it much more independent of ecclesiastical authority than were either the cathedral schools under the bishops or the monastic schools under the abbots. It was also independent of any political or secular control. Under the charter the faculty and students possessed many privileges that theretofore had been granted only to clergy. These included exemption from taxation, exemption from military service, trials by special courts outside of civil jurisdiction, and immunity from arrest by civil authorities.

Universitas was the term originally applied to any group of people organized into a guild for any common purpose, but gradually the term was applied specifically to universities of faculties and students. As these two groups organized themselves into guilds and corporate organizations, a few of the stronger cathedral schools became universities as a protection against the king, bishop, chancellor, or anyone else who attempted to bring them under control.

In similar manner the students frequently organized themselves into guilds for protection against teachers, townspeople, officials, and sometimes even from each other. The entire student body was known as the *Studium Generale*. For living purposes, both social and financial, the students grouped themselves into "nations" according to the country or section from which they came—for example, in the university at Paris there were the nations of France, Normandy, Picardy, England, along with several others. Each elected a councilor every year.

A group of masters teaching the same subject was called a *facultas*, and each of these elected a dean. Deans of the faculties and councilors of the nations made up what was known as the university council, which annually elected a chief executive. The chain of authority was from Pope to bishop to chancellor. Gradually the most important power delegated to the chancellor became the right to issue the *licentia docendi* (teaching license) to students who qualified within the diocese. As a few of the universities gained still greater prominence the Pope often gave to the chancellor the right to issue *licentiae docendi ubique* (licenses to teach anywhere), which meant authority beyond their own dioceses.

One unusual characteristic at Bologna (Italy) was the power of the student guilds to exert control over the administrative affairs of the university. The rector of those student guilds was recognized as the head of the university, and faculty members were obliged to take an oath of obedience to the student rector. Also they had to abide by the regulations of the student guilds concerning the length and contents of lectures—their time of beginning and ending, and length of the academic term.

A student usually entered a university at the age of 14. There he attached himself to a master under whom he studied until he could "define and determine"—that is, until he was able to read, write, and speak Latin. When able to demonstrate adequate proficiency by examination, he was declared a "bachelor." Then for a period of four to seven years he continued his studies under several masters until he could "dispute"—that is, defend his thesis or "masterpiece." A successful defense entitled him to receive his license to teach and he was admitted to the ranks of the masters. From then on he became eligible to compete with the other masters for students and to charge fees for his instruction.

Discipline definitely was a problem. Those special privileges granted to students tended to make them impatient of restraint. Frequent and awkward attempts of youth to assert itself resulted in excessive indulgences and even gross immoralities. Complicating the situation was the fact that the special privileges were extended to students not only within the university grounds but also outside them. Many irresponsible young men exploited their privileges by traveling from one university to another, using the medieval version of hitchhike, begging their way, and sometimes indulging in riotous and unconventional practices. All this was a form of academic freedom that did not tend to make higher education very popular among people coming into contact with students.

The process of transformation from cathedral schools to universities came about so gradually that it is quite impossible to give founding dates for those that came into existence during the twelfth and thirteenth centuries.* Regardless of which has the longest history, the University of Paris (founded circa 1160) was soon acknowledged as the greatest in the Middle Ages. It was a common saying: "Italy has the Papacy; Germany has the Empire; and France has the University of Paris; all is well." As early as the eleventh century Paris was attracting a large number of men to its several noted schools. By the fourteenth century the university had some 40 colleges, including the celebrated Sorbonne. Theology, law, arts, and medicine were the principal subjects at the various colleges.

In the struggle of the university masters to control their own affairs they turned to anyone who would give them help. On one occasion they appealed to the king to assist them against the townspeople, and he gave them the right to strike whenever faculty or students were molested by the town. When another king assumed authority to issue unwelcome orders to the university, the faculty turned to the Pope for help. Later, to gain their ends, they opposed even the Pope. At the University of Paris a significant result of this struggle for autonomy was the growing recognition of the faculty as the full legal body of the university. In time the medieval faculties gained a corporate existence, set their curriculums, issued licenses to teach, conferred degrees, and appointed their own members. In fact, the very idea of a university in its origins was this corporate existence of a faculty, whereas today in

* Most scholars agree that the school of medicine at Salerno in the ninth century was probably the first European university.

the United States the legal corporation for universities is not the faculty but the board of trustees.

Paris had been famed for theology, Bologna for law, and Salerno (Italy) for medicine. In England, about 1167, Oxford achieved the university type of faculty organization modeled after the form used in Paris but not so closely supervised by the Pope or local bishop. Cambridge was established in 1209 when a group of masters became dissatisfied and moved from Oxford. It was, in fact, a rather common medieval practice to set up a new university by seceding from another.

Before leaving this period of history, let us briefly recapitulate. We have seen how the monastic schools kept education alive after the barbarian had conquered the West. We have looked, too, at the training in chivalry given to the children of aristocrats in medieval days. And we have noted the importance of Scholasticism with its effect on the establishment of universities.

One thing more needs to be said. The use of Latin in those universities and in Christian ritual gave rise to the famous Latin schools which prepared boys for higher learning or for the clergy. Thus the Latin grammar schools that later played such an important role in European education actually had their origins in this early period.

Humanistic Education

Among historians the term Renaissance has principally been used to cover the period of the fourteenth, fifteenth, and early sixteenth centuries. Modern times are said to have had their inception with this movement because it represented a speeding up of political, economic, and religious changes as well as intellectual and artistic ones. The chief characteristic of this period, as it affected education, was a growing secularism which had already become a strong though not a dominating force in the later Middle Ages. Humanistic education represented a rebellion against conservative forces, but it took two quite different roads. In Italy individual humanism stressed personal development, culture, and freedom; it produced a revival of classical learning and paganism. In the North, however, it was a social type of humanism, demanding reforms in living conditions and moral life. Both in Italy and the northern countries humanism had two phases: the first was fresh, original, and enthusiastic; the second, narrow and formal.

Francis Petrarch (1304–1374), known as the first modern scholar, insisted that the best portrayal of the development of perfection of human nature is in classical rather than medieval literature. In his enthusiasm to reestablish the glory of the Roman Empire he searched indefatigably for lost classic manuscripts. Although he wrote much lyrical poetry in his native Italian, he took special pride in his accomplishments in writing classical Latin. Stimulated by such an outstanding leader, many humanists asserted the values and superiority of the classical over the medieval (or corrupted) Latin as the best expression of the human spirit—and above all else they stressed style. By the fifteenth century an active interest in reviving classical Greek had also been developed, and soon thereafter Hebrew was promoted as a scholarly classical language.

Since the city-states in Italy were the first in Europe to become wealthy from the trade that followed the Crusades, Renaissance humanism took root in that country. Also, because Italy had been the ancient home of Graeco-Roman culture, its traditions had persisted more strongly there than elsewhere. In Florence, as a typical example, humanism was fostered by the celebrated Medici family of bankers and rulers who spent large sums of money to build libraries and to subsidize such artists as Leonardo da Vinci (1452–1519). Although most of the hierarchy of the Catholic Church looked askance at this new movement, in due time even some of the Popes, including Leo X (1475–1521), proved ardent patrons of humanism.

The humanistic course of study at its best provided for the gaining of a facility in reading, writing, and speaking of basic Latin; extensive study of the poets and prose writers, both Greek and Roman; and familiarity with the lives of ancients through a reading of history and biography. The attempt was made to develop a joy of living and to inculcate an appreciation of the beautiful. Also opened to the scholar was an important field denied his medieval predecessor—nature study.

Physical training received attention from the humanists, not only in the form of swimming, boxing, fencing, riding, and dancing, but also in diet and hygiene. Social deportment and manners were stressed as essential aspects of moral training. Writers declared the importance of moral education even though, in practice, personal standards often gave way to license just as had been the case in the later stages of the Graeco-Roman civilization so idealized by humanists. Moral education definitely was not limited to obedience to religious authority; the attempt was made to make it more practical in its application to life situations. Obviously in some cases the education did not take, partly because men were not used to acting under such a liberal code as humanism represented.

Freedom of thought, creative activity, and self-expression were the aims of humanistic education—a striving for the expression of individual personality through art, literature, nature study, architecture, and music. Versatility and well-roundedness were stressed since it was felt that a blended combination of ability and background, enabling one to meet new situations, formed the path to the most abundant life. The humanist aimed not for life hereafter but for getting the most out of his time on this earth in the way of personal satisfactions based upon high idealism and a sense of adventure. His education was to be the means of living a fine, rich, full life. The Italian humanist, in fact, borrowed from the Greeks their idea of a liberal education—the harmonious development of mind, body, morals. Humanism at its best renewed the emphasis upon individuality and personal self-realization.

The education of the Renaissance was intended mainly for the youth of the upper and wealthy classes. The primary interest of the Church was in the development of scholars and clergy for its future leadership. The rulers were interested in surrounding themselves with trained and loyal followers who would be gentlemen as well as scholars. The middle classes wanted a type of education that would permit them to break into these two charmed circles.

The first classical secondary schools were the Italian court schools. These furnished the model for similar schools in other countries: the *Gymnasium* in Germany, the *collèges* and *lycées* in France, and the Latin grammar schools in England and colonial America. Court schools were so named because they were founded and maintained by the ruling dukes and princes of the Italian cities in connection with their courts. Each of these dictatorial rulers was ambitious to make his particular city a renowned center of humanistic learning. In addition to establishing schools, many of them founded libraries and museums. As patrons of scholars and artists they gave genius a chance to flourish.

Even though the court schools were supported by the ruling family, most of the pupils paid fees. Since these schools were limited to boys, girls whose parents could afford it studied at home under humanistic tutors. Boys were admitted at the age of nine or ten and remained until twenty or twenty-one. Since they attended on a boarding school basis, pupils were educated both in and out of the classroom. Many court schools at first set out to rival the work of the universities, especially since the latter were still antagonistic to humanistic learning. But as the work of those universities became more liberal and was constantly being raised to a higher level, the court schools became in some degree preparatory institutions since they taught pupils how to read, write, understand, and speak Latin—the necessary skills for undertaking university work with ease and profit.

Among the important contributions of humanistic secondary schools were the new methods devised. With the invention of printing, textbooks became more plentiful, obviating the necessity of lectures by teachers. Written themes began to displace the oral disputations that had been so common in medieval schools. Latin and Greek were treated as living and not dead languages, and self-expression was continually encouraged. Discipline was unusually mild because punishment and threats of punishment were not needed as motives for learning. The fact that higher posts of honor and activity in the life of the times were open only to those who had been thoroughly trained in the humanistic manner proved to be sufficient motivation.

In northern European countries humanism aimed not at attainment of individual happiness but at social reform and improvement in human relationships. Classics, translated and properly edited, were the educational tools used to eliminate the ignorance of the common people and also to attack the greed and hypocrisy of some church, state, and business leaders. Literary training had as its objective a religious and social purpose rather than personal self-development. The Italian humanist took religion so lightly that there was practically no conflict with the Church. But the early social humanists bitterly attacked the "moral evils" within the Church while accepting its theological doctrines. Later many of them joined the movement away from Catholicism known as the Reformation.

One noteworthy organization was the non-monastic teaching order founded in Holland in 1376 and known as the Brethren of Common Life. This group developed a democratic type of humanistic education rather than the aristocratic class education of the Italians. Pious and humanitarian in spirit, the Brethren of Common Life assisted poor scholars to support themselves. They proved so successful in teaching backward pupils that many other schools were later placed under their supervision. Formal and meaningless methods were rejected and were supplanted by much of the broad literary spirit of the Italian Renaissance.

Northern humanistic educators were especially interested in the problem of methods. Their theories proved to be far in advance of the actual practices of that time. Desiderius Erasmus (c. 1466–1536) authored two great educational classics in which he advocated a careful study of a child's nature and the liberal use of games and play in school work. He attacked the harsh methods of discipline of his time and proposed more humane and attractive means for bringing a child into line. Erasmus considered it the business of a teacher to help the student, not to display his own learning. He attached no merit at all to besetting the child with difficulties merely as difficulties. His introduction of some independence and individuality into the learning of lessons was most welcome in an age addicted to verbatim memorizing and slavish imitation of the literary style of Greek and Roman masters, especially Cicero.

A few words should be said about Ciceronianism, the overemphasis upon style and sentence structure in the Greek and Roman classic writers, which became so prominent in humanistic education from the middle of the sixteenth century on. This was largely superficial imitation based upon the idea that, to create, one must first imitate the masters of style. The trouble proved to be that very few ever got beyond the stage of imitation. Thus the curriculum became limited to a few selected classics rather than a wide reading of ancient literature. The inevitable result, of course, was that Ciceronianism became as narrow as the rejected Aristotelian Scholasticism.

Moralistic Education

Most American educational traditions can be traced to the Protestant Reformation. Catholicism, in fact as well as in name, was the universal religion in western Europe when the sixteenth century began. But the next 200 years witnessed a series of religious revolts that gave birth to new church organizations destined to play an important role both in Europe and America. These were backed by economic resources of the middle classes and military powers of national states. Protestant reformers, of course, were motivated by intense spiritual convictions. But throughout the previous history of the Church, heresies had been stamped out; therefore, it can be said the Reformation was primarily successful because of the economic and political conditions of that day.

Protestantism denied the claims of Catholicism that the Pope and clergy must be the authoritative interpreters of Christian doctrine. Theoretically, according to the newer viewpoint, the individual gained salvation directly through faith rather than through any mediation of an authoritative priesthood. If carried to a logical conclusion, Protestantism should have allowed each person to interpret the Bible and to believe exactly as he pleased. Such a tolerance was theoretical—it was far from the actual picture. In practice most Protestant groups assumed the role of persecutors of dissenters and, so far as possible, used civil powers to enforce their own convictions upon others. Such was the spirit of the times as reflected in political, economic, and religious life!

Playing the leading role in the educational as well as in the religious aspects of this Reformation drama was Martin Luther (1483–1546), an Augustinian friar, who taught philosophy at the University of Wittenberg. Long before his time the social humanists had been attacking the Church. Critics had persistently demanded that the clergy lead pure lives without exception, that certain ecclesiastical leaders earn their big incomes, and that monasteries make more useful contributions to society.

Most of the critics before Luther had accepted the Church doctrines. It could be only a matter of time, however, before humanistic interest in the study of original Greek and Hebrew sources made inevitable the questioning and attacking of theological beliefs and ecclesiastical practices. When the break from Catholicism did come, there was rather an even division between the outstanding social humanists who left the Catholic Church and those who remained in it.

Protestants substituted the authority of the Bible for that of the Church as the infallible rule of faith and moral practice. Acceptance of the doctrine of innate depravity led the reformers to contend that only an abiding faith in God's mercy could effect salvation—and entrance to heaven largely would depend upon knowing the truth. In order to know the truth one had to be able to read the Bible. This belief naturally provided additional motivation for citizens to want their children to get some schooling.

It should be pointed out that religious moralism as an aim for education was not original with the Protestants. Nearly all primitive and ancient peoples had based their educational systems upon religious and moral, rather than intellectual, concepts. Jesus had fused religion and morality in his teaching, but the medieval Church then proceeded to lay more stress on theological doctrines and ritualistic observances.

Reformers, such as Luther and John Calvin (1509–1564), conceived of education as the preparing of Christian men and women for the glorious life hereafter by providing adequate training in the duties of home, occupation, state, and church. Wherever Protestant influences were felt, schools attempted to integrate the three ideals of intelligence, social virtue, and individual piety. If such an education were to be effective, everyone would have to go to school.

Luther is said to have been the first man to advocate compulsory education. He insisted that the state authorities either establish schools themselves or compel the people to do so—and for the sake of church and state, each family should be required to send its children to these schools. Training of young people should be a state rather than an individual matter, he thought, because of the unreliable whims of parents. Luther went so far as to predict eternal damnation for those youngsters who were being allowed to run about too freely, swearing, stealing, and doing as they pleased.

In Germany, and also in England, the Reformation did bring about a control of the schools by civil authorities. When finally Luther was able to get for both church and school the guardianship of the state, thus planting the seed for modern-day state and national control of education, he did not anticipate secularization of education—the divorce of public-supported schools from church control. His thought was that since a ruler derived his power from God, then as God's representative he had the responsibility of caring as much for the spiritual as for the material interests of his subjects. In comparison, Calvin believed the state was obligated to make laws for the organization and support of schools that would be operated in accordance with the ideas of the pastors. In other words, he would have the church leaders control education. That is what later happened in New England where Calvinistic doctrines dominated.

Protestant education was intended for work rather than play—and the work must be for the glory of God. The Reformation curriculum was a religious one based upon the Bible. In the vernacular primary schools established throughout northern Germany by Johann Bugenhagen (1485–1558) to carry out Luther's educational ideas, the subjects taught included reading, writing, religion, singing, crafts, and physical training. This represented quite an advance in elementary education, but the curriculums of Protestant secondary schools and universities remained largely a continuation of humanistic subject matter.

While Latin, Greek, and Hebrew were considered necessary for a proper understanding of the Bible, Luther did urge the addition of history, mathematics, natural science, music, and gymnastics. In the universities Biblical interpretation began replacing Scholastic theology. In England the dominant aspect of education became a kind of character training, with the stress on good manners as a means of attaining moral conduct.

Protestant reformers were intensely interested in problems of method. However, there was no real progress beyond the theory stage. Reading in elementary schools usually consisted of formal oral pronunciation of words, and memorizing of answers to questions of the catechism; very little opportunity was given for any intelligent comprehension of meanings. In the secondary schools the method consisted of the memorization of rules and declensions in Latin grammar and the learning by heart of long passages from the classics.

Despite theories that sounded beautiful, most of those early Protestant classrooms became gloomy and sometimes terrifying environments under a rigid form of teaching in which the discipline remained extremely harsh. The local church dominated the individual in school even though, theoretically, he was supposed to be determining his own beliefs and personal conduct through his own interpretations of the Scriptures. In reality it definitely was not a matter of teaching HOW to think but rather WHAT to think.

In European countries that had effectively checked the Protestant Reformation movement, the great Catholic Counter Reformation was taking place. The Council of Trent, lasting from 1545 to 1563, eliminated the more offensive abuses that had grown up in the flushed, unchallenged days of ecclesiastical history. Doctrines over which most of the controversies had arisen were clarified. An educational reorganization was considered of prime importance, with the result that teaching orders began to spring up. There was a widespread establishment of new schools in which the teachers had been carefully trained for their work.

The Society of Jesus was organized in 1534 by Ignatius Loyola (1491–1556), a Spanish nobleman who had been converted to religious service while convalescing from battle wounds. The Jesuit schools, for young men only, had as their purpose the training of highly disciplined and loyal leaders to advance the cause of the Church. Specifically, the educational aim was to develop a "Christian gentleman and a Christian scholar." In Jesuit colleges that sprang up in France the curriculum consisted of Latin, Greek, religion, and religious history. But later on the elementary level they borrowed the Protestants' idea of teaching in the vernacular. Moreover, they gave special attention to physical education and encouraged sports and games.

In everything, both in and out of the classroom, the Jesuits placed a premium on motivation and competition. Elaborate devices were developed to stimulate rivalry. Individuals were pitted against each other, classes vied with one another, and honor societies were organized in which membership was gained only after stiff competition. Throughout their entire history Jesuit teachers in both secondary schools and colleges have had the reputation of excellent scholarship and exceptional training—although it must be said that some critics have disagreed with the methods they have used to attain their ends.

Brethren of the Christian Schools, another important teaching order for boys only, was established in 1684 by Jean Baptiste de la Salle

(1651–1719). In these elementary schools, designed for children of workingmen and the poor, the atmosphere was deeply pious and the natural activities of pupils severely repressed. Reading, writing, arithmetic, and religion were taught. Christian Brothers were the first to grade elementary pupils into classes according to their abilities. They also devised the method in common use today whereby the child recites to the entire class and not individually to the teacher as previously had been the custom. Also noteworthy were their normal schools in which, for the first time, children in practice-school classes were used to train the brothers more effectively for their work in teaching.

During the Reformation period some effort was directed toward providing wider opportunities for education among the masses. However, in all the European countries the social class structure was too deeply ingrained to make possible any completely democratic conception. While more educational opportunities were being given to the lower classes, they did not receive the same kind or quality of education as the upper classes. Both Luther and Calvin had much more interest in the classical type of secondary school than in elementary vernacular education. The traditional aristocratic concepts as brought down from the Middle Ages and Renaissance were still deeply entrenched in the Reformation. Nevertheless, the seeds for free universal education were being sown in the efforts made toward providing at least the rudiments of schooling for all.

Encouraging, too, were the proposals being made that girls should be educated as well as boys. In the Netherlands, the Dutch Reformed Church set up what probably were the best vernacular schools in Europe. Stimulated by the practical needs of its commercial cities, the Dutch schools taught the three R's and religion to girls as well as boys. Undoubtedly this innovation eventually influenced the Puritans in England and America as well as our Dutch settlers.

Realistic Education

The third of the great movements in the general intellectual awakening of western Europe, running somewhat parallel to the Renaissance and Reformation, was realism. It was not an original contribution of the sixteenth century; the religious temper, faith in the unseen, authority of tradition and revelation had previously made realism the dominant outlook during the intellectual controversies of the early medieval period. Most certainly those universal propositions laid down by Scriptures and church fathers had been considered real and binding even after being challenged by the Scholastic philosophy known as nominalism—a set of doctrines that had evolved from Aristotle's outlook.

Coming as a protest against the narrowness of both humanists and reformers, this new realism was part of a growing interest in practical realities of life. It represented the beginnings of modern scientific inquiries as exemplified by the work of Nicolaus Copernicus (1473–1543), Galileo Galilei (1564–1642), Johannes Kepler (1571–1630), and Sir Isaac Newton (1642–1727). Realists were centering their attention primarily on the concrete objects in the universe.

But the realists of the 1500's were not teachers. They were speculative individuals who realized that schools of their day were "out of step" with the realities of life—and were failing to prepare for actual living. And yet, while all realists were critical of schools developed by humanists and reformers, they disagreed among themselves as to what should constitute a different type of education. Thus they may be divided into three groups: humanistic, social, and sense-realists.

As pioneers in the movement the humanistic realists made no complete break with the concepts of humanism. Classical languages and literature were considered the only subjects worthy of study, for, as they thought, the ancient writers had reached the highest possible achievements attainable by human minds.

However, their educational ideas, though humanistic in content, were realistic in aim and method. They sought for complete knowledge and understanding of the human society as a proper means of fitting an individual to the environment in which he lives. To accomplish this they advocated the intelligent seeking out of meaning in classical literature, to be studied not for its own sake but for scientific, historical, and social information. Humanists were concerned with diction, structure, and style; the reformers, with religious and moral precepts. But humanistic realists proposed that classical literature be utilized as the best available medium to prepare for the realities of life.

In so doing, they greatly overestimated the capacity of the average man for knowledge; they fell into the common error of judging abilities of others by their own brilliant talents. Thus humanistic realists proposed a curriculum far ahead of that day and age, in some respects even ahead of modern thinking or, at least, practices. Although they stressed a literary type of education, it was much more "down to earth" than that of the humanists. Actually their revolutionary ideas made practically no impression on the organization of schools of their day, but much that they advocated is thought-provoking, even in modern times.*

Probably the most interesting humanistic realist was François Rabelais (c. 1493–1553), an unconventional French monk, scholar, and physician, who effectively used satire to ridicule the schooling of his era. In his famous story of Gargantua, a giant youth is taught according to the methods of Rabelais' day and is drilled in the ABC's so thoroughly that this instruction requires more than five years. Another thirteen years are consumed in the reading of three books, but, of course, in that time the pupil has copied all three volumes in Gothic characters. In the end, placed alongside a young fellow trained for only two years in the newer educational methods, Gargantua succeeds in proving himself to be little else but a "blockhead."

Rabelais was amazingly modern. As a constructive suggestion he advocated an informal method in which reasoning was substituted for rote memory, with study being made pleasant and attractive. This approach to teaching has been the basis for many changes in methodology and content in recent decades, especially in the field of mathematics.

Social realists came from the aristocratic upper classes. They were "men of affairs," interested in the training of their sons for active participation in public life. Their aim was to develop a "man of the world and a gentleman." Education, they believed, must be gained through direct contact with people and their social activities rather than through books. Social realists ridiculed the bookishness of humanistic realists who, they claimed, were preparing for the life of the past and not for that of the present. These critics opposed cramming the memory with facts; they felt that education must provide the basis for sensible choices and decisions as well as for social efficiency and enjoyment of leisure hours. To them the art of living should be the goal of learning—the pupil lives what he learns. While social realists advocated a practical type of education, in no sense was it vocational or professional. Their aim was to make a versatile "man of the world."

Michel de Montaigne (1533–1592) stood out as the most truly representative exponent of social realism. Opposing the idea that a mere study of books provides an adequate education, he suggested an activity curriculum. To him, experience was much more important than words

* In this connection, it is interesting to note that in the 1930's and 1940's some American colleges adopted a curriculum based almost exclusively on the reading of books by world-famous writers. Sometimes known as the "Great Books" theory, this approach to learning has been successfully tried for many years at St. John's College in Annapolis, Maryland.

and books; travel, the best agency for becoming familiar with people and customs; and the world itself, the best curriculum. In his scheme, Latin would be retained as important in the education of the gentleman, but Greek would be rejected as merely the flashy and impractical equipment of a scholar. French and foreign languages would be studied because they were needed for conversation with people at home and abroad. Harsh disciplinary methods so commonly used at that time to command attention would be dropped because learning would be pleasurable and attractive in its own right.

Montaigne had little use for schools and universities. He claimed that fifteen years of such education served only to make the student a greater and more conceited "coxcomb" than when he left home. Like Rabelais, he urged the use of a tutor; and for a short period of time the tutorial system became quite popular among the aristocratic classes not only in France but also in England. However, some of Montaigne's fellow-realists rejected the tutorial plan and began demanding new types of schools which would turn out gentlemen instead of "pedants." Especially in Germany a few such schools were established but they never became common or influential. Those that did operate featured modern languages, mathematics, political history, geography, military arts, and fine manners. It is worthy of note that in the United States today there are a few academies and finishing schools, attended by sons and daughters of the wealthier classes, that still reflect the influence of social realism.

Sense realism represented the complete search for reality as experienced in everyday human relationships. It was a product of the many explorations and discoveries of the sixteenth and seventeenth centuries, and the starting point of the scientific movement in education. Sense realists sought to advance new knowledge rather than limit education to the mere learning of what was already known and written in books. Secrets of nature were to be discovered and utilized for the practical benefits to be brought to man in his everyday living. Religious moralistic education was still esteemed, but an emphasis upon democratic education, especially in vernacular elementary schools, was included. Sense realists proposed a "pansophic curriculum"—one that would include practically all knowledge.

Johann Amos Comenius (1592–1670), a bishop of the small, despised Moravian religious sect, diligently searched every available author and quizzed educational reformers for fruitful ideas in developing his sense-realist viewpoint. To meet the growing demand for a new method whereby students might learn Latin with greater ease and in shorter time, he prepared two introductory textbooks. In these he worked out a concise Latin vocabulary and made use of pictures and words together to impress the learning on the memory of the child.

Comenius's textbook enjoyed extraordinary popularity. His curricular recommendations were accepted as in harmony with the new trend working toward reform in subject matter, but his broad general scheme of applying psychological principles to the learning process was given a cold reception during his own lifetime. Comenius's remarkable treatises on education remained practically unknown for two centuries, and only in recent years has his viewpoint been recognized as forward-looking. To him the school was a manufactory, shaping children into human beings and playing a large part in the improvement of society. He considered the aim of education broader than merely religious, for children must be taught to live not only for church and school but for all other aspects of life. In fact, he proposed a comprehensive school system, with a carefully graded curriculum, to educate children from birth to maturity.

Most of the sense realists were practical educators, interested in the development of schools as the ideal agency for better living. They recognized the importance of the trained teacher, able to study children and to make full use of the natural laws basic to sound pedagogical practices. During the eighteenth century some new sense-realist schools were established in Germany, largely by the Pietist dissenters from the Lutheran faith. The leading figure in this new movement was August Hermann Francke (1663–1727), who developed a group of institutions emphasizing scientific studies. His new University of Halle provided a training school for teachers of the *Volksschulen* just then coming into being. Francke gained support of the king of Prussia, who not only established several hundred schools but also in 1713 and 1717 issued school laws making it compulsory for all parents to send their children. Tuition fees were to be paid for poor children by the communities.*

Sense realists were the first to insist that knowledge comes through the senses, and that the order of learning must be things-thoughts-words. Wolfgang Ratke (1571–1635), founder of experimental schools, is credited with being the first educator to search for the natural order in which the mind develops. Even though he made the error of basing his conclusions concerning the growth of child nature upon analogies involving external nature, such as trees, the general theme of Ratke's

---

* For further discussion of Francke's contribution to German education, see page 168.

theories still dominates modern educational methods. In evaluating sense realists as a group, it can be said they firmly established the principle that basic to educational method is the process of the natural growth of the child. Upon this concept were formulated many practical pedagogical rules that are still in use today.

Rationalistic Education

From the Greek period on, educational theories and practices at times had been influenced and even dominated by rationalism.* Both the Sophists and the philosophers had frequently advocated the power of reason to control human affairs. Rebel cries of defiance to established authority, which had been heard in Rome and even occasionally in the medieval period, became constantly louder during the Renaissance. Then a strong wave of rationalism in the eighteenth century sprang up as a protest against what some regarded as the antiquated and arbitrary authority of church and state; it represented a rapidly growing opposition to displays of bigotry in social and religious life and to despotic absolutism in political government.

Reformation movements of both Protestants and Catholics began losing their uplifting qualities in the welter of bitter hatreds stirred up by religious wars, in which human beings were sometimes tortured or burned at the stake because of differences in manner of belief. At the close of the Thirty Years' War (1618–1648), after each side finally had realized it could not exterminate the other, it was decided to let the religious group in control establish itself as the state religion. From then on Protestants and Catholics settled down to enforcement of conformity to strict dogmas and practices.

In politics, the "divine right of kings" theory had been effectively used to keep existing governments in power. Even in England, where a limited constitutional monarchy had been won, it had been a victory for Parliament and not for the common people. Elsewhere in Europe, legislative assemblies met seldom, if ever, and a favored minority prospered and frolicked at the expense of the overtaxed and impoverished masses.

Political leadership of church and state often joined to check the two recent democratic movements that had been encouraged by both

---

* The term "rationalism" has many different meanings. For example, in a religious sense it has been compared with English Deism and among philosophers it has been contrasted with empiricism and sensationalism. In this chapter, the term is used simply to mean that doctrine which was advocated by those who considered reasoning as the prime factor that should govern man's actions—not faith, loyalty, tradition, or the like.

reformers and realists—freedom of thought for the individual and recognition of the needs of the common people. And so, as if to meet this conservative reaction against individual freedom, there began developing late in the seventeenth century a strong rationalistic movement. But, as we shall see, it soon limited itself to the exploitation of reasoning powers of a small number of intelligentsia and deliberately overlooked the needs of the common man.

Rationalism received its greatest impetus from scientific investigations and interpretations of the universe, especially those of Sir Isaac Newton (1642–1727) whose epoch-making *Mathematical Principles of Natural Philosophy* was published in 1687. The "laws of nature" formulated by Newton remained scientific gospel until the late nineteenth century. His elaboration of the "law of gravitation" and the "law of cause and effect" went a long way in convincing intellectuals that the universe is an orderly system of atoms moving in absolute space and time, essentially simple and uniform in structure, obeying fixed laws that operate in a causal and uniform manner.

Thus the universe came to be looked upon as a great machine, not subject to caprice or divine intervention, but operating naturally in accordance with mathematical laws. Scientific "natural laws" served as the model for scientific natural explanations in other fields of life and thought. Popularity of the Newtonian interpretations brought about new world views, the most extreme of which was materialism. Materialists such as Claude Adrien Helvetius (1715–1771) jumped to the conclusion that nothing exists but matter in the form of atoms operating according to mechanical natural laws. This theory precluded all conceptions of a spiritual world and of a soul.

Rationalism reached its highest peak of popularity in France through the works of the master satirist, François Voltaire (1694–1778). Strongly laced with skepticism, his rationalism aimed to show men how to think for themselves—to test all things whether human or divine by the power of their own reason. The purpose of an education, he maintained, is to free the intellect from all repression and to enable those capable of reasoning to escape from restraints of religious, political, and social authority. An individual properly trained in rationalistic educational methods presumably could control all the aspects of his life merely by means of coldly critical reasoning.

By its very nature rationalistic education was aristocratic. The common man, rationalists believed, did not possess the qualities necessary for reasoning out his problems. Thus it followed that the lower classes were incapable of being educated. Voltaire described these people as destined to reman stupid and barbaric; therefore, unlike the intelligentsia, they needed a God and a king to keep them under control.*

But for the aristocracy of that day intellectual training was given the highest place. The child's schooling included art, literature, philosophy, science, and social etiquette but omitted physical education and vocational education. An aristocratic youth was reared amid the artificialities of a cold, selfish, calculating society. Textbooks consisted usually of pamphlets covering economic, philosophical, and scientific subjects—the more satirical and critical they were, the more popular they proved to be. Heated arguments on philosophical and scientific topics were the vogue and the man who could ridicule successfully another's viewpoint proved himself a "gentleman of letters."

Social education for gentility's sake was a primary consideration of the people who espoused rationalism. Refined manners and language were developed and good taste glorified, but there could be nothing genuine and sincere in a culture that was so brutally heartless and superficial. When appearing in polite society the boy aristocrat powdered his hair and his little sister wore a corset nearly cutting her in two. A typical adult product of this education was the conversationalist who used eloquent words but said nothing. In social life old moral virtues were replaced by sexual looseness, infidelity, and immodesty—the emphasis was on salon and boudoir manners instead of moral training. It is no wonder that when these rationalistic educational ideas were so dominant, personal moral standards sank to such a low level among the upper classes.

Since the rationalists were not professional educators, they organized no new schools and contributed practically nothing in the way of new methods. Characteristically they took great delight in being destructive in whatever they had to say about schools and schoolmasters. Their attacks were leveled against universities for hampering freedom of thought. Although they made use of tutors or schools already in existence, they glorified a sort of self-education through the reading of pamphlets and participation in general discussions held in fashionable salons.

Theoretically, to them, man was a human machine with all his higher mental processes a result of the impressions made by things upon his physical senses. The approved method was to apply analytical

* The Encyclopedists, a group that held the same opinion as Voltaire, were highly regarded by the "eggheads" of that era. So named because they were writing the French *Encyclopedia,* those men reflected their merely academic interest in the masses by their opposition to universal education. One of their leaders, it should be added, was the controversial philosopher, Denis Diderot (1713–1784).

reasoning to every phase of human life and institution, and to reject cynically whatever failed to stand the test. The climax to this worship of reason as the sole means of enlightenment came during the French Revolution in the exalted religious fanaticism that had "Reason" replacing God as the deity.

But it must be said that rationalism eventually left a definite mark on the history of education. The belief that man should rely on his own personal powers to think problems through to logical conclusions resulted in a new and enlarged conception of the intelligent human being. Heretofore, man had been considered a concoction of the physical and spiritual worlds—now he was regarded by some as a product of nature with destiny in his own hands.

Naturalistic Education

During the Renaissance there had been a noticeable shift from spiritual interests in the other world to natural interests in this one. When men began studying nature they became less interested in a divine plan at work on earth. Beginnings of modern science brought with them the certainty that secrets of nature could be revealed and the belief that progress comes from discovering these rather than in searching a body of knowledge inherited from the past.

The Renaissance itself laid the groundwork for the scientific developments of the seventeenth and eighteenth centuries; gradually the restraints of religious dogmatism were being weakened. Doctrines of original sin and the inherent evil of human nature were beginning to be challenged. Montaigne, for one, was struck with the fact that in newly discovered America the untutored savages with no ancient religion or civilized heritage showed such qualities as courage, honor, and integrity. Among the intellectuals there was growing a feeling that perhaps nature was producing a purer and better form of moral conduct than could the oversophisticated civilization of the Christian world.

The naturalism that began in the late eighteenth century represented not only another revolt against the dogmatic authority of church and the absolute authority of state but also a reaction against the artificial conventionalities of rationalism. Just as the rationalist had glorified the intellect, the naturalist idealized feelings. Inasmuch as feelings are common to all human beings, naturalism was a democratic movement.

Practically all schools of that day repressed the natural spontaneity of the pupils, a situation which naturalistic education vigorously attacked. An eloquent and powerful plea was made for a return to the simple life of the peasant home, pictured as one in which the mother herself reared the child instead of leaving him to the care of nurses, governesses, and tutors. Naturalism, in its turn, became such a fad that some aristocratic mothers would breast-feed their infants in the presence of guests.

Jean Jacques Rousseau (1712–1778) stood out as the chief exponent of naturalism with its demand for a return to the simple virtues.* His own life was a direct contradiction of the principles he expounded. Rousseau's domestic affairs were never simple or ideal. Frequently he lived for periods of time as the consort of some wealthy woman. His common-law marriage with a woman of low mentality resulted in the birth of four children, all of whom were soon placed in orphan asylums for adoption. It has frequently been true of great thinkers and writers that a wretched environment or rash personal overindulgence helps them to understand the problems of others. An idealism as great and influential as that of Rousseau is often born of hard knocks and bitter disappointments.

Publication in 1762 of Rousseau's *Émile* attracted the hostile attention of church leaders, both Protestant and Catholic, who regarded it as an ungodly and iniquitous book. He advocated a natural rather than a revealed religious experience. In moral training, Rousseau declared, the child is not to be taught what is right or wrong. Being unmoral, he is incapable of making moral judgments and must learn through the consequence of his own acts—a matter of experience rather than instruction. Religious training should be postponed until the youth reaches his fifteenth birthday because up to that time he is mentally and emotionally incapable of being aware of a divinity.

It was this attitude toward religion that brought down upon Rousseau the wrathful opposition of church leaders. As often happens in cases of censorship, *Émile* became a best-seller of its day, widely read for both pleasure and information. In this masterpiece Rousseau enunciated three great principles that are basic to modern education: growth, pupil activity, and individualization. He was the inspiration for the later educational reforms of Johann Pestalozzi (1746–1827), Johann Herbart (1776–1841), Friedrich Froebel (1782–1852), and many others.

Rousseau agreed with Comenius in advocating the method of instructing through the senses, but he went further in thinking that true education consists less in knowing than in doing. His proposed

* For further discussion of Rousseau, see pages 142 and 302.

teaching methods took into account those inner senses or springs of action known as feelings. The principle of interest was featured—the teacher's proper strategy lay in maneuvering the pupil into wanting to learn. So important to Rousseau were interest and inclination that he advocated a dependence upon them rather than upon constraint to sustain attention and perseverance in the face of difficulties and distractions. He held that the teacher's method should permit a maximum of pupil freedom and that the child should be allowed to follow his own inclinations. Restlessness was not to be penalized—such a manifestation of energy was a necessary apprenticeship to learning. Unless permitted to get about, how was a child to learn about space and objects at a distance?

Rousseau suggested that mothers dress small children in loosely fitting garments to encourage the easy uncoiling of native springs of energy—an idea that has been carried almost to its ultimate limit in the present-day practice of dressing in sun suits and other scant apparel during hot weather. He also regarded each individual as born with a distinct temperament; and he chided teachers of his day for giving the same exercise indiscriminately to all children, thus destroying any special bent some might have and giving to classroom instruction a dull uniformity.

Many of his critics have interpreted Rousseau as saying that freedom is the absence of all restraint. What he did claim was that liberty gives children not more but less right to command others. Freedom requires them to learn by depending more upon their own resources; in so doing, they eventually discover the necessity of limiting desires to their capacities to satisfy them.

This, of course, is Rousseau's much-discussed theory of negative education, or learning through natural consequences. The child has reason to complain if his teacher hems him in with commands or crosses him with prohibitions. However, there is one curb to the child's freedom against which he should not murmur. This is the limit placed upon his actions by physical necessities of nature. A child learns to do what is right and proper by discovering the consequences of his acts. When Émile fails to appear on time for a field trip, the tutor departs without him. If he breaks his window, he must study in a cold room. Thus he becomes conditioned to avoid wrong actions.

Louis René de La Chalotais (1701–1785) and many subsequent critics have pointed out that the idea of encouraging children to profit from their own experiences really deprives them of the benefit of experiences of other people, past and contemporary. As a result, they have said, time is wasted that could be saved. However, Rousseau's general rule for teachers was that they were not to gain time but to lose it! He opposed the acceleration of education and wanted childhood to be held in reverence. It is wrong, he claimed, to be in any hurry to judge a child's actions as being good or bad—nature must be given sufficient time to work out its own solutions, and the child to make his own adjustments before the adult interferes. It is this point in Rousseau's educational outlook that has been under continuous attack by critics, who hold that the subtle forces of nature cannot always be depended upon to find proper desirable expression during the period of rapid growth in childhood.

It should be remembered that Rousseau was attacking the tendency of his day to regard the child as a miniature adult. He disagreed with the established belief that the mind of the child had the same quality as the mind of the adult, which logically meant methods of instruction could be the same for both. Rousseau considered childhood as having its own distinctive character and its own laws of inner development, and it was to these that the teacher's methods should conform. However, while the child did not have the judgment of an adult, his senses were equally acute—and that meant close attention should be paid to sense impressions at all times.

The first person seriously to test Rousseau's theories in a classroom was Johann Bernhard Basedow (1723–1790). His experimental school, called the *Philanthropinum,* probably deserves the distinction of being the first in education to be opened with a deliberate intention of setting aside traditions. Pupils came to classes dressed like children rather than small adults. Latin was taught conversationally, and all sorts of games were used to make learning pleasurable. Handicraft instruction and field trips also helped to motivate interest. Basedow unfortunately was not temperamentally fitted for pioneering a new type of education using such radically novel methods. As a result, shortly after his death the *Philanthropinum* came to an end. Its demise was hastened by the caustic criticisms of antagonistic humanistic schoolmasters who were deeply entrenched as the educational leaders of the time.

Naturalistic education was primarily liberal rather than specialized. Rousseau opposed direct vocational and civic training as being unnecessary and unwise. Education's entire function was to make a worthwhile man, and whoever was well trained for that goal would be prepared to tackle any kind of vocation later in life. However, he did advocate that a child should learn an industrial trade—not for any definite vocational purpose but because it was the best preparation for a wellborn boy to understand social relationships. It also served to raise the pupil above any danger of becoming a human parasite and to discourage the tendency of despising those who must work with their hands.

Rousseau's education for a boy, as set forth in *Émile,* began with the most radical of naturalism; but in the end the product became an idealist. Strange to say, education of the girl destined to marry Émile was hopelessly traditional. Rousseau justified this inconsistency by the argument that girls differ from boys in their nature. He thought that a woman's task was to please men, to be useful to them, to make herself loved and honored by them, to educate them when young, to take care of them when old, to console them, and, in general, to make life sweet and agreeable for them. In other words, woman was to have no individuality—she was never to be trained to think for herself. As for the sex impulses of Émile during adolescence, these were to be directed into activities such as politics, history, and religion. Culmination of naturalistic education was to be achieved in marriage.

Nationalistic Education

A striking characteristic of the political development in the Renaissance was the rapid growth of centralized authority in France and England. While the other European countries were still decentralized by feudalism, these two were getting a head start in the race for worldwide empires.

This general trend to put more political power in the hands of kings was accelerated during the Reformation when the medieval conception of a universal Christendom with the Pope as head was receiving its most crippling blows. Gunpowder, first introduced in the fifteenth century, had made it possible for kings to raise mercenary armies of common men. These proceeded to destroy feudalism by lowering the prestige of the nobility whose military effectiveness had been based upon protective armor and horsemanship. Kings also had discovered a source of ready money in taking over property and funds of the Roman Catholic Church, which in many countries had become enormously wealthy.

Nationalism accentuated national differences by its constant wars, growing use of vernacular languages, and desire for economic gain assisted and protected by the national state. There rapidly developed a feeling that each nationality was different from, and better than, all other nationalities. One crop harvested from these seeds of nationalism has been constant warfare, continuing to the present time and becoming ever more destructive of life and property.

Nationalism emerged as a powerful factor in education when state-controlled-and-supported school systems were being established in the nineteenth century. However, the attitude had had its roots in ancient times. Military authority dominated both Persia and Sparta where the supreme virtue was national patriotism. Among the Jews in Palestine nationalism and patriotism were one and the same thing. Here for the sake of clarity a distinction should be made: patriotism has probably existed from time immemorial—it is a much older concept than nationalism. Originally referring to ties of blood through common ancestors, the meaning of patriotism has been narrowed down to a love for the land where one was born. Nationalism as a term has come into prominence since the Renaissance, particularly since the French Revolution. In addition to ties of place, nationalism includes such various other ties as culture, history, language, race, and traditions.

The nationalistic spirit was generally felt in the upper classes before it spread so dramatically to the masses late in the eighteenth century. The great English "public" schools like Eton and Harrow (a misnomer because they have always been private and exclusive) for centuries had instilled into sons of gentlemen a pride of country and a sense of national destiny despite a curriculum laden with Latin and Greek.

In 1789 the French Revolution challenged the upper-class control of the world. The deposition and decapitation of Louis XVI frightened the other European monarchs into sending a coalition of national armies against the revolutionaries to prevent the spreading of their disturbing and unorthodox ideas about the "rights of man." But the French masses liked the sound and feel of human rights, so they raised a people's army, showed ingenuity in originating two new emotion-stirring devices, a national flag and an anthem, and proceeded to repel the invaders. The morning flag salute and the singing of the *Star Spangled Banner* have been a carry-over from this into American public schools of today.

Early in the French Revolution the Catholic schools had been suppressed and their property confiscated. That left many communities without educational facilities. However, despite the chaos invariably inherent in a revolutionary situation, both educational reformers and political leaders were busy formulating plans for a nationalistic system of schools. These all aimed at a centralization of learning under public control for the dual purpose of maintaining the revolutionary government in power and of improving the state. Needless to say, the proposals embodied a radical departure from the traditional philosophy, administration, curriculum, and methods of former schools.

French revolutionary leaders shrewdly recognized in education an effective propaganda medium for attaching the people more securely to the ideologies of their newly won civic liberties. These, it was realized, had to be incorporated into the new curriculum if a nationalistic spirit were to be maintained. To encourage free expression of political opinion within a republican form of government there definitely was needed a common language that could be understood in all school subjects. Foreseeing the value of propaganda that is so common today, those French revolutionaries advocated the required teaching of "republican ethics." Literature and history also gained a new position of prominence in plans for a curriculum, since it was felt that the best expression of national solidarity was to be found in the legends and folkways of the common people.

So it was in France that the conception of education for national ends arose originally as a defense action on the part of a people threatened by outsiders. After patriotism had spread among the masses, the need was recognized for an educational organization to keep that impulse alive and growing. The Revolutionary Convention took steps to plan the establishment of a national system of schools that would serve to inform citizens of their rights and privileges under a new social order. It was clearly seen that in the education of children there is a powerfully effective instrument to guarantee stability and permanence of a government. This idea was a contribution of the French Revolution.

The French, however, did not get beyond the theorizing stage of a national system of education before conservative elements regained control. And so it was Prussia that first put such a system into operation, and again a national crisis brought the action. But first let us trace the course of events that led to the change.

In Prussia the idea of state support and control of schools had been born during the Protestant Reformation, but, except on a small voluntary scale, it had not been translated into action. While rulers in German states failed to recognize the pregnant possibilities of using education to develop patriotic, loyal citizenship, as benevolent despots they did feel it a part of their duty to maintain schools for the teaching of literacy and religious faith. As early as 1717 decrees had been issued in Prussia requiring compulsory attendance and prescribing how schools should be built, teachers supported, tuition paid, and government aid secured. But the real foundation for a state system of public elementary schools was laid down by Frederick the Great (1712–1786), who believed that the child belongs to the state and not to the home.

In 1763 he issued regulations providing for compulsory education of children, training and compensation of teachers, maintenance of a full term, specification of subject matter, and detailing of methods of instruction.

Thus the framework for the first comprehensive national educational system was laid in Prussia. Even after the death of Frederick the Great in 1786, the momentum caused reforms. A year later a state ministry of education was established and the responsibility for education was taken out of the hands of the clergy in principle if not in fact.

Then in 1794 a General Civil Code (*Allgemeine Landrecht*) made this important statement: "Schools and universities are state institutions, charged with the instruction of youth in useful information and scientific knowledge. Such institutions may be founded only with the knowledge and consent of the State. All public schools and educational institutions are under the supervision of the State, and are at all times subject to its examination and inspection."

But in comparison with Frederick the Great, his successors were weak and reactionary. Even though the above document formed the foundation for secular education, there was little attempt to separate state and church or to exert educational leadership on a central basis. Things grew especially bad after Frederick William III (1770–1840) took the throne in 1797. Politics and corruption reared their ugly heads.

But then came the military disaster at Jena in 1806, and the king was forced into a rude awakening. That defeat at the hands of Napoleon revealed the inadequacy of Prussia's social and economic order, its indifference to the common people, and its corruptness of government. With the nation prostrated, the king inaugurated a series of reforms that brought his government back to vigorous life.

Influential in this movement was a philosopher, Johann Gottlieb Fichte (1762–1814), who saw in education the greatest of all national regenerative forces. In a series of fourteen addresses to the German nation Fichte enunciated a conception of nationalism as the dominant aim of education—he held the school's function to be the building and preserving of the national welfare. With such powerful stimulation, there was put into force during the next quarter-century a series of laws establishing a state system of schools headed by a national department of public instruction with the great Wilhelm von Humboldt (1767–1835) as its first head.

Nationalistic education has flourished in one form or another since the day when it was organized in western Europe. Undoubtedly its worst evils are evident in Soviet Russia. Nowhere in the world in so short a time has there been put into operation such a gigantic educational system for the promotion of national, and incidentally international, ends. It has required some time for the rest of the world to awaken to the fact that in Russia education is being deliberately used with the eventual purpose of dominating the world. Wherever it gains power the Soviet government immediately makes use of the schools for a thorough indoctrination of its theories of government. This process is so rapid, in fact, it becomes self-evident that the groundwork must have been carefully laid long before the actual establishment of Communistic control. The curriculum is arbitrarily set, and teachers must be approved politically as well as academically. Periodic purges of educators are so ruthless and thoroughgoing they defy American understanding.*

Wherever religious and moral training have been retained in nationalistic education, they are considered as agencies in the promotion of patriotism on the principle that law-abiding morality is an essential element of citizenship. Vocational education has been emphasized because the rank and file of the people must be made occupationally efficient to insure the survival of the country in its economic and military competition with other nations.

Physical education is usually considered important because of its values in preparing for vocational fitness and, if necessary, for warfare. It is significant that following each World War, after examination of millions of young men had indicated the startlingly poor physical condition of Americans, there immediately developed physical education movements to remedy the situation. Dictators, who must be efficient to survive, always have taken such matters under consideration before wars begin—not afterward.

Nationalism is the force that has stimulated development of the state-controlled school systems found today throughout the world. Practically all major governments now have come to accept the establishment and maintenance of tax-supported schools as essential to public policy. Under democracies public schools strive to equip future citizens with the knowledges, skills and attitudes presumed necessary for the perpetuation of free representative government. All nationalistic education aims to preserve and glorify the state as organized to protect its people from the dangers of external attack and internal disintegration.

However, dictatorships have brought nationalistic education to a

* For further discussion of Soviet education see pages 178–186.

dangerous extreme. This is exemplified not only by Soviet schools but also by the indoctrination that the Nazis gave children in Hitler's heyday.* As a result, the United Nations Educational, Scientific, and Cultural Organization was established in 1945. The prime reason for UNICEF is to promote international peace through education. Other important aims are to reduce illiteracy, to equalize educational opportunities in the various nations, and to combat doctrines of race superiority.

One last point deserves mention. Of all the great powers the United States is the one that has handled trends toward nationalistic education most gingerly. The power over education resides in the fifty separate states, and there is even now much hue and cry over the danger of federal aid to education.

Psychological Education

Historically, psychology may be said to date back to the conflicting views on human nature of Plato and Aristotle. Plato set up a theory to fit his political and economic proposals as well as his metaphysical philosophy. The universe is divided into a spiritual and material world; human nature likewise consists of spirit (soul) and matter (body). The soul is eternal, changeless, and nonmaterial. The body is born, grows, decays, and is destroyed as are all things of change and imperfection.

Human nature, in Plato's philosophy, is determined entirely by heredity and is fixed from birth. But Aristotle conceived man as being made of form (soul) and matter (body). His scientific studies led him to make more of the relationships between human and lower levels of life. He argued that human nature is a compound of vegetative, animal, and human characteristics. Man's vegetative nature grows, reproduces, decays, and dies just as plant life does; his animal nature has desires, sensory impressions, and active movement as has all other animal life. Man alone possesses a distinctly human nature that no lower form of life has—namely, reason. Such a theory accounts for Aristotle's frequently repeated words: "Man is a rational animal." This difference in outlook between these two great Greek philosophers led to violent intellectual controversies in the Middle Ages—the realists looked to Plato for support and the nominalists depended upon Aristotle.

Psychological education received its modern impetus from John Locke (1632–1704), to whom we shall return later.† Although originally concerned with the academic problem of how the mind works, psychological education led to the development of a careful study of

* For further discussion of Nazi education see pages 170–171.
† For further discussion of Locke's effect on education, see pages 284 and 301.

childhood which, in its later stages, was greatly influenced by the theory of evolution. This movement, which began to affect education in the late eighteenth century, vigorously opposed the common practice of imposing adult standards upon children. Eventually it brought about a better understanding of the learning processes, development of new methods, and improved training of teachers.

When Rousseau (who came almost a century after Locke) proclaimed that education is a matter of the free and unrestricted development of natural powers and inclinations of the individual, he set the stage for acceptance of psychological education. Naturalism had been a reaction against educational practices growing out of the doctrine of original sin and the Calvinists' belief that a child is wicked by nature and that nurture must be used to transform him into a more God-like being. On the other hand, naturalism, unadulterated, proved impractical. It was found to be too negative and entirely too wasteful a procedure to let the child ignore all experiences of his elders and to learn entirely by trial and error.

The psychological approach attempted to reconcile the traditional viewpoint that education is a remolding of human nature from without with Rousseau's idea that education should be a matter of unhampered growth. Psychologists accepted the naturalistic viewpoint of growth as an unfolding of native capacities. However, they regarded this development as subject to help or hindrance. Therefore, by use of proper teaching methods they could guide it into desirable channels. In other words, to paraphrase them, effective education means the stimulation of natural capacities by means of desirable activities.

For nearly a century psychological educational reforms were almost entirely limited to elementary schools, and only in more recent years have they noticeably affected secondary schools and higher education. One of the reasons for the changes in the elementary schools was the work of Johann Pestalozzi at that level.*

Pestalozzi achieved fame not just because he wrote about educational theories; he actually put them into practice for his contemporaries to see. Many observers from distant lands carried home their enthusiasm concerning the work of this Swiss-born humanitarian. He was not, as many claimed, a radical—the man was profoundly religious and always placed moral instruction of children first in his list of important aims for education. He did talk of social reform and allied himself with liberal groups, but the reform he demanded was the improvement of society by helping the individual to help himself.

Although Pestalozzi was opposed by conservatives in France and

* For further discussion of Pestalozzi, see pages 142, 166, and 303.

Prussia, his sympathy for the underprivileged touched a responsive chord, especially among the middle classes. With his emphasis upon practical activities of children, starting with motor skills and leading to vocational competence in trade, industry, and farming, Pestalozzi was able to offer a constructive program to those who were dissatisfied with the exclusively literary and linguistic emphasis given by most schools of his day.

Pestalozzi insisted that the natural instincts of a child should provide the motives for learning. He considered cooperation and sympathy, rather than compulsion or physical punishment, the proper means by which to achieve discipline. Influenced by Rousseau, he believed that free expression would allow the natural powers of the child to develop. Since it is nature that gives the drive to life, he maintained, the teacher's responsibility is to adapt instruction to each individual according to his particular changing, unfolding nature as required at the various stages of his development. Pestalozzi looked upon the child as a unity made of moral, physical, and intellectual powers—all of which could be developed harmoniously through education.

Sense perceptions, thought Pestalozzi, are vitally important in the development of a child's mind. Among the younger pupils especially this would call for reliance upon observations of actual things and natural objects rather than upon books and reading. To help a child develop his sense of touch, sight, and sound, Pestalozzi designed an entire series of object lessons as instructional aids for mastering the fundamentals of language, number, and form. He advocated proceeding from the concrete to the abstract and from the particular to the general, using everyday objects like animals, plants, and tools.

All this greatly impressed visiting educators at a time when children were studying Latin with very little understanding of its meaning. Furthermore, Pestalozzi had developed his methods in such fine detail that it became evident a definite system of training would be necessary to permit teachers to study the child more closely if they were to guide his personal development and to adjust instruction to his particular requirements and interests.

Just as Pestalozzi influenced the course of elementary school education, so the philosopher Johann Herbart affected secondary school training—although, as noted before, the changes at this level took hold more slowly.*

Herbart's two principal psychological contributions to education were his stress upon social and moral character-building and his formu-

* For further discussion of Herbart, see pages 143 and 286.

lation of systematic teaching methods. For 26 years he held the chair of philosophy at the University of Königsberg formerly occupied by the famed Immanuel Kant (1724–1804). There Herbart founded a pedagogical seminar and a practice school for teacher-training in which experimentation was carried on for the purpose of developing new teaching methods.

Herbart, in advocating sound character as the most important aim of education, held that instruction should be primarily moral in its outlook and intent. However, this he considered more a matter of adjustment of the individual to society than a religious conception of morality. He pointed to history and literature as the most effective subject matter for the developing of desirable social attitudes in children. These areas, he said, should be the "core" of study with which all other school subjects should be correlated. Herbart proposed an intellectual approach to the learning process despite his insistence upon moral and social aims of education. He placed importance on development of clear ideas, and, above all else, concentration by the teacher on the problem of interest.

Herbart is perhaps most frequently identified with his "five formal steps." Systematic planning of lessons had been discussed by many earlier writers. Cicero in his *De Oratore* had dealt with the four parts of an oration, and these were later slavishly followed by Graeco-Roman teachers. Herbart, likewise, somewhat casually suggested a four-step outline by which the mind acquires knowledge and reaches conclusions. His followers (known as Herbartians) seized upon this outline, expanded the four steps into five, and made a deadening rule out of this sequence: preparation, presentation, comparison and abstraction, generalization, and application.

It is only fair to say that Herbart realized that instruction must not be stereotyped—to be truly effective it should possess an element of surprise and novelty. He did not regard the "five steps" as a fixed scheme to be followed religiously. Most certainly he did not propose to have this plan carried through in every lesson as was being done by Herbartians at the turn of the present century.

Friedrich Froebel was a contemporary of Herbart and Pestalozzi. In fact, Froebel taught with Pestalozzi and then conducted his own schools in Switzerland and Germany. He was impressed not only with the sense-realism of his colleague but also with the idealistic philosophy of the era. He felt that the school's educative process should start with the small child of three or four years, and that play activities should be the method for aiding growth and learning. Toward this end Froebel sought a variety of play activities to develop the whole nature of the child, moral and emotional as well as intellectual. In these he included singing, dancing, dramatic stories, painting, coloring, clay modeling, and manipulation of objects. He called his school the *kindergarten*, a garden where children grow.

Being a mystic, Froebel assigned to the above activities a large measure of symbolism—objects were considered "gifts of God"; activities, "divine occupations." Everything done in the kindergarten was supposed to lead to a closer identification of the child with the divine spirit and social unity. Sitting in a circle, so he claimed, made each child feel his identification as a member of the social group. Froebel's mysticism did much to discredit the practical value of his ideas; but, stripped of their symbolism, they became tremendously influential in American education. Children gained from adults a new respect for their individuality. A recognition of their dynamic and active qualities meant the beginning of a decline in rigid discipline and the gradual disappearance of traditional formality in classroom atmosphere.

Scientific Education

The foundations of modern science were being laid in the sixteenth and seventeenth centuries against great odds of antagonism, intolerance, and persecution. Interest in science was continuously growing despite this opposition; finally, in the nineteenth century the balance was tipped in its favor, partly as a result of the Industrial Revolution and technological advances.

Credit must go to Francis Bacon (1561–1626), not a scientist himself, for popularizing the values of science through his voluminous writings and his influential political position as Lord Chancellor in England. He held that men were too enslaved by superstition and tradition, relied too exclusively on Aristotle and Scholastic methods, and were more engrossed in niceties of words than in knowledge of nature. His proposal to reform education was a thoroughgoing reliance upon science and scientific methods. In his *New Atlantis* Bacon described a Utopia on an imaginary South Sea island where the aim of society was to increase man's knowledge of nature and where scientific research had developed machines that flew in the sky, skimmed under water, and conveyed music afar. Many of the educational doctrines of sense realism stemmed from the philosophy of this popularizer of the scientific method.

Despite steady advances, Aristotelian methods still dominated classroom instruction in the eighteenth century. Verbalization was emphasized rather than sense impression. German educators had been the pioneers in introducing experimental science into the curriculum. First to teach such subjects were the *Realschulen*.* Johann Hecker (1707–1768) and later Basedow in his *Philanthropinum* progressed even more in this direction. In addition to astronomy inherited from the quadrivium of medieval education, schools began to make such offerings as drawing, geography, mechanics, and natural history. Compasses, globes, and microscopes made an appearance at this time as classroom equipment.

To supplement the conventional bookish schooling some *Realschulen* began building botanical gardens and displaying models of ships, plows, and other common objects. In 1852 these *Realschulen* started to teach chemistry, mineralogy, physical geography, and physics. Continuously from then on emphasis was being placed upon scientific materials as basic for industrial activities.

In those German schools the instructors at first did all the laboratory work, and it was not until about 1825 that even the brightest students were given the privilege of doing their own experimentation. Soon thereafter new types of technical schools were established, largely because the older institutions had been so reluctant to replace humanistic studies even in the face of popular demand.

In America the universities did not allow students to perform laboratory experiments until after 1850, and another half-century was to pass before this experience was granted to high school students. England and France were still more backward in this respect, and as late as 1950 in both countries the best scientific work was being done in technical and special schools rather than in universities and colleges. However, almost everywhere, at practically all grade levels of instruction, the various physical and natural sciences are now included somewhere in the curriculums of schools. Most educators today would go so far as to include science as a basic subject for every pupil on the theory that scientific methods and facts should be a part of everyone's heritage.

In the nineteenth century there occurred rapid developments in pure sciences such as astronomy, biology, chemistry, physics, physiology, and also in the applied sciences like agriculture, manufacturing, transportation. It is significant that practically all these scientific advances took place outside of schools. In fact, one might even say that the

---

* The *Realschule* is a six-year secondary scientific school. The curriculum includes mathematics, modern languages, science and certain practical arts. Unlike the *Progymnasium,* the classics are omitted.

scientific movement developed in spite of, rather than because of, education. Scientific methods and studies gained admission into the schools slowly and against much stubborn opposition. Let us look briefly at this struggle.

Herbert Spencer (1820–1903) vigorously demanded that the new scientific content being developed in the practical, everyday world be given a more conspicuous place in schools and colleges. In his own England the nine great public schools set the standard for all other secondary schools. These placed such great store in the classics that the insistent, ever-growing demand for recognition of the sciences made little headway. An important event did occur in 1879, when Wilhelm Wundt (1832–1920) established in Leipzig the first psychological laboratory. In England Francis Galton (1822–1911) and his contemporaries were developing statistical methods of research in the fields of biology, eugenics, heredity, psychology, and sociology. The first educator to come under the influence of this scientific movement was an American, J. McKeen Cattell (1860–1914), who in 1890 published his *Mental Tests and Measurements,* a volume which introduced new terms into the vocabularies of professional school people.

The scientific method makes use of both induction and deduction. Induction starts out with some question and proceeds by observation and experimentation to a general rule. Deduction begins with an assumed or demonstrated truth and draws its necessary implications. A common example of deduction is the proof of a geometry problem after a solution has been presented.

Every natural science depends for its development upon observation and induction, while inference and deduction supply proofs of its general principles. The scientific method demands that any investigation be objective, impartial, mathematically precise, and subject to verification by any competent observer.

Scientifically inclined teachers insist that all educational problems be approached in this attitude, and that all practices and procedures must be determined in a spirit of inquiry. Impartiality is the aim of every democracy. Therefore, it seems appropriate that America, which had habitually borrowed from Europe in other educational matters, assumed world leadership in establishing a scientific approach to education. This development took place largely in graduate schools of education coming into existence during the present century. Columbia, Chicago, and Stanford were outstanding among the universities that pioneered in the movement.

The first to apply methods of quantitative research to educational problems was Edward Lee Thorndike (1874–1949), who, at Teachers College, Columbia University, inspired his students to use their native ingenuity in constructing devices for the scientific measurement of the results of instruction. It was in 1902 that he taught the first course ever offered in educational measurements.*

In 1913, with the publication of three monumental volumes, *Educacational Psychology*, Thorndike in his efforts to apply methods of exact science to certain educational problems virtually created a new subject matter field. He directed attention of the educational world to an objective approach for discovering answers to problems of the original nature of children, their learning capacities, and individual differences. Thorndike's goal was to make teaching a science in which students form habits of exact study and learn how to apply the logic of statistical measures to all educational problems.

Scientific education has been highly successful in popularizing fact-finding, statistical, and experimental techniques for purposes of determining quantitatively educational processes and results. There have evolved measuring devices for intelligence, achievements, vocational aptitudes, efficiency of instruction, and school building standards, as well as many types of survey techniques. Graduate students in American universities seeking higher degrees now attempt in many ways to question scientifically how individuals may be changed for the better through education. This is all part of the movement to replace subjective and guessing methods traditionally used to determine proper school procedures and to substitute objective and precise measurements. The aim always is for maximum efficiency at a minimum of cost in time and effort.

The earliest American scientific school at the collegiate level was Rensselaer Polytechnic Institute, founded at Troy, New York, in 1824. It has served well as a model for subsequent institutions. Significant, considering the date of its founding, was the college's charter requirement providing that the students were NOT to be taught by hearing lectures and seeing others perform experiments—they were to do the experiments themselves, under the immediate direction of a professor or competent assistant, as the best way to become practical scientists. For its day such a requirement was revolutionary!

In America today there are many, many colleges specializing in areas of science. Moreover, each university has branches in this field. But the establishment of high schools devoted primarily to the subject has not followed along the same lines. New York City's famous Bronx

* For further discussion of Thorndike, see pages 294 and 304.

High School of Science for selected students is the exception, rather than the rule. Even there the students take a broad spectrum of academic courses.

However, the scientific movement has affected American public schools most deeply in the area of measurement and has brought about many reorganizations designed to adjust the learning process more carefully to the needs of individual pupils. Among these have been flexible grading systems, ability groupings, differentiated courses, and various plans for individualized teaching. Special rooms have been provided for slow pupils, speech defectives, mental deviates, "problem children," and the near-blind. Pasadena, California, for one, operates outdoor schools for tubercular children. On a broader population basis there have been established special schools for the feeble-minded, blind, deaf, crippled, and incorrigible children. This more humanitarian approach for aiding these various types of handicapped pupils is a product of the scientific education that set itself the task of destroying prejudice and superstition by substituting fact for fiction.

Progressive Education

And now we come to that movement which has aroused so much interest and controversy in the twentieth century—progressive education. Today the term is almost hopelessly embedded in semantic difficulties because emotionally charged people have either enthusiastically or angrily placed diverse educational movements and experiments under the general banner of progressive education. Thus the child-centered school, the activities program, the core curriculum, the projects method, and the like are all lumped under the general heading "progressive." Actually, such schools of thought or action are either offshoots of the progressive movement or cousins of it, stemming from the same sources.

For our immediate purposes, let us say that progressive education rests its case on the following chief precepts:

1. Individual differences among children must be recognized.
2. We learn best by doing and by having a vital interest in what we are doing.
3. Education is a continuous reconstruction of living experience that goes beyond the four walls of the classroom.
4. The classroom should be a laboratory for democracy.
5. Social goals, as well as intellectual goals, are important.
6. A child must be taught to think critically rather than to accept blindly.

Actually, the reader will see that the above ideas did not come full-blown into the head of John Dewey (1859–1952) or anyone else. Whether one agrees with the tenets of the progressives or not, he must admit that they formed the culmination of the various movements already described in this book. Indeed, one can discern gleams of the movement in the teaching of Socrates and the writing of Quintilian. Certainly the later influence of Froebel, Pestalozzi, Rousseau, and Herbart cannot be denied. There were other "forefathers" too. Let us glance briefly at the work of one of them, and then go on to a more detailed consideration of the entire subject.

John Dewey credited Colonel Francis W. Parker (1831–1902) with being the "father" of progressive education. In the minds of most people Dewey himself deserved this distinction, but actually it was Parker who first extended Froebelian ideas from kindergarten to the elementary grades. In seizing upon the idea of self-activity he did not restrict himself to formal or symbolic patterns as did Froebel. Self-expression was developed on its own account in a variety of forms such as clay modeling, drawing, music, painting, and creative writing.

Such an emphasis on motor activities doomed the traditional conception of quietness in schoolroom order, for obviously a certain amount of apparent disorder must result if motor expression is to be trained. When a child "commits a crime" by breaking the routine in a traditional classroom, immediate punishment ordinarily is effective in settling the disciplinary case and in restoring order. Parker did not believe retribution would truly educate a child. A youngster acquires no habits of learning to rule himself, Parker maintained, when deprived of choice under compulsion of fear.

For three years, starting in 1872, Parker had studied in Germany and thus had come under the influence of European educational theories. He later became superintendent of schools in Quincy, Massachusetts, where his educational reforms attracted nationwide attention. That pioneering in Quincy foreshadowed many of the changes that have since taken place in modern elementary schools and, to a more limited extent, in high schools.

Hard and fast lines between subjects were broken down. Parker was interested in correlating arithmetic, history, reading, and writing so that each would make its maximum contribution to the experiences of the child. He held that subjects were not ends in themselves, that they merely existed to promote the development of each pupil. In his philosophy, the school should provide an environment where children enter into activities because they desire to do so rather than because they are forced by external incentives in the form of marks, awards, and prizes.

Although Parker remained in Quincy only five years, his new methods and curriculum attracted attention even in Europe. Reading, to him, meant the acquisition of meanings—not the techniques of oral pronunciation. Memorizing of textbook facts received less emphasis because real things were being studied. Lessons in geography and science were largely based on firsthand information gained outside the classroom. Nature study achieved a new importance; sand tables in classrooms and sand piles in school yards were used extensively for the development of concepts of structure. Essential skills were taught in connection with other subjects; oral and written use of language replaced grammatical analysis. The fame of these methods was spread by summer school and institute classes for teachers who learned to use these new techniques.

To Parker, the center of the educational process was not objects of nature as they had been to Pestalozzi, or history and literature as recommended by Herbart, but the child himself. Faced with such a revolutionary educational approach it was not long before Quincy parents were criticizing their school superintendent for turning elementary schools into natural history museums and "mudpie factories." Serious doubts were expressed that the three R's could be mastered where long, hard drills were, and exercises in rote were not, encouraged. In fact, so many protests of this type were being made that the Massachusetts State Board of Education conducted an examination of Quincy pupils in old-type subject matter. Those results completely vindicated Parker's new methods by showing that Quincy children surpassed those in other cities trained in the traditional manner.

The renown of this work induced Mrs. Emmons Blaine (1866–1918) in 1899 to give Parker a million dollars to endow a private training school for teachers to be known as the Chicago Institute. It was her announced intention for him to have an opportunity to build his work free from political turmoil and unhampered by the conventional and financial limitations of a public normal school. But before construction of the new building was started, President William Rainey Harper (1856–1906) suggested that it be made a part of his new University of Chicago. So, with Parker as the first head, it was fused with three other institutions into a school of education that opened in 1901. Colonel Parker died the following year, and John Dewey succeeded him.

A "Laboratory School" had previously been established in 1896 by Mr. and Mrs. Dewey and several neighbors. It continued for seven and a half years, closing in the spring of 1904 when Dewey became convinced that its creative independence was being endangered by the dictation of President Harper. That experimental school was so far advanced for its time that not until years later was its true significance understood. Only a few of the thousands of visitors remained long enough to study its theories to the point of understanding them. For those brought up in formal schools where quiet had been the rule, such noisy activities seemed little else but pure unwarranted license. The impact of the Dewey school with its apparent lack of order in organization, administration, curriculum, and teaching came as a distinct shock to most schoolmen of its day.

Within a quarter-century, however, at least 50 new schools had been started as a result of the Dewey influence—rising, so to speak, from the grave of the experimental school that had come to its end in 1904. Noteworthy was the one at the University of Missouri where for 20 years experimentation in curriculum was carried on. School subjects were abolished altogether in developing a program of study without academic compartments and time schedules. School life was a continuing series of child activities in which construction, discussions, excursions, and field trips occupied central roles. Practical problems of administration finally led to the creation of a fourfold organization of curricular activities: handwork, observation, play, and stories. This allowed for retaining flexibility in the school program while giving an improved sense of organization.

It was not until 1910 that Dewey's books began to be used widely in the study of education. As students today can testify, his writing style is quite difficult to read. Interpreters were needed to express in simpler language the master's thought, and these did not appear until after World War I. The most important was William Heard Kilpatrick (1871–), one of Dewey's colleagues at Teachers College. In 1918 Kilpatrick began writing and lecturing on the project method, an attempt to rescue Dewey's problem method which conservative educators had tried to fit into their traditional, formal methods of teaching.

The idea of the project was not altogether original with Kilpatrick as it already had been used in teaching courses in agriculture. The project had previously taken the form of application of principles learned at school, on the farm, or at home. The vitality of this practical instruction encouraged Kilpatrick to make a much broader application of the project as a general method of teaching. In doing this he stressed motivation—his critics, incidentally, claimed he overstressed it. Kilpatrick described the project as any unit of purposeful activity where the dominating purpose fixes the aim of the action, guides its process, and furnishes its drive or inner motivation.

However, the progressive education movement had really begun to catch fire about 1912. During the following 10 years continuous protests, especially in the northeastern section of the United States, were being made against the inadequacies of traditional education. That was the time, it should be remembered, when Woodrow Wilson (1856–1924) was stirring people with his ideas of building a New Freedom. As a product of this dissatisfaction, the Progressive Education Association was organized in 1919 by a group of educators who held that traditional school practices were not founded upon sound psychological and social theories. These zealous individuals confined their efforts largely to the creation of a school environment in which needs and purposes of the child would be paramount, with the teacher a sympathetic guide rather than a taskmaster.

The PEA* began working first on reconstruction of elementary schools; for the moment they shied away from high schools, which were strongly dominated by inflexible college-entrance requirements. The initial attack in reconstructing secondary education came later with the creation of a Commission on the Relation of School and College. What was known as the "Eight-Year Study" freed 30 high schools from conventional college-entrance requirements. These were permitted to experiment with their curriculums, and 300 colleges agreed to accept their graduates upon the basis of recommendation of the high school principal. In addition to information on the applicant's personal interests and activities, the college registrar was presented scores on achievement, aptitude, diagnostic, and intelligence tests.

A follow-up evaluation study was undertaken to see how well the whole group had done in academic subjects, college life, and personal development. Each "progressive" student was paired with one from a traditional high school of equivalent age, sex, race, intelligence, scholastic achievement in high school, and general economic and social background. Analysis by the evaluation staff showed that students from the experimental schools earned a slightly higher total average of grades in college and had gained more academic and nonacademic honors than the others. They likewise were judged as more frequently possessing a high degree of intellectual curiosity and drive, and of being precise, systematic, and objective in their thinking and more resourceful in meeting new situations.

* Not to be confused with Public Education Association, which has the same initials.

Progressive educators asserted with pride that nearly all the controlled experiments comparing work of children in progressive and traditional schools indicated that the newer, less restricted methods resulted in an increase, rather than a loss, in proficiency in the so-called fundamentals.

In 1944 the PEA changed its name to the American Education Fellowship. Although bitter controversies developed between progressives and their critics, no one can seriously doubt the tremendous influence this movement had in reconstructing educational practices. Almost every American school today gives at least lip service to a deep concern for the physical-mental-emotional growth of the child, respect for the pupil's personality, identification of curriculum with life on the level of the child's maturity, and substitution of democratic for autocratic procedures in school administration.

Essentialistic Education

Essentialism is a fairly recently coined term for modern conservatism, but what it stands for is not limited to the twentieth century. In every stage of educational history the conservatives have played an important and often valuable part. The leader of this movement in America for more than 30 years was William Chandler Bagley (1874–1946), of Teachers College, Columbia, who strongly advocated the induction of each new generation into its social heritage as the primary function of the school. He sought to stabilize educational aims and methods through a reliance on the tried and true in experience. Bagley feared the dissipation of educational energies when the teacher paid too much attention to individual differences. He thought school work should concentrate on what is common, or essential, to all—and a naturalistic analysis of the social heritage, not metaphysics or theology, should be used to determine what is essential.

Free-lance progressive schools coming into existence after 1910 as a product of the Parker-Dewey influence almost immediately met the opposition of conservative educational workers, who charged that their philosophy was basically weak and that it tended to sacrifice the social heritage. Many progressive schools of the 1920's and 1930's were accused of coddling pupils and catering to their passing interests. Criticism was leveled especially at the lack of discipline and bad manners among children trained in the so-called progressive way, and also at their alleged failure to grasp the fundamentals.

Conservatives also claimed that progressive education made schooling effeminate and that teachers "sugar-coated the pill" in trying to get pupils to learn. These critics wanted to direct more attention to discipline, systematic work, and the mastery of fundamentals. In other words, they argued that the values of traditional teaching procedures—such as orderliness and strict obedience—must outweigh the merits claimed for the less formal approach. Their charges might be summarized as follows: Mass education opened the doors for schooling above the elementary level to all kinds of children. This resulted in a lowering of educational standards. By stressing pupil interest, freedom, experience, and initiative, the progressives only added to the confusion; by discrediting formal discipline, work for work's sake, and logical sequences in curricular matters, they made an already difficult teaching situation impossible.

These critics heartily disapproved of the tendency to abandon grade standards by adopting a policy of promoting each pupil whether or not he had earned promotion. They held that logical, chronological, and causal relationships had been ignored in favor of incidental learning. To them the work of the progressive school lacked system and organization, thus encouraging pupils to be at loose ends and generally scatterbrained instead of conscientious and diligent.

However, in its heyday the progressive education movement seemed to thrive on the attacks of its opponents who were numerous but unorganized until the 1938 Atlantic City meeting of the American Association of School Administrators. An interesting development, involving semantics, came out of that meeting. Bagley had long been recognized as the generalissimo in the battle against excesses of the progressive school of thought. To avoid the stigma that had attached itself to conservatives and traditionists, he suggested they use the term "stalwart" in the preliminary conference planning a new organization. Bagley did not want to give the idea that this new group represented the type of teacher who stubbornly holds on to antiquated methods even in the face of both common sense and scientific data.

The designation of "essentialists" that finally gained acceptance was coined by Michael Demiashkevich (1891–1938). The above-mentioned discussions led to the formulation of a platform, including a statement of principles, for the Essentialist Committee for the Advancement of American Education, which was born on the spot.

An unauthorized interview between a committee member and the press resulted in the publication of several sections of the Bagley manifesto. Front-page headlines, such as "Bagley Declares War on Dewey," launched the new movement prematurely; the progressives soon hit back with charges of "red baiting" and "reactionaries." The essentialists, they claimed, were proposing to Hitlerize the schools. Bagley himself found it necessary to assert to the press that he considered Dewey the greatest educator of modern times. For several years thereafter the controversy raged on the radio and in popular magazines as well as in progressive journals. There was so much interest, in fact, that the Gallup poll made a survey of public opinion.

As implied before, the essentialists charged that difficult subjects—because they are exact and exacting—had been discredited in order to promote easier ones. Furthermore, they said, the tendency to build curriculums to fit local and provincial needs ignores the essential unity of the American people, who, thanks to private automobiles and other low-cost transportation, are the most mobile in the world. Essentialists held that the major task of Americans living in a modern world is to preserve the democratic forms of government which are characteristic of our culture. Therefore, it is the duty of formal education to transmit a common core of ideals, ideas, meanings, and understandings which constitute the American cultural heritage and which are so necessary for the perpetuation of our democracy. In brief, essentialism fought for a "speaking acquaintance with the past."

But the impression should not be given that the essentialists were interested only in the teaching of history. They placed great importance on the three R's, the fine arts, industrial arts, and health. They went further in advocating that there should be an agreement on a nationwide scale concerning the order and grade placement of subjects and major topics. Such a nationwide plan, they believed, would go far toward solving the problems of children continually transferring from school to school, often from state to state.

Not only does the immature learner have the right to guidance and direction by his elders, essentialists said, but he needs that guidance as a consequence of the extended period of human immaturity that distinguishes man from animals. Accuracy, thoroughness, persistence, and good workmanship should be encouraged rather than ridiculed. To achieve these ends the teachers, not the pupils, should be held responsible for carrying out the instructional program. Admittedly failure is an unpleasant experience for a child, and repetition of a grade in many cases is ineffective. However, far more often than not, the possibility of failure and repetition is the stimulus that keeps the learner to his task.

So went the arguments of the essentialists, but in due time the progressives prepared a variety of refutations. Many were ready to agree that the fundamental subjects must play an important part in a modern school program, a fact that had been so completely ignored by extreme progressives. However, they held that a mastery of fundamentals is never more than a means to an end—that for each individual the real goal in life is an integrated personality. They pointed out that over-emphasis on fundamentals tends toward a dry, meager, and sterile formalism which defeats its own purpose. Therefore, said these moderate progressives, since learning is a modification of conduct or behavior through rich experiences in a controlled environment, it proceeds most effectively when emphasis is laid upon the learner rather than upon school subjects. The only effective type of discipline, they held, is that which is exercised by the learner upon himself.

It is noteworthy that leading essentialists had been quick to defend progressive education against unfair attacks, particularly during the war years when it was made the "scapegoat" for all weaknesses of the social structure. Those defenders pointed out that in many instances where pupils were shown to be below par in standardized-test scores, there had been significant factors other than the use of informal school methods. The following is a summary of some of the factors mentioned:

1. In comparison with incomes of other vocational groups, teachers' salaries were poor—thus causing many of the more capable to shift to more lucrative positions.
2. Wartime conditions necessitated the employment of substandard teachers.
3. Some teachers held down two jobs with a consequent loss of class-room efficiency.
4. Because mothers were working, children were neglected at home.
5. The number of broken families had increased.
6. Underprivileged children coming from states with inferior school systems had been continually moving into better districts.

Some progressive leaders thanked Bagley and his fellow essentialists for their careful and honest appraisal of educational problems. Continuously hammering away at the need for "iron" in education, essentialists reminded Americans of the social-economic crisis being faced. A real service was performed in their unwillingness to let the country forget that democracy is always on trial; that in a complex society the attainment of security and freedom is a conquest and not a gift—and that a literate electorate is absolutely indispensable to preserve a democratic society.

Disputes like the progressive-essentialist one will always be with us. But let us remember that it is difficult to classify schools according to the ideology and methodology of their teachers—most of them vary in degree between the limits of extremely traditional and completely progressive. Moreover, both types of teaching are usually found in the same school system. Even among the faculty in the same building one observes teachers whose methods are traditional, middle-of-the-way, or extremely progressive. A teacher in the span of several years, or even a single year, month, or day, may reflect varying degrees of conservative or progressive ideology. This flux and flexibility—this resistance to neat categories—is one of the products of democracy. When the "pendulum" ceases to swing, that is the time to worry.

Socialized Education

Stimulated by rapid advancements in science and by the Industrial Revolution, human relationships continuously have been gaining new importance. Today, as never before, educational problems are being studied from the viewpoint of their economic, political, and social significance. This current emphasis has been brought about by a realization that the school must take a leading role in preparing its future citizens to live together amicably in a highly complicated world.

The most recent development of the progressive education movement has been the realization that its philosophy bears social implications—that the school should be vitally concerned with the total economic and social scene. This idea developed from the conviction that twentieth-century society had outgrown the educational ideals and practices of the past.

The leader of this new movement was again John Dewey—or rather, it should be said that socialized education may be considered as a new interpretation of what Dewey had been declaring for 50 years. His publication in 1899 of *School and Society* spearheaded the revolt against the religious, disciplinary, and merely informational aims that had dominated education throughout the nineteenth century. Dewey argued that schools should emphasize civic and social experience, vocational and practical usefulness, and individual development. His great service at that time was a restatement of the aims of education in the light of rapid social changes that had been taking place.

To a follower of Dewey, education has two sides—psychological and social; neither may be subordinated or neglected. The psychological nature of a child forms the basis for his education—it is the teacher's responsibility to make full use of his natural, spontaneous activities. Describing original nature as being spontaneously impulsive rather than passive, Dewey divided impulses into four kinds: the social impulses of communication or conversation; the constructive impulses to make things; the impulse to investigate things; and the impulse of artistic or creative expression.

With these impulses in mind, said Dewey, the school must be changed from a place for sedentary listening to one for active doing or working. The teaching process must be planned to allow the child to learn wherever possible by his own experiences and, in that way, to acquire the habit of thinking. A proper solution to any problem demands intelligent thinking, which becomes the principal factor in the ability to cope with new situations. Thinking, as Dewey defined it, is the use of the meanings of past experiences in the interpretation of new situations.

Dewey felt that when the psychological and social approaches to learning are separated, there is produced either a forced and external education in which freedom of the individual is subordinated to a preconceived notion of what society should be, or else a barren and formal development of the mental powers in which the learner has little idea of the use to be made of what is being learned. The school is primarily a social institution because its processes are social—in fact, educational processes are basically no different from those going on continuously in life outside the classroom.

Therefore, Dewey claimed, the manner in which pre-school learning has been taking place should suggest to a teacher the logical starting point for a more systematic encouragement of physical and mental growth. The school ideally should be that form of social life into which can be concentrated those factors that most effectively cause a child to share the accumulated knowledge and skills of the race. Education can be considered as proceeding most satisfactorily whenever the individual is actively participating in social relationships with others.

Dewey desired certain modifications in both methods and curriculum to meet the needs of a new society. He felt that habits of discipline and responsibility so important in the economy of the earlier family system had lost much of their effectiveness. It is the duty of the modern school, he maintained, to prepare its pupils for a new environment that represents those changes in living conditions resulting from recent applications of scientific data to industry, manufacturing, transportation, and communication.

To Dewey, the school is the logical place for bringing about social progress and reform. By means of education society can first formulate its own purposes and then organize the means for their attainment. Thus, in the school, our society has the ideal tool for shaping itself with a reasonable degree of definiteness in whatever direction it wishes to move. That is the essence of a democratic social order as contrasted with the handing down of ready-made concepts so characteristic of autocratic social orders.

Dewey pointed out the general mistake of introducing the child too abruptly to specialized studies which at the time have very little relationship to his own social life—the very basis upon which all growth and training should be concentrated and correlated. In other words, both subject matter and methods in school should be adapted to the child's own peculiar needs. As the best means of preparing a pupil to be introduced to more formal studies Dewey recommended such "expressive" or "constructive" activities as drawing, household arts, music, and nature study. Language, he thought, loses much of its value as a means of social communication because the social element is lacking when it is taught as a separate subject. Instruction in arithmetical processes is more effective, and certainly more fun, when the child plays store and pretends to buy or make change, than is ever possible in the traditional formal style of teaching.

Dewey held that it is not the proper function of the teacher to discipline the child. The most effective moral training results when a pupil assumes the responsibility of disciplining himself as a part of his efforts to enter into proper social relationships with others. Thus, Dewey said, any teacher is on the wrong path when he tries to form rigid habits of obedience within a child. It is much better to create a social environment that permits each pupil to learn for himself what can and what cannot be properly done.

In a socialized classroom situation the teacher repeatedly puts responsibility for decisions squarely on the children unless it seems that an adult's decision is necessary for settling a difficulty. Pupils are helped to formulate rules for their own guidance when it becomes apparent that rules are needed for effective group action. Every possible encouragement is given to the development of leadership. Children set up their own standards of evaluation, and each one is made responsible for completing his job promptly and successfully. Wherever possible, pupils are encouraged to provide for each other's needs. Building good social habits is the primary objective of socialized education.

PART TWO

Evolution of Education in America

Evolution of Education in America

The development of our American public school system to its present gigantic size and complex organization is one of the most interesting stories in educational history. This growth can be termed no less than phenomenal. For example, on the high school level alone, the number of American students was doubled in every decade between 1800 and 1930. Starting with a mere 90,000, the enrollment shot up to four million—and it has since climbed above the five million mark.

But numbers are only a small part of the story. Philosophies evolved into action on many fronts in this new land. The concept of education for all, not just for the privileged, took root in colonial days and flourished later. The idea of state and local control of education eventually prevailed as a result of a latent fear of the tyranny of a central government—a fear that had been planted in the hearts of the early settlers who had fled from persecution in the Old World. Concern for the individual child, although originally urged by European leaders, found its readiest acceptance in democratic America. The handicapped, the very slow, the very young, the emotionally disturbed, the gifted—all categories received attention as the country grew. And even the education of parents and other adults became a widespread practice.

Perhaps the most striking observation that can be made about the growth of American education is to note that it originally reflected European thinking, but that now the Europeans imitate the United States in many aspects of their educational theory and practice. This rapid rise to a role of leadership did not come about easily in the new democracy. In a country so large and so young there had to be many conflicting forces. Let us now trace the uneven course of events from colonial days to the present.

Education in Seventeenth-Century America

The American colonists copied European schools as closely as frontier conditions would permit. Naturally it was England's traditions and customs that prevailed because most of the people had been born there. While population was recruited largely from those ranks of English society where illiteracy was most prevalent, records indicate that the majority of the initial immigrants could read and write. Among the original settlers of Massachusetts Bay Colony it is estimated that one member out of every 30 families had been to college, a ratio comparing well with small towns in the mother country. However, the simple frontier life placed no great premium upon literacy since industry and know-how proved far more useful than book learning. The chores to be done by every member of the family were endless, and working hours were long.

Under such conditions, there was little time or inclination to draw up an entirely new blueprint for education. Therefore, the same church and state control that had characterized the Reformation schools in Europe was at first transplanted to America, especially to Calvinistic New England. The conception of a two-track school system, one for the aristocracy and another for the common people, also made its appearance but never became firmly established. A more democratic viewpoint of education took form as new political and economic institutions began to appear. As early as 1635 the town of Boston voted to establish a school to be supported from the income of a parcel of land set aside for that purpose, to be augmented by private subscriptions. Before the end of the century 30 other New England towns had made similar provisions to finance education, thus establishing a principle that towns should not only take the initiative but should also assume at least partial responsibility for upkeep. Financial support depended upon tuition fees from those parents who could afford to pay and also from fines, licenses, property taxes, and income from town lands and fisheries.

Massachusetts Bay Colony then took two important steps to force reluctant or backward towns to provide educational facilities. The pioneer American school law in 1642 sought to compel parents and masters to see that their children had elementary instruction. Minimum essentials were set up: reading of English, knowledge of the capital laws, the catechism, and apprenticeship in trade. Selectmen were given the authority to enforce this law by fines and compulsory apprenticeship.

It should be noted that this original school law did not establish schools, nor did it even require the towns to establish them. It was the law of 1647 which required towns of 50 families to provide an elementary schoolteacher and towns of 100 families to establish a Latin grammar school for secondary education. Towns were granted authority to levy taxes for the support of teachers, and fines were to be assessed against those that failed to comply. It is noteworthy that many preferred to pay this fine rather than go to the greater expense of establishing a school.

Considerable debate has since developed concerning the importance of those original laws in laying the foundations for the American public school system. It has generally been accepted that they set the precedent for our nineteenth-century state school systems, but some authorities hold that they were merely the means of making sure that the children would be able to read the Bible—a key to salvation in Protestant theology. Regardless of original motive, the important fact is that the government did establish its authority over education.

Actually this system was a carry-over from the Calvinistic conception of state and church responsibility for schools and control over them. With this idea was fused the English tradition of state support for apprenticeship of poor children as set up by the English Poor Law of 1601. The Middle Colonies also attempted to establish such centralized control over schools, but were unable to maintain the practice for long because of the wide diversity of religious beliefs.

Education in the South followed the general practices of the Church of England. Schooling from the very beginning was regarded as a private affair to be provided wherever parents were able to do so. Free education was associated with charity schools for the poor; hence upperclass parents shunned it. This attitude that free instruction was meant only for orphans and children of poor or indigent parents contrasted sharply with the New England tradition of free education for every child.

However, throughout the colonies such legislative acts as making religious instruction and apprenticeship to a trade compulsory for poor children revealed the transplanted English aristocratic class structure. The theory was to use education to protect the rest of society from a working class that might otherwise become vagabond and prove dangerous to life and property. As for the Catholics, they had made early efforts to establish schools but at the end of the seventeenth century they were such a small and maligned minority their schools had practically disappeared in the English colonies.

Especially interesting was the development of education by the Quakers. From the date of their earliest settlements in Pennsylvania, New Jersey, and other colonies, they were active in establishing schools for children of their congregations. William Penn's (1644–1718) "Frame of Government for Pennsylvania," passed by the first colonial legislature in 1682, provided for a system of public schools dedicated largely to the conservation of religious interests. So far as education was concerned, this legislation never went into effect; its operation at that time was impossible because there were so many different denominations. However, Quaker schools usually were established almost as soon as a community was formed, and even after the failure of Penn's ambitious educational scheme they remained under the jurisdiction of the Society of Friends. Most Quaker schools were elementary and concentrated on the inculcation of their morals, mode of living, and religious ideas. For practical trade considerations some attention was devoted to writing and arithmetic. Incidentally, the Quaker meetings were excellent examples of an extensive program of adult education.

The dominant motive for the establishment of all earlier colonial schools was religious instruction. No responsibility was assumed for transmitting the foundations of secular literature, science, arts, and social institutions. Elementary schools provided the rudiments needed for reading the Bible; the education was narrow in scope and meager in content. A bright pupil needed only a year or so to master all the school had to offer.

Social status of early American teachers varied widely from place to place and with the type of school. Those who taught in New England and New Netherlands, generally speaking, enjoyed more respect than their colleagues in the South, where often the responsibility of teaching poor children was thrust upon white indentured servants and sometimes Negro slaves. Qualifications ranged widely from the poorly prepared woman conducting a dame school in her kitchen to the college graduates and ministers who taught the Latin schools. Salaries were derived from tuitions, voluntary gifts, and incomes from rentals of town land. Many were paid in kind with foodstuffs and livestock. For practically all teachers the time and form of payment were uncertain, and the natural consequence was a large turnover with many teachers becoming virtual itinerants. To make a living some of them had to hold down two or more jobs—including preaching, bookkeeping, and even gravedigging.

Frontier environment offered no incentive to the cultivation of true humanistic interests. In that relentless struggle with natural forces, men who were studious sought in the classics a means of understanding the Scriptures. Their sons entered the Latin school at about the age of eight and completed the course at fifteen. Although the teachers were vastly superior to those in primary schools, a surprising number of them were hopelessly inefficient. The better ones were usually young clergymen who divided their time between preaching and teaching, or were waiting for a clerical appointment. Instructional methods were crude, hours were long, and discipline was severe. An indifferent scholar was considered perverted, a dull one a "blockhead." In either case corporal punishment was the cure.

Harvard College (1636) was the first to be established in colonial America—in fact, it was the only institution of higher learning during the seventeenth century, since William and Mary (1693) did not offer collegiate work until after the 1700's.* Harvard had many financial difficulties in its earlier years. Enrollments seldom ran more than 20, and the president served as both instructor and business manager. Keeping an "eagle eye" on the orthodoxy of all instruction were the neighboring ministers, which meant the president was almost always involved in bickerings with his fellow churchmen. Established by the colonial legislature, Harvard's original training course was for the ministry, and it followed the best traditions of the time. No one was allowed to graduate until he could translate into Latin and Hebrew the Greek versions of both Old and New Testaments, and could resolve them logically. The curriculum also included astronomy, ethics, geometry, political philosophy, and physics.

To sum up the growth of American education in the seventeenth century, certainly it can be said that the colonies made some sort of provision for teaching children to read. Of course, for one reason or another, many children were unable to take advantage of this opportunity; nevertheless, the groundwork for free elementary school education was laid.

As for secondary education, only the lucky few entered the Latin grammar schools where they learned Latin, Greek, mathematics, and religion. Intended primarily to prepare students for college, Latin schools proved quite unpopular with the people as a whole because they were not in tune with frontier life. The amounts of the fines assessed for not establishing them were raised several times, and frequently, where Latin schools did exist, they became "class" schools, attended almost exclusively by children of the wealthier families. In brief, the concept of equal opportunity for all Americans was still a long way from realization.

Education in Eighteenth-Century America

As the eighteenth century opened, the colonial educational picture was indeed discouraging. Many New England towns were paying fines because they refused to establish Latin schools. Harvard, the only

* The oldest college in the Americas is not Harvard but the University of San Marcos (1551) in Lima, Peru.

college in English-speaking America, was a tiny ministerial seminary, torn with dissensions and caught in a financial struggle that threatened its very existence. There were a few Latin schools in Virginia and the Middle Colonies but the people showed practically no incentive to establish others. Since the frontier was continually expanding, the maintenance of schools was a difficult problem in many sparsely settled areas.

However, the Church of England, finally realizing its stake in America, in 1701 organized the Propagation of the Gospel to conduct overseas mission work. Before the outbreak of the Revolution, that society was maintaining numerous schools, mostly elementary, and had even invaded Puritan New England with its activities. It successfully raised funds in England and America to establish seminaries for the training of Episcopal clergymen.

Teachers in those days were usually appointed at town meetings. This meant that qualifications were passed upon by townspeople, churches, royal companies, royal governors, and even the Bishop of London in the case of the Church of England teachers. Under such circumstances the most important qualification for teaching was religious orthodoxy. Supervision was conducted by clergymen, selectmen, and committees who paid their visits to classrooms primarily to determine if students were learning correctly the fundamental religious beliefs and the three R's.

Tenure depended largely upon religious orthodoxy and good moral character. Teachers were generally inefficient, and some accounts indicate that many were crude and uncouth. But in their defense it should be noted that the atmosphere in the towns and villages around them was not exactly genteel. Most teachers were men, except for women in dame schools and those serving as substitutes in the summer when men were working in the fields. Planters' wives in the South sometimes carried on instruction as a leisure-time hobby; some even conducted schools for slaves.

Early eighteenth-century Europe witnessed the great rationalistic-thought movement among the intellectuals that came to be known as the Enlightenment. This had many contradictory aspects, but taken as a whole it represented a revolt against traditional authority. In America the Enlightenment served to awaken the individual to a new realization of his potentialities. Interest in reading developed rapidly, showing itself in an increased demand for good literature and especially for current publications.

In the earlier days of colonial history the church and state had jealously controlled and censored the printers, but during the 1700's freedom of speech became firmly entrenched as a principle in American life. With new currents of thought sweeping in from Europe, the Puritan clergy were finding it ever more difficult to maintain a theocratic control in New England. The influx of a wide variety of religious groups into the colonies doomed forever the possibility of a single established church.

During the middle decades of the century, there was a widespread evangelical arousing of religious emotion, a period often called the Great Awakening. Religious leadership gained greatly in power, but this power was held by several denominations rather than by a single church. This spiritual renascence increased philanthropy and altruism either through a broadened sympathy for the unfortunate or fear of everlasting torments in the hereafter. Some of the wealth gained from the flourishing trade was donated to churches, schools, colleges, and philanthropic societies. Because this new support resulted largely from a revival of religious fervor, many schools stressed theological matters almost to the exclusion of all else, thus allowing churches to retain a firm hold on education.

Even though churches continued to set up schools in the eighteenth century, there gradually developed a more liberal conception of education. In time the curriculum became less narrow and religious aims not so dominant. People living in the older settlements enjoyed security and economic improvement. Many of them turned to the educational ideals then being fostered by the leisure classes in contemporary England. Schooling, they felt, represented the road to becoming a "gentleman and a scholar," with the classics as the chief element in the cultural program designed for that purpose. To meet these new demands, many schools emphasized gracious manners, elegant speech, and familiarity with the best of ancient authors. While not entirely replacing religious instruction, this training for the formal social life of the time was definitely a step in that direction.

About the same time a popular demand was growing for schools to take over the functions of vocational training, which heretofore had been almost exclusively the province of the apprenticeship system. In trading centers of the North and East, the fact that Latin schools were usually conducted by masters whose scholarship had been confined to the classics intensified the demand for practical vocational training. In the larger communities along the Atlantic seaboard there began to appear semi-vocational private "English" schools. In 1709 a Boston schoolmaster offered arithmetic, astronomy, writing, and the use of mathematical instruments. Bookkeeping was taught in New York City as early as 1731, and soon thereafter instruction was being offered in such modern languages as French, Italian, Portuguese, and Spanish. These subjects were intended chiefly for those planning careers in foreign trade.

Toward the middle of the century even the Latin schools began to include one or more of the practical subjects. Thus a new motive, that of vocational utility, began to appear alongside college preparation and formal culture. Middle-class fathers, who previously had provided school and college training for sons ambitious to enter the ministry, were now seeking a practical education to help their other sons in trade or business. This created difficult administrative problems, especially when a school had only one or two teachers, as usually was the case in colonial times. Sometimes there were two or three courses being taught in the same building—the Latin school was having "growing pains."

In the 1750's there appeared a new institution, the academy, offering a range of studies designed to serve a variety of purposes, including college preparation. Benjamin Franklin (1706–1790) in 1749 published his "proposals" for the establishment of an academy in Philadelphia, which opened two years later.* He outlined a course of study to include (besides the classics) modern languages, English grammar, rhetoric, literature, history, natural sciences. His announced purpose was to produce a practical, well-behaved, and well-informed man of affairs.

The difficulty of presenting an orderly arrangement of these various subjects was met by organizing them into three schools: Latin, English, and mathematical. A student was given his choice of the three courses. Even though the elective system was employed from a very early date, many of those first academies copied the plan of grouping subjects in parallel courses. Toward the end of the century there appeared many new academies along the Atlantic seaboard, including some for girls. Usually they were private institutions with courses of study determined by both local aspirations and previous training of the masters. This resulted in uneven development—some academies were little more than primary schools while others prepared for college.

While education increasingly became more a local than a church matter, and politically the colonies progressed nearer the Revolution, the idea of state control began to gain headway. All legislatures had passed laws concerning education but outside New England these did not prove effective. New York and Pennsylvania, for example, had tried to establish their own public school systems. Those efforts were balked by the influx of varied religious sects, each determined to operate its own denominational schools.

* This academy was eventually reorganized in 1779 and became the University of the State of Pennsylvania.

However, interest in state control of education was beginning to rise, especially after independence had been gained. Thomas Jefferson (1743–1826) was the outstanding spokesman for this movement in America. In 1779 he introduced into the Virginia legislature a comprehensive plan for reorganization of the state's institutions. He included a proposal for a system of free education in which elementary schools at state expense were to be provided throughout Virginia and secondary schools at state expense were to be set up for the more intelligent youths. The most promising of these students were to be sent to an enlarged and reorganized College of William and Mary, which, in effect, would become a state university. The legislature failed to approve Jefferson's plan, largely because of opposition by religious interests and by friends of William and Mary.*

Jefferson's great contribution was his clear statement of the ideal of free universal education, a goal almost achieved during the following century. Just as soon as independence had been secured, the country was flooded with pamphlets, essays, and articles setting forth theories about educational control in the new republic.

George Washington (1732–1799) was intensely interested in a national university as a means of unifying the nation, and he proposed to Congress that one be established. To help subsidize the project he willed the government some shares of valuable stocks. The first four presidents, in fact, favored the founding of a national university; and at one time or another committees of both houses of Congress reported favorably on it. But no action was taken, and the issue went into eclipse during the slavery controversy.

A most important step toward the building of state school systems was made while the country was still operating under the Articles of Confederation. Two ordinances were passed covering disposition of the vast public lands in the West, claims which the various states had surrendered to the federal government. The Ordinance of 1785 provided that the lands should be surveyed into square plots, six miles on a side, to be known as townships. Each of these was to be further subdivided into 36 sections, or squares, one mile on a side. Income from the sale of the sixteenth section, located in the center of each township, was to be used for common schools when the land was sold or rented.

The Ordinance of 1787 reconfirmed this land policy and set forth the governmental principles to be followed, including establishment of common schools, when the Northwest Territory was settled. These

* Just as Franklin pioneered in the establishment of the University of Pennsylvania, so Jefferson can be credited with the University of Virginia. The original buildings, the organization, and the curriculum were all planned by him.

two ordinances marked the establishment of a new principle of federal aid to education—they represented the eighteenth century's greatest legacy to American free public education in the centuries to follow.

Education in Nineteenth-Century America

Most Americans in 1800 still considered education either a matter of private initiative or a church responsibility. Several of the original state constitutions had ordered their respective legislatures to establish schools, but liberal theories of intellectuals like Jefferson were quite different from practical administration. Enthusiasm for public schools cooled when the propertied class, in control of government, began counting the cost in increased taxes.

As the nineteenth century opened, in fact, there was in progress a clash between two distinctly different kinds of liberalism—that of the French writers who loudly proclaimed the "human rights" of man as opposed to the laissez-faire theories of Adam Smith (1723–1790). Smith's *Wealth of Nations* held that individuals should be free to contract such relations to each other as they found to be personally advantageous, and that government derives its authority from contract, too. In other words, a citizen should not be taxed to educate the children of other people unless he voluntarily consents.

It was this English laissez-faire attitude that in 1800 largely governed the provision of educational opportunities in America. The states held aloof, waiting for the self-interest of parents, churches, philanthropic societies, and individuals to develop whatever education each cared to provide. It was only when the paupers were to be educated, or the rate bills of indigent children were to be defrayed, that the states stepped in with their niggardly contributions.

Yet at the very height of this laissez-faire liberalism there was growing an insistent demand for the states to take positive action in support of wider educational opportunities. This pressure was met with a variety of halfway measures. In some states, private schools and philanthropically supported societies were allotted the revenues from excises, lotteries, and sales of public lands. Others went so far as to pass permissive legislation giving local governments authority voluntarily to tax themselves for schools, should they wish to do so. Our early national educational history was largely the story of efforts to provide schooling at a minimum cost.

Complicating the situation was the Industrial Revolution that had begun in England in the 1730's and was sweeping the United States during the first half of the nineteenth century. Closely associated with this industrial development were rapid advances in science and technology which made possible mass production of goods and their more rapid distribution and transportation. An important aspect of industrialization was the growth of city life bringing with it problems of filth, overcrowding of slums, juvenile delinquency—all threats to health, morals, and sanitation. Capitalism produced the factory system, placed concentration of great wealth in the hands of a few, and spurred the rise of labor organizations. Our educational system reflected these cultural trends and tensions.

A public tax-supported school system was not an original idea. But while such theories sounded fine, no country in the world had ever put one into operation. Even in America this approach was not accepted without a bitter struggle, although the adoption of political democracy as our form of government made it inevitable that education become one of the most important governmental functions. Many conservatives felt that only a relative few would be able to profit; therefore, they fought against establishment of public schools on the theory that working people should not be allowed to rise too rapidly out of their inherited places in society.

However, the reactionaries were swimming upstream against the forces of democracy, humanitarianism, industrialism, secularism, and an expanding population. In general it was a case of the middle-class liberals, reformers, labor groups, and organized farmers being pitted against industrial and business interests, southern aristocrats, conservatives of all classes, and certain religious and non-English-speaking groups who saw in the movement a threat against their private control of religious and foreign-language schools.

Gradually the humanitarian idea gained strength, leading first to the provision of charitable education for the poor by churches. Then free-school societies were formed for the purpose of extending educational opportunities to those children not served by the church schools. Some states began to pass laws providing free schools for poor children. In the 1820's infant schools were formed in the larger cities for those below the ages of seven or eight. Sunday school societies were organized on the model of the original ones in England, to give the rudiments of secular instruction on the Sabbath when juvenile factory workers would be off the job and liable to create trouble because of free time on their hands. But soon the churches took over the Sunday school movement and made religious instruction its whole aim.

An important development at this time was the beginning of the high school. It was a case of changing conditions bringing about modifi-

cations in an existing institution rather than the creation of a new and
entirely different one. Considered the pioneer in 1821 was the English
Classical School in Boston which three years later changed its name
to English High School. This institution, as well as others of its kind,
was not originally designed for college preparation; but as time went
on, college preparatory departments were usually organized whenever
new high schools were established.

Massachusetts in 1827 passed a law requiring towns of 500 families
to establish high schools, and other New England states soon followed
this example. The problem of providing secondary education for girls
was met in Boston and elsewhere by establishing separate schools for
them. Lowell, farther west than Boston, set up a "female" department
that offered courses parallel to those for the boys. That was the first
step toward coeducation. By mid-century high schools had largely absorbed the Latin grammar schools and differed from the contemporary
academies only in manner of support—public funds versus private resources.

In the new territories the settlers brought with them their respective
types of religious and social institutions to which they had been accustomed. This meant New England district schools supported by local
rates made an early appearance in Ohio, Michigan, and Indiana; pauper schools of the lower Atlantic states cropped up in Mississippi and
Alabama. The two conflicting sentiments of the older states went along
with the settlers: they were enthusiastic for schools yet reluctant to levy
taxes for their support.

For a time hope ran high that the land grants would carry the whole
financial burden of education or reduce it to a trifling amount. One of
the great tragedies in American education has been the rapid dissipation of this heritage intended for the people as a whole. For example,
Wisconsin sold thousands of acres of valuable timber land at five cents
an acre to a favored few, and a mysterious fire in the state capitol destroyed the recorded transactions years later when an investigation was
imminent.

The public school system began to take form in the second quarter
of the century. Many state legislatures passed public school measures
only to repeal them the following year. The move to abolish rate bills
in New York State was defeated by popular vote as late as 1850. The
movement that finally awakened the conscience of the country was essentially middle-class sponsored. Led by clergymen, teachers, patriots,
it was an effort to extend education to the economically poorer people
who themselves were either too indifferent or too inarticulate to espouse their own cause. Numerous propaganda societies sprang up in

the 1850's. Occasionally there were resolutions demanding schools by workingmen's societies, but these were few and far between.

The battle for reform is best illustrated by what happened in Massachusetts. James G. Carter (1795–1840), a farmer's son who became interested in education while still in Harvard College, initiated the reform of the Massachusetts school system. In a lengthy pamphlet he pointed a finger of shame at the schools whose inefficiency was so contrary to the New England tradition. As a member of the legislature, with the assistance of Horace Mann (1796–1859), Carter in 1837 secured passage of a law creating a state board of education. He was also instrumental in establishing a state school fund to assist the towns in maintaining more efficient instruction. Later Carter was chiefly responsible for the founding in Massachusetts of the first American normal school.

Having thus created the machinery for competent centralized control and having prepared the means for more adequate preparation of teachers, Carter passed the leadership to Mann who gave up a prosperous law practice to accept the uncertainties of the office of secretary of the new state board of education. That office had no authority except the force of public opinion, so Mann's first task was to arouse sentiment of the people in order to make the legal machinery work.

Mann gave to the new work all his tremendous energy, lecturing passionately, issuing voluminous reports, and publishing his views in the *Common School Journal* which he created. He won friends to his cause but he also stirred up enemies. Property owners contested his pleas for higher taxes; religious denominations called his schools "godless." Even the Boston schoolmasters were peeved by his aspersions regarding their efficiency. Mann's twelve years in office produced terrific agitation, but the battle was being won. The school fund was doubled, teachers' salaries raised, new hygienic schoolhouses erected, school terms lengthened, high schools established, three normal schools opened, and teaching methods improved. His crusade for public education spread to practically every other American state. After serving two terms in Congress, he finished his career as the president of Antioch College (Ohio). Horace Mann, some historians claim, is the foremost educational statesman that America has ever produced. Certainly it can be said that he played a most important role in the establishment of nonsectarian school systems under state control.

Between 1830 and 1860 in nearly every state there was active agitation for public schools. Before the Civil War most commonwealths had already yielded to the pressure of public opinion and had provided state, county, and local school officers; established state school funds;

passed regulations governing the examination* of teachers; and a few had normal schools. Responsibility for schools gradually was being shifted from the local districts to the state at large. There was much sentiment, too, for a tax-supported educational system to which almost everyone would contribute. But it should be noted that despite this democratic fervor, five of the northern states were still operating their schools under unfair rate bills.

In the decades following the War Between the States, home and community life outside the school continued to provide children with the larger part of the experiences needed to fit them for competent citizenship. The war itself had disrupted the development of educational systems in the North as well as in the South, but more drastically in the latter.

However, the closing years of the nineteenth century witnessed the beginning of an expansion that was truly phenomenal. By 1900 more than two-fifths of our population was already living in urban communities, and with this development of industrialization the conditions surrounding children were vastly changed. Cities were growing up and taking form to accommodate the demands of production and exchange with little or no consideration for the requirements of childhood. More and more the schools were forced to supply experiences regarded as essential for the socialization of youth in the areas of manners and morals, health, recreation, vocation, and civic behavior. This urbanization meant longer years of formal schooling than had ever been necessary in the rural environment.

Education in Twentieth-Century America

The American frontier had almost disappeared when the twentieth century began. Theodore Roosevelt (1858–1919) was the first of our presidents to establish a serious action program for the conservation of our national resources, the reckless destruction of which had begun almost as soon as the first colonists reached American shores. Our economic system had never fully exemplified the principles of laissez-faire inasmuch as the government rarely, if ever, had occupied a neutral position. Fostered with an indulgent hand, business enterprises were greatly favored by high tariffs, bounties to railroads, patent rights, and an overgenerous disposition of the rich national domain.

Whatever may have been the inefficiencies or injustices of the system, it cannot be denied that the United States was developing into

---

* At that time oral examination preceded certification. The practice stemmed from an earlier period when clergymen asked questions of applicants for teaching positions.

the greatest industrial nation in the world. Such an economy had operated well enough in the nineteenth century because there was a virgin continent to exploit. But in the 1900's the "shoe was beginning to cramp" as a greatly increased population faced a rapid shrinkage of natural resources and began to discover the impossibility of expanding as rapidly as in the previous centuries. The fact that the five largest American corporations already controlled assets of greater value than the total assessed valuation of all property contained in half the states indicated an unhealthy situation.

A ferment of social reform has continued throughout this century. Reduction in the working day, child labor laws, employer responsibility for accidents to employees, safety and sanitation measures, compulsory accident insurance, public health measures for control and prevention of disease, regulation of public utilities, housing laws, and many other reforms have been fought for and won as a result of a rising social consciousness. But in all these the school has played a minor, or even a negative part, although theoretically the changes in national economy have placed upon education a new and enlarged responsibility.

It should be noted that since 1918 every American state has had on its statute books a compulsory school attendance law. Passage of such legislation indicates the state's tacit obligation to see that nothing in the environment of the school may endanger the lives or impair the health of the children who are required to attend. The communities are obliged to provide not only safe and sanitary buildings but also ample playgrounds, pure water, and proper observance of other hygienic conditions. Medical and dental inspection programs, vaccinations and inoculations to prevent diseases have also been accepted as obligations.

Recognition of responsibility for the health of the school child has justified the maintenance of gymnasiums, swimming pools, and showers with which the better schools are now equipped. Also, the operation of special classes for partially blind, deaf, retarded and subnormal children has been warranted. Another recent development has been maintenance of facilities for hot lunches and, in some cases, provision of free milk and food for poor and undernourished children. What a far cry this is from the era of the Latin grammar school!

Public schools now enroll approximately 90 per cent of all American children between the ages of seven and seventeen, and public funds contribute about 80 per cent of all school expenditures. Faith of the nation in education has been exemplified by the doubling of expenditures for all school purposes every decade since 1880.

The twentieth century has put into operation two new types of school organization—the junior high school and the junior college. The idea of a junior high school began with the efforts of President Charles W. Eliot (1834–1926) of Harvard in the 1880's to improve the elementary school curriculum. His contention was that much of the time spent in grammar grade reviews could be used more profitably in teaching new materials, and that the elementary programs needed to be shortened and enriched. In 1893 the famed NEA "Committee of Ten" favored this revision, and it was advocated that Latin, algebra, and geometry be added to the upper grades of the grammar school; also, that high school courses begin with the seventh grade. A few schools did introduce the above three subjects into the grades, but since the teachers made no real change in subject matter, the experiment failed.

Despite protests of opponents that departmentalization overworked the children and made teachers too narrow in subject matter, the plan was introduced into a number of schools and proved quite successful. However, this departmentalization remained within the framework of the 8-4 plan. It was not until 1906 that the 6-3-3 organization of the junior high school finally took hold. Three school systems (Berkeley, California; Columbus, Ohio; and Concord, New Hampshire) claimed the distinction of having been the first. But according to testimony set forth in 1948, it was Mansfield, Ohio, that took President Eliot's suggestion in 1880 and that same year tried out a junior high school. The plan was soon dropped, but it can be argued that Mansfield was the first city ever to have had a junior high school—just 26 years before the date of rival claimants.

As early as 1902 President Harper of the University of Chicago had recommended the extension of the high school course to six years so as to include the freshman and sophomore years of college. The high school at Joliet, Illinois, acted immediately upon this recommendation and organized a junior college department. In 1907 California's legislature authorized high school districts to offer junior college courses. The movement in that state progressed rapidly, and within 10 years of the organization of the first junior college at Fresno there were 20 such institutions. Their purpose was to bridge the gap between high school and college or to provide advanced vocational training. In the latter case the junior colleges became terminal schools. It should also be noted that early junior colleges—unlike the one at Joliet—were established as separate institutions.

Texas and Iowa soon followed the lead of California, and the junior college movement spread rapidly throughout the nation except for the Northeast where the presence of older institutions temporarily deferred the change. But the idea has really caught on in recent decades. A 1958 report showed that 20 new public junior colleges had been begun that year, bringing the total to some 400 such schools with an enrollment of nearly 800,000 students. In several states (Mississippi, California, and Illinois among them) junior college tuition was free or fees were only slight.

Unlike the junior high school and the junior college, the <u>vocational</u> <u>school</u> was a product of the nineteenth century. Originally a young man who wished to become proficient in a skilled occupation had to work as an apprentice or learn a trade from his own father at home. But the Industrial Revolution brought the demand for a wider and better system that would give specialized training in the handling of new machines. In the 1800's other forces gave impetus to this movement: the doctrines of Pestalozzi and Froebel, the rise of manual training-instruction in Scandinavia, and the extension of opportunity for schooling to the children of the poor.

Vocational training programs gradually spread in the nineteenth century. Some instruction in the use of tools developed in elementary schools; courses in commercial subjects appeared at the secondary school level; and private trade schools like Cooper Union (1859) and Pratt Institute (1887) were formed. Also, in 1888 the first regularly established public vocational secondary school was created as an offshoot of the University of Minnesota. This agricultural high school paved the way for many other institutions devoted to the science of farming.

But vocational training really took a giant step forward in 1917. In that year the Smith-Hughes Act provided for federal funds to assist the states in setting up courses in agriculture, home economics, and industrial arts. Separate vocational high schools soon sprang up everywhere—within the big cities and, on a regional basis, in many counties. Since that time other laws, like the "G.I. Bill of Rights" in 1944, have encouraged the extension of this training into the adult years. Moreover, many industries have set up their own training programs.*

All this interest in vocational schooling has run hand in hand with the spread of compulsory education laws through all the states. The twentieth century has witnessed the flowering of the educational ideals stated or implied in the Constitution. Through the morass of dame schools, Latin grammar schools, academies, and the like we have come

---

* General Motors Institute, at Flint, Michigan, originally was a YMCA school. This was taken over by the Corporation to train employees from all its numerous plants and dealerships. Courses range from three-week training periods to a four-year engineering degree, where the plan leading to a degree is to spend three months in the plant, then three months at school, etc.

to a somewhat orderly plan of state public school systems that provide education for all. Although we have no national school system, the structures and curricula of the various state educational systems are remarkably similar.

But it should not be inferred that the ideal has been reached. Grave problems still exist. Some states are richer than others; consequently, they are presumably able to offer a better quality of education. The issue of "separate but equal" schools in the South has been brought to a head by the Supreme Court's decision (1954) that integration must be effected "with all deliberate speed." Legions of underprivileged children in the North, as well as in the South, are not realizing their full potential. There is a serious shortage of public school teachers and a dichotomy as to what they should teach and what methods they should use. The constantly increasing number of college-bound students has caused an admissions problem in higher institutions—and at that level there is also a growing shortage of teachers.

The above are only a few of the many educational problems that face Americans as they move forward toward the twenty-first century. The authors intend to discuss them, as well as other issues and trends, later in this book.

Evolution of Elementary Education

The Greeks were first to divide the child's formative years into periods: pre-school to seven, formal education to some point in adolescence, and, finally, various forms of post-adolescent training which eventually were segmented into secondary and higher education. Early training of the child remained under direction of the mother; toys, games, and fables were the chief materials of instruction. Then came the mastering of the rudiments of reading and writing, after which the child started immediately on the best of Greek literature. Some elementary instruction in grammar did grow out of reading and writing, and there was also the beginning of a concept of numbers. Later, music and physical training were added to complete the first level of formal schooling.

Roman education, like that of the Greeks, had three divisions with formal schooling postponed until the age of seven. Quintilian (35–100) held that moral training should start before that time but warned parents not to expect too much from children in those tender years. He felt, however, that the sooner a child started the more knowledge he could hope to amass by the end of his period of formal training. Reminding teachers of the waste that follows from attempting to pour water too fast into a narrow-necked vessel, this great schoolmaster cautioned against undue haste and adult pressure in the teaching of reading.

Aesop (c. 560 B.C.) was the most popular author for beginning readers in Rome. Although there is a question as to whether there ever really was an Aesop, we do know that scholars wrote out the fables, first in Greek and then in Latin, and that they became standard stories for youngsters of all Western lands in later centuries. Incidentally, a Roman boy might skip Aesop, but he could not avoid the Twelve Tables— the fundamental law of the land. Memorization of the Tables was an established practice in elementary education.

During the early Christian period a new elementary (or catechumenal) school came into existence for the teaching of church doctrines. Although many early converts were recruited from the underprivileged social classes, the emphasis in schooling was more on Christian aspirations and convictions than on literacy with the inevitable result that the quality of elementary instruction deteriorated.

Then, in the early part of the medieval period, education really took a narrow road. What had survived from Greek and Roman traditions was perpetuated in Latin-language schools maintained in connection with cathedrals, monasteries, guilds, and chantries. Latin was the language not only of the Church but also of the law courts, of civil government, and even of business. Therefore, schools to prepare young men for careers in such fields were conducted for a small, highly selected minority. Since the masses spoke in the vernacular they had no need for schooling.

However, as economic conditions improved toward the end of the medieval period, there came into existence schools teaching in the vernacular, known as "adventure" or "hedge" schools because they were usually private ventures and were held under such impromptu conditions as behind hedges. Especially noteworthy is the fact that a new distinction was developing between elementary and secondary education. In the Graeco-Roman world the difference had been based upon age, with more advanced studies in the post-adolescent period. There was now emerging a distinction based on social class and the language used in instruction.

Thus the modern elementary school took root in vernacular instruction. Some authorities date its origin with the invention of printing about 1450, but most of them place it with the Protestant Reformation in the following century. Martin Luther (1483–1546) replaced the authority of the Catholic hierarchy with that of the Bible, which meant that everyone would have to learn to read in order to seek personal salvation. The new Protestant church services stressed two rituals that required literacy: congregational singing and responsive reading. In certain of the German principalities education was made compulsory, and it was unthinkable that anyone should be unable to read the Bible. Those innovations determined the character of elementary schooling for the next several centuries.

The seventeenth-century Puritans brought to New England what became known as "dame" schools because they were taught by housewives anxious to eke out meager incomes by teaching school while they were engaged in spinning or other household duties. Sometimes these were not private ventures but were sponsored by a religious denomination, a practice common in New York and Pennsylvania.

Leading the way for other New England colonies, Massachusetts by law established elementary schools which for a long time thereafter were known as "common schools." It was natural that reading should be stressed as the skill needed for an understanding of the Scriptures. Since writing was not considered so important, often separate schools were set up for reading and writing. Whenever arithmetic was taught it was relegated to these writing schools. Much of the teacher's time was spent in sharpening quills, setting copies, dictating sums, hearing each child's lessons individually, and, above all, keeping order. These activities usually absorbed so much time there was little left for teaching.

From about 1750 a rapidly growing spirit of toleration served to dampen the fires of sectarianism which previously had been the chief incentive for education. Economic, political, and nationalistic forces began to rival the religious interests. The Industrial Revolution became an important factor because it created the wealth by which free schooling could be furnished. But it was also largely responsible for the poverty growing out of the exploitation of children forced to work long hours on weekdays. Often these urchins proved a menace to life and property during their free hours on Sundays. Some type of schooling seemed a great necessity if only as a defensive measure.

Many good-hearted religious people worried because these waifs were growing up without knowledge of either their letters or catechism. And so in London and nearby towns there developed an extensive system of charity schools. These not only provided free education for poor boys and girls, but sometimes even furnished them clothing and helped them find work.

Such charity schools were sponsored by members of the monied classes as a means of alleviating the pitiful conditions of factory worker families. Established and supported by benevolences, they tackled the problem both at home and abroad. The chief British agency to affect the American colonies was the Society for the Propagation of the Gospel in Foreign Parts, which organized schools across the Atlantic aiming specifically to teach reading, writing, and enough arithmetic to fit poor children for apprenticeships. Since the most important aim of those schools was religious, actually there were four rather than three R's. Discouragement of lying, swearing, and profaning the Sabbath was to be accomplished by teaching of the catechism. Knitting, sewing, spinning, and other practical employments were added later; the purpose was to make the "pauper children" self-supporting.

About this time the monitorial schools came into being, first in England and then briefly in America. These had the virtue of educating large numbers of children at relatively low cost. The schoolmaster first instructed the older children who then served as monitors in teaching the day's lesson to a group of 10 or 12 smaller pupils. These recited aloud and in unison whatever was being taught. Wall placards and charts were used to aid group instruction and to save money by eliminating the expense of books. Subject matter remained principally the catechism, reading, writing, spelling, and arithmetic.

The rising spirit of nationalism set forces into motion that began by replacing Latin with the vernacular languages. Folk tales and literature received new emphasis. The American Revolution brought with it a realization that if people were to rule themselves, they had first to learn how to exercise their newly won liberties. For this they required an education to free them from blind dependence on their leaders. The fact that declamation gained an important place in the common schools during our early national period indicated the eagerness of the people to use their schools to prepare themselves for active participation in democratic processes.

But a more significant result of the spirit of nationalism was the inclusion of history and civics in the curriculum of the elementary schools. Later, along with geography, the whole area came to be known as social studies. Finally, educators borrowed a page from the Athenians and added such subjects as music and calisthenics to promote cultural interest and physical fitness.

However, these nationalistic and political ideals were slow in creating a truly effective educational system—there was much more talk than action. Even into the twentieth century the average elementary school was in session fewer than six months each year, and three-fourths of the instructional time was being spent in formal subjects that were usually taught in a very mechanical manner. Little that was done in school bore any true relationship to the needs of the society in which the pupils were living.

Initial incentive for reform in elementary education came from Europe. The Pestalozzian and Herbartian movements brought with them a vigorous vitality, but soon they became formalized and conformed to the inertia and mechanicalness so characteristic of the American graded schools at that time. As so often has been the case, most of the followers of these imported methodologies got the idea but not the spirit.

Thus it was left to Colonel Francis W. Parker (1831–1902), serving as superintendent of schools at Quincy, Massachusetts, to initiate a more far-reaching and enduring reform to remedy the distressingly jejune instruction. To Parker, the center of educational processes was the child himself; therefore, he concentrated the work of his elementary schools on self-expression, especially in the forms of reading and writing. All other school subjects were taught incidentally to these two. History and geography, for example, were sources to be read for information and enjoyment. Also introduced by Parker as classroom activities were clay modeling, drawing, and field trips—activities which for that time were indeed revolutionary.

John Dewey (1859–1951) articulated, intensified, and broadened the accomplishments of Parker. Dewey considered it an archaic practice for elementary schools to spend four-fifths of their time on verbal studies. In place of such a traditional education he substituted at his famed experimental school a curriculum centering on such occupations as were familiar to a child in his home and community life.

Dewey's school thus started with the household occupations; then food and textiles were traced to the sources of their production, and later were studied in connection with their historical settings. Reading and writing began in a pupil's keeping of his own records; number work was done as a necessary part of the study of occupations like cooking and carpentry. Dewey held that education is the regulation of a process whereby the child comes increasingly to share in the social consciousness. Thus the emphasis in elementary education is to regard the "whole" child, his emotions and individual differences.*

Today there is a far greater demand for teachers in elementary schools than anywhere else. All but forgotten now is the tradition that placed teachers in secondary schools at a higher economic and social

* See also the discussion of Dewey and Parker in the section in Part One entitled "Progressive Education."

level than their counterparts in the primary grades. Making elementary education more attractive to capable young people is the single-salary schedule, in which teachers are paid on a basis of professional preparation and years of experience regardless of the grade level taught.

Moreover, in recent years there has been a growing recognition that it requires real ability and thorough professional preparation to get younger children started properly in the acquisition of learning habits and basic skills. Though said facetiously, of course, there is some truth in the remark that teaching is done best in the lower grades and gets progressively poorer until it is at its worst in the graduate schools of universities. In other words, elementary educators were the first to reorganize thoroughly along modern lines and were soon recognized as leaders in the development of effective techniques of instruction.

Evolution of Secondary Education

When the Greeks rose rapidly to leadership in the economic and political life of the Mediterranean world, they felt keenly the need of educational opportunities beyond the elementary level. A training that developed courage, endurance, obedience, loyalty, temperance, and reverence had been sufficient so long as society remained relatively simple. But worldly success gave rise to considerable self-examination among those Greeks who felt a need to participate in the public discussions of their day, whether political or philosophical. Soon there sprang up schools that promised to give students a mastery of grammar, logic, and rhetoric so indispensable to effective self-expression.

Thus the Greeks developed two types of secondary schools, one in which philosophical interests predominated and the other specializing in rhetoric. Both offered basic training in grammar but for different purposes. It was needed in the philosophical secondary schools as a prerequisite to participation in subsequent logical and ethical discussions of a theoretical or idealistic nature; the rhetorical secondary schools required it as a preparation for the very practical purpose of effective public oratory.*

These two types were taken over from the Greeks by the Romans, who tended to emulate the Athenians in most educational matters. Some adaptations were made, however, especially in the direction of subordinating the philosophical to the rhetorical schools. In fact, the

---

* The teaching of grammar in secondary schools eventually caused such institutions to be called "grammar schools." Today, British grammar schools teach Latin and Greek and other subjects preparatory to college. However, in the United States, the term has become practically synonymous with elementary school.

former practically became a preparatory school to which a boy went before attending the school of the rhetorician. An orator needed more formal training than might be contained in rules of grammar and in some well-known tricks of rhetoric, and so a study was made of the seven liberal arts of the Greeks. The styles of the best Greek and Roman authors of prose and poetry were also examined. This approach represented an introduction to bilingualism. It should be noted that Roman youths were required not only to study famous authors but also to write original compositions as part of their preparation for taking an active part in public life.

Early Christian leaders were hostile to the Roman grammar school which they considered a perpetuation of pagan culture. Up to the sixth century the teaching of grammar and associated liberal arts was frowned upon. Finally it was realized that this long failure to cultivate letters was bringing with it the imminent possibility of an illiterate leadership. Eventually this problem was resolved by reconstructing the aim of the grammar school to train devoted and intelligent leaders for church service.

It so happened that the expanding requirements of the Catholic Church demanded more education at the secondary level at the very time that rapid deterioration of the Roman Empire was affording less stimulus for schools. Eventually those institutions sponsored by the Church opened their doors to youths seeking secular careers. Significant also were the chantry schools, set up when endowments were left by testators to engage a priest to sing masses for the repose of the departed's soul; many of those priests were also assigned teaching duties.

It should be noted that some medieval secondary education had no connection with the Church. For example, there were guild and burgher schools whose names indicate their secular origin and nature. In addition, aristocratic adolescents received training in chivalry.

During the Renaissance there developed the humanistic schools, which still have an influence on secondary education today. In them attention was shifted from the world-to-come to the world in which the student was living. To gain more enjoyment from life, the humanists glorified the literary contributions of ancient Greece and Rome.

They aimed at individual development and personal accomplishment through the process of learning to speak and write elegant Latin, then Greek, and still later Hebrew. Their schools were from the beginning designed for the upper classes, though some admitted free a few talented poor boys. The Renaissance humanistic school served as a model for the later *collège* and *lycée* in France, the *Gymnasium* in Germany, and Latin grammar schools in England and America.

The Latin grammar school which the American colonists brought with them followed the Reformation pattern of northern Europe rather than the Renaissance type of Italy. Students did not seek so much the aesthetic enjoyment of the humanities as personal preparation for service to church and state. Boys entered as early as seven or eight for a course that continued six or seven years and was devoted almost exclusively to the study of Latin and Greek. Successful students could not only read Latin at sight and speak it readily but also write Latin themes in prose and verse. Some had a fair start in Greek and might also have studied Hebrew. These students then could apply for examinations for entrance to Oxford or Cambridge, but in case they did not go to college they still knew enough to continue reading in Latin.

Unfortunately by the time the Latin schools were established in America, their European models had lost much of the humanistic spirit and were absorbed in religious controversy. A meticulous study of the Scriptures in the original tongues was conducted. This meant that the study of the classics ceased to be an end in itself and became chiefly a means to an end. Colonial environment offered little incentive to the cultivation of humanistic interests. A relentless struggle with both natural forces and Indian enemies drove men to religion, and they made use of the classics as a means of gaining a better understanding of the Scriptures.

The inability of Latin schools to adjust to changing conditions brought into existence during the eighteenth century a competing secondary school, the American academy. With the coming of prosperity, secular interests had begun to crowd out religion, and the colonists started taking a keen interest in the scientific movement which in Europe had already gained considerable momentum. There was little or nothing in the Latin school curriculum to prepare young men to take part in these newer movements. Consequently, the last quarter of the eighteenth century saw numerous academies established in the states along the Atlantic seaboard. Some offered little more than primary subjects, while others attempted to teach college and professional courses. The variety and elasticity of their programs can be seen by glancing through their old catalogues. One notices such offerings as composition and literature, modern languages, natural science, and even commercial subjects.

The academy reached its peak of popularity in the second quarter of the nineteenth century, which marked the time for the founding of academies for girls. But it must be remembered that the entire movement was primarily under private auspices. Although the academy served to unshackle secondary education from the domination of the narrowly conceived Latin school, it could not be the final answer in a democracy.

High schools made their initial appearance while Latin schools were still in existence and academies at the height of their popularity. This new secondary institution did not arise, therefore, from disappointment with the academy but rather because its originators were so attracted by the academy program they wanted to duplicate its opportunities at public expense. A school committee in Boston planned the original high school as an upward extension and completion of common school education. Thus, in 1821, the English Classical School was established to follow the elementary education of that time. Its purpose was to provide the foundation considered necessary for successful careers in both mercantile and mechanical pursuits.

The high school proved an immediate success and enjoyed special popularity in the western frontier states. There the people looked with disfavor on a dual, or parallel, system of schools in which elementary and secondary education were distinguished from each other on the basis of a child's social expectations. As the American standard of living improved, a high school education became recognized as a means for individuals to mount higher on the nation's socio-economic ladder to success. However, many problems arose and some are still with us; for example, the dual purpose of preparing a small minority for college while providing terminal educational and vocational training for the majority of students. Under the pressure of such criticism the high school has made many changes, and continues to do so today.

In fact, the junior high school arose largely from dissatisfaction with the traditional four-year institutions. Originally it was contended that a four-year period was not sufficiently long to make adequate preparation for a college education. The NEA convention in 1888 was asked by Harvard's famous president, the great Charles W. Eliot, if elementary programs could be shortened and enriched. To eliminate waste and delay in schooling, he urged that some secondary studies begin in grades seven and eight. Following the impact of that speech, and another stirring address in 1892, a number of grammar schools did departmentalize their two upper grades.

Subsequently, many factors combined to cause acceptance of the junior high school idea. The traditional 8–4 plan had been under criticism because of the large percentage of failures in the first year of high school. Some schoolmen argued that a transitional stage was needed in order to give youngsters special guidance according to their abilities and, in addition, an exploration of vocational or academic avenues. Another point in favor of a change was the enormous drop-out rate in the seventh and eighth grades under the 8–4 plan. Proponents of the junior high school reasoned that a 6–3–3 plan would probably induce the pupils to stay in school at least until the end of the ninth grade.

Psychologists and college leaders like Nicholas Murray Butler (1862–1947) put in a good word for the junior high school, too. They said that children who are passing from pre-adolescence through pubescence should have a school of their own, specifically designed to meet their unique and critical needs, with teachers specially trained to help them in their subject matter and personal development.

But it must not be inferred that there was unanimity of opinion on the junior high school proposal. That was far from the case. Through the 1890's and into the early 1900's national groups of schoolmen with names like the "Committee of Ten" and the "Committee of Fifteen" wrestled with the problem that Eliot had enunciated. One group favored a 6–6 plan; others concentrated on minimum requirements for elementary schools. In the final analysis, necessity was the parent of the 6–3–3 invention. In that period there was an unprecedented number of young people in the twelve to eighteen age bracket. The most economical way to take care of them was to build intermediate schools.

After 1920 the number of junior high schools increased phenomenally. The total rose from 55 in that year to 3,227 in 1952. The U.S. Office of Education reports that in 1959 the figure had reached 4,996. In addition, there were 10,130 combined junior-senior high schools in 1959, whereas there had been only 828 in 1920.

Criticism of the 6–3–3 plan has accompanied its growth. Many parents who went to school under the 8–4 system resent the new arrangement. Some claim that putting so many young children of a volatile age under the same roof is asking for trouble. To some extent this argument is valid in big cities where enrollments in some junior high schools have soared to 2,000 pupils.

Whether the 6–3–3 plan is the best that can be found is a moot question. School systems have worked out all kinds of variations—3–6–3, 7–2–3, 5–4–3, 3–5–4 and myriads of others. Conditions in the local community often dictate the plan to be used. But it can be safely said that the junior high school is now firmly entrenched as an integral part of the American educational system.

Evolution of Higher Education

In examining briefly the evolution of higher education, we must again return to the Greeks where adults grouped themselves informally under such great thinkers as Socrates (469?–399 B.C.), Plato (427?–347 B.C.), Aristotle (384–322 B.C.), and Isocrates (436–338 B.C.). Plato's Academy and Aristotle's Lyceum school continued long after the deaths of their founders. Roman emperors at a later period added stability to the loosely organized groups located in the principal centers of learning by subsidizing the teaching of such subjects as philosophy and rhetoric. That financial support logically brought with it a certain amount of control; nevertheless, higher education in the ancient world never advanced beyond the status of a voluntary aggregation of teachers and students. In fact, since these groups lacked a corporate organization, we use the term loosely when we call them universities. Even in Alexandria, where the Ptolemys had provided imposing public buildings for instructional purposes and an immense library, there was no corporate university organization.

The principal subjects taught in the ancient world were the seven liberal arts. The trivium (grammar, rhetoric, logic) was preparatory to the more advanced studies of the quadrivium (arithmetic, geometry, astronomy, music). Beyond these came the more advanced and professional studies of law and medicine.

The medieval university emerged in the twelfth century from the intellectual life that centered in the cathedral schools, and was brought about by the rapidly growing social atmosphere.* Teachers and students came together informally to pursue their common interests, and eventually found it desirable to adopt the legal form of *universitas,* liberally translated as "corporation." This action made it necessary to get a charter, which could be secured from either the church or state as both were active in medieval times in fostering higher education.

University instruction generally was organized into three levels. Prerequisite was a thorough knowledge of Latin, so the student ordinarily spent his first three years achieving a mastery in this language while he also pursued the medieval version of the seven liberal arts. After completing this initial training satisfactorily, the student was ad-

* See also the discussion of universities in the section in Part One entitled "Medieval Education."

mitted to the degree of bachelor of arts. Thereafter he attended lectures based chiefly on the works of Aristotle. At the end of this period he took an examination for the coveted master's degree. This prize made him eligible to offer his own services as a teacher. The final period of training, not attempted by all, was to enter one of the higher faculties in law, medicine, or theology.

Fifteen was not an uncommon age to enter the medieval universities. This posed the problem of keeping youths protected from the temptation to spend their time in riotous living rather than in diligent application to their studies. One solution was the founding of colleges which at first were merely halls or inns under the charge of masters who enforced discipline based on rules similar to those governing monasteries. Gates closed at sundown; the indolent were strictly reminded of their duties; no frivolity was tolerated. As in due time these colleges became endowed and gained permanence, the master in charge began to assume tutorial functions. Later the professors took up residence in the colleges and gave their lectures there.

In the continental universities colleges never reached the importance that they achieved at Oxford and Cambridge. English universities, in fact, became a group of tightly knit communal colleges built in the form of a quadrangle which facilitated close supervision with masters and students studying together. The university still awarded all degrees, but each college assumed the responsibilities of training its students in the liberal arts and of supervising their morals.

The required instruction at Oxford and Cambridge was largely aimed at training clergymen in Latin, Greek, Hebrew, and the art of disputation so that they could go forth and defend their religious doctrines against all attacks. During the Reformation the emphasis upon mental, moral, and religious discipline favored the system of college instruction as opposed to the less rigidly supervised university instruction. In colleges those of a like mind could live and work together, whereas early universities had a nomadic character.

A continued enforcement of celibacy upon masters and tutors helped to preserve the communal life of the English colleges long after it had disappeared in German universities. It was this English conception of a college with its strict discipline and narrowly prescribed curriculum that served as a model in the early development of higher education in America. Harvard, the first colonial college, was virtually a copy of Emmanuel College at Cambridge University. Harvard was, in reality, a large boarding school for students of more mature age. Regulations for the control of the personal life of students were prescribed down to such minute details as the disciplinary action for wearing improper garb and for taking studies too lightly.

All nine colonial colleges were privately controlled, but each received some financial assistance from its respective legislature. The colonies seemed willing to foster colleges but not to assume the primary responsibility for their support and control. Then came the gradual disestablishment of the various colonial churches by the new states, beginning with Virginia in 1789, so that legal ties no longer existed between the government and the church-sponsored colleges. Inspired by the secularism and democracy of French revolutionary thought, Americans began to think in terms of public control of education. Yale and Harvard fought the efforts of state authorities to make them public institutions, and each succeeded in compromising the issue.

So it was the case of Dartmouth College that set the precedent through a momentous Supreme Court decision in 1819. With the intention of changing the college into a state university, the legislature of New Hampshire undertook to modify the charter granted Dartmouth many years earlier by George III (1738–1820). Chief Justice John Marshall (1753–1835) ruled that the original charter was a contract which the legislature had no right to violate without cause. That decision continued the existence of Dartmouth as a private institution and served as a precedent insuring the perpetuity of all similar private corporations.

Religious and philanthropic agencies thereupon proceeded with confidence to set up private institutions of learning. Within the next quarter century more than 500 charters were granted for this purpose, of which less than 200 survived the rigorous competition. On the other hand, the Dartmouth decision turned the attention of legislatures to the establishment of state universities subject to their control.

In the founding of the University of Virginia secular purposes proved as prominent as had been religious motives in starting the private colonial colleges. Virginia provided instruction in agriculture, commerce, and industry along with the more conventional interests of higher education in law, medicine, and theology. Included within the curriculum were mathematics and science, as well as classical languages. Significantly high among the objectives of instruction was the study of principles and structure of government itself. Further, the studies were to be elective.

Just as English tradition had influenced the nine colonial colleges and French philosophy had affected the University of Virginia, German thinking dominated the University of Michigan. There it was hoped to have an institution that would approach the quality and discipline of scholarship in German universities rather than that of the English communal colleges. It was even proposed to board students about town so that the limited financial resources might be invested in the instructional program instead of dormitories. Here again in the Michigan curriculum secular interests were stressed.

However, state universities did not begin their phenomenal growth until after the Civil War, at which time the lands set aside for educational purposes by the Ordinance of 1787 began to produce sizable incomes. The Morrill Act (1862) made available public lands, proceeds of which were to be used for the establishment in each state of "land-grant" colleges. In some states there were set up separate agricultural and mechanical colleges; in others, the endowment was used in conjunction with institutions already established. Many of these A. & M. colleges later expanded into the field of liberal arts and sciences, a development anticipated in the original Act.

Higher education for women did not take root in this country until the nineteenth century. Many were the arguments against it: women had no intellectual capacity to profit from such an education even if it were offered them; education would make them less refined; and their rate of fertility would decline as the amount of their formal education was increased. But women were daily proving their worth in the settlement of the frontier and in the Industrial Revolution. The American and French Revolutions had stressed the ideal of equality so much that it became difficult to justify the traditional argument of women's inferiority caused by Eve's role in the eviction from the Garden of Eden. Then again, the Protestant Reformation had made it necessary for girls as well as boys to read the Bible. Thus coeducation was gaining ground in common schools. Academies had been established for girls, while some high schools had "female departments," and others coeducation.

Three women in particular were instrumental in gaining higher as well as secondary education for their sex: Emma Willard (1787–1870), Mary Lyon (1797–1849), and Catharine Beecher (1800–1878). All three inaugurated seminaries that later grew into famous women's colleges. Vassar, founded just after the Civil War, was the first institution of collegiate grade for women only, although several others had previously begun work in that direction and later claimed the honor.

While women in the East were having a struggle to secure the advantages of collegiate instruction, those in the West were finding their way to this goal through new institutions open to both sexes. Oberlin

College admitted students of proper preparation regardless of race or sex. Coeducation was the rule from the date of the founding of the new Midwest state universities, and thereafter the women students were not slow in proving their capabilities.

Another development that occurred in the nineteenth century was a drastic change in the structure of the curriculum. Colleges were forced to meet the demands of new generations coming from middle-class families. These students wanted practical information rather than a large dose of the classics and theological courses. Consequently, the elective system became very popular. New degrees, like the LL.B. and the B.S., were conferred as specialization increased.

This movement led to the establishment of technical schools like Rensselaer Polytechnic Institute and the Massachusetts Institute of Technology. In addition, well-known colleges like Harvard and Yale set up separate scientific schools.

In the first half of the twentieth century the elective system was subjected to much criticism. The argument was advanced that students who had specialized in technical subjects knew little or nothing about vast areas of our culture. Consequently, the trend increased toward a modified form of the prescribed curriculum that had originally dominated higher education. Some colleges insisted that every student take a certain core of courses, with very little room left for electives. Others set up a "major-minor" system. Students specializing in one area (their "major") also took a number of courses in a "minor" subject. This system was widely adopted in teachers' colleges. A prospective English teacher, for instance, might take a "minor" in social studies. Thus he not only broadened his education but also increased his chances for getting a position after graduation.

Also, it should be noted that "survey courses" came into vogue as a result of the reaction against specialization. Many colleges formed these courses for freshmen. The purpose was to give the students a taste of several fields of knowledge or a deep draught of a subject in which they were not specializing. To illustrate, a science major would receive a course entitled "A Survey of World Literature." In some cases, this exposure to broader horizons served to awaken students, but in many colleges the survey courses unfortunately were regarded as useless drudgery.

Today the desire for college training is at its peak. In 1956 there were 1,850 institutions of higher education in the United States, as contrasted with 563 in 1870. Moreover, approximately 500 junior colleges have sprung into existence since the end of the first World War.

Because education is the cornerstone of democracy, this phenomenal growth is indeed encouraging to anyone who believes in American ideals.

Another criterion for measuring the rise of higher education is the number of degrees granted to college graduates. Ninety years ago exactly 9,371 students received the A.B. degree or its equivalent. By 1956 the total had skyrocketed to 308,812. In other words, for every student in the graduating class in 1870, there were 33 in 1956.*

On the post-graduate level the figures are even more startling. In 1956 there were 59,258 recipients of the M.A. degree or its equivalent in the United States. Sixty years before that a total of only 1,478 had gone that far. This is a more than 40–1 ratio.

Using the same years for comparison, we find that in 1896 there were 271 students who had reached the Ph.D. level. But in 1956 the figure stood at 8,903. This is approximately a 33–1 ratio. Incidentally, records indicate that in 1870 just one person climbed to the rarefied atmosphere of the doctorate degree.

In the pursuit of college diplomas and early post-graduate work, men now outnumber women in the United States on a two-to-one basis, whereas in 1870 the proportion was six to one. However, the girls still lag far behind in the Ph.D. race. There the ratio is nine males for every female. Yet one wonders how many of those men owe their eminent status to the hard-working, loyal women behind them.

In summary, it is indeed amazing to see how far education has progressed since colonial days. Although Washington's dream of a national university never really came true, that great patriot would certainly be satisfied if he could revisit his country today. The early reality of education for only a handful at the *elementary* level has broadened in this democracy to education for millions at the *university* level.

Evolution of Preschool Education

Now included in the American educational system are nursery schools for children as young as two and kindergartens for five-year-olds. These are operated both as a tax-supported public service and more frequently as private enterprises. This type of work with very young children makes a strong appeal to young women liberally endowed with the maternal instinct.

Youngsters at this comparatively helpless though rapidly developing age do offer an interesting challenge, especially since child psycholo-

---

* All these figures are taken from *Historical Statistics of the United States: Colonial Times to 1957*, published by the U.S. Department of Commerce.

gists are well agreed that the preschool years are the most important in the forming of those lifetime habits that go far to determine future happiness and success. Studies of first-grade pupils indicate clearly that many children are badly handicapped before they begin their formal schooling.

In nursery schools and kindergartens a teacher must possess, above all other personal qualities, patience and understanding. Pre-primary classes are rapidly growing in importance; but whenever adverse economic conditions bring about the demand that schools economize, the first units to be attacked are those that supplement the basic elementary and secondary education. With this in mind let us examine the historical evolution of early-childhood education.

Johann Amos Comenius (1592–1670), a Moravian bishop and one of the great pioneer pathfinders of modern education, advocated a school of infancy in conjunction with the home. He proposed that special attention be given food, sleep, fresh air, and exercise in order to build up a body fit for the habitation of the soul. Robert Owen (1771–1858), English mill owner and philanthropist, proposed taking children as early as three into an "infant school," where they would be provided a sort of informal education emphasizing health and physical training rather than books. Near his own mill he established such a school which was visited by people from many distant points.

A few infant schools were started in America but soon disappeared into the primary grades of the common schools. Unfortunately those who copied Owen's idea overlooked his stress on the spontaneous activities of children. One schoolmaster, in presenting his ideas to a committee of Parliament then studying the infant school, made the extravagant claims that before the age of seven a child should be able to read any book written in simple language, should know the first four rules of arithmetic and many of the elements of geography and natural history, and also have some knowledge of the New Testament. One might be prompted to say, "What a school!"

Probably the best-known pioneer in kindergarten work was Friedrich Froebel (1782–1852). His unpleasant boyhood in Germany made him decide to dedicate his lifetime to the education of very young children. So concerned was he with establishing a school free from the influences of formal education that he called his creation a "garden of children." He did not intend them to be "schooled," but rather to be allowed under gentle treatment to develop freely. He visualized children growing like plants in the congenial environment of the garden and undertook to devise a form of teaching in which they would be educated through their own spontaneous activities. Thus the principles of self-activity and individual expression dominated the work of the kindergarten which he began to develop about 1837.*

Strangely enough, the kindergarten did not take deep root in Froebel's homeland, but enjoyed its greatest development in the United States. The movement came to America during the big wave of immigration from Germany following the Prussian Revolution in 1848. Mrs. Carl Schurz (1834–1879), a student of Froebel, in 1856 started in Watertown, Wisconsin, the first kindergarten in this country. The language used was German, and several other German-speaking communities followed suit. However, the movement in America owed its development not to those German kindergartens but to the work of Elizabeth Peabody (1804–1894) who in 1860 established in Boston our first English-speaking kindergarten. Of some significance was the fact that she had become acquainted with the idea in England where the concept had been considerably changed from the original German model. Miss Peabody's school was a private enterprise, as were others that followed shortly thereafter.

Then in 1873, on the initiative of Superintendent William T. Harris (1835–1909), St. Louis became the first American city to provide kindergartens at public expense. Soon afterwards philanthropic societies began maintaining kindergartens in the other large cities. The movement gained more and more momentum down to the present day. As just one example, we see that in New York City alone a round total of 75,000 children were enrolled in free public school kindergartens in September, 1960.

Many claims have been made both for and against the values to children of kindergarten training, but the research generally has been quite inconclusive. A common technique is to compare children of equal intelligence who have attended with those who have not. Such investigations show little or no difference between the two groups in their learning abilities during later years. Possibly the kindergarten's chief values are that it provides an enriched social experience for the child and helps him adjust gradually to the new and strange environment of school.

This process of socialization and adjustment can frequently be observed in action during those first few days of a term when some children have to be coaxed, or even dragged, by their mothers to attend kindergarten. This initial period is the critical time for most of the tots, but even under the most skilled of teachers there may be a "lone wolf" who

* See also pages 73–74 for additional discussion of the work of Froebel.

sits by himself for days, weeks, perhaps months, before finally deciding to join the activities. Lacking the experience in kindergarten, such a child probably would waste at least a term of his first grade just in getting used to school.

One notable effect the kindergarten has had on the elementary school has been its insistence on beauty as a desirable feature in the classroom environment. Historians describe the grammar school of the 1890's as a dreary place without decorations of any sort. From the very beginning, kindergarten leaders have insisted that the schoolroom, its surroundings, and equipment be made as attractive as possible. Decorative curtains are hung at the windows, and green plants are placed where they may receive sunlight; blocks and other equipment are painted in bright colors. In more recently built kindergartens there frequently are fireplaces, and the furniture is designed to interest and attract the young child. The kindergarten has also been instrumental in introducing into elementary schools the concept of the educative value of motor activity. This, in fact, is the basic principle of the "activity movement" in modern progressive education.

The establishment of separate nursery schools did not occur until about 1900. The work in Italy of Marie Montessori (1870–1952) has had considerable influence on this movement. As a physician, she advocated medical and preventive measures at her Orthophrenic School. Much of her equipment was devised for groups of low intelligence, and she put up apparatus which could be used by the children themselves without help from the teacher. Dr. Montessori's books on the subject have been widely read in America. Probably her greatest contribution has been her emphasis on developing a child's initiative and sense perception through freedom of movement.

In this country the nursery school idea germinated in the work of child psychologists like Arnold Gesell (1880–1961) at Yale, who for years now has continuously studied in his laboratory clinic the reactions of children, beginning at birth.* He came to the conclusion that the first two years of life are far more critical than previously realized. It is now claimed that some of the worst types of phobia, inferiority complex, aggression, and repression of primitive impulses in adult years might easily be eliminated if proper action is taken during the years of infancy.

The preschool movement received a great impetus in America during the 1930 depression years when a considerable portion of Federal Emergency Relief funds was allocated to community nursery schools on

* For further discussion of Gesell and his findings, see pages 312–313.

a temporary and experimental basis. These thoroughly justified their existence in terms of providing good care and diet to small children, many of whose parents were unable to provide adequately for them.

At the present time a few universities operate nursery schools as laboratories for the study of child growth and development. The aim is to provide a natural, wholesome environment in which children can learn to adjust themselves in social situations—an opportunity that is particularly valuable to those who have but a few playmates in their homes or neighborhoods. These nursery children are under close observation and guidance of skillful supervisors who attempt to check the development of undesirable traits and qualities by providing activities intended to develop worthwhile social attitudes and habits. Usually no attempt is made to lay the groundwork for intellectual instruction, but great care is taken to teach the preschool child how to play amicably with others in his group.

An important later development of the nursery school program is the instruction given to parents whose children are in attendance. A school directly influences the lives of children for only a small part of each day, so it is the home that has the responsibility for making effective much of the training given in the school. Some nursery schools are organized on a cooperative basis. Under this plan the mother is required to spend some of her time each week in the school, presumably for the purpose of helping with the work but also for the usually unannounced intention of providing an opportunity for parent education.

Some nursery schools instruct mothers regarding the proper care of their children by means of individual conferences, or group meetings, at which child problems are discussed and questions answered. Development of nursery schools so far has been principally outside of public school systems. Taxpayers habitually shy away from adding to their burdens. That same problem is faced in the financing of public kindergartens.

Adult and Other Part-Time Education

Personal growth and development is a lifelong process. Our schools can provide childhood and youth with only an introduction to the world's vast store of knowledge. Much of the program they begin must be completed in later life. The real tragedy, of course, is that so many virtually stop trying to learn once their classroom days are finished. Others, however, maintain an active and inquiring mind far into their declining years. Adult and part-time educational programs have been greatly accelerated by the scientific studies of Edward L. Thorndike

(1874–1949) and others who refute the notion that learning efficiency declines rapidly after physical maturity is reached. Thorndike's conclusions were to the effect that maximum learning efficiency is not reached until about the age of twenty-five, and that there is comparatively little diminution in learning ability until the age of forty to forty-five.

Since World War I, adult education has become a highly organized division of public school systems in many cities, and there are numerous private agencies that seek to improve the intellectual level of Americans. Let us, therefore, look back into the past to see how this area of education evolved.

Two of the world's greatest teachers of adults never conducted formal schools. The famous dialogues of Socrates as reported by Plato were casual conversations held with such people as he could get to discourse with him. Jesus Christ (c. 4 B.C.–29 A.D.) was an informal teacher of adults, often instructing his disciples or the multitudes that followed him.

Religion has always played an important role in the teaching of men and women. The theological controversies of the Protestant Reformation brought about in the Sunday sermon from the pulpit a form of adult education in which the congregation was kept informed not only on matters of doctrine but quite frequently on politics and current events as well. This practice, as churchgoers are well aware, continues today in many communities.

The town meeting of colonial New England represented a very practical application of adult education, and the Quaker meetings were especially effective in this direction. Before the days of radio, TV, newsreels, magazines, and daily newspapers, the village store came to rival the church as a forum of adult education. Over the traditional cracker barrel, arguments on slavery, temperance, and other critical topics trained the participants not only in knowledge of the subjects under discussion but also in rhetorical and logical skills. Individuals organized themselves into groups for the specific purpose of promoting free-for-all debates and the general dissemination of information.

Lyceums were founded in several localities before 1820. As scientific societies they collected natural history specimens, studied the natural resources of the country, and provided lectures on serious subjects. Considered the founder of the lyceum movement was Josiah Holbrook (1788–1854) who, in 1826, made the important suggestion that the local groups be organized into county, and the county into state, organizations. For several years he devoted all his time to the extension of this movement. His success is shown by the fact that in the late 1830's more than 3000 communities had lyceums.

A national organization, effected in 1831, held a few annual conventions before disbanding. The local lyceums set up individual libraries and held periodic meetings featuring lectures on educational subjects and scientific demonstrations. One of the most enthusiastic promoters was Ralph Waldo Emerson (1803–1882) who frequently lectured for only a five-dollar fee, along with oats for his horse. It is said that most of his celebrated essays were written first for oral delivery from the lyceum platform.

Other organized efforts for the education of youth and adult populations outside of established school and university systems made rapid progress in nineteenth-century America. Philanthropic and humanitarian agencies, as well as ventures for profit, promoted this idea of spreading knowledge to all classes of people. The Boston Mechanics Institute was founded in 1826, and the Society for the Diffusion of Useful Knowledge in 1829. Many organizations sponsored libraries, lectures, discussions, and debates. Employers and philanthropically-minded members of the wealthier classes also promoted adult education in such forms as the Lowell (Massachusetts) Institute (1836) and Cooper Union (1859) in New York City.

In 1874 a religious movement was organized at Chautauqua Lake, New York, as a summer training course for church workers; and eventually local chautauquas appeared in hundreds of communities. Chautauqua in 1878 provided a four-year reading course in religious, literary, social, and scientific studies—and, incidentally, its summer work is still in operation. Also stemming from the religious motivation for youth and adult education were the Young Men's Christian Association and the Young Men's Hebrew Association.

The growth and development of evening schools must not be overlooked. Starting early in the eighteenth century an occasional private school offered evening courses in vocational subjects, thus initiating a movement that has greatly appealed to young adults eager to improve themselves. Originally these evening schools were at the elementary level; then Massachusetts became the first state to pioneer instruction at public cost for those past regular school age. Soon cultural as well as vocational subjects were being offered at the secondary level. Cincinnati, just before the Civil War, was the first American city to establish a free evening high school. This type of instruction gained new importance in respect to literacy and citizenship during the twentieth century when Americans awoke to the fact that there were thousands of foreign-born immigrants unable to speak English.

The idea that gave birth to both university-extension and correspondence courses came to us from England. In the 1850's a college tutor became sensitive to the fact that many adults were not attending the public lectures at Cambridge chiefly because they resided too far away from the university. He suggested adoption of the proverbial Mohammedan principle of "going to the mountain." This idea was given a trial when a professor started giving off-campus lectures of a popular nature on astronomy, later accompanying them with a syllabus, and concluding with an examination. In due time there developed at Cambridge an officially recognized program of university extension.

In the 1880's it was proposed to do the same thing in this country, but the movement really got its start in the early 1890's when a number of institutions began to offer university-extension courses. The mistake was made, however, of having as instructors those who were either unwilling or unable to adapt their academic subject matter so as to appeal to the popular mind. For some years this extension work languished, but in our twentieth century that mistake was corrected. Thereafter growth resumed in the movement to offer late-afternoon and evening courses, both on and off the campus, for those who were otherwise occupied during regular school hours.

Correspondence courses were a product of both this Cambridge idea and the Chautauqua movement.* The lectures of William Rainey Harper (1856–1906) proved so popular that his listeners asked him to outline a continuation of their summer work for winter study. Although a busy man, Harper did agree to furnish this service but soon found himself unable to supervise the work properly. Shortly thereafter this correspondence instruction was improved by making it more systematic and by charging fees in order to defray the expenses of instructors specifically assigned to the work. In 1891, when Harper became the first president of the University of Chicago, he announced a home-study department as part of his educational program. The success of this venture prompted a number of other universities to follow suit in the next two decades.

Continuation schools have had extensive development in European countries but have not proved widely popular in America. In this nation

---

* In 1873 the "Society to Encourage Study at Home" was organized at Boston. However, the "Correspondence University" established ten years later at Ithaca, New York, was the first formal American effort in this field.

they have been associated chiefly with the furtherance of education after a boy or girl has reached the end of compulsory-attendance period and entered employment. Some states permit employment at sixteen provided the youth attends a continuation school, generally for three or four hours a week, until he is seventeen or eighteen. Even girls who marry before the end of legal school age are required to attend. Continuation schools usually are found only in the larger cities, and many have already been absorbed in the more rapidly expanding program of adult education. Some states are now allowing youths to attend night school classes as a means of meeting the requirements of their continuation school laws.

Adult education as a public-sponsored movement began about the time of World War I. A step in this direction was the Smith-Lever Act (1914) that provided for agricultural extension work. The movement was further stimulated by the Smith-Hughes Act (1917) providing grants of federal funds to assist in payment of teachers' salaries in several types of vocational education, including the continuation school.

The first attempt to consolidate adult education facilities for a community took place in Cleveland in 1924. That same year a national conference was called by the Carnegie Corporation of New York, and from then on the term "adult education" came into general use. In 1926 the American Association for Adult Education was organized. This now serves as a clearing house for research, investigations, publications, and promotion of the movement.

It was during the 1920's that adult education concentrated on the "Americanization" of the foreign-born—a direct result of a wave of immigrants after World War I. Public schools were used day and night for classes in English and citizenship, and this practice has continued to the present day. For example, in New York City in September, 1960, there were more than 900 such classes. Most of them, unlike the groups in the 1920's, were attended by Puerto Ricans and other Spanish-speaking people who have been flocking to the metropolis in the last decade. Approximately 11,000 of these men and women were enrolled in New York City's program in the 1959–60 school year.

But the most profound influence on the course of adult education in the United States was exerted by the great Depression of the 1930's. People turned to evening classes either because they wanted to improve their chances for employment or because their jobless state had left them with a great deal of time on their hands.

The Works Progress Administration pitched in on two levels. A WPA program was organized to help the 4 per cent of the adult population which was illiterate. Advanced vocational courses and university courses were organized for high school graduates. In addition, public libraries and municipal museums instituted new educational services and classes for adults.

Probably the most popular aspect of modern adult education suburban programs is the kind that was started in 1935 in the Maplewood–South Orange area of New Jersey. Courses in everything from golf and dog-training to political science and abstract art are given, usually at night, under the auspices of a private group of citizens. In most cases school buildings are used.

Recently the interest in such courses has grown so much that school and municipal authorities have stepped in and arranged programs. Sometimes special coordinators or directors are employed for the sole purpose of administering and supervising the courses. State aid, usually on the basis of attendance, is a widespread practice.

Adult education is one of the strongest and healthiest outgrowths of American democracy. This can be attested by the millions of people who have enrolled in courses in recent years.

Education for Handicapped Children

Several million American children are handicapped in ways that demand specialized educational facilities. That was the startling report made in 1940 by the Fourth White House Conference; and while a great deal of constructive work has been accomplished since that date, the battle has just started. Slowly but surely states, counties, and cities have begun to recognize this responsibility by making possible greater opportunities for physically and mentally handicapped youngsters.

Some states give substantial subsidies to help the local school districts defray the extra costs involved in this specialized service. In hundreds of cities there are now educational opportunities designed to meet the specific needs of the blind and the partially sighted, the deaf and the hard-of-hearing, speech defectives, cripples, also the cardiac (heart) and tubercular cases. Such instructional work requires teachers with some technical training. Also, they need the type of personality that is capable of inspiring hope in young people who have good reason to be worried or discouraged about their chances for success and happiness. With that in mind let us examine the development of education for handicapped children.

Throughout history the lot of the physically handicapped has been very difficult. Occasionally a hopeless cripple like Alexander Pope (1688–1744) rises to great heights of fame, but such cases are rare exceptions rather than the rule. Until recent years those lacking good health or normal bodies had but little in life to look forward to and a minimal chance for success. Then in the nineteenth century there developed a movement stemming from the social humanitarianism of France, the transcendental outlook of Germany, and the romantic ideals of England. Here in America it took the form of societies to prevent poverty, abolish slavery, humanize criminal codes, improve prison conditions, extend women's rights, control intemperance, and help the insane, blind, deaf, and crippled.

From France came our stimulus to educate the blind, resulting in 1832 in the establishment of the Perkins Institute for the Blind in Boston. This idea spread, and schools for the blind began to appear in other cities. Great impetus was given the work by the adoption of the Braille method of reading and by action of Congress allowing materials for the blind to be sent through the mails free. It is conservatively estimated that the number of schools for the blind in this country now approaches the 200,000 figure.

Complete blindness, in which the sense of light is either entirely lacking or so dim as to be of no substantial utility, is chiefly an affliction of the aged. Recent appraisals show that there are approximately 330,000 blind people in the United States, half of whom are over 65. About 13 per cent of the blind are under 20 years of age. The American Foundation for the Blind and the National Society for the Prevention of Blindness have indicated that in 1955 there were about 7,400 school-age blind children in the United States. Since then the figure has almost doubled!

But for every blind child there are at least five who are classified as "partially seeing." Their difficulties range all the way from minor defects to those of impaired vision bordering on blindness. Authorities in the National Society for the Prevention of Blindness state that there are now approximately 78,000 partially seeing children in the United States and that fewer than 8,100 of them are provided with the necessary educational facilities. This is a situation that calls for vast improvement. Much more expenditure of money for sight-saving classes has been recommended.

Sight-saving classes originated in Europe in 1908; and five years later the first in America was started in Roxbury, Massachusetts. These classes are for pupils whose eyes do not permit them to do the work of regular grades, either because their sight would be further impaired by such study, or because their vision is too low to assure progress in school by the usual methods and equipment. Sometimes in high schools a student goes to his regular classrooms but studies and writes his examinations under a special teacher who reads and explains in order to eliminate all unnecessary use of the eyes. Charts and typewriters with extra large letters are typical equipment.

In the elementary grades the organization often resembles a one-room rural school in that the teacher works with all levels. She is assigned a very limited number in order to insure each child as much personal attention as possible. Physical features of a sight-saving classroom include walls painted in light buff colors, indirect lighting, and also pupils' desks that are adjustable and movable. Unglazed buff paper, soft pencils and chalk, maps and books with large type are accepted instructional materials. Some classes make extensive use of the radio and phonograph in order as much as possible to substitute hearing for seeing in the learning process. In passing it should be noted that many of the innovations begun in sight-saving classrooms have been widely adopted for the education of all children.

The first school for the deaf in America was started in Hartford, Connecticut, in 1816 by Thomas Gallaudet (1787–1851), who had become so interested in a neighbor's deaf-and-dumb child that he traveled to Europe to study techniques then being developed. Connecticut established a state school the following year. In 1857, the Columbian Institution was incorporated at Washington, D. C., and seven years later became the National Deaf Mute College, eventually renamed Gallaudet College—the only institution for higher learning for the deaf in the United States.

In this country the earliest efforts to educate those unable to hear depended upon writing and the so-called manual method, or sign language. Horace Mann (1796–1859), among others, was instrumental in introducing from Europe the more modern approach that involves communication of ideas by means of speech and lip reading. Incidentally, when in 1869 Boston became the first public school system to establish a special school to educate the deaf, it was named after Mann.

There are today more than seven times as many children who may be classified as deaf or hard-of-hearing as there are blind or partially sighted. Defective hearing is less easy to detect than faulty eyesight; hence identification is more frequently neglected. In fact, it was not until 1935 that New York passed the first compulsory law for testing hearing, whereas Connecticut had enacted the first legislation requiring vision testing 35 years earlier.

No longer considered reliable are the whisper, watch-tick, and tuning fork tests. The audiometer does an excellent job, and as many as 500 children a day may be examined in groups of 40 each. The children wear head-telephone receiving sets and are instructed to write down the numbers spoken by the phonograph in gradually decreasing degrees of intensity. Audiometers determine in decibels the amount of hearing loss for many pure tones. Such tests need to be made periodically—progressive deafness comes on so gradually and insidiously that frequently it escapes notice until too severe to be corrected. Among adults most cases of deafness can be traced back to their first ten years of life, thus making it important to have frequent check-ups for all young children, followed, whenever required, by medical attention.

The first school organized for speech correction was in Potsdam, Germany, in 1887. For several years it received some financial support from an interested American Medical Association. However, it was not until 1908 that New York City became our first public school system to begin an experimental class that eventually was to grow into modern school clinics doing corrective work.

In the White House Conference report of 1940, it was shown that one million school children between the ages of five and eighteen needed remedial work in speech. Scientists were quoted as believing a very large proportion of the defects to be correctable. Many are not organic but are due to faulty speech habits established while very young. All that is needed to correct the other defects caused by malformation of the speech organs are comparatively minor operations. Causes of speech difficulties are so varied that the corrective work must reach across many phases of school and home life. Treatment may include diaphragmatic breathing and relaxation exercises, speech drills, remedial reading, and conversational exercises carried on in a clinic, a classroom, and in the home. Some case-studies have indicated that pupils with anti-social habits improve their personalities as a result of speech-correction treatment.

Specialized schooling for crippled children is a twentieth-century development. The first such tax-supported school was organized in England in 1899. Chicago in 1900 was next, and in 1904 Massachusetts established the first state school.

A crippled child, in the orthopedic sense, is one who has a defect which causes a deformity or an interference with the normal functioning of the bones, muscles, or joints. On this basis the number of crippled children in the United States in 1940 was estimated at about 300,000. One investigation indicated that 80 per cent of these children had become crippled at an age younger than seven, and that more than 50 per cent of them could have been cured had they been discovered and treated at once!

To meet the educational problems involved in all such types and degrees of handicaps, instruction is now being given in homes, hospitals, and schools. Some cities have erected special buildings with ramps or elevators for wheel chairs to facilitate movement. Additional features are swimming pools, sunlamps, cots, and rooms equipped for physiotherapy.

Other school systems attempt to provide an education in the traditional buildings. A practice in some high schools is to have the crippled children attend the regular classes, coming late and leaving early in order to avoid the rush of other students; often they have their own special room and teacher for purposes of study. A major problem is transportation from home to school, since it is especially difficult for many of the more severely handicapped to come and go without personal assistance. Most city school systems now provide buses, taxis, and similar vehicles.

The aforementioned White House Conference in 1940 estimated that 6,000,000 school children suffered from malnutrition; 1,000,000 had weak or damaged hearts, including 375,000 serious cardiac cases; 382,000 were tubercular with an additional 850,000 suspected cases. In those statistics there was considerable duplication because many children were found to be multi-handicapped, but summed up it meant that about 30 per cent of American school children could be considered in the "delicate child" class. Such figures were indeed both startling and alarming!

Many city school systems have attempted to meet this problem by advancing beyond the traditional classroom program and providing an instructional day more nearly commensurate with each child's physical abilities. Victims of too much irregularity in the home routine learn to develop regularity. Milk is supplied midmorning and midafternoon to the undernourished, and at school expense whenever the parents cannot afford to pay for this service. Our present school lunch and milk programs have greatly improved the health of underprivileged children, whether handicapped or not.

Specially equipped rooms have been set up for cardiac cases and open-air rooms for tubercular children. There are also some preventoriums and sanatoriums. Thus much progress has been made, and the lot of the handicapped child is no longer as dreary as it used to be. Far more is being done today than ever before in the history of mankind to decrease the number of boys and girls who are headed for adulthood under serious physical and mental handicaps.

Morality as an Aim in Education

Morality has always more or less dominated educational aims. The folkways of primitive peoples proved highly effective in making the individual conform to the established pattern of conduct. Explicit rules were evolved to govern such important activities as duties of children to parents, relationships between the sexes, participation in religious rites and ceremonies, and the accepted interpretations of natural phenomena.

Even in the early Egyptian civilization, boys learned the moral precepts contained in the priestly literature, of which the most influential was the Book of the Dead that presented a minute description of how the departed would live in the life hereafter. The copybooks used for teaching the difficult art of writing the Egyptian language contained stories apparently designed to inculcate qualities of virtue, reverence, and obedience. Moreover, among the ancient Jews, morality was stressed above all else. In their case, the precepts for personal actions were drawn from the Mosaic law; and the religious sanctions controlled Jewish manners as well as morals.

The best early accounts of folkway morality among the ancient Greeks are to be found in the Homeric poems, the *Iliad* and the *Odyssey*, which portrayed everyday lessons in such virtues as courage, self-control, temperance, and piety. Religion with the Greeks was a thing of beauty, not of fear, learned by children through participation in games, dances, and dramas that celebrated religious festivals. However, they did not hesitate to use fear of punishment, when necessary, to enforce conformity to the folkway standards of morality. Moral education became less rigid with the Greeks as their economic and political influence spread over the Mediterranean world. They were the first to make a frank recognition that there exists among the various peoples a wide variety of moral codes.

Socrates claimed that no one would knowingly do what is wrong—if one does evil it is merely because he is ignorant of the right or good. However, while he described moral education as a rational process, he was unwilling to go so far as to shift from social convention to individual opinion.

Aristotle criticized this viewpoint of Socrates and stated that mere knowledge about morals is not enough—one must form moral habits by the practice of morals as well. In his scheme of things a special place was assigned to music. He contended that rhythms and melodies, if properly selected, are capable of arousing in the hearer feelings of anger, courage, and affection. In this way he hoped to purge individuals of vicious feelings, and strengthen them in virtuous ones. Happiness, not duty, thus became widely accepted as the basis for the good life; but this happiness, defined by Aristotle as the satisfaction of one's natural impulses and instincts, was that of the community, or city-state, not of the individual. It was not until the advent at Athens of a professional teaching class, the Sophists, that despite vigorous protests the welfare of the state became subordinated to that of the individual.

Even more so than the Greeks, the early Romans were governed by a deep sense of duty to the moral law. They were keenly aware of the spiritual powers external to man to which personal conduct must conform. The religious education of the children in the home effectively maintained a high standard of moral virtues during the days of the Roman Republic.

Later the Christians took over and extended the basic moral code of the Jews. It was this strict discipline governing personal actions that permitted the Roman Catholic Church to rise as the Roman Empire was falling. It can be said, with practically no exceptions, that moral education through the folkways has been authoritarian. From ancient days down to this century, one way for children to learn morality has been the enforcement of obedience to the accepted standard of conduct. And when weaknesses in the culture patterns of those in power begin to spread, as happened in the Roman Empire, a new leadership emerges.

Christianity posed some radically new outlooks on life which profoundly altered the development of moral education in the Western world. Paganism had looked upon life here and now as its main opportunity; Christianity saw earthly existence as merely temporary and probationary, a period prior to eternal punishment or reward. Instead of seeking personal happiness, men were commanded to love one another as brothers. In a period of gross public and private immorality of the decadent Empire, Christians were summoned to renounce lust and greed and to embrace austerity as a manner of life.

The purpose of early Christian education was the restoration of man in the image of God that he had lost because of the original sin of Adam. Repentance became the educational process in which new life was unfolded through catechetical instruction, giving a detailed account of what might and might not be done. Though noble in its aim, this moral education soon came to lay undue emphasis on memorizing at the expense of understanding.

The early Christian pattern of moral instruction changed very little until near the end of the Middle Ages. Then the *Summa Theologica* of Saint Thomas Aquinas (1225–1274) represented the fusing, or compromising, of Graeco-Roman paganism with Christianity. Thereafter a great wave of interest in ancient cultures swept Italy in the movement known as the Renaissance. A strong reaction thus set in against the gloomy outlook of the medieval period. The new humanism glorified those elements in human nature which previously had been so depreciated. The purpose of the education of a young gentleman was to stir his mind with moral sentiments disclosed by the pagan literature of Greece and Rome.

An outgrowth of humanism in northern Europe was the sixteenth-century Protestant Reformation that brought with it much bitter controversy. Those who eventually renounced their allegiance to Catholicism insisted upon the right of the individual to understand God's revelations in the Scriptures in terms of his own intelligence without the intermediation of the Church. Protestantism thus attached importance to training in individual judgment, an educational practice that previously had received little attention because believers had been taught to accept whatever judgments were certified as correct by the Church.

Secularism is defined as the quality or state of being devoted to worldly rather than religious matters. Prior to the Reformation the Church had regarded itself not only as the source of religious education but also as the guardian protector of secular education. Among those factors leading to the eventual divorce between church and state, the scientific and political revolutions of the eighteenth century were important. Pioneering this movement was one of the world's most influential thinkers, John Locke (1632–1704), who wrote extensively about the formation of moral character with but little reference to religious training.

Locke considered that the way to form character is through self-discipline brought about by the individual's denying himself his own desires and following what reason directs as best—in other words, to use will power to control human appetites. Thus was stressed the importance of reason in the formation of moral character, and Locke was confident that a child could be appealed to, through reason, at a much earlier age than most of his contemporaries believed possible.

This emphasis on the role of reason in moral education was in complete harmony with the beginnings of modern science in the Western world. People were becoming deeply interested in the natural law and order that the scientists had discovered at work in the universe. No longer was the world of nature depreciated as it had been in the medieval period. There were some intellectuals called "deists" who even went so far as to have nature replace God as the object of worship.

Jean Jacques Rousseau (1712–1778) sought to discover a "natural law" for education, just as the astronomers had found one for the heavenly bodies. He contended that everything is good as it comes from the hands of the author of nature. Both Catholics and Protestants were shocked at this revolutionary pronouncement. Traditionally they had taken the view that original nature is evil—or prone to evil—and here was a man who stated the exact opposite. Rousseau did admit, however, that the child had weaknesses and needed the help of others.

Reason that developed with age would eventually assist in making up for these human deficiencies, said Rousseau, but not till the child was older. Being amoral rather than immoral during his earlier years, a child should not be blamed for improper behavior. The ideal moral training for a youth is to allow him to suffer the natural consequences of his own acts. Religious instruction, Rousseau held, should not come until at least the age of fifteen; and he feared that even that stage of life might be too early because of the danger that the young man would acquire preposterous notions difficult to eradicate in later life.

This changing of the basis of moral education from supernatural to natural principles definitely was a step toward the secularization of education. Some advocated that morality be taught as a science based upon reason as demonstrated by the common experiences of men of every age. Others took the extreme secular view that formation of character depends entirely upon environment. If such a theory were valid, then mankind had in education a tool which could be used to create for human beings either a good or a bad character. Even the churches were influenced by this eighteenth-century rationalism. It became a common practice to interrogate children on aspects of their catechisms as if the truths of religion had been implanted within them by nature, needing only to be called forth by the skillful questioning of the teacher.

New ideas at this time were fermenting in the minds of educational reformers. Johann Heinrich Pestalozzi (1746–1827) held that moral education should result from the child's native curiosity and that it must stir his emotions. In other words, the child never acquires moral dispositions unless he feels them.

Since Pestalozzi did not follow his ideas with practical applications, it was left to Friedrich Froebel to approach the problem of a change of emphasis in moral education with actual learning situations. He refused even to allow the possibility of evil inclinations within the child's nature. He believed that nature is God's handiwork and to accuse it of evil is blasphemous. According to Froebel, each child is born with a spark of divinity that struggles to achieve a unity with the divine. Learning to be good is not a matter of mastering dogmas, but rather of having an opportunity to be self-active and to grow according to the laws of one's own nature into unity with humanity and ultimately with God himself.

A new pedagogical principle was advocated by Johann Friedrich Herbart (1776–1841), who believed that moral education can best be carried on by presenting those moral ideas to be found in history and literature. Give a child good reading materials, said he, and the ideas he garners from them will build for him a proper character. He did not consider it necessary to provide for the separate cultivation of the intellect, the emotions, and the will. Consequently, he reasoned, there are no distinct forms of intellectual, moral, and practical education. Herbart believed that through the development of the intellect come controlled emotions and a purposeful enlightened will power that expresses itself in desirable action and performance.

Here in America Colonel Francis W. Parker evolved the theory of a child-centered school in which morality is developed through self-effort. He considered all education as moral, and any methods not adapted to the laws of child growth as positively immoral. It was left to John Dewey, however, to develop much of the detail of Parker's ideas. He likewise attached central importance to the child's spontaneous instincts and impulses, insisting that these must have opportunities to exert themselves in social situations if moral education is to be truly effective.

John Dewey was neither an atheist nor an agnostic. But he actively opposed theological or transcendental precepts as the foundations for man's actions. Instead he advocated a scientific approach to morality, and he scoffed at the dualism of those who upheld the methods of natural science in everything but moral questions.

Dewey developed a "problem-situation" approach to morality. Claiming that there is no such thing as absolute good or evil, he accepted moral principles only as instruments for analyzing any given concrete situation. But he insisted that the total situation itself must be the basis for the judgment as to right and wrong—not a set of generalized rules stemming from a belief in a fixed moral reality. As for standards, he taught that the individual should be governed by the customs of society but should make adaptations through the use of his intelligence.

To illustrate the kind of thinking that Dewey opposed, let us say that Richard Roe believes patriotism to be a virtue. Therefore, when his country declares war, Richard immediately enlists. Naturally, as a moral being, he must defend his native land.

Dewey was appalled by such generalized behavior. If Richard were a follower of the Vermont philosopher, he would ask certain questions before making the decision: What is patriotism? Is patriotism the most important consideration in this situation? What are the other factors, pro and con, that should influence the choice of a course of action?

It is easy to see why Dewey's stand on morality was, and still is, criticized by large segments of society. These groups strongly reject his "problem-situation" theory. Although they admit that there are times when one virtue may come into conflict with another, they ask what kind of world would we have if we did not teach our children the importance of cleanliness of mind and body, piety, faith, constancy, courage, and the like under all circumstances.

Like Mann before him, Dewey opposed sectarian religion in public schools. This caused many to conclude that he advocated a "godless" school system. For them, his belief in democracy as a "spiritual community" rather than a form of government was not enough. They argued that in addition to educating children to live as socially competent beings in a democratic world, schools must actively inculcate traditional moral precepts and a belief in God and the supernatural.

The nub of the controversy is whether moral values can be separated from religion. George Washington did not think so. In his Farewell Address he stated: "Whatever may be conceded to the influence of refined education on minds of peculiar structure, reason and experience both forbid us to expect that national morality can prevail in exclusion of religious principle."

Of course, it is true that in a broad sense "education" goes on outside of school as well as in school. The church, the home, and even the street are agents of education for better or for worse. Few people deny that character formation should be an important goal of the public schools, but many object to the intertwining of moral and religious education in the classroom. Their argument is that schools in a pluralistic society must choose what is basic to all religions (the Golden Rule, for instance) and build on the education that takes place in the church and home. The other side answers that it is ridiculous to try to set up such "artificial" divisions. Religion and morality, they declare, are inextricable.

In 1951, the Educational Policies Commission of the NEA and the American Association of School Administrators took a neutral stand on the above issue.* They listed such fundamental moral and spiritual values as devotion to truth, brotherhood, and spiritual enrichment. Shying away from the inculcation of any religious creed in the schools, they recommended that common education be based on "a decent respect for all religious opinions."

The NEA document was a noble attempt, but it settled nothing. A small minority of Americans insist that religion has no place at all in a public school to which atheists presumably have as much right to send their children as any other group. A larger minority avers that a secular school in an essentially religious world is an anomaly. They argue that unless educators take an active part in fostering religion, the moral fiber of future generations will rot away.

With these points in mind, let us turn our attention to the history and present status of religion in our schools.

Religion in American Education

It is a fact that religion was the earliest and most dominant force in the promotion of early American education. And yet today a child in a public school is taught almost everything *except* religion. Some of the reasons for this paradox were implied in the previous section, but the full story needs to be told from the beginning.

Anyone who has read the horrible tale of the Salem witchcraft trials knows something about the fanaticism that the colonists were capable of exhibiting. Puritan children grew up in an atmosphere perpetually saturated with dour Calvinistic pessimism and suspicion. Since the only hope for salvation lay in the Bible, it was incumbent upon every good Puritan to learn how to read and to see that his offspring did so, too. Hence it was that Massachusetts, in 1642, passed the first American school law compelling parents (and masters of apprentices) to send their children to school. Another law was enacted later to impress upon the populace that the elders meant what they said. This law stipulated that any group of 100 or more householders should organize and maintain a school. Thus universal, compulsory, community-supported education got its start in the New World.

* National Education Association, *Moral and Spiritual Values in the Public Schools.*

The Puritans welcomed none but their own faith to Massachusetts, and those adhering to the Church of England persecuted Puritans and Quakers alike. Roger Williams (1604–1683) and William Penn (1644–1718) began the battle against the spirit of intolerance at a time when religion and education were practically synonymous. So long as colonial communities remained religiously homogeneous there was a minimum of conflict between church and secular educational interests, but this strict orthodoxy began to lose ground as newcomers with varied religious beliefs continued to arrive in America.

Slowly but surely the scientific and political revolutions of the eighteenth century created new interests that competed with religion for the attention of colonists. Nevertheless, on the eve of the American Revolution, all our public as well as private schools included religious instruction in their curricula. Even after political freedom had been won, many states passed laws requiring religious tests for the certification of teachers—some even delegated the supervision of their schools to church authorities. Massachusetts and Connecticut retained the Congregational, and Virginia the Episcopal, as the "established" churches; that is, churches deriving their financial support from public revenues. Such a situation naturally made possible state support for church schools.

While it was legally possible for each new state to maintain an established church with its system of schools, members of the Constitutional Convention (1787) recognized that religious heterogeneity prevailed on a national scale. Thus the First Amendment, part of the so-called Bill of Rights, declared in favor of religious freedom for all by enjoining against a privileged position for any religion. Therefore, one by one, the individual states followed the example of the federal government and disestablished the state churches, thus aiming at religious freedom locally as well as nationally.

This development logically led to the eventual exclusion of religious instruction in the public schools, although secularization of tax-supported education did not take place immediately following the legal separation of church and state. Massachusetts, in 1827, after more than a quarter century of bitter controversy between orthodox and liberal interpreters of Calvinistic doctrines, took legislative action and directed school committees not to purchase or use, in any of the schools under their jurisdiction, school books calculated to favor any particular religious sect or tenet. In compliance with this legislation Horace Mann, as the state's first school superintendent, steadfastly insisted on keeping controversial sectarian religious materials out of the public school curriculum. The orthodox Calvinistic minorities thereupon proceeded to attack Mann personally for this policy, but eventually he won his point.

But Mann's attempt to placate the Protestant leaders got him into trouble with another group. Urging that the Bible should be used in all schools and that no teacher should attempt to interpret it, he made his famous statement that the Good Book would "speak for itself." This aroused the Catholics who believed that the Bible should be read under the guidance of their authorities. Furthermore, they observed that Mann was talking about the King James version—a Protestant Bible.

It should be noted that there were approximately 1,600,000 Catholics in the United States in the middle of the nineteenth century. Although this figure represented a vast increase over their original number in colonial days, they were still a relatively small minority. The Protestants were in control.

This was borne out by events in New York in the 1840's. The practice in that state had been to apportion its limited funds for education to various church schools. When the Catholics asked the state legislature for a share of the New York City funds in keeping with their percentage of the population, a great outcry was raised. All through the county the issue was hotly debated, and anti-Catholicism ran rampant. New York solved the problem by discontinuing its subsidies to private church schools. The legislators recommended that the state support a public school system instead. They claimed, incidentally, that the number of allotments to church schools was increasing so much that the shares for each were becoming too small to be effective.

The Catholics fared no better in other parts of the country. As they sought appropriations, the states amended their constitutions to include safeguards against the use of public revenues for sectarian instruction. The result was that practically all formal teaching of religion disappeared from the public schools except for the reading of the Bible. Even on that point the decisions of state courts have differed as to whether or not such reading should be considered sectarian instruction.

Another result of the rift in the nineteenth century was the rise of the Catholic parish school. Bishops made it clear to their people that they must finance their own schools and make their children attend, or else commit a mortal sin. Thus it has happened that approximately half of the ten million Catholic children of school age are enrolled in parochial institutions. And the figure would be greater were it not for the fact that these facilities are lacking to accommodate the others. It should also be noted that at least nine of every ten children now attending non-public schools are in Catholic schools. Thus we see that decisions reached a century ago relative to the "separation of church and state" have caused the subsequent rise of a vast parochial school system.

A movement in the 1940's to introduce some form of religious instruction into public schools received its impetus from the Third White House Conference held in 1939. Both lay and clerical leaders of many faiths expressed their concern about the lack of religious knowledge among Americans. They pointed out that modern youth is reaching maturity with but little appreciation of the role of religion in modern life, an ignorance of the contents of the Bible, and no adequate understanding of the relationship between an evolving democracy and the Hebraic-Christian tradition. It was charged that the public schools prepare children in everything but religion. Religious needs, these critics argued, should receive equal consideration with the other needs of young people.

It was Protestant leadership that first suggested the "released time" program whereby public school children may be excused an hour each week to receive religious instruction. Statistics have indicated a peak attendance of more than a million children in a thousand different communities, the largest single enrollment being 123,000 pupils in New York City in 1958. Catholic leadership at first opposed this plan but soon agreed to cooperate. As it has happened, in public school systems conducting released-time programs there are enrollments of 80 to 100 per cent of the Catholic pupils, whereas the percentages of Protestant and Jewish children are much smaller; New York City statistics indicate but 14 per cent of the Protestant and 5 per cent of the Jewish children participating.

In 1948, the Supreme Court rendered an important decision threatening the entire structure of this released-time plan. A mother, wife of a University of Illinois professor and an avowed atheist, had brought suit three years earlier, seeking to halt the practice in public schools in Champaign of releasing a period a week of regular school time for religious instruction. Pupils had been grouped according to faith (Protestant, Catholic, or Jewish) as indicated by their parents on cards distributed by the school authorities, but supplied and paid for by the Champaign Council on Religious Education. There was no extra cost to the taxpayers. Those children not attending religious classes went to study halls.

Basing its decision upon the First Amendment, the Supreme Court ruled that the state's tax-supported public school buildings were being illegally used for the dissemination of religious doctrines. The justices held that the practice violated the constitutional requirements for separation of church and state. The opinion seemed to rest not alone on the fact that public school buildings were being used for religious instruction but also on the school board's cooperation with the program. It was further held that compulsory attendance was used, at least indirectly, to help sectarian instruction.

That decision left both educators and religious leaders confused and puzzled. They wondered whether the pupils then under some other type of released-time plan would have to drop it. Or did the ruling apply only to those programs where school buildings served as religious classrooms? In New York City the board of education decided that its plan, whereby children are let out of school to attend the religious classes elsewhere, was still constitutional. In Georgia the question arose as to whether the Supreme Court ruling had knocked out a state law requiring daily Bible reading in public schools. The attorney general's office decided that it had not.

The National Education Association also pointed out that the typical opening exercises, such as reading the Bible and repeating the Lord's Prayer, were not directly affected by the decision. The eight-to-one majority decision stated: "The First Amendment has erected a wall between the church and the state which must be kept high and impregnable." The one dissenting opinion held that aid to religious sects was only a "by-product of organized society" and not to be condemned any more than the long-established practice connecting religion with government—for example, the use of chaplains in both the armed forces and in Congress.

In a 1948 Gallup poll 94 per cent of the Americans quizzed answered in the affirmative to the question, "Do you, personally, believe in God?" and 68 per cent answered yes on the question, "Do you believe in life after death?" That same year two important articles appeared in current magazines. The *Journal of Psychology* reported an analysis of the religious beliefs of 500 Harvard and Radcliffe students, finding that all but 6 per cent of the men and 10 per cent of the women had been given religious training in childhood; the majority said they were still religious in practice. But half of those examined had no convictions about specific doctrines; 15 per cent denied experiencing deep religious feelings; 25 per cent professed orthodoxy of some kind; 20 per cent were agnostics; 12 per cent atheists. However, 70 per cent said they felt the definite need of some kind of belief.

Also in 1948, *Religious Education* carried the charge of a teacher writing anonymously: "The Christianity with which America is familiar is distorted, confused, and almost absurd." This startling statement

was based on a study of 50 examination papers from a college sophomore class whose members all came from religious homes, had regularly
attended Sunday school, and had just completed a semester's survey of
religion which included five weeks of Bible study. Out of the 50, so
the author claimed, there were only eight or nine religious literates.
The rest generally were under the impression that there is no difference
between the Old and New Testament—their answers had the figure of
Jesus appearing "here and there through it all, tempting Job, helping
the prophets, and giving the Ten Commandments to Moses." Several
other studies have confirmed a general lack of accurate knowledge
concerning basic religious matters. This is indeed a challenging educational problem!

Academic Freedom in Education

The courage to speak freely and to inspire others to do likewise has
characterized the world's greatest teachers; oftentimes those bold
enough to do so have had to suffer serious consequences. Most famous
of the martyrs to the principle of academic freedom was Socrates, whose
fearlessness in developing ideas that powerful Athenians did not want
to hear resulted in his being condemned to death. Since men in power
invariably are suspicious of anyone who may upset the *status quo,* there
have been frequent struggles for the individual to maintain the privilege of saying what he thinks is right and proper.

In the Middle Ages we find another celebrated example of this
struggle. Peter Abelard (1079–1142) gained fame in Paris by his manner
of teaching logic. Outspoken and stimulating, he was just the type of
teacher to attract youthful attention at a time when the usual methods
of instruction involved dry lectures, reciting of propositions and
counterpropositions, citing of authorities, and presiding over aimless
disputation. When finally Abelard was forced to leave Paris, many of
his students followed him wherever he went. Like so many outstanding
teachers, it was characteristic of Abelard that he aroused either violent
dislike or equally devoted loyalty.

The medieval Church looked with horror upon anyone who advanced new ideas; consequently, there arose countless struggles to gain
academic freedom in the universities of that time. Later, as nationalistic
states took form, many of their rulers attempted to control the contents
and manner of what was taught. In 1542 the Court of Inquisition in
Rome began to decide questions of doctrine, to try suspected heretics,
to punish those convicted of heresy, and to keep a watchful eye upon
spoken and published statements of doctrine. The Spanish Inquisition

was conducted under state control with pitilessness, secrecy, and terror. In both Italy and Spain universities and schools were closely watched to prevent development of liberal ideas in either religion or science. Protestants were as severe as Catholics in this. Calvin, for example, made effective use of terrorism in stamping out opposition to his way of thinking.

This battle for academic freedom has been fought chiefly at the level of higher education. But the struggle there has not always been fierce in every country. Let us consider Germany, for instance. As a gesture of enlightened interest in the welfare of the people the despotic rulers of German states allowed a vital intellectual life to develop as early as the eighteenth century. Down to the time of Adolf Hitler (1889–1945) Germans had proudly ascribed the superiority of their universities to two conditions: freedom of investigation and freedom of teaching. Curious as it may seem, their universities were scholarly republics flourishing within autocratic kingdoms, with professors accorded opportunities for free and unbiased research such as scholars of no other country enjoyed. Not only were they free to search for truth and to impart it without hindrance, but they evolved a form of university organization that actually necessitated progressive thinking on the part of faculty members.

In contrast, most of the active research in France developed outside the universities, often in connection with the Institute of France, one branch of which is the Academy of Science. English universities also lagged behind those of Germany in academic freedom. Not until 1871 were they freed from doctrinal tests for all degrees, fellowships, college and university offices.

In American schools at all levels of instruction religious interests were so dominant until the middle of the nineteenth century that orthodoxy as dictated by the controlling church remained the most common qualification for teaching. From then on, however, a new conception of liberal education emerged as traditional objectives began to be challenged by the informational, social-civic, vocational, and personal-development aims of education. Currents of social and economic unrest brought about reforms in curriculum and methods of presentation of subject matter moving in the direction of greater academic freedom. In institutions of higher learning the strict administrative supervision that had so closely controlled all phases of student life began to weaken in favor of more freedom for the individual to develop his own sense of responsibility and to gain self-reliance.

Society owns and controls the public schools; therefore, legally it has the right to prescribe what may or may not be taught in those schools. Prior to the Civil War, certain institutions attempted to prevent campus discussion on the subject of slavery. During World War I the German language was legislated out of many schools as a result of the propaganda demanding that we hate the enemy. In the 1920's those teachers who joined labor unions or were outspoken in favor of the right of labor to organize were sometimes subjected to the so-called "yellow dog" contracts, in which discharge was stipulated for anybody who joined a union.

In religion the clash between fundamentalism and modernism was dramatically highlighted in 1925, when a high school teacher, John Thomas Scopes (1901–   ), was brought to trial because of his classroom teaching of the doctrine of evolution in violation of a Tennessee state law. Scopes was prosecuted by William Jennings Bryan (1860–1925) and defended by the famous criminal lawyer, Clarence S. Darrow (1857–1938). Nationwide attention was centered upon the rights of teachers to rely upon scientific findings rather than upon the literal interpretations of the Bible in describing the origin of man. For several years thereafter the teaching of evolution remained a highly controversial subject, and today a few states still have on their statute books laws that prohibit the teaching of evolution in their public schools.

"Red scares" were numerous in the 1930's, and some teachers with strong New Deal leanings were labeled Communists. Congress enacted an appropriation bill for the schools of the District of Columbia that carried the notorious "red rider" clause forbidding any teacher to teach Communism—the administrative interpretation of this legislation construed it as forbidding even the mention of Communism in classrooms of the city of Washington. There was nationwide furor over this action, and the legislation was soon repealed.

In 1949 the University of Washington "fired" three long-established professors—two because they admitted having once held membership in the Communist Party and the third for refusing to answer such a question. Liberals as usual went to their defense; the NEA and other educational groups investigated the merits of the cases; and members of several state legislatures applauded the action. One especially unfortunate feature of these so-called witch hunts is that certain liberal schoolmen with no Communistic leanings were traduced sometimes because disgruntled students, with a personal axe to grind, would maliciously start false rumors to embarrass the object of their wrath.

Much of this started in the 1920's when patriotic and veteran organizations successfully lobbied for legislation in many states requiring a daily flag salute. Since then, because of fear of Communist infiltration, a few legislatures have required all teachers to take oaths of loyalty. Most of the teachers resent this stipulation, not because they are disloyal, but because they dislike being singled out as a group for suspicion of their integrity.

A similar situation arose in 1959. Because of the Russians' successful Sputnik, a cry was raised in the United States for the training of more scientists. As a part of the ensuing National Defense Act, Congress allotted scholarship grants to students in need. But the scholarships hinged on their signing an oath that they were not Communists. The reasoning was that federal money should go only to loyal young men and women. However, many colleges and universities refused to accept the scholarship money under those circumstances. Students, too, resented the requirement. They argued that it served no valid purpose because a real Communist would have no qualms about perjury.

The outstanding issue of the 1935 NEA meeting was this question of academic freedom. Stirred at that time by passage of the so-called gag laws in state after state, and by the efforts of certain newspapers and patriotic organizations to pin the "red label" upon many educators, the liberal elements among the NEA delegates were determined to commit the association to a strong declaration for academic freedom and for the protection of teachers unjustly accused of subversive teaching. The resolution that was passed committed the NEA to the same type of protection for other teachers as was provided for its faculty members by the American Association of College Professors. The right to present differing viewpoints on any and all controversial subjects was demanded in order to aid students to adjust themselves to their environment and to changing conditions.

The NEA was authorized to appoint a five-member committee on academic freedom, three of whom were to be classroom teachers. The duties listed were to make known to teachers and friends of education any proposed legislation threatening freedom in teaching and to take necessary steps to combat such legislation; to investigate and report upon cases of discharge of teachers in violation of the principle of academic freedom; to seek public support for the right of teachers and administrators to academic freedom; and to assist in every way possible efficient teachers deprived of their positions in violation of the principle of academic freedom.

One NEA study in 1939 under the title, *The Limits of Academic Freedom,* indicated that while few teachers were being dismissed, demoted, or otherwise disciplined for exercising free speech, the majority were dealing cautiously with and speaking guardedly on controversial subjects because of fear of punishment. This would indicate that there are practical limits to academic freedom; evidently many teachers steer away from classroom discussion of topics that arouse the public. The NEA stated that the subjects considered "most dangerous to teach" included religion, sex, politics, and economics; and that the groups most active in limiting academic freedom were school board members, parents, school administrators, and church clubs.

It should be noted that few difficulties in the area of academic freedom are encountered by teachers of good taste and sound scholarship. Academic freedom is not a license that permits careless handling of the truth—it does not permit libel or similar practices. Certainly teachers should have the right to state their views on any issue if all sides of the question are presented in such a way as to place students in a position to formulate their own beliefs. In the United States the teacher's obligation fundamentally is to enlighten rather than to advocate. Therefore, in his classroom he has no right to be eternally a propagandist for any personal or unusual doctrine, creed, or dogma.

This means a teacher should state his views before a class calmly and judiciously, always with the stipulation that they represent his opinions only, which need not be accepted by members of the class. Moreover, if the teacher is to exercise this right of academic freedom, he has the responsibility of being well-informed on many sides of all important controversial questions.

Economic Influences on Education

The situation in which people are barely able to make both ends meet is called a subsistence level of economy. For instance, by hunting, fishing, or farming many individuals secure only enough food to survive. Should their efforts be relaxed ever so slightly, they endanger their own livelihood and render precarious the existence of those dependent upon them. Under such circumstances cultural advance is either impossible, or at best accidental, and, of necessity, education is informal. Thus it can be said schools are products of a surplus economy; that is, one in which production exceeds consumption.

Whenever there is a surplus economy formal education follows, and until the nineteenth century such schooling had been a privilege enjoyed almost exclusively by the economically favored classes of society. For example, the annual overflowing of the Nile River enriched the soil of the Egyptian valley to the point where crops not only sustained the life of the population but yielded a substantial surplus that was sufficient to allow a favored minority to utilize their leisure in studying the more subtle forces affecting human nature.

The Athenian Greeks were especially successful in achieving for the minority of free citizens self-improvement of the highest type reached in ancient times; their leisure resulted from the economic prosperity built on a surplus derived from commerce. In fact, to them schooling and leisure were almost synonymous. Plato significantly noted that children of the rich were the earliest to begin their schooling and the last to leave off. An age of economic prosperity in Athens produced such other great teachers as Socrates and Aristotle and brought about the development of a whole class of professional teachers—the Sophists.

Reaching unprecedented heights in wealth and power, Rome organized not so much the spirit but the form of an educational system for the upper economic classes. Significantly, Rome's period of educational decay paralleled its economic decline. The fact that the later emperors found it necessary to subsidize schools with funds from the imperial treasury reveals that the standard of living was falling below the point where private initiative could be depended upon to finance education. Then, during the medieval period, a profound economic depression settled down on all the western half of Europe except Moroccan Spain. With very little of surplus wealth or leisure, schooling in the so-called Dark Ages became but a shadow of its former Graeco-Roman greatness.

However, in the contemporary eastern half of the old Roman Empire where commerce still continued to thrive under established law and order, education flourished. Then western commerce began to revive during the Crusades, and there was accumulated an economic surplus sufficient to initiate a rebirth of formal education. Ever since the Renaissance the standard of living in the western world has remained generally high enough to maintain a relatively good standard of education for at least favored minorities of the population.

History shows that education has had cycles of rise and decline coinciding with economic ups and downs. When times are good, education flourishes; when bad, it is seriously neglected. These cycles have been more pronounced in industrial than in agrarian or even commercial economies. Some critics claim that education for the masses has been largely a defensive measure on the part of the property-owning classes on the theory that it is cheaper to keep children under control in an organization such as the school than to let them run the streets and have to pay for the damage they do.

Such was basically the purpose of the Sunday school as devised in 1780 by Robert Raikes (1735–1811) to relieve the pitiful condition of poor children in the newly industrialized areas. So long as they worked in factories from sunup to sundown they were under control, but on Sundays when they were free it was a different matter. By 1785, Raikes' idea had developed into an organized movement, and before the end of the century it was estimated that at least a half-million children were attending Sunday schools.

Frontier conditions in colonial America came close to destroying the respectable amount of education our forefathers brought with them from Europe. All the grim necessities of fighting for survival (clearing the land, tilling it, erecting shelters, and hunting for food) brought living standards very close to the subsistence level. Even when there were schools in frontier communities, farmers proved somewhat reluctant to send their boys because they represented a substantial labor value at home. However, interest in education revived as wealth began to accumulate on the Atlantic seaboard. Similarly, in the continuous westward extension of our American frontier, formal education flourished only when that part of the country became settled and prosperous.

It was during the nineteenth century that the Industrial Revolution opened the way in the United States for an accumulation of such gigantic resources that for the first time in the world's history it seemed possible to fulfill the dreams of Thomas Jefferson (1743–1826) and others to provide education for the children of the entire nation. Unfortunately, the Industrial Revolution was not an unmixed blessing. While creating the wealth to be taxed for educational purposes, it also subjected the necessary revenues to the vicissitudes of the economic cycle. Financial depressions have often followed periods of industrial prosperity and overexpansion, and such cataclysms have always hurt the schools.

And yet, in the face of many setbacks, the Jeffersonian ideal was approached more closely with each passing decade. Looking back, it almost seems inevitable that the free public school would evolve and expand because of the many forces in its favor. The character of the country changed as new factories sprang up in city after city and railroads spread across the land. Vast hordes of immigrants were disembarking at the great ports, and urbanization was taking hold. Most important, the common man began to use the powerful weapon of the ballot to affect legislation through his leaders. The large property owners who were opposed to the taxation of wealth for school purposes soon found it impossible to stem the tide.

Some proponents of legislation to liberalize educational opportunities sprang up, even from the upper-middle class. Men like James G. Carter (1795–1849), Horace Mann, and Henry Barnard (1811–1900) argued that public schools were necessary to prevent crime and pauperism, to aid in the Americanization of the immigrants, and to keep the country from becoming a caste-ridden society. Mann, in particular, stressed that public schools would give the economy a boost by increasing the productivity of the poor.

Of course there were some who protested that the state had no business in education—that it was a private and religious matter. Schooling, they said, was traditionally a leisure-class privilege; since the poor had no leisure, they had no need for education. But these tories were opposed by others in their own spheres who felt conscience-stricken at the thought of depriving any child of his "God-given right" to be enlightened. Furthermore, the labor organizations that had been formed early in the nineteenth century began to make themselves heard. Despite the resistance of the aristocratic and agricultural interests, organized efforts were made to establish child labor laws and compulsory education. There ensued a long and bitter struggle for the financial support to produce well-trained teachers and to erect adequate buildings.

The reactionaries eventually lost, and after the Civil War the free public elementary school became an accepted American institution. The form and content of the education also changed. A victory for the rising middle class was won when the academy gave way to the public high school. In fact, the latter was often called the "poor man's college." Its curriculum gradually came to include those subjects shunned by the old Latin schools. By adding science as a practical subject (previously it had been viewed only as an interesting but nonessential area), the high school also reflected the Industrial Revolution. The same observation applies to the introduction of manual arts, modern languages, and commercial subjects.

In the twentieth century, as has been noted, the United States developed into the world's wealthiest and most powerful nation. It was the land of big business, and the biggest business of them all was education. To illustrate: in 1900 only 6.4 per cent of the 17-year-olds in the country graduated from high school, but by 1956 the figure had zoomed to 62.3 per cent. Today some 40 million children go to school in the United States.

Labor leaders have always played a great part in the expansion of education. They campaigned for the child labor laws that were enacted after 1905; they fought for the enforcement of compulsory education laws; and they successfully advocated the extension of the upper age limit to 16. Their reasons have two economic foundations: education means the acquisition of the skills that lead to better-paying jobs, and too early an entrance of youth into the labor market causes an over-supply of cheap workers.

Mass education has had its support from the business world, too. Today's scholar is tomorrow's consumer, and his education will enable him to earn more money to buy more products. Furthermore, industrialists now realize that Communism feeds on poverty and ignorance; hence, it behooves those who thrive on a system of free enterprise to support public education.

This is not to say that the feeling is unanimous. Schools must be supported by taxes in one form or another, and taxation can become so severe in our economy that it generates everything from resentment to hardship. This is one reason that school budgets are often voted down at the local level and financial aid to education is fought at the federal level. The great question is whether the United States can continue its commitment of education for all without foundering on fiscal reefs. A related problem that is now being investigated is to what extent mass education has caused the quality of each child's schooling to depreciate.

PART THREE

Elsewhere

PART THREE

Elsewhere

From the beginning, European traditions deeply influenced American education. Some of the effects served to hinder the ideals and stated purposes of this "brave new world." Up to 1767 the Yale catalogue listed students according to their social positions rather than alphabetically, and as late as the middle of the nineteenth century our colleges and secondary schools were teaching only modifications of the seven medieval liberal arts to the privileged few. Not until the Morrill Act (1862) providing for land-grant colleges did higher education break with the classics and offer practical courses. Finally, the 1945 "Harvard Report" somewhat reluctantly concluded that today "the aim of education should be to prepare an individual to become an expert both in some particular vocation . . . and in the general art of the free man and the citizen."

And yet it cannot be denied that Europe also had its positive effects on American schools. In particular, the culture of three world powers— England, Germany, and France—furnished our founding fathers and our educators with guidance and leadership.

Generalizations are risky and often misleading, but to give focus to this chapter the following statements might be made. From England we inherited our basic culture, our interest in the humanities, our ideas about the curriculum for a college-bound student, and even our decentralized control of school systems. From Germany we learned a great deal about organization and methodology in a school system, the extension of schooling to the very young child, and the approach to education at the university level. And from France we obtained a reinforcement of our belief in the "natural rights" of all men.

The Scandinavian and Mediterranean countries and other lands of Europe also have left their mark on American education either through their religions, their individual leaders, or their flow of immigrants. But space does not permit the treatment of all these divergent forces. Instead, this chapter ends with a discussion of the evolution of Russian education because recent historical events have led to an interest in the comparison of American and Soviet school systems.

With these viewpoints in mind, let us look briefly at the development of education in certain European countries in order to gain a better perspective of the course of American education.

Evolution of Education in England

England made little or no provision to fill the educational gap that was left when the Church of England replaced Catholicism and the foundations of the monastic and chantry schools were confiscated by the royal crown. Parents taught their children whatever elementary education they could, hired a tutor whenever able to do so, or depended upon the parish priest to teach them their letters. As the mercantile class accumulated wealth some provisions were made for charity schools, but English elementary education in its beginnings was rather haphazard and unsystematic. Philanthropic interest was chiefly centered in developing a classical secondary education where the money invested would show to better advantage.

Some of those funds donated to Latin grammar schools helped lay the foundations of England's nine public schools—a name that confuses Americans since they are institutions endowed and managed privately.* The desire to give free instruction to talented poor children was an original motive in their endowments, but these public schools were attended by the well-to-do to such an extent that to many people they are today synonymous with British snobbery.

The emphasis that these "private" public schools have always placed upon sports and other physical activities deserves comment. The spirit of fair play in athletic contests has been traditionally relied upon to develop moral habits, sportsmanship, and the ability to "take it." Some historians point out that Great Britain's rise to the status of a world power was primarily due to the development of outstanding leaders through strict public school discipline, enforced largely by the students themselves.

During the Reformation the warring religious factions agreed that the classical structure provided the best secondary education for training the leaders needed by church and state. Christianity's historical documents had been written in the classical languages, and the Renaissance humanism had established the classics so firmly as the foundation

* England's nine public schools: Charterhouse, Eton, Harrow, Merchant Taylor's, Rugby, St. Paul's, Shrewsbury, Westminster, and Winchester.

for education above the elementary level that their validity was seldom seriously questioned. Both Catholics and Protestants relied whole-heartedly upon the classics to the point that they became deeply entrenched in American as well as in European grammar schools. In the newly established Church of England, however, English replaced Latin. That meant the language of parish schools taught by Anglican priests also came to be English. Puritans stressed the use of the vernacular tongue in their elementary instruction, and it became common in the so-called Dissenters' Academies taught by their ministers.

The "two-track" system was a characteristic of European education transplanted to America that failed to flourish in our frontier environment. In England this system consisted of basic elementary education for the masses and classical secondary schools for the upper strata of society. The humanities were recognized as the mark of religious scholarship, political superiority, and good breeding.

Those educators who saw possibilities for reform in vernacular language or science were always hard put to uproot the classics. Grammar schools of Reformation England made a great condescension to the practical interests of the commercial classes when occasionally the art of letter writing was included in the curriculum.

Since English tradition held that schooling is a private matter for parents to provide as best they can, during the eighteenth century the control and support of education remained in religious or private hands. Schools were supported by Anglican parishes, dissenting churches, private endowments, and subscription societies set up for that purpose. The typical English solution for meeting the needs of the poor was to depend upon those who could afford it, and had the heart to do so, to give free education as a philanthropic deed.

There were a few eighteenth-century voices being raised in favor of state support for education, but usually the reasons were far from noble. Adam Smith (1723–90), author of *Wealth of Nations* (1776), urged public education for the poor as a means of giving them a useful occupation and a better realization of their position of inferiority in society. He believed that, if properly educated, they would not be so apt to menace the lives or destroy the properties of the better classes of society. Thomas Malthus (1766–1834), proponent of the "survival of the fittest" theory in population trends, also expressed the desire to use public education as a means of protecting the economic interests of the propertied classes.

In nineteenth-century England it was generally accepted that self-respecting parents would pay tuition for their children's education.

Deplorable working and living conditions faced by the laborers in factory towns gave great impetus to the philanthropic measures that had begun in the previous century. Also, the religious revivals of that time were influential in moving toward a democratizing of education. All this prompted the conservatives in England to form additional voluntary societies in order to provide at small cost sufficient education to satisfy the common people.

Numerous charitable agencies set out to furnish "ragged schools" for the underprivileged—industrial schools, orphan schools, reformatories, and soup kitchens. Religious denominations organized school societies to provide charity education. The three most common types of English schools, all transplanted to colonial America, were: Sunday schools that gave instruction to children who worked in factories the rest of the week, monitorial schools that put education on a mass production basis, and infant schools for the very young children of those mothers who worked in the factories.

Several investigations found such shocking lack of opportunities and gross inequalities that agitation rapidly developed for the government to do something to help the situation. At the beginning of the nineteenth century many bills were introduced into Parliament, but until the 1830's the Tories were able to defeat such proposed legislation. Their opposition was motivated largely by fear that education would make servants insubordinate to masters. In 1833 Parliament began granting financial aid to assist certain voluntary bodies in providing schools. A regular grant for primary education thus became established, so naturally a form of control by the state was evolved. In 1839 a special committee of the Privy Council was set up to consider all matters affecting the education of the people.

Not until the Forster Act (1870) was a state system of schools put on a stable basis. This provided in England and Wales for the establishment of popularly elected school boards to set up and manage schools in areas not covered by voluntary societies. Thus there began a dual system with two types of grant-aided elementary schools—one sponsored by the churches and the other by school boards. The latter were empowered to levy local rates or taxes for the purpose of education and, if they wished, to make attendance compulsory from the ages of 6 to 13. The Act of 1899 created a central authority covering elementary, secondary, and technical education. Its primary duties were as follows: to enforce attendance; to pass on physical equipment, buildings, and qualifications of teachers; and also to make suggestions and to give aid in matters of curriculum and methods.

Education progressed more rapidly in the twentieth century. The Act of 1902 abolished the school boards and made the county councils, country-borough councils, municipal-borough councils, and urban-district councils the local education authorities. These were given the power to provide or to assist in education other than elementary. The Act of 1902 also lessened the financial difficulties of the voluntary schools by requiring the local education authorities to maintain them in return for control of all their education except religious training. This legislation led to the establishment and rapid development of secondary schools maintained entirely by local authorities. It also granted financial assistance to a number of secondary schools already in existence, provided for the development of technical education, and led to establishment of training colleges for teachers.

Both World Wars revealed to British statesmen the dangerous weaknesses of their school systems. The Fisher Act of 1918 raised the age of compulsory education to 14 and made provision for establishment of part-time compulsory attendance at day continuation schools for children from 14 to 18 who had given up full-time schooling. However, the post-war depression prevented the latter provision from being put into effect.

The Act of 1944 created a ministry of education. In this body were included not only central administrative officers but also inspectors authorized to report on the efficiency of schools, assist teachers, serve as the local agents of the ministry on administrative matters, and act as expert advisers on educational theories and practices.

This Act of 1944 organized education into three progressive stages known as *primary, secondary,* and *further education.* The last term, strange to Americans, covered educational provisions for adolescents leaving school before the age of 18. *Primary education* was organized for children from 5 to 11; it was also the duty of each local education authority to provide nursery schools for children under five whenever such service was needed. Incidentally, it was decided that no child should be "failed" in nursery or primary school; grade advancement was to be based on chronological age only. At age 11, children were required to take examinations of the achievement type to determine the kind of secondary school each should attend.

In order that older children might receive the education best suited to their abilities, the Act of 1944 provided for three types of secondary schools; the grammar school, somewhat like our college-preparatory high school; the modern school, offering a general education closely related to the personal interests and local environment of the students;

and the technical school, closely related to agriculture, commerce, and industry—much like our vocational high school. These three types of *secondary education* were set up in separate schools or included as different courses within the same building. Based on achievement, there were opportunities for free interchange of students from one type of school to another. The original choice of the kind of secondary education was made at age 11, but for all students this decision was reviewed at 13 and any necessary adjustments were made at that time.

Great Britain's ever-increasing interest in education for all has been manifested throughout the last few decades. Today attendance is compulsory for children from age 5 to 15. Moreover, in 1959 a new building program for technical education, costing 54 million pounds, was established for the period from 1961 to 1964.

A country with such a great cultural heritage would naturally be expected to continue its interest in higher education. There are presently 16 universities in England; Wales and Northern Ireland have one each; and Scotland has four. In a recent year there were almost 100,000 full-time students in universities. Although that figure represented little more than one per cent of the children then attending the public schools, it should be noted that approximately 80 per cent of the university students were assisted by scholarships or grants.

The need for providing new teachers for their bulging classrooms has been uppermost in the minds of the British. In 1958 the Minister of Education announced plans to increase the capacity of teacher-training colleges by 12,000. But many educators in England predicted that the need for additional new teachers would be far greater than that. Like their American cousins, the British are reaching toward more democratic goals in education but are finding it difficult to supply the manpower and the facilities.

Evolution of Education in Germany

Early in the nineteenth century several prominent Americans returned from Prussia enthusiastic about the schools they had visited. Also, American thought was influenced by the report on the organization of German schools made in 1831 to the French Government by Victor Cousin (1792–1867). In the 1850's Froebel's kindergarten idea began its growth in this country. After a visit to Prussia in the 1860's Edward Sheldon (1832–1897) brought some Pestalozzi-trained teachers to Oswego, New York, to help improve the teaching of his staff. Oswego's experiment became so well known that normal schools in other American states adopted Pestalozzian methods.

Herbartianism had a similarly popular vogue in the United States during the final two decades of the century. Herbart's ideas became so widely used in American teacher-training institutions that in 1895 there was formed the National Herbart Society, later renamed the National Society for the Study of Education. Until the 1930's most American educators looked upon German universities as the best in the world because of their unusually high standards of teaching and research.

Considering the above influences of German education upon American schools, let us turn our attention to it and see how it evolved. The Renaissance period is usually considered the starting point of modern education. At the time England and France were laying foundations for their later world empires Germany was still politically decentralized. Town authorities fought church officials for the privilege of setting up their own schools. In due time the German towns won this right by appealing to the local ruler for support against the local bishop. Sometimes they even carried their appeal to the Pope, indicating perhaps that "school politics" is not exclusively an American or even a new phenomenon.

As town and church reached agreements for the joint operation of the schools, a public-parochial educational system was being established in Germany. Frequently the priest would do the teaching while the town paid his salary and looked upon him as a public official. As for the curriculum, Renaissance education in the German states as elsewhere was intended mainly for youths of the upper and wealthy classes; therefore, its ideals centered on humanistic classical studies and the cultivation of gentlemanly graces.

During the Reformation period the aims of education were being broadened, with some opposition developing against the separate Latin schools for the aristocracy. Provisions for vocational education and interest in teaching trades to poor children indicated the growing economic and political influences of the time. The middle classes were attempting to widen the scope of vernacular education to make it meet more adequately their commercial needs. The growing use of printed books brought about a wider dissemination of Luther's German translations of the Bible, his catechism, hymnbook, and the schoolbooks written by the reformer himself and his followers.

Two of these, Johann Bugenhagen (1485–1558) and Philipp Melanchthon (1497–1560), urged the Protestant rulers to study their schools and to reform them by civil authority. Often the transformation of Catholic into Lutheran churches did bring with it a reorganization of the schools. As a result of surveys of Melanchthon and others, several of the German states and free cities issued codes for the conduct of schools. Also influential was Johannes Sturm (1507–1589) who laid the foundation for the German *Gymnasium* by his division of secondary schools into regular classes that were taught by different teachers. Another important development was the *Ritterakademian* for children destined to live their lives in court. They were taught dueling with sword and pistol, riding, music, heraldry, geography, history, mathematics, science, and vernacular languages.

The religious enthusiasm of Pietism, a reform movement among Lutherans urging a more sincere and active religious devotion, stimulated the creation of a public religious system of schools in the various German states. August Hermann Francke (1663–1727) established virtually an entire educational system: a free school for poor and orphaned children, a vernacular school at the elementary level, a Latin *Gymnasium* for secondary students who could afford to pay, and a *Pädagogium* or higher school originally intended for nobles but eventually developed into a type of combined scientific academy and teacher-training institution. Francke received sufficient financial and moral support from the king of Prussia to establish several hundred schools in which the communities paid tuition fees for poor children while those who could afford to pay did so.

Prussian school laws of 1713 and 1717 made it compulsory for all parents to send their children to school, and in 1737 a general code provided government aid to build schoolhouses and to pay schoolmasters. The Prussian School Code of 1763 laid the foundation for a national system of elementary education and was chiefly the work of Johann Hecker (1707–1768), a Pietist clergyman who had worked with Francke. Attendance from ages five to thirteen was made compulsory, and definite school hours were prescribed. State inspectors supervised the schools, but church officials prepared the examinations. To obtain a license, teachers had to be approved by both state inspectors and the church consistory. That 1763 law prescribed in rather minute detail the qualifications of teachers, curriculum, and textbooks.

Full state control came in 1787 when a code took the supervision of schools away from the clergy and created a state ministry of education. Also instituted was a "leaving examination," one that secondary school graduates had to pass before being admitted to the universities. All this represented a highly centralized educational system under state control for authoritarian purposes. But at that time certain important middle-class aims came into prominence, too, as the demand arose for practical subjects preparing youths for various trades and occupations.

For a few years after the defeat of the Prussian army by Napoleon Bonaparte (1769–1821) at the Battle of Jena (1806) it seemed highly possible that this disaster might bring some liberalism into the authoritarian educational system. The philosopher Johann Fichte (1762–1814) urged that education be used to unite the German people and to regenerate their spirit by linking the ideals of nationalism with those of liberalism. He preached that class distinctions should be wiped out and that all Germans unite under a strong national state.

However, in 1815 the Congress of Vienna brought with it a reactionary nationalistic control in which repressive decrees were issued and the liberals hunted down and silenced. Again in 1848 there was a resurgence of the liberal movement that soon collapsed. Pestalozzian ideas of the regeneration of society through education began giving way to religious, disciplinary, and military obedience. Education was used as a tool to make the common people satisfied with their appointed position in society and, above all, loyal to the monarch.

The two-track educational system had become firmly established by 1830; schooling was compulsory from six to fourteen, and, wherever possible, separate schools for boys and girls were maintained. At the age of six about 90 per cent of the school population went to the *Volksschulen* while the upper-class children attended the *Vorschulen* as a three-year preparation before entering one of the secondary schools at nine years of age.

Prince Otto von Bismarck (1815–1898) was the man who crippled German liberalism and created a militaristic empire. In his *Kulturkampf,* a policy against any outside interference in the affairs of Germany aimed especially at the Catholic Church, Bismarck sought to remove all control of schools from the clergy. This led to the school inspection law of 1872; but after the abandonment of *Kulturkampf,* inspection largely reverted to the clergy, regardless of the law.

The 1872 law did recognize that the different religious groups in the states constituting the German Empire were to be reconciled to state control by setting up schools as Protestant, Catholic, or Jewish—whichever happened to be the dominant local group. Wherever a community was divided, the difficult alternative was to maintain separate schools or to give special religious instruction for each of the different faiths.

In 1871, Kaiser Wilhelm II (1859–1941) issued a decree to teachers, informing them that their prime purpose as educators was to combat the dangerous doctrines of socialism and Communism.* The dictum was obeyed. By the beginning of the twentieth century German education had become a highly centralized nationalistic agency, designed to produce patriotic subjects who knew their place in society, promptly and efficiently followed orders, and remained loyal to the emperor and the fatherland. Thus, in avoiding one evil, the Germans embraced another.

It was this type of single-purpose education that helped build the gigantic manpower machines for human destruction in both World Wars, for Adolf Hitler (1889–1945) carried even further the educational objectives of Chancellor Bismarck and Kaiser Wilhelm. Only once did nationalistic aims yield to humanitarian objectives. Following World War I the Weimar Republic tried to reverse the aristocratic and centralized character of German education by making opportunities more flexible and by increasing the chances for advancement for the masses of German children. In order to adapt schooling for local needs the Republic granted German states more authority in educational matters.

But Hitler's rise to power ended this brief period of liberalism. Nazism took over the government in 1933 and soon revealed its opportunistic nature by attacking anything that people disliked and by claiming to do everything the masses wanted. Control of the schools was an initial step in gaining mastery over the political, economic, social, and cultural life of the people. This meant destroying the power of the federated German states in educational as well as in political matters.

To achieve such an objective the hold of the churches over schools had to be broken. This involved destruction of the aristocratic two-track system with the consequent decline in secondary education. In order to replace the old aristocracy and the prosperous middle class with people inspired to give unquestioning loyalty to the party, there was developed a "mass school" idea designed to instill the Nazi ideology into growing youth. Out-of-school physical activities were substituted for the highly formal, bookish, and overintellectualized character of most of the pre-Nazi schools. In fact, the sixth day of each week was taken from class work and devoted to Hitler Youth activities.

When in 1945 the United Nations occupational authorities began

* The German social philosopher and political leader, Karl Marx (1818–1883), had published the first volume of *Das Kapital* in 1867. Previously, in 1848 along with Friedrich Engels (1820–1895), he had published the world-shaking *Communist Manifesto*.

their work in Germany the problem was to create a democratic educational system to replace the very thorough job of Nazification done by Hitler's schools. Complications arose from the fact that England, France, Russia, and the United States all had zones of control. There was a serious shortage of qualified teachers. De-Nazification had involved about 70 per cent of the 50,000 German instructors in the American zone, and the process of reinstatement was very slow.

The American Military Government issued a report three years after the end of active warfare that showed its zone as having only 2,900,000 books for the 3,000,000 pupils—fewer than one per child. A Catholic nun had but one book, so she painstakingly made hand-lettered copies for each of her 40 pupils. This 1948 report indicated that German students had been reeducated in basic mathematics, some languages, geography, and to a lesser degree in physical sciences, art, and music. But to erase Hitler's militaristic and racial concepts of history the Allies had accomplished practically nothing, largely because of disagreements among the four powers on proper interpretations of past events. Another investigation showed that textbooks used in the Russian zone contained considerable Soviet propaganda apparently aimed to arouse distrust of democratic processes.

After 1948 the situation in West Germany improved somewhat, but it is still far from satisfactory. On the whole, teachers avoid discussion of the crimes of the Nazis; many of them find it hard to decry Hitler because they had once been his genuine or ostensible supporters. In this failure to inculcate an antipathy toward Nazism, the teachers are supported by a great number of parents who want to shun discussion of the entire issue because it raises unwelcome specters of their guilt or shame. And so, German youth are given little more than an outline history of the Nazi era. They learn the facts, but few are taught to deplore them. This is a problem that worries the rest of the world. The German economy has boomed in the last decade, and there is no doubt that the country has the potential to become a world power again. The question remains whether Germans will use their knowledge and talents in constructive ways after the bitter lessons of the two World Wars. A large part of the answer lies in the schools.

In Germany today approximately 80 per cent of the children between the ages of six and fourteen are receiving an education. Most of them spend eight years in elementary schools and then attend vocational schools for another three years. However, about 20 per cent of them at the fourth-grade level are siphoned off and sent to the German equivalent of our "secondary schools," to prepare for university study, business careers, or specialized vocations.

This screening at so early an age has recently been criticized by German parents, just as a similar system in England and France has raised a barrage of complaints. The ten-year-old German boy who wishes to qualify for the *Gymnasium* must pass examinations in his native tongue and in mathematics. The tests are grueling three-day affairs lasting five hours each day. Even if he is successful, the student has no assurance that he will go on to the university. He must pass a probationary period, and failure to measure up means his relegation to the ranks of the laborers in his adolescent years.

German children attend school six days a week—not five. Furthermore, they get far more homework than American children. A recent Gallup poll showed that the typical ten-year-old in West Germany spends 297 hours each year on homework, as compared with 106 hours for the American child of the same age—and only 39 hours for the typical British ten-year-old! The same survey indicates that at fourteen a German student puts in an average of 89 minutes per night on homework while the American of the same age spends 73 minutes daily on this out-of-school activity. The British teen-ager, incidentally, again does the least. He averages only 50 minutes daily on homework.

Another aspect of German education that should be mentioned is the teacher's concentration almost solely on the intellectual advancement of the child, in contrast to our American philosophy that the school should be concerned with a pupil's social and emotional growth. It is debatable whether the German approach should or can be emulated in the United States today. While it is true that the average German child learns his geography and his mathematics better than his American counterpart, it is questionable whether he grows up to use that knowledge to the best advantage. The German *Gymnasiums*, like the Russian schools, are highly competitive places; they lack the warmth, spontaneity, and friendliness of American high schools. Indeed it has been posited that the repressive and non-social characteristics of German schools and homes are the seeds for the Kaiser Wilhelms and Adolf Hitlers of the past and future.

Perhaps the answer to this problem is the "middle way" recommended by the ancient Greeks. American schools would do well to study some of Germany's tenets in the education of the gifted, while German schools might take another look at their effect on the human personality and on attitudes toward citizenship in an interdependent world.

Evolution of Education in France

Paris held the distinction of having been the first great medieval center of learning, but during the Renaissance the French universities proved hostile to humanism. Their faculties were so resistant to this new type of learning that even the French kings were unable to prevail upon them to change. It was natural that the universities would resent such outside interference. They had struggled through the Middle Ages to wrest their right of self-government from the hands of both church and state. Hence it happened that in order to have an institution hospitable to humanism, Francis I (1494–1547) found it necessary to set up the Collège de France. Municipal governments at Bordeaux, Lyons, Montpelier, Orléans, and Reims also established institutions to promote the new classical learning.

As has been the case with all vital and vigorous educational movements, humanism, once established, lost its vigor and became formalized. Typical of its critics was Petrus Ramus (1515–1572), who adhered to the naturalistic interest in science and mathematics in attacking both the Aristotelian Scholasticism of the universities and formalized humanism. He set out to reform each of the seven liberal arts by improving the materials studied and by making methods of acquisition simpler and easier. His aim was to make knowledge apply more readily to actual social situations, to free it from ecclesiastical control, and, above all, to emphasize science and mathematics. Ramus wrote new textbooks that became quite popular in European countries, and later in colonial America.

It was not a churchman, teacher, or scientist, but a man of affairs and letters, who most effectively combined humanism and naturalism in his attacks upon formalism, verbalism, and blind reliance upon authority. In his sophisticated essays Michel de Montaigne (1533–1592) urged that the proper education of a gentleman should include the classics as a source of wisdom in action and not merely as models of literary style; modern languages as well as classics; history, travel, and wide social contacts; and physical education. In America Thomas Jefferson advocated and tried to put into operation many of the ideas of Montaigne.

During the Reformation period Catholic leaders in France showed themselves more willing to expand and reform secondary education than they were to provide common education for the masses. There was but little serious thought given to changing the traditional aristocratic conception of medieval and Renaissance education. In the seventeenth century, however, the French *Estates General* did call upon the Church to establish schools in all towns and villages and to institute compulsory attendance. Before the end of the Reformation period there were several Catholic orders promoting elementary education. The purpose of founding most of those schools was to provide free education for poor children of the working classes, the dominant aim invariably being to prepare youth to become good Catholic men and women. As opposed to the academic curriculum given to the upper-class children, the training of the masses was of a practical nature.

In the eighteenth century the religious rivalries that marked the Reformation had largely given way to rivalries over commercial and nationalistic interests. The Church conducted its schools with very little civil control. However, Louis XIV (1638–1715) did issue edicts covering what the university professors could and could not teach, and he required instruction in French civil as well as in canon law.

Governmental extravagance, economic disasters of the colonial wars abroad, heavier taxation, and irritating social injustices eventually led to the French Revolution (1789–1799) in which the "Declaration of the Rights of Man" enunciated the liberal principles that formed the basis of most of the democratic constitutions of the nineteenth century. The doctrine that men are born free and equal brought an entirely new slant into education—it was to be free, compulsory, and secular.

The French Revolution in setting out to create a new and more democratic society dramatized how important education might become as a tool of nationalism. Several plans were proposed, but the more detailed was by the Marquis de Condorcet (1743–1794). He planned a complete state system—elementary schools throughout the country within walking distance for all pupils; intermediate schools located in all medium-sized towns to provide more advanced education for the common people; and secondary schools, or institutes, in the cities to give not only a classical education but also a wide variety of subjects adapted to the needs of the people. Condorcet further proposed nine lycées to replace the traditional universities in higher and professional education, and at the very top there was to be a National Society of Arts and Sciences through which scholars could exert influence over the entire educational system.

The end of the French Revolution prevented this plan from being put into operation, but its ideas were embodied later in the school laws of France and other nations. However, in attempting to establish a state educational system the National Convention confiscated church property and suppressed the teaching orders. The new emphasis upon the political use of education to make better citizens began to take hold.

Napoleon secured for France a large measure of law, order, efficiency, and even equality before the law—but he did not allow democracy. In order to strengthen the centralized power of the state and to weld France into a united nation, he found it advisable to reach an agreement with the Catholic Church by restoring it to a privileged position through the Concordat of 1801. However, he did refuse to return the lands the Republic had confiscated, and he preserved some measure of religious liberty by refusing to recognize Catholicism as the only religion in France.

Napoleon was less interested in elementary education than in secondary schools. Through the latter he expected to train a loyal and efficient body of officials to help carry on his government. His *Law of 1802* returned elementary schools to church control and at the same time provided the framework for a state system of secondary schools under private control. The *lycée* of the larger towns became the standard secondary school of France, the preferred way to prepare for entrance to universities. This institution developed into a residential boarding school, received national funds for building construction and teachers' salaries, maintained a humanistic course of study, and, by charging fees, catered principally to the aristocratic classes.

The *collèges* of the communes (the smallest political divisions in France) also led to the universities but were not so well endowed as the *lycées* because they had to depend more for financial support on the local community. The *Law of 1802* also established higher faculties of law, medicine, science, technology, and theology.

During the period of restoration of the Bourbon kings from 1814 to 1830, the Church was given much more of its former status in the schools—thus completing the retroactive cycle that Napoleon had begun. Priests were appointed as principals and teachers in public schools, and the licensing of private teachers was through bishops rather than state authorities. However, when the constitutional monarchy was established in the July revolution of 1830, secular interests regained much of the ground they had lost.

Victor Cousin visited Prussia in 1831 to study the organization of German schools, and his report formed the basis for the legal establishment in 1833 of the framework of French primary education. Each commune was required to provide a building and pay the teachers for a public primary school. Poor children attended free but fees were charged those parents who could afford to pay. The private religious schools continued in operation, but their teachers had to be certified by the mayor of the commune as well as by church officials. It was stipulated that no child in the public primary schools could be forced to receive any religious instruction against the wishes of the parents.

In the principal cities of the legal and political subdivisions known as *départements* there were authorized higher primary schools, designed to offer vocational preparation in agricultural, commercial, and industrial subjects appropriate to each region. The *Law of 1833* also provided for establishment in each *département* of a primary normal school for the training of teachers. In the late 1830's infant schools were set up for children of preschool age, primary schools for girls, and so-called adult classes for boys beyond fourteen and girls over twelve. Primary education was still neither free nor compulsory but it was headed in that direction.

France more than any other European country has continuously changed governments, and each shift has involved the educational system. When Louis Napoleon (1808–1873) became emperor largely on the strength of his famed uncle's reputation, he saw to it that bishops and other church officials gained strategic positions in the control of education, thus making it easier for the clergy to teach in the public, primary, and secondary schools. "Liberals" in the schools were hunted down, exiled in certain cases and discharged in others, while the normal schools were kept under close surveillance to prevent them from becoming "hotbeds" for the growth of radicalism in social, political, or educational ideas.

The disastrous defeat by Prussia in 1870 overthrew the Second Empire, and under the Third Republic democratic ideas regained ascendancy. The modern form of French education was realized in the 1880's through a series of laws promoted by Jules Ferry (1832–1893). Fees were abolished in the primary schools and compulsory education required between the ages of six and thirteen. The ministry of public instruction was given complete control over the details of curriculum, selection of textbooks, examination and appointment of teachers, and payment of salaries in the primary schools. There also developed a much stricter supervision of private religious schools.

Regardless of form of government—monarchy, empire, or republic—French leaders have believed in a strongly centralized system of state education. The Third Republic brought with it many democratic trends, but these did not prove strong enough to eliminate the two-track system of schooling that has always provided one type of training for the upper classes and still another for the masses. Occasionally attempts were made to grant secondary school scholarships to talented poor children, but until 1933 the *lycées* virtually limited their membership to the privileged few. That year there began the process of abolishing fees.

In the meantime practical education had been gaining ground in the higher primary schools, and beyond them there developed technical and trade schools as part of the two-track system. A chief feature of this training was the glorification of France based upon the authoritarian role of the teacher, strict discipline, unquestioning obedience by pupils, and rigid adherence to state curriculum and textbooks.

The Socialist and Republican forces brought about the Separation Act of 1905, stipulating that within ten years all teachers in the elementary schools were to be laymen and all religious teaching orders suppressed. While the Third Republic had allowed no religious instruction in public schools, a half-holiday per week was set aside for children to receive such instruction out of school if parents desired. Then in 1942 in Vichy, France, partly because it suited the Nazis to create dissension, the ban on religious teaching orders was lifted and state funds once more allocated to their schools.

Under the Fourth Republic there was set up the Langevin Commission which made a two-year study of the question of educational reform. Its report appeared in 1947, recommending a thorough democratizing of the schools, elimination of the two-track system, and extension of compulsory education to age eighteen.

Moreover, the National Assembly adopted the commission's suggestion that progressive American teaching methods and curricula be incorporated into the first years of secondary instruction. *Classes nouvelles* (new classes) were soon formed on an experimental basis; their success led to far-reaching curricular reforms.

The Fifth Republic under President Charles de Gaulle (1890–   ) came into power in 1958. So many more pressing political and economic problems faced this new government that education for the moment seemed forgotten. A broad reorganization was undertaken, however, in the next year. The goal suggested by the Langevin Commission was almost reached when the upper limit for compulsory education was set at age sixteen. It was also decreed that all pupils, rich or poor, should be provided with the same program in the elementary school.

The De Gaulle cabinet set up an intermediate cycle for children aged eleven to thirteen. After careful observation of each pupil's scholastic aptitude, school officials were authorized to channel the children either to general long-term instruction in the *lycées* or the general short-term instruction terminating at age sixteen. Pupils were also allowed to elect vocational training at age fourteen.

A survey in 1957 had revealed that 80 per cent of the young people whose fathers were professional and businessmen and higher civil servants entered the *lycées,* but only 20 per cent of the laborers' children did so. In an attempt to correct this imbalance in educational opportunities, the De Gaulle government has planned a new system of awarding scholarships, based on financial need and scholastic potentiality.

Since the seven-year *lycée* course leads to an A.B. degree—a prerequisite for entrance to a university—it is reasonable to expect that the De Gaulle plan will produce a greater number of university graduates from all walks of life. At present France has 22 universities, five of which are operated by the Roman Catholic Church.

In summary, France is a prime example of states that have moved away from their original class distinctions in education. Like many other people, the French have advanced gradually and unevenly to the position that the state has an obligation to provide a free education for all children and to see that no parents deny their offspring the opportunity to go to school for eleven or more years. Although French schools are still a long way from the attainment of democratic ideals, they are now solidly advancing along that road.

Evolution of Education in Russia

Communism today is seriously challenging democracy on a worldwide front. The dramatic success of its aggressive policies suggests an unusually effective and highly specialized educational system. Although Russian education has contributed practically nothing to organization or procedures in American schools, for self-defense, if for no other reason, we need to examine its history and perhaps discover what "makes it tick."

The Russian Slavs had long had a Byzantine culture and religion before being conquered in the thirteenth century by the Mongol Tartars and thus established the beginnings of the modern Russian state. Near the end of the seventeenth century the Russians had begun an expansion westward by taking lands from Poland and Sweden.

Peter the Great (1682–1725) invited Europeans to visit his country, sent students abroad, and made trade agreements. He also introduced Western clothes and customs, established hospitals, printing presses, and schools. This westernizing process was continued by Catherine the Great (1762–1796), who expressed her hopes of establishing schools throughout the land. Despite sporadic attempts by some of the succeeding czars, in the nineteenth century Russia was far behind most European countries in social reform. Nevertheless, there was an active spirit of liberalism kept continuously alive largely by secret organizations.

The czars of Russia did very little to establish or maintain educational institutions. The universities would not admit the peasant or working classes and, in turn, were spurned by the nobility as being the "breeding ground" of dangerous revolutionaries. That suspicion seems to have been justified both by the constant agitation for social reforms and by general support of the Revolution of 1905 that followed the disastrous Russo-Japanese War. For such activities the universities lost much of their autonomy, but were on the point of regaining it during World War I when plans were in progress to emphasize scientific investigations rather than specific preparation for public service. Attended primarily by the middle class, the universities opposed the proletarian Revolution of 1917. When the Communists came into power, partly in retaliation for this opposition one of their first acts was to abolish entrance requirements, examinations, and degrees, and to open the universities to all persons over sixteen regardless of sex.

Recognizing that education represents a most effective tool in the creation of a classless society, the Communists immediately set out to secularize, socialize, and centralize all Russian schools. They confiscated church property, abolished private schools, and began establishing a universal and free educational system completely under state control. Naturally this has involved a process of trial and error, but while the administration and classroom methods of Soviet education have frequently changed, the aim always remains the state promotion of Communism by use of the schools to eliminate social classes. Even informal education that goes on continuously outside the classroom is regulated directly by the state, with propaganda definitely an integral part of all training.

An unbiased evaluation shows that between the two World Wars the Communistic educational system in a shorter period of time accomplished more to raise the literacy of an entire nation than had ever before been achieved in all recorded history. Statistics concerning the USSR are notoriously unreliable, but within the first quarter-century since the Russian Revolution it is claimed that illiteracy was reduced from about 60 per cent to less than 10 per cent. At any rate, our observers abroad have been amazed by the growth in the reading ability of Russian citizens. This improvement is all the more remarkable because the government, which supplies all the textbooks, has been obliged to print them in 90 languages. In those schools where some other speech is the vernacular, Russian is taught as a "foreign language." Incidentally, it should be noted that 10 per cent of Russia's income has been spent on education, as contrasted with 3 per cent in the United States.

In the period immediately following the Revolution there was urgent need for trained scientists, technicians, and mechanics. The high command decided to stress vocational education and to develop special schools, called *rabfaks,* to be closely associated with factories and collective farms. But in integrating education with production the educators met a problem; factory workers and peasants had received so little previous schooling that they were unable to do even ordinary arithmetic, much less to understand the concepts and methods of science.

To meet this situation the leaders went to the extreme. The new *rabfaks* had neither entrance nor final examinations, and no tests in between. Consequently, their educational results were pitifully poor. One must credit the Communists that in building a gigantic educational system in such a remarkably short time they have been quick to learn the errors of their ways. These *rabfaks* were soon improved and now maintain creditable standards. Also, in 1922 the universities were made a part of the state system of education, and numerous other higher schools were established in a program intended to prepare specialists and scientific workers for the various occupations. While the university entrance examinations were restored, preference was given to students of proletarian background, many of whom received maintenance at state expense while in attendance.

The Russian Revolution, in fact, was a proletarian movement, one in which leaders and workers of necessity had to be transformed quickly into Communists if it were to be successful. The schools were required to emphasize political and social as well as general or vocational subjects, and to attack "religious superstition."

The initial problem lay in the fact that the great majority of the teachers, because of their middle-class origins, were opposed to the Revolution. Nevertheless, those teachers had to be used until either they were converted to Communism or others could be trained to replace them. Thus there was developed a policy of supervising the instruction to make certain it followed the party line. To do so with a minimum of personnel the students were ordered to participate in every phase of school administration. They took charge of discipline, curriculum, and financial management of schools. In fact, many became so active in the work ordinarily done by teachers they had but little time to study.

In 1928 this control in the administration of the schools by students was withdrawn. The change in policy resulted from investigations that showed the schools of the first decade of Communistic control were failing to teach thoroughly the essential elements of the sciences, mathematics, history, geography, and native languages. Thus, as soon as it was felt that the teachers had become loyal Communists, they were again put in full charge of the schools, and students were told rather bluntly and abruptly to study and not to meddle in their management. With the teachers' return to power, very strict discipline became the rule of the classroom. In fact, in the 1940's elaborate decrees were issued to instruct children to obey without question the orders of their teachers.

The effort had been made in the 1920's to reform Russian elementary education according to the American pattern; at that time John Dewey (1859–1952) had visited the country to lend his moral support in instituting the progressive education idea. During the first Five-Year Plan the Russians used a combination of project method, student freedom, and political ideology to instill Communistic ideas in the younger generations. Individual grades and competition were abolished as a hold-over from capitalistic ideology—the ability to perform in group cooperative work was extolled as the ideal.

Reaction developed in the 1930's with vigorous protests against the insufficiency of the educational program, lax discipline, and poor methods of teaching—more specifically, the minimizing of the teacher's function and failure to check the work of individual pupils that had led them to a general lack of personal application in their studies. It was charged that the attempt to make the project method the basis of all school work actually had ruined education. What we would call child psychology was also assailed because, the critics claimed, pedagogy had uncritically adopted reactionary and unscientific theories evolved abroad to the effect that a child's fate is irrevocably determined by his heredity and environment, thus not taking into consideration the powerful factor of planned socialistic education.

These criticisms were effective in bringing about the re-establishment of the teacher's complete authority and stricter discipline. The pupil was held responsible for conscientious work, strict obedience to the teacher, diligent study, passing marks in examinations, good grades, as well as personal appearance, manners, and conduct. In 1931, education at the elementary level became compulsory. Not only did schooling become free in all schools, lower and higher, but even in elementary schools a program was started for many pupils to receive state financial aid while in attendance.

At first the Russian secondary schools subordinated everything to the political and economic theories of Karl Marx (1818–1883). These have always remained powerful educational influences; but new emphasis is now being given to history, literature, the humanities and arts—as well as to science and technology. Russian history is taught for three or four years, and occasionally the world hears that some historian has "discovered" that certain inventions and explorations were accomplished not by the individuals long credited for them but rather by some Russian historical figure.

Studies of American and English history, English grammar and literature are occupying an increasingly important place in Russian schools. Even Russian art and literature are being studied for their intrinsic qualities rather than simply as tools for achieving a classless society. Seemingly, some intellectual and cultural ideals have been fitted into Soviet education without diminishing its fundamental political character.

When the schools were opened to everyone, girls as well as boys, it was proclaimed that absolute equality had been achieved not only between the sexes but also among the numerous races within the Soviet Union. In 1943, however, separation according to sex was ordered in secondary schools of the larger communities although coeducation was retained in the smaller ones because of a lack of building facilities. Explanations ranged from the desire to give girls more time in such studies as home economics to the necessity of providing military training for boys.

The present keynote of Russian education is regimentation down to the minutest detail. When a child first enters school he receives a card containing 20 regulations, which he signs as soon as he learns to read and write. This pledge must be with him at all times, and its signing means he has read the rules, understands them, and swears to obey them. He must exhibit this card to school authorities whenever requested to do so. Each pupil is fully aware that one infraction makes him subject not only to punishment but even to expulsion. Thus a child has definite instructions not only to be punctual, diligent, polite, and respectful, but also to "do all homework without assistance," to "give up his trolley seat to the sick or aged," and to "assist in the care of little brothers and sisters."

The Soviet educational system now consists of nursery schools, often located in factories where the mothers work, all-day kindergartens for children between the ages of three and seven, four-year primary schools for ages from eight to twelve, three-year secondary schools from thirteen to fifteen, and three-year upper-secondary schools to the age of eighteen.* Parallel to these regular secondary schools are specialized educational services for the peasants on collective farms and for the underprivileged in cities. As in Germany, Soviet schools are in session six days a week.

In addition to the universities at the top of the Russian educational system, there are now agricultural, scientific, and technical schools. Also in existence are special schools for the handicapped, classes specializing in removal of illiteracy, part-time schools for employed adolescents, several types of adult education, and both intermediate and higher schools to train leaders for the Communist Party.

Since there are two sides to every question, it is interesting to note the reactions of six Soviet educators who made a month-long tour of the United States in 1958. In a newspaper interview they said they "admired" the modern school buildings, the varied extracurricular activities, the excellent equipment, the skill and enthusiasm of the teachers. Also they offered criticisms: the pace of instruction in many classrooms was similar to that of a "slow-motion film," and mathematics instruction in the United States contained easier problems for students than at the same age level in the Soviet Union.

On the other hand, American educators who have made extensive visits to the USSR have not always returned with ecstatic reports. They claim that the Soviets have built their educational system largely on Pavlov's conditioned-reflex theory and that true creativity and critical thinking are given little encouragement. Moreover, they are wary of the glowing statements issued from Moscow since it is well known that the Soviets twist facts and figures to suit their own purposes. Another important point is that there are tremendous differences in the quality of educational facilities and methods in different parts of the USSR, despite centralized control. Our observers state that in the vast and remote rural areas the educational level is far below that of the large cities.

As a corollary, it should be noted that the cultural level of people

---

* In some areas this organization has been superseded by the 10-year schools, known as "complete secondary schools," or by 7-year schools. In some non-Russian-speaking republics, an extra year is provided for the study of the Russian language and literature.

in the Soviet Union is still inferior to that of the West. This factor must be considered when we compare our educational system with theirs. As just one example, Soviet technical and vocational schools have been forced to teach young people certain skills that many American youths pick up as part of their everyday life. The adolescent Muscovite is not likely to have a "hot rod," a transistor radio, a record-player or any of the great variety of other machines and gadgets that surround a child in the United States. In other words, our way of life is an educative force in itself—and the Soviets are frantically trying to catch up through this program in their schools.

But let us make no mistake. When Nikita Khrushchev (1894–   ) threatened that the Communists would "bury" us, he was talking more in terms of economics and education than missiles. The Kremlin is convinced that the West is decadent and that its citizens lack dedication or purpose. Therefore, the Red leaders are confident that they can make their school systems vastly superior to ours in a very short time. In fact, they contend that they have already surpassed us in many areas of the curriculum. For example, they point proudly to their well-advertised language program.

Some of the Soviet children study a foreign language in the kindergarten. A larger number begin the study in the third grade. Among the languages they are taught are Arabic, English, French, Hindi, and Urdu. Also, in the non-Russian-speaking republics the study of Russian begins in the second grade.

Except in remote rural areas, all children are required to take six years of a non-Soviet foreign language. This instruction begins in the fifth grade. Those who go on to higher institutions must complete five more years of intensive language study to earn a diploma. Thus a prospective Soviet teacher of English has had at least eleven years of instruction in the language.

English is a language that gets a great deal of attention in the USSR. According to the Deputy Minister of Education, about 75 per cent of all students in higher education study English; 60 per cent of all language majors are in that subject, and higher institutions have 77 English faculties. From one point of view, this emphasis may be considered wholesome because knowledge of a language has always been an aid to understanding the people that speak it. However, one can be sure that the Soviet officials have less altruistic aims. The advantages for purposes of espionage and attempts at world domination are obvious.

The belief that Soviet interest in foreign languages is merely pragmatic is borne out by the fact that discussions of the culture and mores of other peoples are not woven into the language lessons. Soviet teachers treat the subject like a code that must be deciphered. Their methods, incidentally, are traditional and analytical, although it must be noted that in higher education they are now making excellent use of language laboratories.

The main thing to keep in mind about all Soviet education is that it is like a monstrous machine that turns out literate and skilled products to suit the single-minded purpose of the Communist Party—service to the state. The raw materials for these products come from a vast area, almost three times the size of the United States, and are rooted in their own traditions and customs. For example, the USSR has approximately 180 minority groups speaking more than 125 languages and dialects. But they are all given a similar initial processing and at a certain point on the assembly line they are inspected and sent to designated compartments for further refining. At the end, they come out neatly labeled— technician, teacher, farmer, soldier, professional Communist, or whatever other brand of worker is needed.

The entire system is quite cold-blooded but highly efficient in terms of Communist goals. And, as noted before, the authorities are quick to retool when the machinery falters or when a better product is demanded. To illustrate, in 1956 a boarding school program was started for selected children of widows and working parents. Khrushchev's idea was to train these pupils for future leadership in adult society. The forerunners of this program were the successful military and naval boarding schools, Suvorov and Nakhimov, established by decrees in 1943.

Additional reforms were instituted in 1959 in an effort to establish a balance between academic and manual training and to see that students gained experience in socially useful and productive work. Today, like the United States, the USSR has a tremendous variety of programs. These include the aforementioned schools for adults, correspondence secondary schools, evening schools for rural youth, and part-time schools. There are even special establishments for illiterates and semi-literates; and there are schools for exceptional children like the bright, the retarded, and the handicapped.

In visiting all these schools, our observers have been impressed by the intense concentration of the Soviet children. As in most other countries on the continent, corporal punishment is used more sparingly than in the United States. Pressure is brought to bear on the pupils in other ways. The most effective, apparently, is the thorough and continuous indoctrination. The Soviet child is taught, literally from the cradle on, that it is his duty to help prove the superiority of a socialistic state over the "capitalist world."

This system has its frightening Orwellian aspects. One conceives of robots responding to button-pushing. It is certainly not the kind of educational program that Americans would wish to imitate in its entirety. Nor would we want to adopt education-by-decree, even though it is expeditious and apparently efficient. However, we do need to realize the grave danger that the Communists will outdo us through education unless we set aside petty differences and institute important reforms of our own in the support and management of our schools.

PART FOUR

Leadership

PART FOUR

Leadership

It is almost axiomatic that any organization is as good as its leadership. Schools are no exceptions. The personality, scholarship, and efficiency of a principal will affect the morale of an entire faculty and will even shape the attitudes and work habits of many pupils. For example, in a certain rundown neighborhood there are two schools—both equally unattractive from the outside. But on entering P.S. X, the visitor is pleasantly surprised by the bright displays of pupils' work, the friendly attitude of the children, the smiles on the teachers' faces and the air of businesslike attention to work. In contrast, the atmosphere at P.S. Y is tense; the halls are drab and cheerless; hubbub is silenced by the angry shouts of an adult; and everybody is impatient for the dismissal bell to ring. Why the difference? Anyone who takes the trouble to investigate a little further can answer in two words—"the principals."

Principal A is affable and kind. He is brimming with confidence and energy. He knows how to help teachers solve their classroom problems. An organized person, he plans his work so that he gets around the building sometime every day. Children welcome him. They beam when he greets them by name and occasionally makes a personal comment to one of them. Teachers like to see him, too. They know he will give them a pat on the back for their current achievements and that he will take action to surmount the difficulties they have run into. They tell their friends what a grand place P.S. X is; consequently, recruitment is no problem.

Principal B is an introvert. Essentially he was born to be a follower and not a leader. He lacks self-esteem. And so he hides away in his office where he handles innumerable picayune details week after week. He is like a stranger to the children—the man who sallies forth from time to time to scream at them and maybe to pluck one of them into his office for a good scolding. The teachers neither like nor respect him. His classroom visits precipitate harsh and critical notes. Afterward his victims find themselves venting their wrath on their pupils. They say to each other: "I'm transferring out of here as soon as I can." To the young applicants they confide: "Don't come here. It's like purgatory. And please don't quote me."

If such is the effect of the principal on a school, then one can imagine the importance of a superintendent of schools in relation to a whole community. Of course, it is sometimes true that a competent superintendent is hindered by a backward or arrogant majority on the board of education. But in most cases superintendents of high caliber do not succumb. Either they fight a wrongheaded board until progress is wrought or they quietly move elsewhere.

Thus it can be said that our American schools are largely what the citizens of each community make them, and that the primary factor in the relative worth of their schools is their choice of leaders. If a populace selects civic-minded and intelligent board members, they in turn will carefully pick a superintendent who will carry out a constructive program. And as the leader of the schools he will set the right tone for the principals and teachers. The children—and indeed the entire community—will benefit.

Since leadership is so vital to the welfare of a school system, let us now look at its various aspects. In this chapter we shall touch upon leadership not only at the local level but also at the federal, state, and county levels. Perhaps the best place to begin is with a general survey of the field of administration of schools and the opportunities it presents for alert, ambitious educators.

Administration as a Profession

The school administrator's job, whether the principalship or the superintendency, is most complex. It involves more than mere organization of classes and administration of routines. Some of the facets of the educational leader's position are: improvement of instruction through various supervisory methods, public relations, leadership in the planning or operation of the school plant, problems in finance and budgeting, extracurricular activities, health and guidance programs, adult education, staff morale, and programming for children and teachers. The list could go on and on. And under each of the above categories many subdivisions could be made. Suffice it to say that the administrator's task is a challenging one and requires, at the very least, intelligent and balanced people who enjoy excellent health.

Today more and more school systems are demanding that the administrators have at least an M.A. degree and a background of courses in supervision and administration. In cooperation with graduate schools of education some communities have set up an internship program whereby likely candidates for administrative positions earn while they learn. In other words, they get the necessary experience by assisting the present administrators; at the same time the college checks on their progress and gives them credit for the apprenticeship. This system has been found especially valuable in school systems where a current administrator has indicated his desire for retirement after a few years. A smooth transition is provided while he "breaks in the new man."

The field of education offers to men opportunities to secure positions of leadership and responsibility much more quickly than does any comparative professional work. In rural areas, many a college graduate has gone immediately into a principalship, or even a small superintendency. On the other hand, those young men entering the larger school systems invariably find greater competition. Many possessing ambition and natural leadership qualities remain classroom teachers through their entire professional careers for lack of opportunity to prove their executive abilities. It is a common situation in some of the larger, better paying school systems that the high school staffs contain many bitter men who feel, justifiably or otherwise, that they are victims of discrimination every time a promotion is announced.

Nevertheless, the opportunities for men are vast in relation to those for women. Many an inferior man is promoted in preference to some superior woman possessing much more executive ability, merely because he wears trousers. It can be truly said that the average woman who rises to a position of educational leadership had a much more difficult struggle to get there than that faced by men in similar positions. Some critics of women administrators say that they are inclined to be too conscientious concerning relatively insignificant details; others claim they are a little too dictatorial, largely because of their sensitivity to the real or imagined fact that so many people resent any woman's having a position of authority. Research studies indicate that most men and women teachers much prefer to work under a man. Perhaps this attitude stems from the fact that for centuries the distaff side had been given no real chance to take positions of leadership in the world.

Several of the larger cities have had women superintendents—Chicago and Los Angeles, for example. It is quite common in the larger systems to have women assistant superintendents, especially in the field of elementary education. In recent years the fair sex has been holding down some important high school principalships, but their greatest avenue of promotion has always been the elementary school principalship. For example, San Francisco until the 1940's employed nothing but women as heads of elementary schools.

Regardless of who is the administrator, one of the facts of life is the extreme importance of the school board members. Under our present system of local control any voter can be elected a school trustee if he secures enough votes. Many of the best citizens, well qualified to give intelligent and faithful service, refuse to run when urged—they don't want to be involved in a nasty "school political fight." This sometimes leaves for the position men and women who have no further qualification for the work than a selfish desire to swell their own egos and to be glad-handed by teachers made conscious of the necessity of such tactics as insurance for holding down their jobs.

Now this situation is not true in all cases, perhaps not even in a majority of them, but it is common enough to present a serious problem. Certainly an administrator must earn the respect, if not always the warm personal affection, of his board members. Each time there is a trustee election the new members must be "educated" as to the purpose of the broad policies he is trying to implement. Many of those elected date and limit their knowledge of schools back to their own classroom days when pedagogy was far more simple than it is today. This is not a hopeless job over which one needs to become a cynic—it is all part of the price of leadership.

Then there is the question of parents, and some of them can be truly annoying problems. The very child who drives his mother almost frantic at home mysteriously becomes an angel in her mind when he arrives at school. Americans are notably softhearted when it comes to children—they have swallowed "hook, line, and sinker" the naturalistic school of thought that a child, when left to his own resources, is certain to develop into a worthwhile human being. Thus the parents continuously compromise at home, bribing immature youngsters to take a necessary dose of medicine and even to be good on occasion, when it would be far simpler and easier to tell them what to do and see that it is done. The school has to step in and do a straightening-out job, and often when teachers get too enthusiastic about making a social creature out of some wild undisciplined human animal, the superintendent or principal receives the fury of a wrathful parent.

Success in administrative work requires a great deal of tact, but it also needs courage to stand up for what is right and proper regardless of the immediate politics in the situation.

This leads to the question of the strategic position of a building principal. He has over him a superintendent to whom there must be accounted not only his own errors in judgment but also those of his teachers. Under him he has a staff of teachers and, except in extreme cases, they must be backed in what they do even though admittedly they should have shown better judgment. To do otherwise means to lose the confidence of those upon whose work and loyalty his own success depends. Of course, after an error in judgment the matter needs to be talked over with the teacher as insurance against repetition. But in almost all cases a principal of necessity must support his teachers—the task is to get them to think along his own lines of procedure so that future problems may be avoided. A principal who protects his teachers against parents and pupils, or even the superintendent, usually earns their active and enthusiastic loyalty.

Finally, a good administrator must understand and use the better techniques of educational research. A few books and treatises on this subject had appeared before 1900. Thereafter prospective school officers turned in increasing numbers to the universities for training for their growing responsibilities, and there developed a systematic treatment of the principles applicable to education. Research eventually included the study of the legal machinery of schools, powers and duties of school boards, school finance, buildings and equipment, and functions of the respective school officers.

This application of statistical methods to the study of problems of school administration came in response to the demand for greater efficiency in the operation of school systems. During the early 1900's notable studies of the drop-out rate of children and a host of wasteful school practices encouraged the general use of statistical procedures in the study of such problems. From these beginnings arose the departments of research that most state and city school systems now maintain.

Federal Government in Education

Strange as it may seem, the United States Constitution does not contain a single word about education. But even before its adoption in 1787, Congress operating under the Articles of Confederation had passed the Ordinances of 1785 and 1787. Thus at its very beginning our federal government had demonstrated a deep interest in a national program for educational improvement. Nevertheless, this important omission from the Constitution has caused considerable speculation, especially since today so many Americans are directly connected with public or private schools as trustees, administrators, teachers, clerical workers, custodians and janitors, lunchroom employees, or students.

It must be remembered that schooling in the early days of our country was almost entirely the concern of the family, church, or private agencies. Also, among the American colonies educational practices differed so greatly that there could be but little agreement.

However, the private journal of James Madison (1751–1836) indicates that at one stage in the drafting of the Constitution, in a list of enumerated powers to be assigned the federal government, there had been included the control over an educational system. This specific reference to education was later deleted. But it is interesting to note that two of our early presidents, Thomas Jefferson in 1806 and Madison in 1817, had advocated a constitutional amendment granting the federal government powers over education. Congress accepted the proposal of neither man, and further efforts to centralize education in this country were doomed by the rise of Jacksonian democracy and the states-rights movement.

Many European countries have developed highly centralized national school systems through which direct control is exerted over what shall be taught and who shall teach it. In our nation the schools have been decentralized; in other words, the control is largely centered in the individual states, not the federal government. But, both directly and indirectly, Congress has shown a strong interest in the educational improvement of the people. Attention has been brought to bear upon such pressing problems as the Americanization of immigrants, a lowering of our disgracefully high rate of illiteracy, and ways and means of meeting through education the unemployment problem of the nation's youth caused largely by the Industrial Revolution.

Although the Constitution makes no direct reference to education, it contains no prohibitions of educational activities by the federal government. The first school authorized directly by Congress was the United States Military Academy at West Point. Established in 1802, it has been supported entirely by federal funds and conducted under the auspices of the Department of War, now the Department of National Defense. Entrance requirements and academic standards have remained unusually high. Upon completion of the four-year course the graduates are given commissions as Army officers. In order that the government may be assured of some return on its investment, the new officers are pledged to continue in service for a period of at least eight years from the time of their enrollment at West Point.

In 1845, Congress established the United States Naval Academy at Annapolis, Maryland. Similarly, other schools intended to develop leaders for national defense have since been created and supported by federal funds.

In 1803, when Ohio was admitted as the seventeenth state, the federal government put into action its epoch-making proposals written into the Northwest Ordinance (1787). Land was surveyed in townships of 36 sections, and "Section 16" (one square mile) was set aside for the support of public education. With certain exceptions, such as Texas, this policy was continued as each new state was admitted. Then, beginning in 1850 with the admission of California, the gift consisted of two sections of public land. Since the admission of Utah, in 1896, four instead of two sections have been received.

The total of these land grants to schools has been estimated as more than 140,000 square miles. In addition many other federal grants have been made, both conditional and unconditional, including saline lands, swamplands, and the internal improvement grants. At different times the federal government has also aided the public schools by money grants and has made donations to normal schools, universities, and other types of educational institutions.

The United States has been very active in promoting vocational education through both land and money grants. The original Morrill Act (1862) gave each state 30,000 acres of land (or the equivalent thereof when public lands were not available) for each senator and representative then in Congress. All proceeds from the sale of these lands were to be invested at 5 per cent and used for the "endowment, maintenance, and support of at least one college where the leading object shall be, without excluding scientific and classical studies and including military tactics, to teach such branches of learning as are related to agriculture and mechanic arts."

Thus, substantially supported by the Morrill Act and subsequent legislation, 69 land-grant colleges or universities have been developed but not along identical patterns. Each of the 50 states has at least one; Puerto Rico also has one; Massachusetts has two. In the southern states there are 17 additional land-grant colleges established predominantly for Negroes. These institutions were specially provided for by the second Morrill Act (1890). The same legislation called for federal appropriations to each land-grant state. Among the institutions established as a result of the Morrill Acts are the state universities of California, Colorado, Illinois, Maine, Minnesota, Nebraska, Ohio, West Virginia, and Wyoming.

The Hatch Act (1887) made possible the establishment of agricultural experiment stations by providing annual cash subsidies of $15,000 to be used in connection with each land-grant college. Later acts increased this sum substantially, as did the Bankhead-Jones Act (1935). That legislation, however, changed the basis of distribution, providing that 60 per cent of the grant for experimental stations be distributed to the states according to their rural population and the other 40 per cent be granted for research conducted by agencies designated by the Secretary of the Department of Agriculture.

The Smith-Lever Act (1914) provided federal subsidies to be used in extension work in agriculture and home economics. It set up classes, conferences, meetings, institutes and traveling demonstrations. It also included county agents—highly trained men to work among farmers, and women specialists to help housewives. This legislation was quite important because it marked the first time in the history of federal aid that states were required to match the funds voted by Congress.

Not until the twentieth century did there develop a movement for federal aid to vocational education at the high school level. Certain organizations including the NEA, National Association of Manufacturers, American Federation of Labor, trades and agricultural groups, began to advocate the extending of facilities for vocational education in the public schools. Various individuals and groups interested in this problem met in 1906 and established the National Society for the Promotion of Industrial Education. Their labors bore fruit a decade later.

The Smith-Hughes Act (1917) provided federal funds for annual distribution to the states for vocational education in public schools of less than college grade. These appropriations, on a state-matched basis, were intended for development of trained teachers and supervisors of agriculture, home economics, trade and industrial subjects; and for studies in vocational education.

The George-Deen Act (1937) provided for further development of vocational education in the states and territories, and more than doubled the amounts of money previously available. This act recognizes as worthy of federal aid such distributive occupations as salesmanship.

Even though the United States does not have a nationalized system of schools, there is a centralizing agency that has special jurisdiction in the territories and over such groups as the American Indians. Beginnings of the Office of Education can be traced back to 1838 when Henry Barnard (1811–1900) went to Washington, D. C., in search of reliable facts but found none. The efforts of this great educational leader finally brought about the congressional act of 1867 creating the Federal Department of Education.

Primarily because of the opposition of some of the states the F.D.E. was reduced two years later to the Office of Education and placed in the Department of the Interior. In 1870 the name was changed to Bureau of Education, but in 1929 it again officially became the Office of Education. Ten years later, in connection with the general governmental reorganization act of 1939, it was transferred from the Department of the Interior to the Federal Security Agency. Reorganization of its work, effected in 1946, had the Office of Education operating under eight major divisions: school administration, auxiliary services (libraries, health, lunchroom, radio, TV); central office services (for example, editors, statisticians); international education relations; elementary education; secondary education; vocational education; and higher education.

In 1953 Congress established a Department of Health, Education and Welfare. Since that time the Office of Education has been a part of that division of the Cabinet. The office is still headed by a Commissioner of Education. In the past the tenure of this official has varied from one to 17 years.

It was truly fitting that Barnard should have been appointed the first commissioner, but he served only three years. In the basic law creating this position the three main duties enumerated were the collecting of statistics and facts, diffusing of information about the schools, and otherwise promoting the cause of education. Appointment for an indefinite term is made by the President with the Senate's consent.

So far as federal appointments go, this important office has been relatively free from politics. However, in 1948 Commissioner John W. Studebaker (1887–) resigned in protest, claiming that the Office of Education was being swallowed up by the Federal Security Agency and that education on a national level was not being accorded the independence which has always been so essential in the American management of schools at the local and state levels.

Many educational leaders believed that this controversy served to dramatize the need for an independent educational agency headed by a national board of education on somewhat the same pattern as state and local boards—a move that had been supported long and consistently by the NEA and other organizations concerned with education. In recent years Vice Admiral Hyman G. Rickover (1900–), an avowed critic of modern schools, has recommended the formation of another kind of national board—one composed of influential citizens who would propose goals and standards which the individual schools could then accept or reject. It is his contention that the establishment of such a board would put pressure on local laggards to improve the quality of their education.

Another suggestion along this same line has come from James E. Allen, Jr. (1911–   ), New York State Commissioner of Education. He asks for a National Council of Educational Advisers whose function would be to make recommendations not only to the schools but also to the President and to Congress.

Critics of the proposals for some sort of national curriculum planning express fears similar to those voiced by the opponents of federal aid to education. They warn that our democratic system may be undermined, that problems vary in each of the states, and that national standards may cause us to neglect attention to individual differences among children. An outstanding proponent of this point of view is Hollis L. Caswell (1901–   ), ex-president of Teachers College, Columbia University. He favors assistance to local efforts through the establishment of several "educational laboratories" connected with universities. But he concedes that national minimum standards for the preparation of teachers in each of the subject areas might be a good idea.

In the spring of 1961, Sterling M. McMurrin (1914–   ) jumped into the controversy. As soon as he was sworn in as the new United States Commissioner of Education, Dr. McMurrin indicated his intention to make the Office of Education "a national forum" of ideas from educators and laymen rather than merely a center for the collection of data. He indicated that his office would enter the field of curriculum for the first time in its history and that he would attempt to get the best minds in the country to draw up "model curriculums" in all subjects and make them available to all school districts. However, Commissioner McMurrin was careful to state that his office would not set up a "national curriculum" and impose it on the schools.

Keeping in mind the arguments pro and con for a national approach to education, let us now turn our attention to the system that presently operates in the United States.

State Control of Education

"The powers not delegated to the United States by the Constitution, nor prohibited by it to the States, are reserved to the States respectively, or to the people." So reads the Tenth Amendment, ratified in 1791. By implication it has brought about the interpretation in various court decisions that education is one of the unmentioned powers reserved as a state function. The reasoning is that the 13 original states were in existence before the adoption of the Constitution, and that their voluntary formation of the Union caused them to surrender but a portion of their sovereign rights. As a matter of record the colonies of Massachusetts, Connecticut, Pennsylvania, New Jersey, and Maryland had all attempted to establish school systems before the Revolutionary War.

As mentioned previously, although the Constitution by its failure to mention education did not grant the federal government any specific powers, neither did it prohibit them. In "promoting the general welfare," Congress, it has been traditionally understood, may establish and support schools for specialized training in the national interest; also, contributions for the aid of general education may be offered through legislation. But the legal status seems to be that the federal government is acting as an outsider or private party in contracting with each sovereign state; it can neither levy taxes upon state property for the support of such schools nor directly administer them. However, Congress has been able to enforce certain stipulations regarding the use of land and money grants by implied threats of discontinuing them. In this way there has been exercised a control over agricultural, home economics, and other types of federally subsidized vocational instruction.

It can be said there is an American school system but no national system of schools. There are, in fact, 57 school systems—one in each of the states and territories and one in the District of Columbia. Their similarities are far more significant than their differences, a situation brought about partly through the Office of Education, though its services are largely limited to an advisory capacity. Also working toward this end are the few controls exercised by the federal government over how its land and money grants may be used.

But far more important in interstate communication on scholastic matters has been the multitude of national organizations and committees made up of all kinds of educational leaders and, in some instances, of interested representatives from other occupations. The reports of these groups have had wide circulation among both teachers and laymen. No other nation can claim as wide and free a dissemination of published materials on educational subjects. There exists today in this country an amazingly large number of journals that rival each other in presenting new ideas, methods, results of experiments, and even "gripes."

Another great factor linking the school systems of the various states is the mobility of teachers, pupils, and articulate parents. Ours is a nation of rovers. In moving frequently from one state to another, people bring with them the customs and ideas of their original regions. Nor should we forget the role played by school superintendents. Always in search of higher salaries and better working conditions, these administrators play their own game of "musical chairs." Although some do remain in the same school system where they began, others move from place to place, accepting better positions and bringing to one state the ideas they have gleaned in another state.

Furthermore, the curriculum of school systems in the various states is influenced by nationwide book companies. In rural areas and small towns the syllabus is often governed by the content of the textbooks put out by these companies.

Finally, a kind of professional control exists through the power and prestige of outstanding colleges and educators. In the 1920–1940 period Teachers College played a dominant role. More recently, James B. Conant's (1893–   ) reports on senior and junior high schools have caused schoolmen in all parts of the land to evaluate their work in terms of his criteria.

The educational system in each state is based upon its constitution and statutes, and depends upon the interpretations of these as made by the state school superintendent, the state attorney general, and the courts. Thus each sovereign state determines for itself the most important issues in education, extent and manner of financial support, powers of the local school boards, minimum qualifications of teachers, compulsory school age and enforcement thereof, textbooks to be used, what shall and may not be taught. Such uniformity as prevails within each American commonwealth has been accomplished through the policies of the state board of education, the personal leadership of the state superintendents or commissioners, and the work of the professional staff members in state educational departments.

Even though the state may operate institutions of higher learning and special schools, ordinarily it is not engaged directly in common school education. In America such schooling is traditionally a local matter. Each state establishes the legal framework within which local communities are authorized to operate schools. Thus elementary and secondary schools are essentially local institutions; the main function of the state is to enforce some degree of uniformity in their support and procedures.

Responsibilities for schools have been delegated to counties, cities, towns, villages, townships, and other local districts. These powers and duties originally resided within the legislatures which are the supreme lawmaking bodies in state government. Whenever a legislature wishes to increase or decrease the powers and duties that have been delegated to local school officials, this may be done merely by changing the laws, so long as such changes do not conflict with federal and state constitutions. This means that legally school officials and employees are agents for the state to carry out its educational policies; they are responsible to the people of their community only because the state has delegated them that responsibility.

In each state there may be one or more boards that have educational functions. Several have governing boards for the state university, the land-grant colleges, and sometimes for other state-supported institutions like state teachers colleges. The foundation for state educational departments was laid in 1784 in the establishment of the Board of Regents for New York. To that body was granted supervision over colleges and academies throughout the state, and since then the institutions incorporated under its control have been jointly known as the University of the State of New York. It should be noted that this is not truly a university but rather a state educational department, and also that it did not gain control of public school education until 1904.

There was no other state educational board organized until 1825, when North Carolina created a body known as the President and Directors of the Literary (or permanent) Fund. Other boards were then started in various states for special purposes, but only limited powers and duties were assigned them until Massachusetts established its State Board of Education in 1837. Connecticut followed in 1838.

There are various patterns in the composition of state boards of education. Some have ex-officio members, such as the governor, attorney general, and secretary of state. These men usually are more interested in the development of their own efforts and sometimes are inclined to pay little attention to educational matters. In other states all members are appointed or elected; some boards have combinations of ex-officio appointed or elected members. Utah is unique in that members of the state board of education are elected by local school board members.

The trend today definitely is away from ex-officio members and toward appointment, rather than election, of public-spirited citizens who are willing to give their time to the cause of education. The function of the state board varies from that of merely advising the state commissioner of education, as is the case in Massachusetts, to large control of the entire educational system in certain other states. The New York Board of Regents has greater powers and duties than the state board in any other commonwealth. The tendency of legislatures has been to grant the boards an increasing amount of control, and in most states this now includes supervision over all public schools.

These powers and duties are exercised with the assistance of the chief state school official. Again it was New York that was first to make provision for such a position when in 1812 its legislature enacted a law providing for a state superintendent of common schools. In January, 1813, the appointment to this office of Gideon Hawley (1785–1870) made him the first state superintendent in the United States. There is today a variety of names used for this office but most common are the titles of Superintendent of Public Instruction in 21 states and Commissioner of Education in 12. The term of office is usually set by law at either two or four years, but a few states now prescribe an indefinite tenure.

The office is explicitly provided for in the constitutions of more than two-thirds of the states. Many of the features frequently prescribed are: manner of selecting the incumbent, eligibility requirements for the position, term of office, salary, and certain of the powers and duties. The state superintendent, it should be noted, often must work under handicaps placed on his office by the constitution and statutes that went into effect many years ago when living conditions were entirely different.

In some states, unfortunately, there has developed a two-headed organization in which at times the state board of education and the state superintendent are at loggerheads with each other concerning policies and administration. This occurs quite often when the state board is appointed by the governor and the superintendent gains election by popular vote. The trend today is toward appointment of the state school chief by the board with which he must work. This not only maintains harmony but also attracts outstanding individuals who might refuse to face elections at stated intervals due to the unpleasantness so often attached to political races. The importance of this office can be more fully realized when it is remembered that, in the number of people employed and the amount of money expended, public education is by far the largest of all businesses in each of the American states.

Especially since World War I the state has been gradually regaining a large measure of the authority over schools that previously it had delegated to local districts. Many educational leaders are of the opinion that there should be an even greater degree of centralization of educational functions in the state government. They complain that especially in small towns they are at the mercy of "amateurs" on school boards.

This situation has frequently led legislatures to adopt the administrative policy of placing schools in rural areas under more rigid control than the big city school systems.

County School Administration

The county form of government was imported from England. During colonial times religious and economic conditions favored the town unit in New England while the larger county seemed much better suited for purposes of government elsewhere. Later, as the sparsely settled territories were being made into new states, the county rather than the town became the intermediate governmental unit between the village or rural inhabitants and the state. There are today more than 3,000 counties which vary in size from 22 to 20,175 square miles (San Bernardino County, California) and in population from approximately a hundred citizens in certain sparsely settled rural areas to more than 6,000,000 in Los Angeles County, California. These counties as intermediate units are charged with much of the administrative routine and detail of government, including education.

The office of the county superintendent of schools began about 1835, and by the 1870's was common in most of the older states, New England excepted. Thereafter this office frequently was created even before a territory became a state. As need for such an officer developed, his work was legalized by an amendment to the constitution, or inserted when the constitution was being revised. Sometimes his position was created merely by legislative statute. In certain instances it was evolved out of some other county office, such as auditor, treasurer, or probate judge. In a few southern states and Iowa the county superintendency grew out of the presidency of the county board of education. In the earlier years of this position the duties were almost entirely clerical—keeping records, making reports on the number of schools and their attendance, and enforcing school laws.

Most county superintendents are still being chosen on a partisan or nonpartisan ballot at either a regular or special election, even though authorities favor their selection by a professional county board of education in order to take the schools as far as possible out of local politics. The most common term of office is still two years but gradually it is being increased to four. Sometimes the incumbent is ineligible for reelection after serving four years—a restriction that has been attacked on the grounds that it robs an important office of the value of experience. Some states today are beginning to require a certain amount of teaching experience and a supervisory certificate for eligibility to the county superintendency—records show that some occupants have had as little as a fourth-grade education. Other states, in reorganizing their basic structure, have abolished the office.

In addition to such administrative details as making annual reports to the state superintendent, preparing teacher payrolls for the county treasurer, notifying local districts of the amount of school funds apportioned to them, and filling vacancies on district boards, the county superintendent serves as supervisor in enforcing the use of the official course of study. As an inspector he examines school property and premises, orders the necessary repairs and alterations, sets his own teachers' examinations, and examines those pupils about to graduate from elementary schools. As a legal representative of the state he interprets the school laws and acts as technical adviser to the local boards.

Usually the most important work of the county superintendent is with rural and village schools outside the larger city systems. He and his staff have the important responsibility of helping these rural people educationally, socially, and economically. In making available satisfactory educational facilities for pupils in agricultural regions, the county superintendent must consider such factors as migrations of population, income and taxes of farmers, and the occupational changes and expectations of the people.

It must be remembered that about half of the public schools in our nation are in rural areas and small towns. The county superintendent has a special obligation toward such pupils in aiding their teachers to become more effective, and this has always been an extremely difficult assignment because of the tremendous turnover in rural schools. Such schools traditionally have been the place where many teachers get their initial experience before joining the big city school systems.

The office of county school superintendent is much more important in some states than in others. Under a merger law in Pennsylvania, communities supervised by county superintendents continue to administer their local schools under the direction of a county board of directors. This body, elected in convention by the school directors of each county, is selected from the membership of local boards and functions under the guidance of the county superintendent. In Louisiana all except three cities are organized on the basis of parishes (the equivalent of counties), with a great deal of power lodged in the central boards of education. In Florida the city and county superintendency are combined, but the chief officer is known as the principal.

Utah is an excellent illustration of a strong county organization. It has 29 counties and only 40 school districts. Except for the first- and second-class cities of more than 75,000 population, all towns, villages, and rural areas are included in these county school districts. The first county consolidation became effective in 1905, and then 10 years later Utah made county consolidation mandatory. Now a county board of education of five members is chosen from representative districts, and it appoints a county superintendent to serve as its executive in the operation of schools throughout the county.

One of the most significant reform movements began in 1869 when Massachusetts enacted legislation permitting the consolidation of school districts, and in 1882 finally abolished the district system and restored the old town system from which the district system had evolved. Ohio in 1892 became the first state west of the Alleghenies to permit the union of two or more districts to form a consolidated school. Within the next 15 years 20 more states had authorized the consolidation of schools, and other states operating under some form of county unit began the work of consolidating local rural schools into larger units.

By pooling resources on a county basis there can be provided fewer but better schools, served by county buses and manned by better paid and better trained teachers. Colorado, Illinois, Indiana, Kentucky, Louisiana, Mississippi, North Carolina, North Dakota, Ohio, Oklahoma, and Texas have achieved especially notable results in their consolidation efforts. Some other states have not been so successful. Throughout its history this consolidation movement has met vigorous opposition from many enthusiasts for local and decentralized control. These citizens express fears that the county or state may usurp their rights. As examples of the struggle the respective cases of Illinois and Oklahoma may be cited.

Even before the consolidation movement got really started in Illinois, the 11,000 local school districts had been reduced to 9,000; by 1950, after the movement had gained momentum, there were but 3,000. The legislature had passed a law in 1945 permitting counties to set up survey committees and had given each county three years to make final recommendations for the merging of its school districts. Many areas did not wait for the committees to report but began immediately to organize what are called community school districts.

As reported in newspapers of that time the change was not easy. Educators and civic leaders had to fight "farmer stubbornness," a fear of increased taxes, and the opposition of local politicians bent on maintaining the status quo. But two factors favored the new approach: a shortage of teachers aggravated by an inability of smaller districts to match the higher salaries of city schools, and the examples of successful consolidated schools that were well publicized by the Illinois State Department of Public Instruction.

And now the Oklahoma story. After the State Supreme Court had upheld the new law abolishing 1500 one-room schoolhouses (legislation designed to cut the state's school costs and to boost its educational standards) trouble spots appeared here and there. Typical was the case of Waterloo. It was one of the 300 tiny Oklahoma communities that had appealed for exemption from the law and had been turned down. The parents complained that their children would have to wait in the early morning darkness, frequently in bad weather, for the school bus to take them on a two-hour ride to the city of Edmond.

The wife of a school board member lamented: "There are two churches. Half goes one way; half the other. But everybody used to meet in the schoolhouse." Also saddened was the teacher, a local woman, who had to seek employment elsewhere. Said she: "Every morning I got up with the sun, drove my 1938 Ford over dirt roads to the schoolhouse and lit the fire in the old stove. After that I swept, dusted, and oiled the pine floor. When my fifteen pupils arrived—some on foot, some on horseback, and some, in muddy weather, on tractors—the room was warm and clean. The new schools may have everything else, but they won't have the spirit of the old place."

Local School District System

Education in the United States is state-controlled, but most of the actual administration has been delegated to subdivisions known as school districts. These have various legalized names, such as city, county, town, township, common school, consolidated, central, community, joint-union elementary, township high, union high, and county high. Their average size in square miles ranges from five in Illinois and New York to 2,055 in Utah. Enrollments vary from one-room schools with about five pupils to the New York City public school system that enrolls in excess of a million children in its elementary, junior, and senior high schools.

Statistics in 1940 indicated there were then approximately 420,000 school board members. At the time those figures were released, in several of the states there existed the ridiculous situation of more trustees than teachers—many rural schools had governing boards of three or more members to direct the work of a single teacher. Since then steady progress has been made in the consolidation of school districts and the consequent elimination of trustees. Significant increases in state aid have been bringing about a transfer of powers and duties from the local administrative unit to the larger intermediate one, frequently the county.

Nevertheless the local school district remains as a powerful force in the shaping of American education. In order to understand how firmly this system is entrenched in the United States, let us look briefly at its historical development.

The early New England town usually was a small, compact settlement occupying an area extending several miles beyond the limits of the village; and it was truly a civic, religious, and social unit. The first American school laws passed in 1642 and 1647 by the colony of Massachusetts required the maintenance of schools under penalty of fines. Such town schools were at first supported in large part by tuition fees, later by pro-rata assessments on parents whose children were attending the school, and still later in some towns by a general property tax.

As people began scattering into outlying areas and found it impossible or inconvenient to send their children to the town for schooling, they demanded that the schoolmaster divide his time, teaching a few weeks in each of the rural communities. After considerable insistence there reluctantly was put into operation a makeshift plan known as the "moving school." When a teacher's time was being spent in the rural areas, children in town had no schooling. This for obvious reasons proved unsatisfactory to all parties concerned, so finally the outlying communities asked the towns for their portion of the property tax and agreed to maintain their own "district" schools independently of the towns.

In response to this demand the Massachusetts law of 1789 set up school districts. School committees in the respective districts were given the jurisdiction over education that had formerly been exercised centrally at the town meeting. Thus the law virtually destroyed the town system of school administration under which, in certain places, strong educational programs had been developed. Each school district was now empowered to raise money by taxation, select teachers, and determine details of instruction and supervision.

By the 1830's most school districts had become very small; most of them employed only one or two teachers and enrolled no more than a hundred pupils. Whenever the number of children in a community taxed the capacity of a school, it was customary to subdivide the district and set up a new school. In rapidly growing cities this process of subdivision proceeded until there were 10, 20, or even more school districts within the city limits. Inasmuch as each of these districts was a separate taxing unit that maintained its own school independently of the others, there resulted much confusion and inequality of educational opportunities. Many of the districts were run by men with little interest in educational progress. Moreover, even under the most wise and prudent management some districts were too poor to maintain respectable schools.

Eventually this problem was solved by the centralization of authority under a city school board with a superintendent as its chief executive. Providence, Rhode Island, in 1836 was the first to establish the office of city school superintendent; and other cities soon followed. However, there were certain notable exceptions. For instance, in 1853 Chicago still had seven school districts, each administered independently of the others. The city council that year appointed a school superintendent as the initial step in unifying the work of these various districts. Four years later the state legislature abolished the separate districts in Chicago, a move that at last brought about a unified school administration.

Unfortunately the district unit resulting originally from frontier conditions persists in rural areas in some states even to this day. Before the invention of automobiles and the building of good roads, the isolation of rural populations and simplicity of educational facilities encouraged the maintenance of small school districts. To organize rural schools into more efficient and economical larger administrative units has been a bitter and protracted struggle that today is still far from over. Many times proposals to enlarge local units for administration of schools in rural areas have met with defeat in state legislatures, especially in northern states. In the South, by contrast, all local governmental units traditionally have been large, partly as a result of the plantation type of agricultural life.

Some authorities now advocate that local districts be done away with entirely and that education be completely controlled by the state. Delaware, in effect, has accomplished this goal; and in recent years a number of other states have moved in the direction of adopting the state as the unit for financing all public education. This plan, of course, means eventual state control.

In the American states there exists considerable variation in the form taken by school districts. But essentially there are two types: one has direct control through an independent board of education; the other exercises indirect control since it is dependent upon some other governmental agency. Far more common is the first named, a direct control resulting from selection of school board members by popular election.

These independent boards sell bonds, collect taxes, and make use of the proceeds for the public schools of the district, subject only to the state and local laws, regulation of the state educational department, and public opinion. Usually the actual tax collections are assigned to the regular county or city assessors and collectors, who are legally obliged to carry out the instructions of the board of education regarding the turning over of school monies to the proper officials.

Under the dependent type of control the school board members are responsible to some local official or governmental body, such as mayor, city council, county commission, or county court. Sometimes they are elected by popular vote, but usually they are selected by the political leaders. Such school boards must depend upon some other governmental body to provide the necessary revenues for operation of the schools. Their budgets are subject to review and modification by other governmental groups, perhaps the city council or county court. School plants are usually erected out of general bond issues, and funds for the current expenses in operating the schools are appropriated from the general funds of the controlling governmental unit.

Educational authorities generally feel that local school districts should be politically and fiscally independent of city and county governments. They fear especially the effects of confusing educational and political issues—educational goals all too often are wrecked by politics. On the other hand, experts in the field of municipal government are equally agreed that education can be more efficiently controlled and financed when it takes its proper place alongside the other municipal governmental functions. They feel there is no more justification for the independence of schools than there would be for independence from the general city government of such departments as police, fire, health, and street-cleaning. Although the majority of the American people presently side with the viewpoint of the educators, this issue is by no means resolved.

Local School Board Control

Serving in the United States today as school board members are about 300,000 men and women, most of whom receive no compensation other than for expenses incurred in line with their duties. These people help direct one of the world's greatest financial investments that involves the management of valuable property, the annual expenditure of large sums of money, and the employment of a million teachers and tens of thousands of other employees. It is they who legally control a gigantic public enterprise that serves directly about 38,000,000 boys and girls and touches the lives of millions of men and women.

Yet many critics claim that the school board is the weakest link in our educational system. They point out that boards of education are frequently influenced by partisan politics and that some boards when appointed are the products of the "spoils system." Despite progress made in recent years toward establishing better professional relationships between board members and teaching staffs, often individuals are elected who have "an axe to grind," or else like to feel the satisfaction of making teachers "play up to them." Theoretically teachers should enjoy academic freedom and security of tenure, while the school board speaks and acts for all citizens of the community, unhampered by the influence of class or political restrictions. These, unfortunately, are ideals still far from universal attainment—but let us again take a brief glance backward to gain a better perspective as to the level we have reached.

The earliest colonial schools were planned and managed by the whole community—all the citizens had a voice in what was being done. It naturally followed that schools would be controlled locally since they were generally the result of community initiative and enterprise. With the passage of laws permitting and sometimes ordering the creation of schools supported by public taxation, the need for a group to administer educational matters became pressing.

When control via the town meeting proved impractical for the building of a schoolhouse or the employing of teachers, it became customary to appoint temporary committees. Then permanent committees began to replace the temporary ones as the amount of school business increased. Responsibility for enforcing and administering school laws at first was placed in the hands of such religious and civil officers as ministers, selectmen, magistrates, grand jurymen—officials chosen primarily for the performance of other duties rather than school affairs. It was not until a century after the passage in the 1640's of the first school laws that the direction of educational matters came to be invested in a special board charged with the administration of the school as its primary duty.

Although the 1946 yearbook of the American Association of School Administrators under the title of *School Boards in Action* did much to clarify the situation, there still exists confusion as to what are the exact functions of school boards.* This was indicated by the variety of names originally given to boards having control over schools. The term "board of education" is today the most common designation, but there are in

---

* The 1956 yearbook of the same organization was entitled *School Board–Superintendent Relationships*. It provided a more particularized account of the roles and responsibilities of board members vis-à-vis administrators.

use such names as "school committee," "school board," "board of school supervisors," "board of school directors," "board of school trustees," "board of school inspectors," "board of school commissioners," and "board of school superintendents."

The size of school boards has varied widely, depending upon the functions delegated to them, the processes by which they were formed, the area of the districts, and the general organization of the state school systems. Membership of the earlier boards varied from more than 60 to as few as three. With the advent of professionally trained superintendents, business managers, and other educational specialists who gradually assumed the administrative duties, there naturally resulted a reduction in the size of the boards. This sometimes came about as a result of an amended city charter whereby representation on the board was changed from a ward basis to representation at large.

Later some states fixed by law the maximum number of board members for school districts. For example, Ohio in 1913 restricted the size of boards for city districts to five or seven members. Pennsylvania classified its school districts according to population and fixed the size of boards accordingly. New York City, with its population of almost 8,000,000, now has a board of education of nine members appointed by the mayor. A membership of seven to nine is generally considered ideal for cities and five for the smaller districts. Incidentally, in New York City there are also 54 local school boards, each with five members, under the control of the central board. The local groups exercise very little authority but serve to keep headquarters aware of district problems.

During the present century there has been a growing realization of the potentially greater efficiency of smaller school boards; large ones are likely to degenerate into debating societies where there is much talk but little accomplishment. Big unwieldy boards usually make necessary the appointment of numerous committees, with the result that the board members cease acting as a unit. Frequently it is difficult to obtain a quorum for a meeting, and even when there is a quorum, matters of the greatest importance are often decided by a majority of those present who are but a minority of the full board membership. Also, those serving on large boards may fail to realize the importance of their position; each assumes that since he is only one of a large group his vote will count for practically nothing.

On the other hand, a board limited to three members may tend to become much of a one-man affair. There have been all too many instances of an individual, or the group he represents, dictating educational policies that neglect the general welfare. Every graduate school of education has at least one master's thesis detailing cases of serious damage to schools because of domination by selfish board members. Two cases from California can be cited as typical.

One superintendent was "fired" unceremoniously—an act which has been quite a common occurrence in numerous communities. Unlike the great majority of schoolmen finding themselves in similar situations, this ex-superintendent did not seek employment elsewhere but remained to establish himself in a thriving business. In due time he was elected to a three-man school board, and from then on his main ambition in life seemed to be to fortify his own ego by making life miserable for the local teaching staff, especially the superintendent. In each annual election to fill one vacancy, that community was so closely divided that a matter of three or four votes usually decided whether or not the ex-superintendent would have the balance of power to permit him to carry on his personal feud against the educators in office. At any rate, the inevitable result was a continuous turnover in teaching staff and a poorly stabilized educational service. As always happens, the greatest losers were the children of that community.

And here is the other "horrible example." A woman superintendent of an elementary school district had served for 17 years in a community where the three churches stood on the same street. She managed to avoid the fate of her predecessors who had joined one church and then had found the other two-thirds of the town against them—this wise woman retained her church membership in nearby Los Angeles. However, there arrived the time when she felt that an especially ornery lad had to be thrashed in the interest of maintaining order over the entire school. The erring youngster was disciplined with a witness present in accordance with California's legal restrictions.

It so happened that the boy was the son of a hot-tempered citizen who had not fared well in school himself. And so he became the spearhead of one of those all-too-common local movements to oust the superintendent. Logically his first step was to get elected to the school board to be in a strategic position to make things disagreeable. Then the following year a crony of his gained membership on the three-man board. This, of course, doomed the tenure of the woman superintendent despite her 17 years of satisfactory service.

Most Americans accept the school board plan of control "for better or for worse," content that no matter what may happen to the efficiency of the schools it is, after all, the democratic way to do things. Not many years ago there were consistent demands that school boards be abolished and that education be made the responsibility of trained professional people. Critics pointed out that the annual turnover of teachers in the United States sometimes was running as high as 30 per cent, and, before tenure became so well established, often exceeded 40 per cent. It was observed that in Australia, by contrast, the annual turnover was less than 2 per cent.

Australia is a much younger country. When ready to create a school system, educators and laymen came to both the United States and European countries to observe, investigate, and recommend whatever administrative procedures and teaching techniques they considered should be adopted at home. Those visitors paid us the great compliment of copying more American than European procedures. But they turned thumbs down on our plan of local school board control. Australia established a centralized school system in which professionally trained personnel determine salaries, tenure, promotion, and other factors that make for the efficiency and stability of a profession. Noteworthy were figures released in the 1930's showing that about 60 per cent of the Australian teachers owned their own homes at that time. In America it was then estimated that probably less than 10 per cent were home owners. This figure, fortunately, has been greatly improved in recent years, thanks to teacher tenure laws.

It is fortunate that some able men and women do seek positions on local school boards, despite the fact that they must serve without pay and will frequently find themselves involved in nasty community fights. An all-important fact is that education is basically a responsibility of our whole society, and not of a professional group alone. Local school board control, as an example of the workings of democratic government, is at once the strength and the weakness of the American school system. It is strong in that all the people have a direct interest and voice in school affairs; weak, because the system is vulnerable to the attacks of scheming politicians and self-seekers.

The *American School Board Journal* has been published for many years, thus indicating the interest of members in their work. The fact that school trustees are beginning to recognize their position in the management of schools as policy makers and not administrators is encouraging. A very significant development in recent years has been the banding together of school boards in the common cause of education. Board members have been joining county and state organizations to discuss their mutual problems, and the state associations are now linked together in the National Council of State School Board Associations. Moreover, the National Association of Public School Boards and Members was established in 1938. Finally, it should be noted that many board members are now attending the annual conventions of the American Association of School Administrators, as well as their own national conventions.

Legal Authority of School Boards

The legal status of school districts is unique. They are quasi-corporations resembling business corporations, but they exist only for the performance of certain limited public duties and not for profit. Such powers as their corporate boards possess are derived from the state; their authority is controlled, extended, or limited by the state just as it sees fit. Nor should it be overlooked that there are several kinds of powers exercised by school boards.

Mandatory duties are those expressly demanded by statute, such as the taking of the school census. Ministerial duties are the ones prescribed exactly, thus involving no exercise of judgment; but when statutes specify what must be done without directing how it is to be done, such duties are said to be directory. Duties which involve personal judgment and the weighing of values are called discretionary; since these are not mandatory, they may or may not result in action. The courts are in quite general agreement in granting wide implied discretionary powers to enable boards to perform the duties considered necessary to the best interests of the schools.

In the absence of specific statutory authority, courts have ruled that discretionary powers permit boards to employ a school superintendent, physicians, and nurses; to require physical examinations; to employ and discharge teachers; to exercise disciplinary control over pupils; to allow students to do practice teaching in public schools; and to insure school property. However, boards have been denied exercise of discretionary powers in performance of whatever acts courts have deemed in conflict with statute law or beyond the purpose for which schools are established. Schools may employ nurses, dentists, and physicians to examine pupils but cannot give treatments since that represents an invasion of the field of medicine and is alien to the powers of a school district.

It is important to note that discretionary powers cannot be delegated because they involve the judgment of the school board. Thus the superintendent may interview teachers and be responsible for having contracts prepared and signed, but the actual appointment must be made by the board itself. However, as previously stated, courts have generally proved very lenient in their interpretations of discretionary powers so long as it appears that the boards are acting in good faith.

Unless the statutes require that contracts shall be in writing, oral contracts are valid. Under common law a simple majority of those present may bind the corporate board. This means that blank ballots usually have the effect of voting in favor of letting a given contract. School boards, like individuals and corporate boards, have the legal right to withdraw bids before contracts have been consummated. They may also rescind their own action before it has been acted upon by the other contracting party. Board members as individuals do not have the power to act for the district; they must act together in session, at which time their action becomes that of a corporate body.

However, boards may ratify at a later date such irregular contracts as the ones made by board members acting individually, those made by employees acting without previous authority from the board, and contracts made informally when the school board has not been in corporate session. But a board can ratify no contract that extends beyond its contractual powers. Ratification may be either formal or implied; the latter takes place when a board, after obtaining knowledge of the material facts, acquiesces to the contract. When the material facts are known, acceptance of services or use of property commonly constitutes ratification in the eyes of the law.

Occasionally some organization makes a request to use school property on either a rental or free basis and is denied that privilege. That, most courts now rule, is a discretionary power of an implied nature over which school boards exercise control. But, in general, courts have not permitted school properties to be used for activities essentially conducted for commercial gain. The reasoning is: schools are not business corporations; hence they have no legal right to enter business ventures. While boards may possess the right to allow school property to be used for certain activities so long as such use does not interfere with school efficiency, they cannot be compelled to do so. However, in all these matters the statute law of each state governs the situation as to the specific powers of local school boards. In decisions of the past few years, the courts have been permitting wider use of school property for community activities.

In selecting teachers, school boards are granted broad discretionary powers. They may prescribe qualifications in addition to those required by statute so long as such requirements are not arbitrary, unreasonable, or contrary to public policy. Thus boards may make sex a factor in the employment of teachers; they may refuse to hire those who are affiliated with certain unions and organizations. Also, any rights of taxpayers or patrons to direct a board in its selection and dismissal of teachers are practically nonexistent. Generally speaking, it can be said that the law commits the government and conduct of schools to the discretion of the board and places it beyond that of patrons. So long as the board employs such certified teachers as the law authorizes it to employ, the patrons cannot interfere by injunction or otherwise, merely because other more competent and satisfactory teachers might be found.

School boards possess wide discretionary powers to regulate pupil management and conduct. In the absence of statutory limitations it is left to the board to determine who shall be admitted to the school and what the requirements for admission shall be. Courts have held that boards possess the authority to exclude pupils from school when they have physical or mental defects, or when for other reasons their presence is judged to be detrimental to the best interests of the school. Negroes in the South have heretofore been excluded from white schools, but recent Supreme Court decisions have made racial segregation unconstitutional.

Boards have the right to make reasonable rules governing the conduct of pupils both in school and off the school grounds during school hours—or at any time so long as the rules enacted are necessary to the general discipline, morale, and welfare of the school. In one unusual case that came to trial, a pupil's father was fined because the lad made faces and swore at a passing teacher while standing on his own front porch on a Saturday morning. The court ruled that the teacher's value to the community had been impaired by such actions.

A teacher or school administrator may suspend a pupil temporarily; but only the board has the authority to expel him, and courts have held that expulsion does not extend beyond the current year. However, it has been held that when the presence of a pupil is detrimental to the discipline of the school, and the board declines to expel him, a teacher may refuse to teach and can recover his salary for the term of the contract. Also, in the absence of statutory regulations, boards are limited in their authority to require a pupil to study specific subjects, but they may withhold his diploma unless a prescribed course of study is followed.

Origin of Administrative Officers

When increasing enrollments in the early American schools brought about employment of more than one teacher, it was found advisable to appoint one of them as head teacher or "principal" as he later came to be called. Thus the principal was the first professional officer with administrative and supervisory duties. However, neither the principalship nor other administrative positions developed extensively before the nineteenth century. After 1830 the trend toward extreme localization of school control began to reverse itself. With the new movement toward centralization there came a tremendous growth of educational administration and supervision in the cities and in the state school systems.

Enthusiastic executive leadership of individuals characterized the evolution of administrative officers. In other words, the man made the job. The first city school superintendent was appointed in Buffalo in 1837. Louisville, Kentucky, also claims the honor of having established the office that year. More superintendencies were created as school committees in big cities found their responsibilities to be increasingly time-taking and onerous. For instance, one trustee in Springfield, Massachusetts, complained that to execute his duties faithfully would require two whole days of the working week, and he simply could not afford to give that much time. As another example, minutes of one school committee pointed out there was no one charged with the duties of looking into the best type of school architecture, deciding what is good teaching and helping teachers to correct their deficiencies, looking for good replacements in case vacancies should occur, organizing new schools, and seeing that important business comes before the school committee. Such circumstances seemed to point to the need of having someone give his full time to the management of the schools. Consequently, before the Civil War nearly all the larger cities had created the office of superintendent of schools.

The concurrent rise of public education and rapid growth of cities so expanded municipal school systems as to put them financially in the class of "big business." Appropriately, then, educational adminstration was largely patterned on the corporate form of organization that had proved so successful in the business world—the school board became the legislative body making the policies, and the chief executive officer was made responsible for the actual administration. However, a long struggle has been waged to have school boards accept the spirit as well as the form of this type of administrative organization. Even today some school boards insist on meddling in the field of administration.

We now think of the superintendency as demanding the highest professional qualifications, so it is hard to believe that the early incumbents frequently were laymen rather than educators. In some cases the school committee appointed one of its own members, generally the secretary. In Los Angeles, 13 of the first 21 superintendents were laymen—businessmen, clergymen, doctors, lawyers.

But in many school systems from the very beginning a principal or teacher was selected to become superintendent, and in the course of time it became customary to appoint only educators to the position. Sometimes the mayor or city council had the power of appointment, making it quite possible for political considerations to prevail to such an extent that the office failed to attract well-qualified men. In certain cities the school superintendent had to run for office in popular elections. That situation prevailed in San Francisco in the 1920's.

In the evolution of the office the initial duties were administrative and supervisory. As an administrator the superintendent had the responsibility of keeping records and of making reports to both his local board and state educational department. He saw to the repair of school buildings and looked after supplies. When compulsory attendance laws were enacted, their enforcement was his responsibility. In supervision the superintendent's job was to coordinate the instructional program as a whole. As there developed a graded system of schools, he logically was in the best position to regulate promotions and to inspect the work going on in the various buildings and classrooms. It was he who developed the early courses of study. Incidentally, it was unthought of at that time to seek the cooperation of those who actually did the teaching.

At first many laymen opposed the creation of the superintendent's office out of fear of "one-man control." Nor did the taxpayers relish the thought of establishing a new administrative position requiring a higher salary than that of a teacher. Also, some principals and teachers fought it because they wished to retain things as they were in the loose way permitted by decentralized administrative control. But the greatest opposition came from the school board members themselves because many of them were reluctant to transmit their powers to any other authority.

From colonial times the legal control of public schools has been vested by statutes in the school boards, and not until quite recently has the office of superintendent gained statutory recognition. Under a legal situation in which his powers were merely delegated to him, each superintendent wielded just as much power as he was able to win from his board by gaining their confidence in his personal and professional abilities. This accounts in large part not only for the indefinite boundary line between the powers of the board and those of the superintendent, but also for the uneven growth of this office in different cities. All too many boards still delegate only petty clerical and technical supervisory duties and refuse their executive officer any real powers in such professional matters as selecting teachers and making budgets.

Business affairs of the earlier schools were managed by the school committees. Sometimes a member, usually the clerk, was made the special business agent and paid a salary for his services. Connecticut in 1841 passed a law authorizing a "school committee" to be responsible for business affairs and school properties, and a "board of school visitors" to oversee instructional matters. The duties of the first-named committee eventually were placed in the hands of a "director of schools," and the latter in those of a superintendent.

Thus it was that the office of business manager was evolved along with that of superintendent; and there developed a dual control of schools which generally proved unsatisfactory because of the inevitable conflicts involved. The better plan of school organization now places the business manager subordinate to the superintendent of schools. In the earlier history of school districts business affairs were simple and required but little time or training for their management. Today the complex business organization of a modern school system demands adeptness in budgetary procedures. This involves such matters as financial and unit-cost accounting, purchasing and distributing supplies, and weighing immense construction expenditures against the funds available.

Organization of Supervision

Supervision is that phase of administration that deals directly with the development and management of the school life of pupils. In colonial times supervision was first performed by the local pastors and later by school committees. It consisted of visits to the school, inspection of classroom and equipment, and oral examinations of pupils to ascertain their mastery of subject matter. Those last-day-of-the-term sessions were certain to be nerve-racking for the teacher whose work was being judged through quizzing of the children.

After it had become necessary to employ a superintendent, inspections by laymen gradually ceased, and this responsibility was delegated to the new administrative officer. Thus the first professional supervisor (in most school codes) was the superintendent charged with the duties of visiting the schools, directing the work of the teaching staff, and inquiring into the proficiency of instruction.

However, in those earlier days of the superintendency the principals and teachers continually resisted the efforts to unify the educational program through supervision. The principals still had direct access to the school committee and frequently made use of it when they disapproved the acts of the superintendent. In fact, many of the failures of nineteenth-century superintendents were due to this political maneuvering of the principals. So long as the superintendent lacked real administrative powers of selection, promotion, transfer, or dismissal, his success often depended upon his political know-how.

At the turn of this century the responsibility of superintendents for the general direction of the instructional program had been fairly well established, at least in the elementary field. High school principals retained considerable independence for an even longer period, and there are still school districts where the secondary school program is just beginning to become completely integrated with programs in the lower grades.

Along with the recognition that supervision is an integral part of the general administrative program, there came the realization that the building principal occupies the most strategic position for performing its functions. The principal serves as an organizer, manager, and supervisor—in this last capacity he actually should be a teacher of teachers. The objection is sometimes raised that a principal cannot be expected to have an expert knowledge of all the various subject fields in the curriculum; therefore, the reasoning goes, he seldom is qualified to supervise all phases of instruction.

It is true that in the past most principals relied heavily on their own teaching experience as a criterion for evaluating the work of faculty members. Of course, the practical value of their basis for judgment should not be underestimated. Intelligent supervisors were able to recognize good, bad, or indifferent instruction whether or not they were intimately acquainted with the subject fields or grade levels. Certain precepts, rooted in common sense, apply to all good teaching.

However, the idea that a would-be principal must receive specialized training for the job has spread in recent decades. Graduate schools of education now enroll thousands of men and women studying for administrative positions in towns and cities throughout the country. Large cities like New York put candidates through a battery of grueling examinations which test not only their potential ability in administration and supervision but also their knowledge of all the areas of the curriculum.

In the smaller school systems, theoretically at least, supervision should consume a major portion of the superintendent's time. But in the larger systems it commonly is delegated to subordinates and now has been developed into a highly specialized service. Regardless of how much of this work is delegated, responsibility for its results still rests on the superintendent.

Until recent years supervision was focused on the teacher. It was largely a matter of evaluating personalities, determining cleverness or lack of it in discipline, and checking on the details of classroom procedures. Such supervision emphasized uniformity and demanded strict adherence to detailed courses of study that had been designed to inculcate certain knowledge and common skills. There were two fundamental criteria: Could the teacher control the class? Were administrative edicts being strictly followed? This led to the development of rating cards to be filled out by the one supervising at the time of a classroom visit. A question long debated was whether or not the teacher should be shown the rating card inasmuch as it was kept on file for possible use against him at some future date. Naturally many teachers resented this form of paternalism and sneeringly labeled supervision as "snoopervision."

When such new subjects as art, manual training, music, and physical education were being introduced into the curriculum, there arose a need for special supervisors. The initial task of establishing a new subject is to construct a course of study to be adapted to the various grade levels of the school system. Then, because so few of the regular teachers have had previous experience with the new teaching field, it usually becomes necessary to institute a program of teacher-training. Finally there comes the work of directing and supervising classroom instruction in the new area.

However, as soon as any special subject becomes established as an accepted part of the curriculum, teacher-training institutions begin to include it in their program of preservice training for prospective teachers. Thus, after a subject has become implanted in the curriculum, the necessity of having special supervisors usually disappears. Logically those special supervisors are selected because of their expert knowledge and training in a particular field, so there have always been the dangers of overemphasis and of failure to correlate with other subjects. This is one of the reasons that some large cities have dropped such supervisors.

Twentieth-century research has caused changes in the concepts of supervision. Application of scientific methods to the problems of education now makes it possible to produce more accurate evaluations of teaching procedures. Measuring results of the school program in terms of the changes effected in pupils has brought with it an intense interest in the nature of the child and his needs in relation to the social order. As a result, supervision is focused not so much upon the teacher as upon the pupil and upon the changes wrought in him by his experiences in school. "Creative supervision" is one of the labels given to this new approach. It concentrates on the task of providing for the growth and improvement of teachers, for building flexible and dynamic courses of study, and for providing educational diagnoses as the means of insuring adequate growth and development of the American school population. The new definition of a supervisor is "one who frees teachers to teach." He is a leader and helper, rather than a critic.

However, so long as human beings are just that, supervision will never entirely escape the dictatorial tendencies of strong-willed or blindly stubborn individuals in positions of authority. In the 1920's, for example, one large western city had a woman supervisor who was so enthusiastic over the project method then sweeping our educational world that she insisted that each elementary schoolteacher must have her class build a project. Some of the less timid souls virtually defied the supervisor and delayed the building of a project. It was not long before they heard in no uncertain terms directly from the superintendent to whom the supervisor appealed. From then on teachers remained long hours after school to erect the projects depicting life in Japan, China, and elsewhere. It made no difference that the children had very little to do with building the more artistic projects; those were the ones that received high praise and formal recognition in the superintendent's bulletin. The poorer projects, amateurish because the children themselves had done the work, brought forth sarcastic remarks and veiled threats of retaliation. In the meantime much of the remaining school work became badly neglected—and certainly that supervision was detrimental rather than helpful.

In following the twentieth-century trend of trying to make education a science, supervisors began to encourage teachers to engage in research projects themselves. It was thought that carrying such work through to completion would improve their grasp of instructional problems. As a similar means of subtle supervision following World War I, teachers were included on committees for curriculum revision in the hope of upgrading the quality of instruction.

Over the years in school systems large enough to employ a number of administrative officers there have been developed two general types of supervisory organizations, but it would be difficult to find any that could be called a "pure" type. In the more common dualistic plan teachers are responsible to the building principal for discipline, records, reports, promotions, and other matters outside those immediate instructional activities under the control of subject supervisors. Both principals and supervisors, in turn, are responsible for their activities to the superintendent's office. Of course, it depends largely upon the policies and attitudes of the superintendent, but there is always the danger that the authority of the principal may be subordinated to that of the subject supervisor, or authority of supervisor to that of the principal. The dualistic supervisory organization frequently invites personal jealousies and conflicts; its success is conditioned upon a clear statement and understanding of policies and lines of authority, a proper coordination of the work, and efficient leadership by the superintendent and his staff.

Line-and-staff supervision is so called because of similarities to the organization of army personnel. Superintendents, principals, and other administrative officers represent the line; heads of such departments as personnel, buildings and equipment, tests and measurements, and curriculum are the staff members who have little or no authority over the line officers and teachers. There is a direct and definite line of authority down from the superintendent through subordinate executives to the teachers. Those possibilities of conflict so inherent in the dualistic system are eliminated by the simple process of divesting the staff of authority. The job of staff officers is to furnish such services as conducting experiments and investigations, analyzing and diagnosing problems arising in operation of the educational program, and providing the schools with necessary materials.

Development of School Finance

Since instructional programs and buildings require large expenditures of money, finding ways and means to finance them has always been a basic problem in the management of schools. The study of educational history from ancient to modern times shows that until relatively very recent years the chief sources of financial support were private. The student usually paid for the privilege of being instructed, which meant that education was largely limited to the upper economic classes.

Among the earliest ways of making instruction available to more than just the economically self-sufficient were charitable gifts contributed to the support of schools. Such donations became quite common during the Renaissance, but the support always had the unfortunate characteristic of being neither regular nor dependable. Somewhat greater stability was achieved in the later chantry schools as developed from endowments left to engage a priest to sing masses for the repose of the testator's soul. Teaching duties were frequently assigned, and with good management those chantry bequests made in the form of trust funds could insure to a school a more or less steady income for a considerable period of time.

When the Industrial Revolution began in England during the

eighteenth century great wealth became concentrated in the hands of a few individuals. This brought about an enormous increase in the size of trust funds. In America the British mercantile theory of trade delayed our Industrial Revolution. That fact and the frontier conditions postponed the accumulation of great fortunes; and so, educational trusts or foundations were somewhat late in making an appearance.

However, motivated almost entirely by religious fervor, there started early a small but steady flow of philanthropic gifts to Latin schools, academies, and colleges. These continued throughout the seventeenth and eighteenth centuries, and thereafter their size and number increased rapidly. As fortunes were being accumulated from the tapping of our vast natural resources, princely endowments were laying the foundations for some of America's great universities. This lavish philanthropy has continued to the present time, checked only by increasingly heavy income and inheritance taxes.

After the Civil War, with the South prostrate, there appeared still another type of foundation. Its object was not to subsidize teaching directly, but rather to supplement and assist schools already in operation. Typical was the fund established in 1867 by George Peabody (1795–1869) of Massachusetts, amounting in time to $3,500,000. The trustees were instructed to administer it for education of whites and Negroes in the war-ravaged states. Peabody wisely made the provisions of the trust elastic enough so the money could be disposed according to changing needs. Both white and colored schools were established in cities and towns; states were assisted in setting up school systems; salaries of rural school supervisors were paid, and teachers' institutes financed. In 1875 there was founded a normal school at Nashville, later to become the George Peabody College for Teachers.

John D. Rockefeller's (1839–1937) initial gift of $40 million to set up the General Education Board, and an approximation of this sum by Andrew Carnegie (1835–1919) to establish projects like the Carnegie Institute and the Carnegie Foundation for the Advancement of Teaching, are twentieth-century developments. But probably the most far-reaching foundation is the one established in 1936 by Henry Ford (1863–1947) and his son Edsel Ford (1893–1943). In 1959 alone the Ford Foundation made new grants and appropriations totaling approximately $114 million for education and other areas of national importance. The Ford Fund for the Advancement of Education has sponsored experiments and research to improve the schooling of youngsters all over the country. Vast sums of money have been allocated not only to curricular projects but also to new kinds of school buildings and to scholarships for promising students.

The average citizen applauds all this philanthropy since it helps the younger generation and costs the taxpayer nothing. But there are many who decry appropriations by big companies as a tax dodge. Furthermore, some schoolmen worry that various private foundations may insidiously dictate the course of education by their very selection of projects to underwrite. They feel that greater public support of schools must come through a broader tax base at the local level or through some kind of federal support. Their essential claim is that the schools have become "beggars" because they have relied for finances almost solely on the local property tax.

When a government is authorized to tax property, it is true that the authority may be used to such an extreme that the property will not be worth the tax. Despite dangers involved in granting governments this authority to tax, such a power is absolutely essential. Otherwise government would not be possible and a political state could not exist. Aversion to a general property tax for schools was general everywhere in early nineteenth-century America. Rather than tax themselves directly even in periods of rapidly increasing interest in education, citizens had recourse to taxes on marriage licenses, billiard halls, and liquors.

The most common method of raising money in the middle and southern states was by lotteries, and at first the religious denominations found little or no objection to their use. Whenever schools, academies, or colleges wished to raise money in this way, the usual procedure was to apply to the state legislatures for permission. If approval came, the state sometimes even supervised the lottery. Columbia University and the University of North Carolina, in their earlier years, were aided by lotteries which are now almost universally condemned.

Prior to the 1840's even the largest of American cities had no public schools in the present meaning of the word. So-called school societies, supported principally by local subscriptions, gave instruction to poor children. Most famous of these was the New York Free School Society, organized in 1805 under the leadership of De Witt Clinton (1769–1828). It was chartered as a nonsectarian organization to provide education for those poor children who were not already attending the schools of any religious society. During nearly a half-century it financed numerous schools, trained teachers, and educated more than 600,000 children.

From time to time the state and city contributed to the support of these schools, and in 1831 the legislature authorized the grant of a half-mill tax. In 1835 the New York Free School Society turned over its buildings and equipment to the school board in New York City for the use of public schools for all children regardless of the economic status of their parents. Likewise, in Philadelphia and Baltimore, similar societies educating poor children laid foundations for later tax-supported school systems.

An important step in the development of the idea of public education was the introduction into America of the Lancastrian monitorial schools, as promoted in England by Dr. Andrew Bell (1753–1832) and Joseph Lancaster (1778–1838). This was, in effect, a "production line" administrative teaching plan in which a schoolmaster instructed monitors, who, in turn, taught groups of younger boys. It proved very popular where large numbers of children were to be taught by a single master—one teacher could control the instruction of as many as a thousand children. In some cases the per-pupil cost was reduced to less than a fourth of that required to maintain a pupil in a private school of that day.

This mechanical system showed very little concern for the immaturity of the children, and its chief recommendation lay in its devices for cutting down school costs. It did prove to be a big step forward in selling people the idea of taxing themselves for the support of public schools because at first glance it appeared as if education would be quite inexpensive. After this service had been performed the monitorial system sank rapidly in public esteem. The thought began to dawn that if there were to be tax-supported schools, they might just as well be the best.

Nevertheless, progress toward public school systems was slow. Taxation had been the outstanding issue of the Revolutionary War and was still so fresh in the public mind that political leaders moved very cautiously in proposing tax measures for any purpose except protection of life and property.

In such laws as were passed by state legislatures, usually the people in each community were given the right to say when, if, and how they should be taxed. Expenses of maintaining those earlier schools were partially met by granting to them any income from public lands set aside for that purpose, or from gifts to the schools. Collection of school money through rate bills was also carried forward from colonial times. New Jersey used this method as late as 1870, although rate bills had disappeared in most states during the first few decades of the century. Since families were charged on those rate bills according to the number of children in school, the larger households that usually could least afford it were penalized most.

As the frontier expanded with the westward movement of population, it was soon discovered that the cheapest and easiest way to reduce rate bills was through the sale of the nation's vast public domain. Connecticut was perhaps the first state to sense this possibility, and in 1795 established a permanent school fund of $1,200,000 by selling its claims to lands in Ohio. The management of this fund was exceptionally good, and by 1820 the income from the invested principal had grown so large that many communities stopped taxing themselves for schools or curtailed expenditures as the amounts paid by the state increased. Thus the unforeseen and unfortunate result of this excellent handling of a state school fund was that the quality of education actually declined!

Other states, especially the new western ones, were not so skillful or so honest in their management of permanent funds (sometimes called "literary" funds). For the most part the lands set aside for public schools by the Ordinance of 1787 were shamefully dissipated. Many states discounted the future growth of the country and sold their public lands for mere pittances; others made poor investments of the proceeds derived from the sale of their lands; some squandered their permanent school funds by borrowing from them and later repudiating the indebtedness. A few states tried later to make amends for this gross mismanagement by recognizing the amount of the lost endowment as a perpetual debt to the treasury on which the state pledged itself to raise annually by taxation the equivalent of the interest on the lost funds. This chimerical financing scheme (accomplished by "juggling" bookkeeping accounts) actually increased, not eased, the burden of taxation for school purposes.

Public school finance went through the stages of permissive legislation, then local option allowing the people in each district to decide whether they should tax themselves, and finally legislative enactments making school taxes mandatory on a statewide basis. Once the idea of taxation had been accepted, attention was centered upon the problems growing out of this relatively new method of financing schools. Taxation on real property became increasingly inequitable as the nation was being changed from agrarian to industrial. In those districts with thriving industries it proved much easier to raise money for schools than it was in rural districts. Less visible and thus more difficult to reach for taxation purposes was wealth represented by intangible assets—stocks and bonds, interest-bearing investments, and bank accounts.

Another complication has been the fact that the children most in need of educational advantages and the wealth of the nation so frequently are not located in the same areas. Ways and means of making more equitable distribution of educational opportunities are urgently needed.

Of the many remedies proposed in recent years, three have received the most serious attention. Already in process of fulfillment is the movement to enlarge the geographical size of administrative and attendance units. The second suggestion, as mentioned previously, is to relieve the local property owner by establishing a new kind of tax base. The third idea—federal support—will be discussed in the final chapter of this book.

Business Administration of Schools

Considering the amount of money spent today on schools, the American educational system is definitely "big business"—and it has frequently been under fire from taxpayers for real and alleged extravagances. Indubitably there has been prodigality in the disbursement of funds, but probably much less waste than in the expenditure of public monies for other purposes. In recent years school executives have been developing a science of business administration patterned somewhat upon the practices of thriving industries in which the managers know the cost of materials, labor, distribution, and overhead of every article produced.

Business executives are able by cost accounting to predict quite accurately how production costs will be affected by certain changes in manufacturing processes. While school superintendents are now able to account for, and even to forecast, future educational costs, there is definitely a limit as to how far scientific analyses can be carried when the products are human beings. The business world has a dollars-and-cents measuring rod of its profits and losses; the vocational, cultural, and spiritual values of the classroom defy immediate and exact measurement.

Not only administrators but also teachers and parents should understand how school monies are derived and spent. Such information may lead those whose vision seldom extends beyond their own immediate environment to appreciate the problems involved in keeping a school system properly financed.

It is especially true that those responsible for helping prepare the budget and for determining the curriculum ought to have available the per-pupil costs for housing, administration, supervision, supplies, instruction, and such school services as library, attendance, lunchroom, and the like. Some superintendents do object that such a policy puts the administration "on the spot" in justifying its distribution of financial support to a few favored projects. But usually when parents and teachers have been given an honest picture of educational costs, they tend to make greater efforts to stretch the taxpayer's dollar to respectable lengths.

Financial transactions are governed by the budget, which can be defined as a systematic statement which forecasts the probable expenditures and the anticipated revenues during a stated period of time. Specifically, the school budget is a spending plan that represents the policies adopted by a board of education for the fiscal year. To conform to the school term this usually runs from July 1 to June 30. In the past many budgets have merely been lump-sum guesses of income and expenditures. Modern business practice now demands that a budget be based on past records and carefully prepared estimates. Also included should be detailed information as to the source of receipts and reasons for unusual expenditures. The well-planned budget states its items so specifically that if any reductions are necessary, they will have to be made in terms of lower salaries, fewer services, or cheaper materials. At least the facts are there to make possible a sensible attack in the matter of required reductions.

Budget making is definitely the responsibility of the superintendent and his administrative staff; but, ideally, practically every employee contributes to the finished document. When on July 1 the officials of a school system begin the administration of an annual budget, they should also be starting the preparation of the budget for the following year. Some school boards still prepare their own budgets and even pointedly ignore the superintendent as an "impractical schoolmaster." This practice is highly unethical since the board's responsibilities are to review and approve, or demand changes—not to spell out in detail the original budget. If the superintendent lacks the ability to perform this all-important function, then he should be replaced by a better qualified man.

Ideally, as noted above, budget making is a combined effort of many people. The board sets the policy and in this framework the superintendent works out the particulars after consultation with his staff. When a budget is approved, it controls all fiscal matters pertaining to the school system and is binding alike on the school board and all its employees. Deviations from the budget are justified only in cases of extreme emergency, and then only after securing the consent of the approving authority.

It has been unfortunate that in many districts the approval of the school board is not final. The school budget is involved in the general city or county finances, thus making it subject to political considerations. In those states where the law requires that expenditures be limited to income, no choice is given in the matter of exceeding budgetary allowances. When the funds are expended, the school program must be curtailed or even stopped altogether.

Such dire possibilities create a tendency on the part of those making the budget to allow for plenty of leeway between estimates of expenditures and sources of income, so as to increase the likelihood of there being a balance at the end of the year. This deliberate practice of "padding the budget" leads to wasteful expenditures at the close of the school year wherever funds remain to the credit of the school district.

In the business management of a school system where many thousands of dollars are expended each year, it is highly essential that an accurate system of financial accounting be established, one that is as simple and uniform as thoroughness permits. For the most part school financial accounting systems have been patterned upon commercial practices. There was but little uniformity in public school accounting prior to 1912 when the Department of Superintendents of the NEA prepared a report on uniform records which has since been adopted rather generally as a standard method for recording financial data. It was indeed an important step forward when cost accounting was introduced into school administration to supply data for answering such questions as the per-pupil cost of maintaining attendance service and of teaching each elementary grade and high school subject.

In the management of public school monies there are involved collections, disbursements, and the protection of reserve funds. Because of constitutional requirements or legislative enactments, tax collections used to be poorly adjusted to the needs for funds. In some instances the major part of the school year had passed before local taxes became available for school use. That resulted in large-interest bills on temporary loans for payment of salaries and similar expenditures.

An important principle of business management is that every disbursement should be made by checks carrying the signature of both superintendent (or business manager) and board president, or some other bonded official authorized by the board of education to perform this function. Payment should not be made for goods except upon a properly rendered statement which has been checked against the materials actually received. If an endorsed check states the nature and time of the service rendered, it serves as sufficient receipt. On the other hand, a petty cash account always invites trouble. Many school systems manage without a petty cash account, purchasing stamps by check to the postmaster and running bills for such services as express, freight, and telegraph that are paid monthly or weekly by check.

Supplies constitute the small nonpermanent materials (exclusive of textbooks) used for instructional purposes, maintenance, and operation of the school plant; supplies are consumed with use. In contrast, equipment embraces the larger and more permanent items used in furnishing and maintaining the school plant; equipment is usually considered as lasting two years or more. Teachers frequently fail to realize that instructional supplies and equipment needed during the school year should be determined long before they are actually used. The earlier this need is determined, the more opportunity there is to consider source, quality, and price well in advance of need. The economic law of supply and demand operates to the extent that supplies and equipment can be bought for less during April and May, whereas the pressure of last-minute deliveries brings about a consequent rise in prices during August and September.

In small school systems the superintendent determines his supply budget by consulting teachers, clerks, and janitors as to their needs. He also checks storerooms to see what there is on hand; he studies the purchases and expenditures made in previous years. In addition, the probable changes in enrollment, curriculum, and methods must be given due consideration. These same procedures are used in the larger systems, but of necessity many of the responsibilities for determining needs are delegated to business assistants, principals, and supervisors.

Evolution of the Modern School Plant

Previous to the nineteenth century schools were rarely held in buildings specifically designed for educational purposes. In ancient Greece teachers frequently taught their followers in temples or on porches. Roman schools often met in *tabernae,* actually little more than booths off the street. Students in the medieval period usually found shelter in churches, while in both Europe and America in the seventeenth and eighteenth centuries many schools were held in homes of the masters or in buildings rented for that purpose.

Whenever the colonists found it necessary to build a schoolhouse, invariably it was a dingy, boxlike structure. A typical school had low ceilings, poor lighting, uneven heating, bad ventilation, and shocking sanitary facilities. Pupils sat on benches without backs and had only the crudest of equipment. Often these conditions worsened as the schoolhouses fell into sad states of disrepair.

The foremost leaders in the struggle to provide better housing were Horace Mann (1796–1859) and Henry Barnard (1811–1900), who made it a special objective of their state educational departments to try to improve the condition of school buildings. Barnard in 1848 authored *School Architecture,* the first outstanding American book on this subject.

Our earliest buildings were designed for ungraded schools in which children of all ages were gathered together in a single room where the teacher heard their lessons individually or in small groups. No notable change in architecture was made when the Lancastrian monitorial system came into vogue although the dimensions of the schoolrooms were increased virtually to the proportions of a hall. In order to provide the master with a commanding view of his entire class, it was necessary to have a teacher's platform or to build the school floor on an inclined plane.

Adoption of the grade school plan in the 1840's made necessary the provision of an individual room for each grade. About that same time auditoriums began to appear. Afterward they went out of favor, but still later their importance was renewed by a growing emphasis on music and dramatics. By 1900, innovations in the curriculum caused a demand for special rooms for kindergarten children, and workrooms for pupils interested in manual training, domestic and fine arts. The increasing popularity of gymnastics and athletics resulted in the addition of gymnasiums to school plants, and the inclusion of vocational subjects made necessary the addition of shops. Finally this sort of specialization, as begun in the design of individual classrooms, became the rule for entire buildings. And so, elementary schools are now being designed differently from secondary; technical and commercial high schools differ from academic; and, more recently, schools for the handicapped are being built on different functional plans from those for normal children.

After considerable trial and error it was discovered that in the construction of school plants the greatest economy of space and materials could be achieved in the shape of the letters E, H, I, L, T, and U. Such architectural planning allowed for the erection of additional rooms to accommodate future increases in school population. Brick and cement began to replace wood as building materials; and central heating plants were installed, eliminating the individual units for each room. Research studies indicated that unilateral lighting rather than windows on all sides should be used to prevent harmful glare on pupils' eyes. It was further determined there should be a ratio of at least one-fifth window space to floor area. Therefore, in the transition from the nineteenth to the twentieth century the classrooms were constructed on a more scientific basis and were much more conducive to health and efficiency than were the rooms in which colonial children had been taught.

Notable advances were also made in school equipment. The first major improvement came when the bare rough benches were replaced by seats with backs. The early desks were designed for two, three, or more; later, individual seats were installed. At first these had been screwed to the floor in fixed rows, but the coming of progressive education with its greater emphasis on freedom finally led to movable equipment. Such other conveniences as cloakrooms for children and closets for teachers made their appearance in due time; and now, at least in high schools, the cloakrooms have generally been supplanted by lockers.

The life of a school building varies from 20 to 100 years. If properly planned and maintained a well-built, fire-resistant structure will serve three, four, or more generations. This durability, however, has not always proved itself an unmixed blessing, as witness those buildings still in use with small windows, high ceilings, and antiquated architecture. Many of these remain as eyesores, still being used but lacking those elements needed for efficient modern education. School boards of previous eras "got their money's worth" in sturdy construction values, a fact dramatically shown in the 1933 Long Beach earthquake when the older buildings easily withstood the shocks while the newer, more beautiful ones crumbled, with the resultant charges of graft and corruption. If the school plants being erected today are to stand the tests of both time and educational progress, there must be a long-range view of probable changes taking place not only in education but also in the social and economic structure of American civilization. For this reason, educators are now giving considerable attention to demography—the statistical study of population.

The problem of predicting school enrollment trends is a complicated one. First, national factors must be considered. For instance, in the 1950's school planners had to take into consideration the "baby boom" in World War II and in the Korean conflict. Apparently more buildings would be needed for those infants as they reached school age. The respite provided in the 1930's, when population expansion had been temporarily halted, was definitely over.

But national statistics cannot be used alone on the local level. Migration patterns must be taken into account. For example, in recent years certain cities in New England suffered a decline in population because their industries had closed down. On the other hand, the population of some southern cities boomed because new factories were opening every year.

New York City is an interesting example of how an out-migration pattern has been balanced by an in-migration flow. On the one hand, upper middle-class families have been moving to the suburbs; on the other hand, Puerto Ricans and Negroes from the South have been pouring into the city. Moreover, the flow has not been a steady one, but has been affected by the economic conditions. Thus, if there is a recession the number of Puerto Ricans landing at the airports declines sharply. The word gets around quickly in San Juan that jobs in the great metropolis are hard to find.

In growing suburbs school planners must study the curve of the population expansion over the last few decades and must keep records of construction of private homes and apartment houses, not only as to volume but also as to quality. Low-cost housing units bring more children than do expensive developments. In this connection, the telephone company's analysis of the number of families gained or lost in a given area is sometimes used as an aid. The local census, which includes the number of preschool children in each family, is also a valuable yardstick.

Emotional and spiritual factors make the job of the school planner even more complicated. For example, if people are dissatisfied with the program of the public school and if they can afford the luxury of tuition fees, they will send their children to private schools. Furthermore, an upswing in religious fervor will cause an exodus from public to parochial schools.

The above has been only a partial account of the many intricacies of enrollment prediction. It can be readily seen why many communities have hired experts to make elaborate surveys of school plant needs. Graduate schools of education have given this service to certain cities and counties. In some cases state educational departments have made large-scale surveys.

A plant survey consists of a statement of building needs for a period of 10 or 20 years, a detailed analysis of the existing plant, and recommendations for the alteration and expansion of present facilities. It presents a program showing approximately when and where schools should be built, specifying the enrollment capacities of these plants, and the facilities to be included. In the case of growing cities there is usually included a schedule for maintenance, alterations, disposal of obsolete buildings, and construction of new ones. However, it must be stressed that merely making the initial school plant survey is not enough; it should be followed by a continuing study of enrollments, population shifts, and proposed educational changes.

In the selection of school sites the first consideration is accessibility not only to the present pupils but also to those to be served in the future. Wherever possible schools should be located so that pupils need not pass through industrial sections or slum areas. Environment of a school, ideally, should be attractive and reasonably quiet; railroads and business streets are to be avoided. The better locations, of course, are in residential areas. Nearby parks, playgrounds, and libraries are desirable.

In construction of schools there are many important considerations, such as heating, ventilation, fenestration, acoustics, size and purpose of classrooms, lunchrooms for teachers, workshops for janitors, fireproof storage rooms, and sanitary facilities. Above all else, schoolhouses must always be built with the thought in mind of protecting the lives and health of the occupants. Every time there is a fire resulting in the death of school children, the point is vividly driven home that protection of pupils must be the first thought in the planning and constructing of school buildings.*

Evolution of Child Accounting

Child accounting is defined as the keeping of essential records of each pupil's activities. In the early American schools there was an almost complete absence of accounting procedures; teachers apparently were too busy drilling children in formal subject matter to devote any time to recording their accomplishments, failures, potentialities, and needs. Reports of the school boards included only the number of buildings, teachers employed, and pupils enrolled; the percentage of attendance and tardiness was regarded as the appropriate index of educational efficiency.

The present system of child accounting is concerned not only with statistical data but also with diagnosis, classification, and sometimes remedial work for each child enrolled. Chicago is the city that gets the credit for having given impetus to this system more than a century ago. By the close of the Civil War the "Chicago Rules" were being used in almost a hundred cities. They dealt almost entirely with methods of determining the total number of pupils actually enrolled, the number

* For recent trends in the construction of school buildings, see Part Seven.

who should be in school, the average daily attendance, and ways to calculate the percentage of attendance. As time went on, this emphasis on attendance led to some statistical hocus-pocus. In order to show as high a percentage as possible, it became a common practice for schools to mark as "temporarily left" any pupil absent for five days. One of the "burning questions" in the 1930's was whether even those five days should be counted as absences.

The United States census, beginning in 1870, collected and reported data concerning school children. About that time the NEA became active in seeking to improve methods of collecting educational statistics; soon afterward committees were appointed to consider the problem. However, those initial NEA reports continued to deal only with mass statistics and did practically nothing to encourage the seeking of information concerning the individual pupil.

The first publication of age-grade statistics appeared in the 1904 annual report of New York City schools, in which it was shown that 39 per cent of the elementary pupils were retarded. This may be considered the starting point of modern child accounting because of the general discussion that was aroused. Several important research studies followed, notably those in 1907 of Edward L. Thorndike (1784–1949) and in 1909 of Leonard P. Ayres (1879–1946). Then in 1912 the NEA evolved a system of uniform cumulative records to be used for each pupil; and in 1918 there was published the Strayer-Engelhardt series of school records. Two years later superintendents of several city school systems organized a rather informal group that appointed a research committee to develop uniform terminology and standards for child accounting.

Since an important feature of this whole area is compulsory education, let us briefly review the paths that Americans have taken in requiring children to attend school. Throughout the early American educational history there was a conflict between the English concept that schooling of a child is a parental responsibility and the theory that basic to the preservation of the democratic way of life is a general diffusion of knowledge among the people. In New England attempts were made to make education compulsory, but the English concept generally prevailed in the middle and southern states.

The first law compelling the child's attendance at school was passed in 1852 by Massachusetts. By 1885 all the New England states and 15 others had compulsory education statutes, with Kentucky in 1896 as the first of the southern states to enact such legislation. When Mississippi passed its attendance law in 1918, the entire nation had compulsory education in varying degrees of effectiveness.* Naturally enough, this movement accompanied the rise of industrial economy; those states predominantly agricultural were the last to fall into line. Child labor laws, which were largely intended to check abuses in urban factories, were important elements in the trend. As opportunities for employment were closed to young people, the situation dictated that school attendance be required.

Among the states there is today a wide variety of requirements as to the age when compulsory education begins and ends. The earliest legislation sought to compel attendance only for sufficient time to assure society that children would acquire the rudiments of learning as indicated by the ability to read and write. Thus, taking the child from the age of seven or eight and covering annual periods of only 40 to 80 days, compulsory education usually continued over a period of four to six years. Gradually this required age span was extended to cover the period of elementary schooling as we understand it today. Later it was increased to cover high school graduation, or at least the age of 17 or 18. These attendance laws have brought with them the necessity of systematic and accurate child accounting, showing what pupils are in actual attendance and whether all those affected by the law are in school and attending regularly.

The basis from which all child accounting must start is the school census. This involves the tabulation of every individual within the age limits of the law. Some school systems try to include everyone from birth until the legal age of maturity is reached. Census records furnish information to the authorities as to how many children of all school ages live within the district; where they live; who is legally responsible for them; how many belong in the school; at what date they arrive at compulsory school age; at what date they pass out of the jurisdiction of the law; how many are in public school, in private school, or out of school; and what their records of nonattendance have been, with the reasons therefor.

Sometimes census information is collected from the children at school rather than by canvass of the home. Inevitably inaccuracies occur—one fourth-grader did not reveal that he had three sisters, all of school age, none enrolled. It later developed that the parents did not believe in schooling for "women."

In the earlier days of state school systems the census was usually the sole basis for distribution of state apportionments to the local

---

* As an outgrowth of the segregation issue, compulsory attendance laws were repealed by South Carolina (1955), Mississippi (1956), and Virginia (1959).

districts. The dishonest practice of "padding" census rolls as a means of getting more state aid was quite common. Comparison of those states distributing their apportionments on a census basis with those using average daily attendance (ADA) indicated that invariably where schools received funds for only the actual days of attendance there was a much more efficient enforcement of compulsory attendance laws. Today many states use a combination of census and ADA.

A continuous census is now in operation in certain school systems. It permits an uninterrupted individual record of every child defined by the legislative act as being of school age. This reasonably informs the authorities as to whether those children who legally belong in school are actually there. Such records are checked constantly against membership and attendance in the schools of the district. In some cities there is kept a "spot record" of all the residential properties as they are rented, but usually there are a few houses occupied by transients who move in and out as the spirit urges them. Those are the people most likely to neglect enrolling their children in school. Moving van companies sometimes cooperate as part of the machinery that must be set up in order to add promptly to census rolls those children moving into the district.

Problems of enforcement of attendance laws are likely to be multiplied whenever illiteracy, low cultural standards, or economic stresses prevail. The situation is also complicated by attendance of many pupils at private schools, where, perhaps, the officials may not be as aggressive as public school people in carrying out the provisions of the compulsory education law. Likewise to be combated is that insidious propaganda of cartoonists and comedians who picture schools as something that children naturally hate.

However, irregularity of attendance ordinarily involves only a relatively small percentage of the pupils. Most parents are anxious to have their children go to school regularly for the benefits to be derived from formal education. Of course, there are legal as well as illegal reasons for absences. Death in the family, illness of the pupil, serious sickness at home, and lack of clothing are quite different matters from nonattendance caused by truancy, parental neglect, work at home, or illegal employment. There is little that can be done to hold down the legal absences except to establish a spirit of active cooperation among parents and pupils by impressing them with the fact that days lost from school can never be adequately recovered. But for those who are habitually truant an organized approach is needed.

Truancy was, in fact, the attendance problem that first challenged the attention of school people. Originally those working to enforce the law were called truant officers, a name that has persisted despite recent changes in emphasis. Many of those first truant officers were recruited directly from police departments. In recent years the general practice has been to employ for attendance work teachers with specialized training, and to substitute the techniques of social workers for the more conventional enforcement methods.

This change in attitude grew out of research studies that followed World War I. The data showed conclusively that the major causes of absence are illnesses, social and economic conditions, and very severe maladjustment cases that require institutional care. Investigation has indicated that only a relatively small percentage of nonattendance is directly due to truancy or other forms of delinquency. Our present thinking seeks to advance remedies based upon understanding the errant child rather than forcing him to attend school simply because we have the legal right to do so. In other words, prevention and not punishment is the answer.

Attendance departments are now developed to the point where they have responsibilities for the continuous census, enforcement of attendance, issuance and control of work certificates, placement service, and the follow-up of nonattendance cases. Since the welfare of the child is the central point of concern, there necessarily must be close coordination with the juvenile court, health department, and all other community services working in the fields of child and social welfare. Larger city school systems can afford highly specialized attendance departments, but limited budgets often hinder such a service in town and rural school districts. However, this problem sometimes has been solved by the joint efforts of several districts in pooling their financial resources to establish a cooperative attendance service, quite often on a county basis.

Improvement in compulsory school attendance laws and in methods of enforcement has resulted in increased enrollment in schools. Whereas in 1900 only 79 per cent of the physically and mentally able children in the United States were being educated, in 1958 the figure stood at 97 per cent.

The increase in enrollment in secondary schools is particularly heartening. In the 1899–1900 school year only 519,251 pupils in the age group 14–17 were attending secondary schools. At the time there were more than six million youngsters in that age bracket. Hence only eight out of every 100 were taking advantage of the chance to continue their education beyond the eighth grade. But in 1957–1958 a total of 7,874,000 were enrolled out of a possible ten million. Thus the ratio rose to slightly more than 77 out of every 100!* This phenomenal rise has led to two opposing schools of thought which will be discussed in the next section of this book.

Pupil Classification and Progress

Schools have become more humane than they used to be in the days of the hickory stick. A significant contribution in this direction is the progress made in the psychological measurement of individual differences. That such differences exist had been noted throughout the history of education—Plato in his *Republic* had sorted children and proposed that they be prepared to become philosophers, warriors, or artisans according to whether they possessed gold, silver, or lead talents of mind. Later writers mentioned individual differences, but it is one thing to note them and quite another to analyze them. The conventional method was through examination and recitation. The first to try to achieve precision by casting psychological data in mathematical terms was Johann Herbart, but it was Thorndike who made educators measurement-conscious.

Today, administrators and teachers are continuously faced with the perplexing problem of how to meet the varying needs of individual pupils. High schools, until this century, were attended for the most part only by those of average or superior intelligence. Such a situation made student bodies reasonably homogeneous. But all that has changed.

In the modern industrial world very few of our youths have farm chores, and since child-labor laws prohibit the others from working in factories there is no place for them to go but school. If only to keep children off the street and juvenile delinquency under control, everything possible is being done to encourage school attendance on the part of those who in years gone by would have dropped out somewhere in the elementary grades. This policy has brought about a heterogeneous high school population in which the amount of overageness caused by nonpromotion keeps pointing to the urgent necessity of more efficiently adapting the school program to the capacities of the children concerned.

It is at this point that educational philosophies conflict. The traditionists feel that education should be a standardized process from which there shall be no deviation or letting down. According to these educators, children lacking the abilities or attitudes necessary to achieve

* These figures were obtained from *State Legislation on School Attendance* (Jan. 1, 1960), a publication of the U.S. Office of Education.

the required standards should be eliminated from school as soon as they have acquired the rudiments of learning. The school, they say, is a selective agency which serves to retard and eventually eliminate from its ranks the very slow and the very reluctant learners.

The more modern philosophy holds that the purpose of education is to provide for each individual pupil those opportunities which may enable him to develop his capacities and to attain the most efficient citizenship and highest degree of happiness of which he is capable. Under such a philosophy the primary objective of classifying pupils is their welfare rather than the mastery of a standard body of subject matter. Thus it is held that the school program should be adjusted so as to teach how best to live and work together in an industrial economy where individuals perform a variety of functions.

American education has been severely criticized because it does a fair job of educating the average child but a wretchedly poor one for those both above and below average. Soon after the beginnings of the graded school it was recognized that some pupils were finding it difficult to keep up with their work. Many became discouraged and eliminated themselves by dropping out of school. Other children were able to complete their assigned tasks in a short time, then loafed—or, being bored, found pleasurable activity in disturbing others in the classroom. Not properly challenged by their school tasks, many developed habits of slovenliness that handicapped them in later life.

There have been numerous attempts to solve these problems. Some of the plans involve administrative adjustments, such as breaking up traditional class organization to permit more individualized work. Others are based upon changes in teaching procedures—for example, differentiated assignments to pupils.

In Batavia, New York, an additional teacher was employed in each large class to give assistance to the slower pupils as a means of preventing them from failing. This system, incidentally, by eliminating non-promotion, helped to save taxpayers' money. On the other hand, in North Denver, Colorado, special attention was devoted to the more capable children. These were released from their regular classes for short intervals and allowed to devote their attention to some work under a special teacher.

Cambridge, Massachusetts, divided pupils into two groups, allowing the brighter ones to complete an eight-year course of study in six or seven years. Promotions occurred three times a year, or at the end of each three-month period. It worked out that once each year a pupil could be transferred from one group to another without skipping or repeating any work. It should be noted that this type of administrative planning encouraged the vogue for semiannual promotions, with the objective in mind of causing retarded pupils to lose only half a year, and permitting brighter children to "jump" grades when acceleration seemed advisable.*

Winnetka, Illinois, became famous because of its plan for individualizing instruction, an idea developed in 1919 from a plan used as early as 1888 in the schools of Pueblo, Colorado. The curriculum was divided into two parts: the common essentials (consisting of knowledge and skills needed by all pupils), and group activities. Work on the common essentials was completely individualized for each pupil. This area was divided into units—each with assignment sheets, worksheets, diagnostic-practice tests, and final tests. A child worked at his own rate on each unit and, when finished, compared his results with the appropriate answer sheet. If he found he had passed the unit, he proceeded to the next one; if not, he went over his work to correct the deficiencies.

When a pupil had completed a group of units, he asked the teacher to give him a final test on that group. If successful, he proceeded to the next group of units; if not, he did more practice work and requested a re-test. Before advancing to the next unit a child had to secure 100 per cent on every test. Then a portion of his school time each day was occupied by group activities for which marks were not given. This program was centered around the arts, literature, music, playground, shopwork, social sciences—in fact, almost anything calculated to stimulate creative work and to develop social consciousness.

The Dalton, Massachusetts, so-called *contract plan* (1919) was based on the three principles of freedom, cooperation, and budgeting of time. Each unit of work was designated a "job," one of these being outlined for each 20-day period. The job plans were made by the teacher or pupil, or both, and included several related phases of school work. The pupil signed a contract to complete each job and worked at his own rate of speed, but before advancing in any favorite subject he had to finish all the work as specified in his contract. A pupil budgeted his time to suit himself, and had a job card on which he daily recorded his progress for each subject.

There was an organization period of about 15 minutes each morning during which pupils of each "house," as homerooms were called, met with the "house teacher" to plan the work for that day. Then came the laboratory period, usually lasting from two to three hours, in which

---

* In this connection, it should be noted that as early as 1870 St. Louis had inaugurated a plan for promoting at intervals of five or six weeks.

pupils worked on their problems and were permitted to go freely from one subject matter laboratory to another according to individual needs and interests. Finally, a conference period of 30 or 40 minutes permitted the pupils of each room to assemble and, as a group, discuss their jobs. The afternoon sessions were usually devoted to such activities as art work, household and industrial crafts, music, and physical education.

The Morrison plan was developed in connection with the high school at the University of Chicago. Like those at Winnetka and Dalton, it stressed the unit assignment but attempted no radical change in school organization. The change was in teaching procedures and had the virtue of being easily adapted by any teacher in any grade or subject. The essence of this plan was to pre-test, then teach those elements where weaknesses were shown in the preliminary test; test the results of this additional study, again tackle those weaknesses shown by the test; teach, and test again to the point of actual mastery of subject matter. The Morrison plan was built around group rather than individual instruction; hence provision for individual differences had to be made through special coaching for slower pupils and supplementary work for the brighter ones.

These typical plans have been presented briefly because of their historical significance. Also, they may suggest ideas to young teachers when in the classroom they themselves are face to face with the perplexing problem of individual differences. But most important is homogeneous grouping that had such a vogue back in the 1920's and is still common in a modified form in most schools of today. Actually complete homogeneity would be impossible to attain—no two pupils are identical in all physical and mental characteristics.

The plan is to divide pupils into groups according to their abilities as determined from mental tests, achievement tests, average scholarship, or teachers' ratings of academic ability or intelligence. Regardless of how the groups are determined, the brightest are scheduled for the same classes and the dullest work together, as do those classified in between. Outlines of the work to be covered stipulate much more to be done by the more intelligent than by the duller ones.

In its heyday there was much criticism of homogeneous grouping. Parents of the better families, where by chance there might be a dull child, were bitterly opposed. Experimental evidence indicated that the greatest effectiveness of the plan was with the duller children, the least with the brighter ones. Homogeneous grouping was undemocratic, some critics claimed. They feared that bright children would become conceited, and dull ones suffer from inferiority complexes—all of which can only lead to social cleavage in a democratic society. Proponents held the system to be democratic in that it met the needs, interests, and abilities of individual pupils.

Perhaps it was against the administration of homogeneous grouping as it was handled in the 1920's that there could be voiced the most serious of criticisms. Individual differences exist in teachers as well as pupils. A brilliant instructor may inspire a bright class whereas a slow-witted teacher invites their open ridicule. Some teachers are endowed with the patience needed for handling duller pupils; others visibly show they are "bored to death" with those who seemingly can't make progress. Thus, for the sake of efficiency, teachers should have been assigned those groups with whom they could do their best work. Yet many high school principals, with but little thought of how such assignments might affect the work of the children, avoided unpleasant complaints from their teachers by assigning each his equal share of fast, average, and slow classes. Similarly, many elementary school principals "rotated" the homeroom assignments of teachers regardless of their abilities.

Administration of Discipline

Today as always one of the chief administrative problems is discipline. Since it can make or break superintendents and principals, naturally there has been a great deal of controversy over what policies should be adopted. Most research on the subject indicates that inability to control pupils is by far the greatest cause of teacher failure leading to loss of position. The importance of discipline has been somewhat belittled in professional literature by extreme adherents of the progressive education school of thought. These "radicals" themselves have been under attack as being responsible for students' lack of respect for constituted law and order.

The answer to the problem of discipline is far from simple. Certainly excesses in catering to children can create situations bordering on anarchy. On the other hand, harsh and inflexible handling of children is one way to fill the mental institutions of tomorrow. And it must be remembered that the school does not operate in a vacuum; its approach to children is deeply affected by conditions in the homes and by the current mores of society. For example, American parents in the twentieth century are much more inclined to indulge their children than were their forefathers in the seventeenth century.

Discipline was harsh in the colonial Latin schools—teachers gen-

erally seemed unable to comprehend child nature. If pupils were indifferent, they were perverted; if dull, they were "blockheads." In
those earlier schools, when men were the teachers of all except the
youngest tots, pupils habitually were punished with whippings and
similar forms of cruel physical torture.

The traditional school held the theory that society must avenge
itself upon the offender as a means of establishing fear of ever repeating the offense. Out of this doctrine developed the frequent use of
corporal punishment. It was really a sign of progress when a child was
not beaten in view of his classmates, but was taken out in the hall where
the sound of the thrashing could be heard though the punishment was
not seen.

Some teachers argue that psychologists fail to appreciate the problem of keeping a reasonable degree of order in the classroom, especially
if the children have been either pampered or neglected at home. Their
claim is that appeals to reason frequently receive but scant attention
unless backed by a little physical emphasis—or the threat of force. This
argument was recently advanced by the High School Teachers Association in New York City which supported a bill to legalize corporal
punishment.

But New York City offers an example of another approach to the
problem. In the mid-fifties an outbreak of lawlessness among students
culminated in the suicide of one junior high school principal and the
death of several adolescents. Shortly afterward the board of education
gave the principals the power to suspend on the spot any student whose
actions indicated that he was a menace to the safety of the other youngsters or his teachers. That year fewer than 100 of the million children
in the New York City schools were suspended, but there was a noticeable return to law and order in the classroom. One junior high school
principal declared: "There are only a few hoodlums in our school.
Before this year they got away with everything but murder. Now that
they know I can put them out without a lot of red tape, they are watching their step."

A large part of the problem of discipline can certainly be solved by
alert and firm administrators who have the power to act and who at
the same time set a friendly tone—not a harsh and cold one—in the
schools they run. But the heart of the matter has always been the personality and ability of the classroom teacher.

Some teachers are born disciplinarians. They accomplish near-
miracles every day with volatile children, not through a display of
force but through more subtle methods. Administrators have found

such teachers to have the following qualities: deep concern for individuals they teach; careful attention to routines and preparation; integrated, mature personalities; pleasant voices that are well modulated; ability to motivate interest in any given lesson; thorough understanding of the background of each child; objectivity that does not allow for personal resentment of children's actions; and calmness in the face of all emergencies.

The problem, then, is to find teachers who have all or most of the above qualities. This is not easy. Too often the misfit enters the profession—the kind who says: "I'd like teaching a lot if it weren't for the kids."

Progressive education has intensified the problem because its basic tenets demand superior ability on the part of teachers. It is a difficult challenge to teach in schools where children are deliberately encouraged to think for themselves and to express their opinions. It is far easier to control a class when the prevailing philosophy is that children should be seen and not heard. The martinet need not be resourceful. Passivity through dictatorship is a simple goal in comparison with activity through democracy.

Today, even in well-managed schools where standards of behavior are understood and accepted by the student body, there are occasional conflicts. Children are subject to emotional outbreaks, clashes of personality, and tendencies to put up a fight for what they consider their individual rights. When this happens, disciplinary measures would seem to be in order.

But punishment should be natural; it should fit the crime. If a pupil loses his temper and throws an ink bottle on the floor, the obvious punishment is to have him clean up the mess—not to make him solve arithmetic problems after school. If punishment is to be used, it must also be impersonal and constructive. Some teachers have discovered that the practice of letting pupils suggest and carry out their own punishment is more likely to develop the desired self-control than the imposition of penalties from above.

But there is another school of thought that puts little faith in punishment. In recent years psychologists like Gesell have insisted that retribution, strict discipline, and the like are measures that merely keep the problem temporarily in check—only to have it erupt later in a more serious manner. They state that punishment treats the symptoms but neglects to concern itself with the cause. This approach to discipline has led to the current emphasis on pupil guidance.

Evolution of Pupil Guidance

The guidance movement actually began outside the schools as an attempt to give adults assistance in selecting vocations and securing positions. The idea had been maturing in the mind of Frank Parsons (1854–1908) for some years prior to the day when he received philanthropic backing to open in a settlement house the Boston Vocation Bureau. Although that was the first organization to dispense personal advice on vocations, there previously had been considerable literature addressed to people seeking economic success. Parsons himself operated on the belief that it is better to choose a vocation than to hunt a job. His technique involved making a survey of job availabilities and then having the individual analyze himself. He sought to inspire proper self-evaluation by means of rating sheets.

In a broad sense guidance has always been a basic interest of the school, but as an organized activity it definitely is a twentieth-century contribution. Guidance in colonial times was limited to a few vocational subjects. As early as 1709 a private schoolmaster in Boston was offering practical arts, and in 1731 bookkeeping was being taught in New York City. Toward the middle of that century even the Latin schools began to offer one or two of the newer vocational subjects.

Then, when the early high schools were established, patrons of the practical arts looked hopefully to them for training that would lead to proficiency in trades or businesses. But in this expectation they were disappointed. Those early high schools were unable to overcome the inertia of academic tradition; they responded to the demand with brief courses in bookkeeping and little else. This exclusion led eventually to a growth of vocational schools of many types, including technical high schools, full-time and part-time trade schools, and continuation schools.

It is indeed surprising that the high schools themselves did not initiate a program of vocational guidance, considering the citizens' intense interest in practical arts. After the idea was born, however, educators were quick to advance the movement. Parsons' idea was so successful that the Boston school committee in 1910 ordered the appointment of vocational counselors in all its high schools. During the next five years many other cities provided for organized vocational guidance work.

Then in 1913 the *National Vocational Guidance Magazine* began publication. Thus the movement received wide publicity and spread chiefly in the larger cities. These programs of vocational guidance have varied considerably. Sometimes they consist merely of series of lectures given by men locally prominent in their fields. The trouble here, granting the speakers know their own lifework, is that so few of them know how to talk to school children. In other cities the programs are more extensive. They include courses in occupational information offered as part of the regular schedule of studies, visits to industrial plants, the administration and interpretation of intelligence and special aptitude tests, and counsel given by trained personnel workers.

In its beginning the guidance program was aided by another movement that was gaining momentum at about the same time; namely, scientific measurement of individual differences. Tests administered to draftees of World War I indicated for the first time approximate ratings of the intelligence required in the various occupations. They also gave some promise of practical values in helping to select men for special duties. Taken as a whole, however, tests have generally proved more successful in identifying vocational interests than in measuring aptitudes.

As psychological studies of individual differences gained acceptance in the educational world, there was realized the need for a guidance program much broader than mere vocational counseling. That was the point where educational guidance entered the picture, and originally it concerned itself only with the child's school career as it could be kept in harmony with traditional scholastic studies.

In its broadest sense guidance is concerned with every phase of life activities. The educational implications cover such matters as adjusting the individual to the educational process, selecting the proper curriculum, and choosing the college for advanced training. Vocationally it is concerned with giving assistance in choosing an occupation, preparing for it, securing a position, and being trained to make satisfactory progress. In this area the counselor makes an attempt to save youths from floundering about after leaving school, to warn against going into "blind alley" jobs, and to make each individual aware of his own potentialities and limitations.

All guidance is concerned with ethical character and moral sense—indeed, some teachers claim that when they undertake to discipline a pupil, at that point they are actually giving character guidance. Civic guidance ideally should enable a child to become an efficient citizen in local, state, and national government. Guidance in matters of health should assist the individual to develop and maintain the best physical and mental health of which he is capable; guidance should also deal with the development of those personal qualities which make an individual an efficient family member. Finally, it becomes increasingly important in our industrial world that guidance be directed toward awakening children's interest in more satisfying and worthwhile leisure-time activities; when the "human products" of a school habitually patronize poolrooms or read cheap comic books, it may be that the school has missed an important point in its guidance program.

On the other hand, it must be reiterated that even the best guidance program in a school must operate within the framework of the world outside its walls. When the standards of a community are too lax or too rigid, the school guidance program is handicapped. Moreover, counselors often find themselves confronted with children whose home life has been a jumble of unhappiness and neglect. Some are products of broken homes; some are "latchkey" children whose parents work long hours; many are in a state of sullen shock as a result of their blighted environment; and others are spoiled egocentrics—victims of "smother love."

Because the early influence of the home is so important, psychologists have been saying for many years that the least the school can do is to establish a personal guidance program in the primary grades before the problems of pupils and parents solidify. Recently, several towns and cities have begun to follow this advice. For example, in 1960 the officials of the New York City schools announced their intention to place a full-time guidance counselor in every elementary school.

In organizing and conducting the vocational aspects of a high school guidance program the initial step is to secure the kind of information that is needed by youth in preparation for taking over more important places in the business, industrial, and social worlds. The immediate task is to place each student in the proper curriculum that leads either to college or a job. Some high schools operate placement services; others merely answer employers' requests to the principal or counselor. In any case, there should exist cordial working relationships with both college registrars and businessmen so that the school is trusted in its recommendations.

Some years ago a vice-principal in Erie, Pennsylvania, was scheduled to be demoted. The officials there felt he had outlived his usefulness; they said that educationally he was a "Model T" who was handicapping the school's further progress. That superintendent and board of education got the surprise of their lives in the ensuing uproar. It seems this vice-principal for years had been placing graduates in good positions because employers trusted him; over a 20-year period his "boys" were holding many key jobs in the city. He early had learned the value of cooperating with other agencies such as business and industrial organizations, labor unions, welfare agencies, civic groups, parent-teacher associations, mothers' clubs, churches, and higher educational institutions.

The practice among larger schools has been to supplement the regular teaching staff with guidance counselors who have had special training in the field. Their responsibilities include: preparing and using personnel records; administering intelligence, achievement, aptitude, and interest tests; helping students work out their program of studies; giving individual counsel; teaching group guidance units designed to prepare young people to meet more wisely the problems with which they are sure to be confronted; and referring special cases to various staff services, such as health and placement officers.

This work involves continuous study of individual differences and students' adjustments or failures. Counseling may be given partly through group instruction, as in life-career and try-out courses. But basically it is a more personal service involving individual conferences at school and even visits to the home. It is now recognized that guidance should be given to every student, not to the "problem cases" alone—each child is a case worthy of special attention.

Counseling suffers from a shortage of proper manpower. Many now in service have had the necessary training if college credits are the criteria, but lack those personal qualities every true builder of human character must have. Also, the mistake has often been made of assuming that men and women of many years' successful teaching experience are thereby qualified to become successful counselors. Teaching experience is certainly essential, but far more important are a genuine liking for and appreciation of youth, sympathetic understanding of human weaknesses, and a thorough knowledge of occupational possibilities and requirements.

The theory that every classroom teacher should simultaneously serve as a guidance counselor has recently been advanced and popularized. It is rightfully held that teachers are in a strategic position to arouse interest, to develop proper attitudes, to encourage special abilities. Theoretically this is splendid. The brutal truth, however, is that all too few are really qualified to guide and counsel. Some efforts are being made to remedy this situation through in-service training, but lifetime habits and attitudes are not so easily changed. Except in rare cases this homeroom plan of guidance seldom works. The average teacher who carries a full teaching program each day is not likely to be in the proper frame of mind to serve his group as an inspiring counselor.

It is much easier to theorize on what a teacher should do than to have such homeroom guidance programs properly carried out. In many high schools the guidance program of this type becomes a mockery. Even those teachers with the proper attitude and background are too busy checking attendance records, reading announcements, and handling other details. The homeroom guidance period at best represents very uneven counseling service—students with teachers they respect and trust are indeed fortunate; those under tyrannical "hellcats" or weaklings do not fare so well.

Some school administrative staffs have earnestly endeavored to build truly effective guidance programs. These are to be commended if the emphasis can be kept on "guidance" rather than the "program"—in other words, if the ideals and services to be stressed can be kept within the perspective of the students and do not become too academic or adultish. To illustrate, in a 1938 survey of a Pennsylvania high school the investigating committee was presented with one of the most comprehensive guidance programs ever attempted. A full period each week was being set aside for specific instruction. Teachers were given carefully prepared mimeographed outlines. Some of them were enthusiastic; others did not hide their dislike for the program as being something that interfered with their jobs as teachers. But, all in all, apparently a fine piece of guidance work was being done.

After observing several guidance classes in action and being duly impressed, the survey committee stopped several students as they were passing down the hall and proceeded to question them. One girl frankly said she was so "sick and tired" of hearing about her "personality" that the word nauseated her. A boy complimented the definite efforts to teach him and his classmates the value of good manners and the proper etiquette in social situations, and testified that he personally had gained much from the instruction. "But," asked he, "why don't they tell you how to ask a girl for a date without getting goose-pimples? Then what to do, and maybe what not to do, when you're out with her?" Apparently there was something missing even from this pupil-guidance program!

Utilization of the School Library

After a 1933 survey of the then current practices among this nation's elementary and secondary school libraries, the American Library Association formulated certain objectives. All pupils were to have access to books so that they might be trained to love and read that which is worthwhile, to supplement their school studies by use of books other than texts, to use reference books easily and effectively, and to make intelligent use of both school and public libraries. Every secondary school was to have a trained librarian and every elementary school a regular library service, with the librarians having the same status as teachers or heads of departments of equal training and experience.

It was further recommended that every teacher-training institution require a course in the use of books and libraries, as well as a course on the best literature for children. Every state was to provide for the supervision of school libraries and the certification of school librarians. Finally, it was stated that the public library should be recognized as a necessary part of instruction and should be liberally supported by taxes just as are public schools, and for the same reason.

The American Library Association has constantly held that school systems not making liberal provisions for training in the use of library facilities are not fulfilling their obligation to reveal to our future citizens the opportunity to know and use these valuable resources as a means of education. The admonition of the librarians holds true today, but in the time since the above objectives were formulated, school libraries have come a creditable distance toward their realization.

Libraries were important in our earlier colonial history. For example, John Harvard (1607–1638) left more than an endowment of money to the institution that now bears his name. He bequeathed his library of more than 300 volumes toward the foundation of the college. Such a collection was not unusual. In fact, several of our New England forefathers had personal libraries numbering over a thousand volumes and are reported to have valued their books above all other earthly possessions.

The Union Library in Philadelphia was organized in 1746, and 20 others were founded during the next quarter-century. This movement gained momentum in the post-Civil War period, but as late as 1870 the Library of Congress (which now contains more than 12,000,000 books and pamphlets) had only 183,000 volumes, and there were but six other libraries in the entire nation that had as many as 100,000. Chicago and Philadelphia, in fact, were without free public libraries until about that date. But early in this present century Andrew Carnegie (1835–1919) gave a decided impetus to the founding of municipal and college libraries by contributing many millions of dollars toward their building and endowment.

Thus it can be said that the school library movement definitely has been a twentieth-century contribution to education. Some states before 1900 did enact laws permitting the support of school libraries from public funds, but rarely was advantage taken of those laws. Before World War I a few states, notably New York, began to establish standards and to take other steps toward the development of school libraries. Then in 1920 the school library idea was crystallized into a national movement in which professional library groups, regional crediting associations, and state educational departments actively participated by preparing specifications and offering counsel. As a result of these activities adequate libraries are now recognized as indispensable to the secondary school program, and they are beginning to develop in elementary and rural schools.

Library service vitally affects all the curricular and extracurricular activities of the school. In fact, many of the newer buildings are being functionally planned with the library as the starting point, since it serves all departments and, ideally, should be the center of the educational program. The more modern school libraries consist of a well-equipped and pleasant reading room and an adequate supply of books and other reference materials.

The worth of a collection of books for a high school library can be judged by the following criteria: number of volumes, balanced distribution, appropriateness for secondary school purposes, and recency of publication. Nationwide studies have revealed a need for improvement in all four categories, particularly in balanced distribution.

A simple method of securing a rough index of balance in the books of any library is to check the number of volumes in the various areas of the Dewey decimal system whereby fiction titles are listed alphabetically by author, with nonfiction books arranged according to key number and decimals. As early as possible, depending upon their intelligence and maturity, children should be made familiar with these Dewey classifications.* As matters stand today, the majority of students reach college in ignorance of basic facts concerning a modern library system—some remain in that state even after they have obtained baccalaureate degrees.

The value of any library can also be judged by the number using it, the general atmosphere, and the personalities of the staff members. The last point is most important. Only occasionally now do we encounter a librarian with a "dyspeptic" outlook on life who apparently takes pleasure in keeping children ill at ease. Most librarians today are well trained and are glad to help youngsters in the interesting adventures of

* Dewey decimal system: 000 General Works; 100 Philosophy; 200 Religion and Mythology; 300 Sociology; 400 Language; 500 Natural Science; 600 Useful Arts; 700 Fine Arts; 800 Literature; 900 History.

acquiring new knowledge and of getting acquainted with the world through the medium of good books.

The typical classroom procedure of days gone by was to confine study to specific assignments within a single textbook and to test pupils only on the material covered. That was in harmony with the *Old Librarian's Almanac* which advised that books be kept behind stout gratings, or, to quote: "It were better that no Person enter the Library (save the Librarian Himself) and that the Books be kept in Safety, than that one Book be Lost, or others Misplaced."

Since those early days of the sanctity of books, the school library movement has been passing through three stages of development, all of which can still be found here and there in American schools. At first schools had no library facilities at all, and instruction was limited to textbooks; then small collections of reading matter were placed in classrooms without much regard to their possible educational utilization; and finally, the development of the library has come to be considered the most important element in the school program—an intellectual laboratory, so to speak.

Modern teaching methods no longer place reliance on a single source of information; they suggest the consulting of a wide variety of materials. Pupils are even being encouraged to find conflicting points of view in statements of alleged facts on the theory that such is the way to teach them how to discriminate between truth and propaganda. Under such a system of learning, a well-stocked library is indispensable. But specific instruction in how to get the best possible use from good books is also needed. In recent years this viewpoint has led to the development of a new type of faculty member, the teacher-librarian, who not only protects the books from theft and mutilation but also has a working knowledge of source materials and the ability to refer pupils to the appropriate ones they need to consult.

In many elementary schools, in lieu of a central library, books are distributed among the rooms where they are placed on reading tables for use as occasion or opportunity permits. Such a plan is only a halfway measure for the lower grades and is totally inadequate for secondary schools; the older students need a separate library organization because the modern curriculum calls for so much individual research and for a wide variety of supplementary reading materials.

At one time the library and study hall were considered as two separate and entirely different units of the high school plant. There still are schools with the traditional study hall, a large room with rows of fixed seats, where attendance is compulsory and supervision resembles police methods of law enforcement. But a movement has been afoot to combine the library and study hall. Librarians have opposed this combination on the plea that the atmosphere deteriorates into a situation where enforcement of discipline is the major concern. Nevertheless, many high school principals have abandoned study halls and enlarged their libraries. They encourage freedom of action just so long as each individual considers the others who are working. Discipline commonly consists of the denial of library privileges to those who persist in abusing them.

Experts who plan the construction of new buildings recommend from 15 to 20 square feet per pupil as a standard for libraries. Depending upon such factors as the type of school and general plan of instruction, the library should be large enough to accommodate from 6 to 15 per cent of the enrollment in larger schools and an even greater percentage in smaller ones. Library tables vary in height from 22 inches in the primary grades to 30 inches in senior high schools. To avoid having pupils face the light, it is recommended that tables be arranged with their long axes perpendicular to the windows.

Financial limitations make it difficult for smaller schools to provide adequate library facilities, a problem that has brought about the development of state, regional, and county cooperative plans. Some state departments of education are now maintaining a service of lending books to village and rural schools, either on request or on a circulating schedule. As an example, the California Department of Education has developed an outstanding state library division which exercises general supervision and lends books to county libraries. These in turn do the actual distribution work of circulating books among the smaller schools. Certain other states have developed countywide school library organizations. These usually operate as a part of a statewide plan in cooperation with county libraries, or sometimes as independent school services. Regardless of how the program is administered, the book truck arriving on regular schedule at an isolated school usually marks a "red letter day" for those children.

Extracurricular Administration

Athletics, clubs, debates, dramatics, and school publications are the most common extracurricular activities. The general public usually is better informed about these than about any other part of the educational program—townspeople are often more likely to be critical over a losing football team than the fact that children in a certain grade are not learning academic skills.

From an administrative viewpoint extracurricular activities can prove to be unusually troublesome—Detroit invariably assigns a sizable squad of police officers each time the local high schools compete on the gridiron. The athletic program, in fact, can save or doom an administrator, especially in small towns with a great deal of local pride. But sports are only one part of this vexatious problem. Dances and club activities sometimes get out of hand; a teacher may produce a play that brings acrimonious criticism down upon the head of the school. Or the student newspaper staff publishes a story that startles everybody, including school board members.

True, some administrators show very little common sense in how they handle the situation. A few unalterably oppose and hinder a worthwhile extracurricular activity that is already deeply rooted; others practice a laissez-faire policy that sometimes leads to embarrassing situations. And some well-meaning enthusiasts needlessly disrupt the entire instructional program of their schools by placing too much emphasis on preparation for social or showy activities. Periodic fiestas, bazaars, operettas and carnivals—to say nothing of weekly pep rallies—often afflict such schools with hardening of the intellectual arteries.

Generally speaking, it may be said that extracurricular activities grew up as a protest against the inadequacy of the regular, narrowly prescribed curriculum. The more progressive schools of today appreciate their educational values and possibilities. Thus extracurricular activities are being encouraged and supervised in an orderly and thoughtful way. Some schools are setting aside special periods of each day or week for their promotion; and a few are even giving credit toward graduation to those who engage in them. Moreover, in many schools participation in certain club activities or varsity sports is denied to those whose grades are not up to par.

The big administrative problem is to get proper personnel to exercise subtle but firm control over the situation. There are many teachers who repel children; at least they do not attract them. Such instructors probably would have but few in their regular classwork if students were not arbitrarily assigned to them. Thus, when students are allowed to select club activities sponsored by different teachers, the greatest share of the work and responsibility falls on a few willing and capable shoulders.

Then there is the question of just how much of the actual direction should be made by the teacher-sponsor. Adults have been "through the mill"; they see the mistakes younger people are apt to make in their trial-and-error attempts to accomplish something they think they want to do; and they are tempted to dictate what should or should not be done. In voluntary extracurricular activities even more than in regular classroom work too much adult direction destroys for students the values of the project. Ideally, of course, the teacher is there, ready and willing to give advice, but not until the students specifically ask for counsel or are about to give up.

This brings up the question of student government. Certainly, so far as theory goes, it provides ideal training for young people soon to take their places as full citizens in a democratic society. Student government can be made a success, but usually it falls short of achieving its projected goals. The truth of the matter is that most student government below the college level is faculty-dominated. The student council, let us say, makes a decision that may not represent experienced thinking, but at least it is student thinking. The new rule becomes effective when, and if, the principal accepts it. Of course, a principal must administer his school in accordance with school board policies as the superintendent interprets them to him. That means there are certain things he cannot permit. It is a wise principal who confers regularly with his student leaders, establishes mutually cordial relationships, and keeps them informed concerning the limitations he must place on student government.

The secret of success is to pave the way for the democratic election of capable officeholders, and then to give them the moral backing to do a good job. Recently on a certain Texas college campus a new dean of students found a very demoralized student body. Everybody seemed to be "knocking" the school, attendance at athletic contests and dramatic productions was poor, and many students were transferring to other institutions. The new officers of the student body had done practically nothing to warrant the honor they had been given. Obviously, the low morale stemmed from the lack of leadership and direction.

After the new dean had taken office he made it an administrative habit to confer regularly with all students holding important campus positions and to ask what progress was being made in their work. He was extremely careful not to dictate what they should do, but was rather demanding that each do something to justify his holding down the job to which he had been honored by election. The first-year result was almost revolutionary. Each class put on an assembly program, also a dance, and was active in ways unheard-of in previous years. The student senate of its own accord initiated an honor system and felt responsible for its success. Elections were spirited and the fraternity influence largely removed. During that one year student morale was reborn and everybody, faculty as well as students, much happier.

Certain principles of organization, administration, and supervision have proved quite effective in gaining the desired values from extracurricular activities. Common sense dictates that all organizations be supervised by the school and be made subject to its general rules of conduct. This, of course, does not mean too much supervision—just enough to prevent the enthusiasms of young people from outweighing their judgment. In elementary schools this supervision needs to be of the parental type; in junior and senior high schools, that of "big brother" or "big sister." Generally speaking, the aim is to develop the students' sense of personal responsibility and their social growth—in the larger sense of that adjective.

Introduction of any program of extracurricular activities needs to be gradual, and should arise from the regular curricular work of the school. The number and type of these activities should be determined by the size of the enrollment and the needs of the school. Some student bodies are so overorganized that they can hardly help but do a poor and hurried job. The number of activities in which a student is permitted to participate needs to be limited for two reasons: to prevent overloading of the ambitious, versatile, or popular student to the possible detriment of his health and regular studies; and to distribute the values of participation among a larger number of individuals.

However, no general agreement exists as to how this participation should be limited. Some schools have established a point system in which each activity is rated according to the time and energy it requires, and assigned a certain number of points. The maximum number of extracurricular points that may be carried each term sets a limit to the activities a student may have. Other schools govern individual participation according to the student's average grade in subject matter. A major trouble encountered in the various plans set up to control the activities is the likelihood that the administrative machinery may become so big and unwieldy as to defeat its own purpose. Some plans reported in professional journals would seemingly require the talents of an expert bookkeeper if they really do what the authors claim for them.

Administrators should see that no activity is accepted as a part of the school program unless it gives substantial promise of developing civic, social, or moral consciousness. Certainly there needs to be complete democracy in any activity sponsored by a public school. Fraternities, for example, are entirely out of place in high schools—a fact that many legislatures have recognized by banning them. Yet from time to time one hears that certain groups of parents have risen in anger because local authorities have decided to enforce the long-established state law prohibiting fraternities in public high schools. Probably what is needed in such cases is an intensive and well-publicized adult education program to make such parents aware of the true role of the school in a democratic society.

Some very sad experiences in the past have shown that the school buildings, whenever possible, should be the place for all school functions. Certainly this simplifies supervision. In any case the place of meeting needs to be approved by the school. Time and location of all meetings and activities should be definitely scheduled. In order to avoid conflicts some schools keep in the office a calendar on which each event must be listed before becoming official.

It is also important that expenses incident to all extracurricular activities be kept as low as possible. For example, in planning a prom, the class officers must see to it that the cost of the tickets is kept within reasonable limits. Without proper guidance they may be prompted by youthful enthusiasm to hire an expensive "name band"—thus causing embarrassment and hardship to some of their fellow students who cannot afford such luxuries.

Finally, as many principals can ruefully testify, the school must closely supervise all extracurricular funds and accounts. Any laxness that invites carelessness or dishonesty is heading in the direction of trouble. Strict supervision of extracurricular funds usually brings more economical expenditures. Such a policy performs a real service in guaranteeing the financial integrity and also protecting the reputation of those persons responsible for handling the funds.

Administration of Pupil Transportation

Almost one-third of the public school pupils in the United States receive transportation privileges at the taxpayers' expense. Most of these children get free round trips five days a week in school buses. Some travel in station wagons and other small vehicles. In big cities like New York, thousands go to and from school at reduced rates via the subways and regular bus lines. And in places like Detroit, regular taxicab service is provided in exceptional cases.

The emergence of pupil transportation into this massive, expensive program began shortly before World War II when the movement toward consolidation of school districts was gaining ground. Since then, progress in the field has been truly astonishing. In the 1957–58 school year, according to a report issued by the U.S. Office of Education, there were 170,689 vehicles in use. Of that total 151,523 were buses. Close to $420 million was spent for the transportation of 11.3 million children—an average of about $37 per child. In contrast, only 356,000 pupils were riding to and from school at public expense in 1920. They totaled less than 2 per cent of the children enrolled in public schools at that time.

The history of pupil transportation dates back to 1840, when the precedent was set by a Massachusetts school district. Then, in 1869, that state passed the nation's first school transportation law. It allowed any town to raise and appropriate money to be expended by the school committee at its discretion for the conveyance of children to and from school.

Other states soon followed the lead of Massachusetts. All the early laws, it should be noted, applied only to elementary schoolchildren living farther than a certain distance from school. Moreover, the laws were permissive in nature: school boards were at liberty to decide against transporting children no matter how far away the pupils lived. Even when transportation was provided, it was legal to charge a fee for each child.

Recent state legislation has served to broaden the program and to eliminate or reduce inequities. Secondary school students are usually included today, and transportation is often mandatory beyond a certain radius. Also, the practice of making parents of the young riders pay fees has come to be regarded as unfair. Instead, many states now give financial aid to districts with transportation problems. In some cases the money grants amount to quite a large sum; but in several of the poorer states the assistance is a mere pittance.

At first, pupil transportation was arranged through contracts with farmers who supplied a horse and wagon. In a few areas railroads and boats were used. But when our nation became motorized, the school bus was gradually accepted as the best mode of conveyance. In keeping with the custom of the past, contracts were signed with private owners of buses. Then school boards found that it was cheaper to buy their own vehicles and hire the drivers themselves. Today it is a common practice for school districts to own a fleet of buses and to operate shops for repair and maintenance of the vehicles.

To illustrate the widespread character of the trend, in 1961 more than 70 per cent of the buses were school-owned, but as late as 1935 the figure was only 20 per cent. This sudden surge of schools into the bus business was caused not only by a desire to economize but also by the realization that the entire operation should be an integral part of the educational program. Buses owned by the school districts are readily available for field trips and other excursions. Close control of discipline and safety can also be maintained.

Safety, of course, must always be the first consideration when transporting children. Practically all states now have statutes or regulations setting the maximum speed (usually 35 miles per hour or less) for school buses. Many states require all cars on both sides of the road to halt whenever a school bus stops to pick up or discharge its young passengers. Flasher lights are now standard equipment on most buses, as well as emergency doors, push-out windows, fire extinguishers, and first-aid kits. Regular drills are conducted to teach the children how to use the equipment and how to get out of the bus in case of an accident.

Assembly programs and classroom lessons on bus safety are an accepted part of the transportation program today. Principals are aware that one of the causes of accidents is boisterous behavior that distracts the driver's attention from the road. Therefore, most schools draw up a list of rules for conduct on buses. These usually work out best when the children themselves have a hand in the formulation and enforcement of "do's and don't's." But the chief agent for enforcement must always be a responsible school official, such as the principal. School supervisors now realize that the bus driver needs as much support from the front office as the teacher. Consequently, in many districts the authorities are clamping down hard on youthful extroverts who give vent to their pent-up exuberance the moment they step into the bus. In some cases such offenders have even been suspended from school for the "good and welfare" of their fellow riders.

But even the best administrators exercise only remote control except on those occasions when they ride the school bus to check various aspects of the safety and efficiency of the operation. The key person is, of course, the driver himself. He should be selected carefully on the basis of an interview conducted by a school authority, and a physical examination. The interviewer should use such criteria as mental alertness, maturity of judgment, attitude toward children, personal habits, and general character. The physical test should pay special attention to vision, hearing, condition of the heart, and blood pressure.

Once a driver has received a written contract from the board of education, he should be acquainted fully with the policy of the school district, the route he must travel, the best methods for handling children, and the actions to be taken in case of accident. Some districts give drivers instructions in caring for buses and even use their services as extra mechanics at the repair shop while the children are at school.

Other areas set up clinics, conferences, and workshops for drivers. New Mexico Western College, for example, annually holds a short summer session course for bus drivers from all over that state.

On the other hand, the sad fact is that a great many districts exercise only a minimum of care in the selection of drivers. Although the very lives of the children are in the hands of these people, they are often hired because they happen to be the only persons available for part-time work. Several states do not require special licenses or training for school bus drivers, an error of omission that is deplored by safety experts. They point out that the buses are unwieldy vehicles and often must be driven over hazardous roads. In some parts of the country, snow and sleet are ever-present perils in winter; in other sections, rain and mud make many a journey rough indeed.

One interesting trend is the use of housewives as drivers. The part-time work for "pin money" appeals to many women—and they usually do a competent, conscientious job. Needless to say, their acceptance has not been universal. Prejudice against women drivers still runs rampant despite statistics in their favor released by the National Safety Council. Some school boards have refused to hire housewives for another reason. They ask: "Can you picture a woman tinkering in a garage on one of our big buses?"

Another practice in some states where the licensing laws are lenient is the use of students as drivers. Often these are college boys who can fit the job into their schedules. At times they are older high school boys. The practice may seem horrifying to some, yet the accident rate of these students is reputed to be very low.

In fact, much evidence supports the claim that the school bus is probably the safest form of transportation in the country. It has been estimated that the total weekly distance covered by school buses runs to almost 20 million miles. Yet in a typical year (1957–58) only 7,186 accidents were reported. This comes to one accident for approximately every 94,000 miles traveled. Fatalities are relatively few, and most of them occur when children are crossing highways, either to board a bus or to reach their homes after alighting.

A great deal of the credit for the safety record of school buses can be attributed to the local administrators and drivers. But a share of praise must go to the people who have participated in national conferences on school transportation. The first of these took place at Columbia University in 1939. Representatives of 48 state departments of education set up minimum bus standards at that meeting. Later conferences in 1945, 1948, 1951, 1954, and 1959 improved the original agreements and formulated new recommendations. Manufacturers, businessmen, engineers, safety experts, and community leaders worked with educators to evolve safe, economic, and efficient methods for handling the transportation of children.

Out of some of these conferences came the designation of "school bus chrome" as the official color of the vehicles throughout the nation, and all motorists soon learned to recognize the medium-yellow hue as a signal to be especially careful. At least two important publications resulted from the meetings: "Minimum Standards for School Buses" and "Standards and Training Programs for School Bus Drivers."* Both are widely used in districts that wish to initiate or improve transportation programs.

The first step in the establishment of a pupil transportation project is the adoption of a clear, succinct statement of policy. Experience has proved that the policy is usually accepted when it has grown out of conferences and workshops with all concerned. It should include the objectives of the program, the responsibilities of drivers and other personnel, the safety precautions that will be taken, and the decision as to which pupils are entitled to transportation.

A description of the rules and regulations should follow. Like the policy statement, this document should be neither too inflexible nor too vague. Certainly it should be altered or expanded as needs arise. On the other hand, it should serve as a bulwark to protect administrators from pressure by parents who want exceptions made for capricious or selfish reasons.

One of the decisions must involve criteria for eligibility for transportation. Four standards are usually considered: distance between home and school, pupil's capacity to walk, incidence of hazards on the road, and size of the school enrollment.

At one time distance was practically the only criterion in many districts. Two miles was generally set as the maximum that an elementary schoolchild should be required to walk. But as the volume of traffic increased, the distance was decreased. Now one mile is usually the yardstick for elementary schoolchildren, and the distance is often less for pupils in the kindergarten and primary grades. For secondary school students the distance is often set at two to three miles.

As mentioned above, hazards must also be taken into account. Traffic flow on cross streets is an important factor, as well as the speed

---

* In the 1948 conference it was proposed that state departments of education accept primary responsibility for planning state-wide programs to train bus drivers. This recommendation has been implemented in most states.

of the vehicles, the availability of crossing guards, and the existence of traffic lights or stop signs. Other considerations are of all types: construction projects along the walker's path, storm damage, flooded areas, dangerous corners, gangs, feuding groups, and unsavory adults in the neighborhood.

Sometimes school boards need the wisdom of several Solomons to decide whether or not a group of children should be transported, at least temporarily, when unusual conditions prevail inside the prescribed boundaries. Sometimes, too, they must consider whether or not an individual child's handicap is great enough to warrant giving him the privilege of transportation. In such cases, the best procedure is to base the decision on the recommendation of the school doctor. In some instances, the principals are saddled with the responsibility of weighing the merits of a specific case. Those who have been through this particular mill recommend that accounts of the discussions with mothers and the reasons for the decisions be written out and forwarded to the superintendent and the parent concerned. Thus the principal has a ready reference should criticisms ensue or should a similar case come up.

An important administrative responsibility is the planning of transportation routes. A first step is the preparation of a master sheet showing the name, age, grade, and residence of each child entitled to transportation. Often the school also secures data about young children who will be enrolling in the near future. A map should also be drawn up to show the exact boundaries of the school district; the location of the school or schools; the routes of the buses; and any barriers or hazards like railroads, bridges, streams, and steep hills. Types of roads—paved, gravel, or dirt—should also be indicated. Other information to be posted should include the place where the buses are housed, the residences of the drivers, the capacity of each bus, and the total number of children to be served.

Technical assistance in mapping routes is given by most state education departments. But experienced administrators have found that sometimes what looks good on paper may be far from ideal in practice. Therefore, long before the opening day of school they accompany each bus driver to check the route and determine whether or not any improvements can be made. Sometimes such a "dry run" results in a change in the number of stops to be made, or a slight deviation in the route because of an unforeseen hazard.

Once a route has been determined, all school patrons affected must be notified as early as possible before the school term begins. Sometimes major readjustments are required from year to year because of conditions on the roads, shifts in school population, or rezoning of school boundaries. Some districts announce such changes in the newspapers, but it is even more advisable to send a notice to the home of each child on the route. Ideally, conferences with the parents should be called before the modifications are made. But when this procedure is impossible, it is best to send to the homes a clear explanation of the reasons for the new system. Many a young administrator has learned that one way to stir up a hornets' nest is to change established bus routes arbitrarily, even when such an action may bring about better bus service.

The length of each route must be determined largely by the time required to traverse it. Except in unusual cases, no child should be made to spend more than an hour per trip on a school bus. If funds allow, 45 minutes is an even more sensible maximum. It should be noted that the bus ride is often only a part of the child's journey. In many rural areas he must walk a considerable distance to the bus stop or be transported there by his parents.

Accurate and detailed information as to costs of purchasing, maintaining, and operating school buses is usually required by state law. The perennial problem is to keep costs at a minimum without lowering the quality of service. Numerous factors must be considered in this cost-accounting process; the size of buses, conditions of highways, weather, and depreciation are a few of the matters to be weighed. In planning an economical pupil transportation system it must be remembered that each unused seat represents a financial loss, since the major costs consist of drivers' salaries, gasoline, oil, and repairs—all of which remain practically the same whether the buses are loaded or half-empty. Transportation tests the quality of administration! This is especially true in many school districts where the costs of bus service are second only to the outlay for salaries of teachers and supervisors, and where a new school bus represents the largest single item to be purchased.

In this connection, certain trends have emerged as a result of experience. For one, it has been found more economical to buy the larger transit-type buses. Although in isolated instances smaller buses may prove to be cheaper to operate, the average cost per pupil is usually less when the seating capacities of the buses are 48, 54, or 60.

Some school boards purchase the chassis and the bus body separately in order to save money. Others find it economical to sell their old buses outright rather than trade them in for new ones. The general practice is to replace buses after ten years of service, although variations in rates of depreciation are very great.

As noted previously, school districts are tending to own and operate their own maintenance shops. Not only is this practice safer, it also increases the life expectancy of equipment. Moreover, the cost of repairs is cut as much as 90 per cent. In some cases, the shop also fixes lawn mowers, ditch diggers, and other school equipment; and in a few districts it serves as a practical laboratory for students interested in becoming mechanics.

Finally, there is a movement toward the appointment of transportation managers or directors. These are men with special training in such areas as traffic administration, school problems, and even engineering. One factor that has deterred the progress of this trend is the scarcity of people with proper orientation and experience for such important positions. Only a few colleges have recognized the need and have provided appropriate courses. It is expected that this lag will be corrected as the pupil transportation problem continues to become more acute. At present, many school superintendents and principals are complaining that they cannot be expected to double as experts in the routing and maintenance of buses. One superintendent who must sign the shop report each week confesses privately that he has only a vague idea of what the items mean. He proceeds on the general assumption that the mechanics are honest and efficient, but he worries lest events may some day prove his trust to have been misplaced. Like many others in his position, he would welcome a transportation manager.

A word should be said about the transportation of pupils enrolled in non-public schools. At first such children were prohibited from receiving free transportation organized by local boards of education. When protests arose, the courts handed down rulings that it was unconstitutional to grant the privilege to any but public schoolchildren. However, in 1947 the U.S. Supreme Court held that a New Jersey statute authorizing the transportation of parochial school pupils at public expense did not violate the Constitution. The issue is still in doubt, because situations differ and because courts have handed down seemingly contradictory decisions.

Recently, several states have passed laws similar to the one enacted in New Jersey. New York has stipulated a ten-mile distance for the transportation of children in non-public schools. Local boards in that state now find themselves paying from $850 to $5000 per pupil each year for rides to and from school. In 1961, one father in the Albany area was offered a $1300-per-year deal to drive his two daughters to a private school in his Cadillac! This was the most economical way the school board could find to remain within the law.

New York, incidentally, transports more pupils each year than any other state. Recent reports show North Carolina to be first in the number of buses used—followed by Ohio and Texas. Nevada transports the fewest pupils; in 1957–58 it was the only state to spend less than a million dollars on the program.

Behind the entire pupil transportation movement is the American ideal that every child is entitled—and should even be compelled—to receive an education. For many years this goal was considered impracticable in rural areas. Schools were entirely too far away from many isolated dwellings, and thousands of farmers had neither the time nor the desire to transport their own children. Temporarily the situation worsened when school districts were consolidated. But thereafter a wave of pressure on local and state authorities caused the ideal to come close to a reality—mainly through the use of the school bus. This is the reason that many Americans proudly look upon the school bus today as a symbol of democracy rolling forward. For one of every three schoolchildren in the nation that bus, or some other vehicle like it, is the magic carpet to a fuller life.

Evolution of Public Relations

Some of the techniques of public relations are as old as civilization itself, but the term is comparatively new. Its first known use was about 1905, when it appeared in the vocabulary of the business world but did not gain common usage. Not until World War I did the expression become popular. Even then it was something of a joke, with many considering it but a pompous disguise for the lively, imaginative press agents so commonly associated with theatrical people. Actually it was heralding the advent of a new idea in management—the beginnings of the customer-is-always-right era in business and of the parents-are-always-welcome-to-visit-THEIR-schools period in education.

Both business and educational leaders have begun to realize how essential it is to operate in the public interest. Schools have awakened to the necessity of giving taxpayers a clear and honest understanding of the social and economic factors that have brought about recent needs for increased financial support. It no longer can be taken for granted that the school program is understood and appreciated by everyone in the community. To many the school is an antiquated institution far removed from practical realities of life, with teachers going around in an "intellectual fog"; to others, tax monies are largely wasted "because the kids don't know nothing."

Although the field of public relations has grown into an established profession in recent years, there still remains considerable difference of opinion about it. To one person it consists largely of publicity, to another it seems to lie chiefly in the field of promotion, to a third it means a program of self-advertising, and to a fourth it gives clues to public opinion and thought. Primarily and essentially public relations is a matter of planning, shaping, and carrying out of policies and procedures that eventually will be reflected in good will.

Public relations may be good, bad, or indifferent; but this aspect of the school's responsibility cannot be avoided. It is, in reality, merely a recognition of the necessity of making the philosophies and acts of one segment of public life understandable to the general population—it may be aptly called the art of getting along with the public. Just as an individual makes a vivid or a negative impression on others, so does a school system with its administrative officers, teachers, janitors, and other employees. Unless the values of public education are properly impressed on the public consciousness, inevitably it will suffer a decrease in support and understanding. Thus it is of vital importance that people know the full truth about the schools—their objectives, services, organizations, problems. A cynic once remarked, "It's not that the people don't know enough, but that they know so much that ain't so." A public relations program endeavors to take the stinging truth out of that statement.

During the present century American public schools have undergone some rapid and profound changes. Until very recently those in charge have been completely absorbed with the internal problems of organization and management. Thus the pressure of other important matters and the failure to understand the vital necessity of communication with laymen have kept school executives from giving adequate attention to the problem of intelligently informing the public concerning its schools.

In the meantime increased enrollments, longer school terms, better trained teachers, and richer courses of study have caused the operation and maintenance of schools to cost increasingly more. Citizens, being human, are almost certain to complain about these increased costs unless they are given the opportunity to understand that gone forever is the simplicity of the social structure served by the little red schoolhouse in the days of our grandfathers. As a recognition of this need of keeping the public informed, many states have enacted statutes requiring that at regular intervals school boards report to the people on the condition of their schools. Those who pay the bills have a right to know the full details about the educational program.

Effective public relations programs are not spontaneous, revival-like affairs. No longer is it considered sufficient or wise to flood tax-payers with propaganda on the eve of a bond election, then completely ignore public good will until it is time once again to launch another building program. Plans must be made for at least a year in advance, preferably longer; the details should be discussed and formally adopted by the school board, administrative staff, and teaching personnel. Whenever teachers are made to feel an important part of the program, they are not likely to look upon it as something handed down and enforced from above. Since teachers have frequent and personal contacts with the people of a community, their enthusiastic support is vitally essential.

In the actual planning of a program the first step is to list all the needs of the school system, then to select the most urgent ones for initial consideration. At this point trouble is liable to occur, especially if the public relations program is being developed in a democratic manner—each individual naturally considers his own interests first and may close his eyes to what really constitutes the most pressing needs. Here is where administrative tact and, perhaps, a bit of compromise must be called into play so that the program of action, as finally adopted, may not suffer from sniping by disgruntled laymen and teachers.

In the planning there must be taken into consideration just what agents and agencies are available, and how effective each can be. Agents within the school system include the board of education, administrative officers, supervisors, teachers, pupils, office staff, custodians, janitors, student organizations, and parent-teacher groups. Agents outside the school are parents, editors, reporters, radio station managers, businessmen, officeholders, and other community leaders. Inside-the-school agencies include school board publications, research bulletins, reports of pupil progress, personal and form letters to parents, student publications, and courses of study. Among agencies outside the school are newspapers, radio and TV stations, signboards, civic clubs, and such community activities as the chest campaigns and safety-first drives.

Some of the methods commonly used to bring the school to the people are exhibits and displays of school work, parades, and movie films. Also helpful are informational talks by educators and their supporters, provided, of course, they can make creditable presentations.

The story is told of Mr. J., a big-city principal, who took over a school that had an undeservedly bad reputation. Discovering that only an infinitesimal percentage of the pupils were "bad apples," he decided to publicize the good deeds of the great majority of the hard-working, cooperative youngsters. A community newspaper was persuaded to run a column giving credit to these children. Each week Mr. J. fed the editor with names and details. The practice not only sold newspapers but it raised school spirit.

Mr. J.'s next step was to inaugurate a "Citizen of the Month" award. Every class submitted the name of the most industrious or most improved pupil each month. These children received certificates in the assembly—and their names went to that newspaper. But Mr. J. did not stop there. He sent letters home to the parents telling them that they were the ones who really deserved the awards because they had promoted "juvenile decency" by the excellent upbringing they had obviously given their offspring. He invited these parents to the next evening meeting to receive their own awards. This practice, continued each month, raised attendance at parents' meetings from a mere 50 to 300. Once he had them in the auditorium, Mr. J. made sure that they were informed about all the fine activities their children were engaging in during the day. Three years later Mr. J.'s school was rated as "good" to "excellent" in a community poll. Parents who had formerly falsified their addresses to keep their children out of that school now transferred them in—and relieved their consciences at the same time.

As may be inferred from the above, an important part of a public relations program is the job of securing the cooperation of parents. In this connection, a word should be said about the National Congress of Parents, a very controversial subject in some educational circles. This movement on a national basis dates back to the founding in 1897 of the National Congress of Mothers. The name was changed in 1908 to National Congress of Mothers and Parent-Teacher Associations, and the present name was adopted in 1924. Thousands of units are now established, with a total membership approaching the five million mark. The local units keep the Congress informed of the needs in their communities and try to implement the program of the Congress within the individual schools.

Some schoolmen are quite bitter about PTA interference in strictly professional matters—it cannot be denied that a few PTA's have attempted "to run the school," with educational chaos resulting. Occasionally PTA workers use the organization to gain their own selfish ends; some have been guilty of using pressure to influence administrative policies. But such cases are the exception rather than the rule. PTA's, most educators agree, have helped to get parents and teachers better acquainted. Unfortunately many teachers have been inclined to hold back and not throw their wholehearted support into the activities of the organization, but this can scarcely be held against the parent members. On the PTA credit side is the elimination of many difficulties that involve parents, teachers, and pupils, as well as the stimulation of community sentiment for better schools.

In its final analysis the problem in public relations is to maintain a pleasant working relationship between the schools and the public, one that enables people to understand educational objectives and affords opportunities for the citizens themselves to register their own feelings to the extent that they become a vital part in making the schools what they are.

It is important to remember that to gain public confidence all information must be reliable and available. Unfavorable publicity can be minimized but not suppressed—people are not slow in discovering what and whom they can believe and trust. Further, those who issue information should have no axe to grind other than the desire to promote the welfare and progress of the pupils. Unselfishness in purpose is definitely needed for success in any long-range public relations program.

To be effective publicity must possess clarity and interest, which means that information should be humanized. The average community consists of individuals having a multitude of interests, various culture patterns, and different levels of education. This heterogeneity presents a problem in communication, but a good public relations man can present even somewhat technical data in such a manner as to be understood and appreciated by most of the citizens.

Some cities have carried this principle so far as to send out reports in the various languages. Philadelphia, for one, has broadcast radio programs in several tongues in order to inform the city's foreign-born of their privileges and responsibilities in public education. The recent tendency toward simplifying informational services has been taking the form of pictorial reports, circulation of motion pictures depicting local school activities, and the holding of open house or similar events for the purpose of bringing parents to school so that they may see firsthand the work as it is actually being done. An outgrowth of the last-mentioned practice has been the establishment of American Education Week. This event is observed nationally each November.

Continuous publicity that is interesting but dignified has proved its effectiveness in keeping the public well informed concerning its investment in public education. This continuity in information service has gone a long way to erase the traditional impression that teachers have a public-be-damned attitude—except when a bond issue or salary rise is to be voted upon. But the most important part of a public relations program will always be word-of-mouth communication. Schools must depend upon the good will of those whom they immediately serve. All the organized publicity in the world cannot give a school system, or an individual school, a good reputation when it is obviously bad.

PART FIVE

Psychology

PART FIVE

Psychology

As civilization developed, people gradually broke away from superstition and turned to philosophy to find the meanings of life and man's place in the world. Eventually the philosophers turned to science for facts to guide their thinking, and scientific methods for study were established. A whole new body of knowledge evolved, and psychology came into prominence.

Now let us look briefly at the historical development of psychological thinking since it has left an indelible impression upon modern educational practices. It is interesting to note that a man who achieves fame beyond his own period of life is often an extremist. And so it has been in psychology—a few of those who veered farthest from the accepted doctrines of their day became historical personages whose ideas now serve as milestones to mark the progress of our thinking.

Plato, Aristotle; Faculty Psychology

Translated, the Greek word *psyche* means "soul." Thus it would seem logical that psychology originally meant the study of the soul. However, to the Greeks "soul" had no more religious implication than does the word "mind" in modern-day language. It was the Christians, at a much later date, who developed the concept of the soul as being the immortal part in man as distinguished from the body. As early as 500 B.C. the Greeks had advanced beyond the primitive idea of man within man. For them that was too simple an explanation! Nevertheless, they found it necessary to retain the idea of an invisible something in their explanation of behavior. That mysterious unseen element they named *psyche*. Such a speculative and philosophical approach to the problem of learning was for many centuries the one generally accepted throughout the Western world.

Plato (427?–347 B.C.) was the first man on record to ask himself just how ideas enter the mind. He identified mind with ideas and insisted that ideas exist in their own right, independent of man. It was his doctrine that ideas merely reside in the body during life. They are there when one is born but are not yet fully developed. In other words, ideas are innate at birth. Learning occurs through sensations received via the senses, and these sensations serve to arouse corresponding ideas that have been slumbering in the mind since birth.

Plato drew a sharp distinction between mind and body. To the learning process the mind's contributions are ideas; the body's contributions, sensations. This, of course, is pure dualism; mind and body are separate entities. In Plato's thinking any source of error in thinking is due to the senses—it is the limitations of the body that handicap the mind. Such a dualistic treatment of mind and body was not original with Plato. But he was mainly responsible for fastening it upon education, and this serious miscomprehension continues to plague the educational thinking and practices of today despite its complete discrediting by modern science.

It was also Plato who began the long, endless dispute between heredity and environment, nature versus nurture. He himself leaned strongly in the direction of heredity, propounding that learning must be a development of capacities from within the individual. The purpose of teaching is to bring out that which has been within the learner from birth.

Aristotle (384–322 B.C.) followed in large measure the philosophical footsteps of Plato despite his much greater concern with physical and biological sciences. He did differ in not considering the mind as something apart from the body. Rather, he regarded it as an integral part of the functioning of the body itself. He believed that ideas are produced by the influence of the environment upon the organism. His scientific studies led him to make more of the relationship and similarities between human and other animal life.

Aristotle used the word "soul" virtually to mean life. Human nature, he held, is a compound of vegetative, animal, and human characteristics. Man has a vegetative nature that grows, reproduces, and dies as does plant life. He also possesses an animal nature that has desires, sensory impressions, and active movement the same as other animal life. But distinctly characteristic of man is reason—a power that lower animal forms do not possess.

In the centuries following Aristotle there developed wide support for describing the *psyche,* or soul, in terms of its functions, or faculties. That was the psychology of the medieval Scholastics. It continued, in fact, as the most widely accepted psychology of the Renaissance and post-Renaissance periods. The chief controversy among its proponents revolved around the number of faculties and their precise description. A few insisted there was but one faculty; others that there were as many as two dozen. In the process of time the five faculties of Aristotle were reduced to three: knowing, feeling, and willing. Also, more attention was given to the faculties that have become familiar to teachers: judgment, memory, imagination, and attention.

For many centuries the mind was conceived of as a bundle of powers, or faculties, each of which was capable of separate existence and independent function. Will, imagination, and memory were thought to exist and function by themselves. "Pure reason" was discussed as though it were an entity existing and functioning entirely independent of other faculties. Psychology was the study of these mental powers. A Yale University faculty report, in 1828, set up "development of the powers of the mind" as the supreme aim of education. The classics and mathematics were looked upon as the best means of bringing about the development of the intellectual powers.

The nineteenth-century phrenologists carried this conception of the mind as a bundle of powers, or faculties, to the point where each faculty was assigned some nook or cranny in the brain. They argued that anyone having a great deal of a particular faculty would necessarily have a bump on his skull at the point where this power was supposed to be located. Modern research has shown that the only type of brain localization to be found is localization of types of functions: visual, auditory, tactual, and the like. When today we stimulate that part of the brain thought by the phrenologists to be the center of religion, the individual twitches his leg!

Faculty psychology (the word itself comes from a Latin root, *facultas*, meaning a capacity or power to act) tended to magnify the role of the intellect in learning at the expense of that of the senses. Educators in the ancient and medieval eras, and even in recent years, accepted this overemphasis. They considered as variable and unreliable any knowledge derived from sense impressions; only the intellect was stable and dependable. Thus education was made needlessly difficult. The abstruse was favored; the experimental and concrete were largely neglected.

Formal Discipline; Transfer of Training

"What a child studies doesn't matter much, so long as he doesn't like it," might well have been the slogan of a teacher guided by the formal discipline approach which for hundreds of years remained the accepted doctrine in the instructional process. The advocates of formal discipline reasoned that the mind needs a broad general training—the more difficult the better. Once a mind is well trained by intricate mental tasks, the individual is properly prepared to tackle any of life's perplexing problems.

John Locke (1632–1704) and formal discipline have been almost synonymous because of his significant statement in the opening pages of *Some Thoughts Concerning Education:* "As the strength of the body lies chiefly in being able to endure hardships, so also does that of the mind." Undeniably those words express the essence of the theory, but not all authorities agree that Locke meant to advocate any such doctrine. As a matter of record, some of his writings indorse formal discipline and others oppose it. He very definitely believed that the school should be a pleasant environment to fit the needs of the individual. In any event, formal discipline was not original with the great English philosopher.

At the time Locke was presenting his significant theories on education most of the vernacular schools were ungraded and had poor equipment, long hours, and wretched physical conditions. The primary attention was given to the acquisition of verbal symbols through unrelieved memory work, reading, lectures, and recitations. Rigid assignments and drills formed the mental discipline while severe beatings and similarly cruel punishments served as the physical discipline.

Learning to read was a matter of practicing the alphabet, building up syllables, and copying down words and phrases. Advanced language work consisted of learning the formal rules of grammar, conjugating verbs, declining nouns, and drilling in style and composition, always with the aim of disciplining the child's mind or sharpening his faculties. Should one today visit schools throughout the United States, explore the byways as well as the highways, and observe the variety of methods now in use, he would still find a surprisingly large number of instances of the same kind of schooling that prevailed when Locke was evolving his educational theories. Let us glance briefly at the battle of American schools to overthrow formal discipline.

The idea of culture had largely determined curriculum and teaching methods during the first half of the nineteenth century, but this was gradually being displaced by formal discipline during the second half. For some years prior to the Civil War many academic authorities had been urging the study of the classics for disciplinary values as well as for culture. It had been during our earlier national period that newer subjects managed to enter into active competition with the classics, especially for those young people who did not intend to go to college.

Conservatives were duly shocked, belittling the new subjects as being too simple and too poorly organized to meet the rigid requirements of mental discipline. This ridicule served its purpose. Instructors of the more modern studies hung their heads in shame as, in accordance with the generally accepted psychological principles, they were compelled to acknowledge these criticisms as being just. Efforts were made to remedy the deficiency. English teachers in trying to make their instruction sufficiently difficult even considered the possibility of using Anglo-Saxon! Mathematics was first to gain the honor of satisfying the requirements of the advocates of formal discipline, and by 1850 was being regarded as equal in value with the classics as a means of general mental training.

In 1892, the NEA appointed a Committee of Ten on which President Charles William Eliot (1834–1926), of Harvard, served as chairman. With the assistance of several committees of subject-matter specialists a report was made the following year in which agreement was reached that college preparation is not the main function of the secondary schools. Then this committee proceeded to nullify the revolutionary reform value of its statement by declaring that the same subjects taught in the same manner form the best preparation for both college and life. Sample curricula were set up, and in these the academic subjects were strongly emphasized.

It was further agreed that for the purpose of mental training each major subject should be pursued for a considerable period of time. That, of course, meant education would necessarily be limited to a few established fields of knowledge rather than give a wide choice that might better suit the needs and fancies of individual students. However, some degree of subject selection by high school students was recommended.

At about the same time that this report by the Committee of Ten appeared, a vigorous attack against formal discipline was launched by the early Herbartians. From then on, addresses on the subject became increasingly more frequent in meetings of the NEA and other educational groups. This formal-discipline controversy served to make many teachers more critical of their own efforts to the point that some even began experimenting in order to replace the old and useless with something more modern and effective in the training of youth.

In much more common use today than formal discipline is the term "transfer of training." Both belong to the same school of psychological thought. When knowledge or skill acquired in the study of one subject, let us say Latin, makes it easier to acquire mastery over other subjects, for example, French or mathematics, such a mental process is called transfer of training. This implies that acquired mental capacities spread to other learning situations in which there has been little or no practice. Such reasoning has frequently been used to retain in the curriculum those subjects that have lost their practical utility and would logically be removed as "dead timber" except for their alleged disciplinary values.

There has been considerable controversy as to whether Locke ever meant to advocate transfer of training. In recommending a curriculum for young gentlemen in his *Conduct of the Human Understanding*, he did say: " . . . not that I think it necessary that all men should be deep mathematicians, but having got the way of reasoning, which that study necessarily brings the mind to, they might be able to transfer it to other parts of knowledge as they shall have occasion." But some of Locke's other writings seem to commit him to direct opposition to such a theory. He felt that learning should not be imposed as a task, but that it should be made a pleasant experience. He believed children learn much more quickly and effectively when some natural incentive is used.

Increasingly through the centuries a need has been felt for scientific procedures in the collection and collation of psychological data. Experimentation began about 1860. Some date this starting point in 1879 with the establishment by Wilhelm Wundt (1832–1920) of his laboratory at the University of Leipzig. New methods began replacing the approach through philosophy, which had depended upon personal observation and introspection. One of the problems for which this new experimentation sought to discover an explanation was whether transfer of training did take place and, if so, to what extent.

These pioneers had to devise their own materials and procedures. Using nonsense syllables to test mental associations the German philosopher, Hermann Ebbinghaus (1850–1909), in 1885 published his investigation of memory, an aspect of life about which philosophers had long engaged in discussion. An inconclusive experiment to test the transfer-of-training doctrine was reported by William James (1842–1910) in his *Principles of Psychology* which appeared in 1890.

A few other experiments were made before 1901, the year Edward

L. Thorndike (1874–1949) and R. S. Woodward (1849–1924) presented their study in *Psychological Review* under the title, "The Influence of Improvement in One Mental Function upon the Efficiency of Other Functions." Their evidence showed the transfer, where it occurs, to be due to similarity of contents, techniques, or principles—not to development of any particular psychological faculties or functions.

Almost immediately it was advocated that the idea of transfer of training be completely abandoned. But today, with hundreds of additional experiments completed, it is definitely known that transfer does occur even though there is far from unanimous agreement on the amounts or upon any single explanation as to how transfer may be secured. Positive transfer has been found in about 90 per cent of these experiments. This usually has been in small amounts, ranging from practically zero to as high as 20 per cent of improvement in the trained function or skill.

Most experiments show that the amounts of transfer are greater with young and very intelligent pupils, or when materials used in training and testing are similar. These amounts can be increased by teaching and studying if transfer is kept especially in mind. The learner who searches for principles and generalizations is able to make much broader applications of his acquired skills and knowledge than others who do not.

In general, the amount of transfer can be increased by emphasis upon the learning principles involved rather than by mere repetition. Thus it can be said that whenever material is so taught as to facilitate transfer, some degree of subject matter or method is likely to be carried over into another field. However, it seems to make no difference what subject is being taught—no subject automatically transfers to other subjects or to life situations outside of school. Summing it all up, experimentation has failed to show that any school subject possesses intrinsic values to train the mind better than another of equal difficulty.

In the earlier years of American education, only a small select minority of young people attended secondary schools. They logically were the ones with superior intellects and economic backgrounds. That meant subject matter naturally had higher cultural and transfer values for those of our grandparents who were being educated than is derived by most of today's heterogeneous high school population. So long as only bright students with academic interests attended, the degree of transfer from subject matter necessarily would be more than it is possible to obtain from the same or similar subject matter with the present enrollment of, on the average, less capable students. This lowering of high school intellectual capacity automatically has lessened possible transfer values.

Empiricism and Association of Ideas

From the time of the Athenian Greeks, the controversy over the nature of knowledge developed two major approaches now known as rationalism and empiricism. Rationalism holds largely to the traditional outlook that the mind is a separate and spiritual faculty which has the power to reach out and grasp the essential principles of the ultimate universal truth.* It is sympathetic to idealistic and religious thinking. Catholic leadership as the great upholder of the rationalistic viewpoint places scientific knowledge on a level definitely below that of the intellectual conception of knowledge.

Empiricism relies upon sensory experiences as the source of knowledge and upon human intelligence as the guide to personal conduct. It leans upon scientific investigation for its evidence. This challenge to rationalism was kept in abeyance, with only an occasional protesting voice here and there, until John Locke (1792–1856) gave it fresh impetus with his unique philosophical-psychological presentation. To understand the emergence of this empirical viewpoint we must make a brief historical review of the development up to the eighteenth century, the so-called period of enlightenment, when some of the most creative movements of Western civilization emerged from the seething political and social welter of French life.

Sciences of ancient civilization rose out of practical experiences in response to particular needs. Arithmetic came from the everyday necessities of shopkeepers and taxgatherers. Medicine made notable progress within a narrow range, and then became a dead formalism. Ancient peoples did not think of general principles but of concrete applications. They lacked free imagination, except in the case of the Athenian Greeks. It was they who introduced scientific thinking into the world, largely because they let their minds soar above the realm of the mundane and reach the level of the universal.

But in their intensive development of the intellect, even the Greeks ignored or underestimated the importance of sensory experiences. In trying to explain learning, Plato had found himself in a predicament.

---

* In this section the term "rationalism" is treated in its philosophical sense, rather than in its historical sense. The latter has been previously discussed in Part One under "History."

He was unable to understand how new ideas could enter the mind from without. So he evolved the theory that learning is the remembering, or bringing to light, of ideas with which the individual was already familiar before birth. Likewise, in the faculty psychology of Aristotle, mental faculties were thought to be innate, with the senses serving to irritate those faculties into action.

In the early Christian period Plato's "innate" ideas were merged with the doctrine of original sin, based upon Adam's temptation by the serpent in the Garden of Eden. Under this concept, education was centered upon keeping human weakness under control. In harmony with such a philosophy severe beatings were the approved method for chasing the "devil" out of the child both at home and in school.

Especially prominent also in the early writings of the Catholic Church was the idea that Christians had to be schooled in self-denial to meet the trials which would beset them. Preparation for martyrdom was to be undertaken systematically; a child was asked to keep before his eyes the vision of the martyr's heavenly rewards. Thus abnegation and flagellation long held the upper hand. They had great influence upon educational practices. Vestiges of that influence can still be found upon occasion in modern-day classrooms where teachers "rule the roost" as though each child were a perverted little devil from whom Satan's influence must be driven as the prerequisite for successful education.

This was not the view of Saint Thomas Aquinas (1225?–1247). In bringing natural reason and supernatural faith into harmony, he had some positive and refreshing things to say about the pupil's nature. He spoke of the "active potentiality" of knowledge within the learner, and he claimed that an individual could realize his potential through self-development. As for the role of the teacher, Saint Thomas drew an interesting analogy in his *De Magistro:* "As, then, a doctor is said to cause health in a sick person through the operation of nature, so man is said to cause knowledge in another through the operation of the learner's natural reason—and this is to teach."

But for a long time the philosophy of Saint Thomas was either neglected or misunderstood. Meanwhile the early Christian ideas, as partly enunciated by Saint Augustine (354–430), prevailed. Although Saint Thomas had preceded Locke in maintaining that all knowledge comes to man through the senses, church leaders distrusted the human body as a possible impediment to the salvation of the soul. The effect of such thinking was to place the emphasis on a child's potential for evil rather than good. This pessimistic viewpoint reached its extreme in the Calvinistic doctrine of the innate depravity of the child. Since philosophy and theology influence education, for centuries the schooling of children was largely governed by such doctrines. However, the struggle against this domination began to gain momentum in the eighteenth century. And so we return to John Locke.

It has been said that Locke was a philosopher by virtue of the fact that he was primarily a psychologist. Few men have revealed more profound insight into the human mind. He insisted that ideas and knowledge come from the experiences of the external world, reaching the human mind in the form of sensations and perceptions. He pointed out the way in educational method for more attention to the development of all the senses of the child, not merely through reading as had been the practice before his time, but also through the senses of sight, hearing, taste, touch, and smell. Consistently Locke stressed the importance of the physical development of the body, the principle which today is known as a sound mind in a sound body.

In the building of his theory concerning learning, Locke could find no justification for the doctrine of innate ideas. He studied closely the works of writers and concluded that not even the idea of God is everywhere to be found in the minds of primitive peoples. He compared the greatest peoples of history, the Greeks and Romans, and discovered they did not hold the same conceptions of justice, right and wrong, as were being held in his own day. Locke concluded that there is not a single idea known to the human mind which can truly be said to be universal and therefore innate. Thus, through observations and practical experiences, he identified both an outer and inner source of knowledge—the outer source being the five senses; the inner source, those experiences received from the operation of the mind in its conscious mental activities.

In renunciation of Plato's conclusions Locke presented his *tabula rasa* theory. His *Essay Concerning Human Understanding* proposes that the mind in its original state is a "sheet of white paper, void of all characters." An infant is not born with a preexistent mind or soul, or with innate ideas concerning God, justice, morality, or other values; a newborn baby merely possesses a *tabula rasa* (blank tablet) upon which perceptions from the outside world are impressed or printed. Ideas, values, and knowledge originate in the experiences of the external world and in contacts with other people. Locke then explained the origin of ideas as a matter of impressions being made upon the mind through the senses. The mind is purely passive and receptive; it plays no active part in hearing a sound, seeing a light, or in other perceptions which come to it. All virtues and powers are worked into an individual from the outside through the formation of habits.*

The most prominent psychology of learning in the nineteenth century was associationism. It denied the validity of faculty psychology and attempted to reduce all mental processes to that of association. Mind and consciousness, according to this theory, are formed by a process in which simple perceptions of external objects become associated in the individual with other perceptions to produce more complex perceptions and ideas. Once again educational psychology was indebted to Locke for an important contribution—the phrase, "association of ideas," the starting point of associationism.

However, again this idea was not original with Locke. In searching for the "key" to memory, Aristotle had noted how recollection of a given item could be helped along by trying to remember some other item closely associated with it. The Greek philosopher presented a systemized plan to facilitate memory; contiguity of one idea with another, succession of ideas in a series, similarity of ideas, and contrast of ideas.

Extremists in associationism ruled out Locke's "inner faculty of reflection" and put their exclusive emphasis upon the five outer senses as the sources for ideas. Traditionists, especially those within the Catholic Church, bitterly attacked them for so completely eliminating the role of the mind in stressing the body as the exclusive instrument for learning.

The doctrine of association of sensations and ideas, a position that came to be known as "sensationalism," was developed by David Hume (1711–1776) and expanded by David Hartley (1705–1757). To them the basic natural law of learning was that sensations, repeated often enough, would leave their traces in the nervous system. Thus, if different sensations should be associated frequently enough, the occurrence of one sensation would call up a memory of another. In this way, said these theorists, simple ideas could be built into complex ideas merely by association.

This became an important doctrine in educational psychology, especially for those seeking a mechanical or physiological explanation of the learning process. Hartley, a physician, attempted to reduce all ideas to sensations, and all sensations to nerve vibrations. He claimed that all associations occur because the associated ideas have been to-

* For previous discussion of Locke and his theories, see pages 70 and 141.

gether in the mind. But such an extreme position was difficult to maintain. Critics pointed out there are many ideas together in the mind that do not become associated, and that these "basic laws" of association fail to explain why certain associations do take place and other possible ones do not.

To meet such valid criticisms the doctrine of Hume and Hartley was modified by their followers. Aristotle's precept that the mind seeks and selects what is remembered was revived. Moreover, to bolster up other glaring weaknesses of extreme associationism, there were proposed secondary laws of association: recency, frequency, duration, liveliness, and finally, primacy—the idea that the first association of a series tends to be stronger than the later ones.

Despite much discussion and controversy for more than a century following Locke's pronouncement of an "association of ideas," it remained for Johann Herbart (1776–1841) to gather the loose ends in the exploration of the bases and limitations of associationism. This Herbart did in formulating his theory of learning known as "apperception," a term he borrowed from a famous philosopher of the previous century, Gottfried Leibnitz (1646–1716).

Herbart held that perceptions and ideas become associated in many combinations; that an apperceptive mass of experience is built up in the individual and constitutes the structure of his mind. Thus, when two ideas become linked in experience, a stimulus from external causes recalls not only the original idea but also the other idea that has become associated with it. This doctrine of apperception directed attention of teachers to the importance of commencing the learning process at the point where a child's experience has placed him.*

Genetic Psychology and Pragmatism

Genetic psychology is the study of behavior in terms of the origin and development in the individual and in the race. The initial impetus came from the publication in 1859 of *The Origin of Species* by Charles Darwin (1809–1882). Limiting his investigation to the realm of biology, Darwin set forth the hypothesis that the evolution of living organisms is due to the everlasting struggle for existence resulting in the survival of the fittest. The popular interpretation, of course, is that man's immediate ancestors are apes.

The Christian world was shocked by such a theory, but that shock did begin a new epoch in human thinking. Despite bitter opposition nearly every subject of human interest came in gradually for a complete

* For previous discussion of Herbart and his theories, see pages 72 and 140.

reorganization in the light of this new viewpoint. The most perplexing problem that faced this new theory of biological evolution was to account for the human mind and soul. It was this challenge of reconciling man's life with the evolutionary hypothesis that motivated the thinking of G. Stanley Hall (1846–1924), called the first of the new scientific psychologists, just as Herbart is considered the last of the great philosophical psychologists.

Trained at Leipzig in the laboratory of Wilhelm Wundt (1832–1920), Hall returned to the United States to introduce during the last quarter of the nineteenth century this new European approach to psychological problems. He wanted to do for the human mind what Darwin and his followers had been accomplishing in piecing together the various lines of evidence for the evolution of biological life from cellular forms to the complex human body.

Hall's explorations went into uncharted areas of mind reaction in both the animal and child worlds. His fundamental theory was that mental and physical life are always parallel. Mind and body have evolved together; physical life began in a single unicellular creature, so also did the mind. Through millions of years and infinite changes, said Hall, the human body has become what it is today—the mental life has accompanied physical change at each and every step of this development. Hall's interest was not so much in theories of learning, attention, memory, and forgetting. His efforts were focused on the child, and "child-centered" became a rallying cry of forceful importance.

This movement began to gain momentum with Hall's publication in 1883 of *The Contents of Children's Minds on Entering School*. Data for this volume were collected by teachers of Boston and vicinity, who asked beginning children individually a series of questions which Hall had prepared. There were about a hundred items covering their knowledge and understanding of common, everyday things—what they knew about plants and animals, things they could do, their ideas about religion. This study indicated, much to everybody's surprise, that there is very little that children of six can be safely assumed to know.

Hall's studies and those of his students were largely conducted through the questionnaire method; frequently neglected were the uses of observation and experimentation as the basis for evidence. This questionnaire method is now in considerable disrepute because of serious inaccuracies; for example, those introduced by hearsay and untrained introspection. Despite such admitted weaknesses the questionnaire at that time afforded valuable new information and led to the development of the more careful scientific studies of the present time.

Hall's greatest contribution was to focus attention upon the need for studying child development.

More spectacular though probably less significant than Hall's methods of gathering data was his genetic theory of interpreting them. Profoundly influenced by the biological thought of his day, he proposed the "recapitulation theory" which assumes that a child's development from birth repeats the pattern of human historical development. Play activity, he thought, is recapitulation—the social stages in the history of the race are recapitulated in each child's educational development. Hall believed that for each advance made by man in his progress from savagery to civilization there is a corresponding stage in the normal growth during childhood. For example, primitive life includes climbing, swinging, babbling, chasing, hiding, and hunting. Nomadic life includes wandering, traveling in gangs, fighting, and engaging in team games. And finally, every civilization has had its resemblance to adult occupations.

According to Hall a teacher must be a close student of human nature so as to be able to take full advantage of opportunities for setting up the learning process when each of these stages, in its turn, appears. Recapitulation is not always complete in every individual, which, of course, explains the exceptions to the general rule. But when and if it is complete, the teacher may expect the appearance of certain types of conduct. Fighting, for example, though no longer socially approved, is but a natural mode of expression at a certain age, and is useful as a mode of adjustment to the environment.

Hall's famous theory of "catharsis" (compare its medical meaning) is to permit these childish actions, not to inhibit them—allow them to run their course; in other words, get them out of a child's system. If these tendencies were permitted expression at their normal time, so Hall believed, they would spend themselves and disappear. If inhibited, there was always the danger they would find harmful expression later in life. This theory, incidentally, is closely related to Aristotle's ideas on the blood-and-thunder aspects of Greek tragedy.

Many of Hall's doctrines, like recapitulation and catharsis, were vigorously attacked. Most of his critics were more scientific in their own procedures, relying less on speculation and more on facts to support their views. In recent times Hall has been receiving less attention relative to the scientific work he accomplished, or even the inspiration he gave those who studied under him, of whom Yale's Arnold Gesell (1880–1961) is doubtless the most famous. Many writers today are content to discount his merits by stating that Hall risked everything on the recapitulation theory, and lost when that theory fell into disrepute. However, this is rank undervaluation of the true importance of the man.

The word "pragmatism" was first introduced into our language by Charles Sanders Peirce (1839–1914) in an article published in the January, 1878, *Popular Science Monthly*. William James elaborated on it in his *Principles of Psychology* (1890). Pragmatism emphasizes and deals with real things. It lays stress on practical results as standards in conduct. To every theory it applies the test of its functioning in actual practice—"If it works, it's all right."

Historically, pragmatism is considered the most distinctively American nineteenth-century contribution to intellectual life. The frontier, with its wilderness to be conquered and the constant struggle for existence, had shaped a mood not in sympathy with any tradition in which everything has a fixed place in relation to the whole and in which truth is looked upon as uniform, fixed, and eternal. The combination of this characteristic temper in American life and the example of Darwinism led James to formulate a pragmatic psychology, which for modern living conditions he considered far more appropriate than traditional European doctrines.

Psychologically, pragmatism points out that interest, attention, selection, purpose, bias, desire, emotion, and satisfaction all color and control our thinking processes. It insists that the individual's thought is both personal and purposive—also, that there is no such thing as "pure" thought. In other words, any judgment which is not prompted by motives and inspired by personal interest is psychologically impossible.

John Dewey (1859–1952) led this pragmatic reaction against long-established conservative viewpoints by drawing together the philosophical traditions of naturalism and empiricism. These Dewey blended with the new scientific evidence from biology, anthropology, Gestaltism, and social psychology. Through the pioneer experimental school which he conducted at the University of Chicago from 1896 to 1903, and through his teachings and writings Dewey has had the greatest influence upon modern educational development throughout the world.

While Dewey's fame is primarily that of a philosopher, it should be noted that his earlier work was in psychology. He showed the necessity of connecting the school with life outside the classroom, and of giving children an intelligent understanding of the world in which they are living. He held that real education must be based upon the nature of the child; that knowledge is a part of one's intellectual equipment and resources. The mind to him is a process, a growing affair. Development depends upon exercise of its functions, and requires constant stimulation from social agencies. One learns to do any specific thing by doing that specific thing. Books may give explicit instruction on the art of swimming, but one actually learns to swim by getting into the water and swimming.

In his *School and Society* (1899) Dewey insisted that the school cannot be a preparation for social life except as it reproduces the conditions typical of social life. In *How to Think* (1909) he gave almost classic expression to the principle that all learning takes place in attempts to remedy or remove the inadequacies in past experiences, and that this learning should become the process of making use of past experiences as resources in developing the future. These and other pragmatic principles have served to modify and improve school practices not only in our country but in many others as well.

Dewey insisted upon constant experimentation as a means of learning more about the child's nature so that school practices may be better adapted to its effective development. A child's nature is inherently active and bubbling over with the impulse to do something, so it is the function of education to direct these impulses into desirable channels. He divided impulses into four kinds: the social impulse of communication or conversation; constructive impulse to make things; impulse to investigate things; and impulse of artistic or creative expression.

Thus Dewey stressed the fact that the psychological nature of a child must not be divorced from the social situation. Rather, it is to be used for directing his energies into socially useful channels. He advocated changing school procedures to the end that the child is given opportunities to learn by experience. In other words, one learns to think by managing experiences. This of necessity means a change must be made to transform the classroom from a passive, listening basis to an active doing or working one. The proper solution to any problem requires intelligent thinking; therefore, thinking becomes the principal factor in the ability to cope with new situations.

In fact, Dewey's definition of thinking is to bring the meaning of past experiences to bear on the interpretation of new situations. In order better to develop this ability to think, school methods and subject matter should be adapted to the child's interests and needs. In his earlier experimentation Dewey had found that a general mistake is made in introducing children too abruptly to special studies that have but little relation to their own social lives. He felt the social life of the child should be the foundation upon which to base his growth and training. Such expressive activities as music, drawing, nature study, manual arts, and household arts should be used as the steppingstones to introduce the child to the more formal subjects. Whenever this social element is lacking, said Dewey, a school study loses much of its value.*

Structuralism and Functionalism

United in their opposition to faculty psychology, those who advocated empirical emphasis upon sensory experiences as the basis of learning began to differ among themselves and to split into new groups, or "schools." Of these, structuralism is historically important because it is the source from which our current American psychology evolved. Sometimes called the psychology of consciousness, it is concerned with knowing, feeling, and willing. Knowing is analyzed into concepts, percepts, and sensations, which are the elementary and structural elements of thinking. Hence the name structuralism.

Representing a transitional step from philosophical to experimental psychology, structuralism made some use of laboratory science but still depended chiefly upon traditional introspection as its method for analyzing and classifying mental states. Structuralism grew out of the English associationistic psychology that had continued from the seventeenth through the nineteenth centuries. It was Wilhelm Wundt, in his Leipzig laboratory from about 1879 to 1920, who brought structuralism to maturity after becoming involved in a long controversy. The question was whether psychology should merely study mental processes as "contents" of the mind which were found to exist, or if it should describe how these processes function. Structuralists believed that psychology should have definite and organized subject matter comparable with that of the science of physics.

Wundt thought of sensations as those experiences which are aroused when a sense organ is stimulated and the incoming impulse reaches the brain. These he classified as seeing, smelling, hearing, and the like. To him there was no fundamental difference between sensations and images. In addition, so he reasoned, there are qualities known as feelings which include those experiences not coming from any sense organ, or from the revival of sensory experiences.

The highest development of structuralism was reached in the hands of Wundt's English-born student, E. B. Titchener (1867–1927), who from 1892 to 1925 directed the research of so many students at Cornell

* For previous discussion of Dewey and his theories, see pages 79, 87, and 143.

University. Further development of structuralism by Titchener was basically the same as that of Wundt. Mental states are made up of sensations, images, and feelings. Simple feelings are classified as pleasant and unpleasant. All other feelings, in reality, are compounds of those two fundamental ones.

Structuralists found sensations and perceptions to be the primary ingredients of simple mental states. Complex mental images and ideas are then built up by the process of association, in which sensations and images are linked together within the individual's experience. In simpler words, mental states that occur together will recur at some later time when, and if, similar stimuli appear.

It is impossible to understand structuralism without comparing it with functionalism. The general mental laws of structuralism are opposed to individual differences of functionalism. Americans now definitely favor the latter viewpoint. Stated in simple terms, structuralism is an "IS" psychology; functionalism, an "IS FOR" psychology. Structuralism deals with contents or elements, such as visual or gustatory sensations, beliefs; functionalism, with acts or operations, such as seeing, tasting, believing.

Functionalism considers consciousness an activity with a biological end—an activity of special use in allowing the organism to adapt itself to the circumstances of its environment. Structuralism is narrower and more rigid. Essentially it is an introspective psychology, aiming at the analysis of experience into elements. Because it considers that part of human life inaccessible, structuralism makes no entrance into the wider biological sphere—and that is exactly what functionalism does.

Throughout his life, despite the losing battle against functionalism and other new forms of psychological thought, Titchener remained stubbornly true to the Wundtian tradition. He believed that a science should deal only with things as they are found to exist. This excludes all references to the meanings of the processes, which he considered a speculative problem in the philosophy of values. He further warned against the common error of confusing descriptions of mental processes with descriptions of the stimuli which set them off, the so-called stimuli error. Titchener wanted to experiment on the normal human mind, not the abnormal. He had little interest in those features that distinguish one individual from another, and in this he differed from the more popular psychology known as functionalism.

Functionalism goes considerably beyond structuralism in breaking away from faculty psychology—it applies the evolutionary theory more fully to human behavior. Darwin's concept of the utility of functions greatly influenced William James who began teaching at Harvard about 1870. Having prepared originally for the medical profession, James was especially sensitive to the possibilities of a close connection between psychology and both physiology and neurology. Resorting only to introspection himself, he begged off from the obligation of explaining in exact terms the mind-body relationship. In avoiding this point he suggested that teachers content themselves with learning the ways in which psychological life functions.

James took issue with those who viewed the learner as a sort of passive receptacle. His oft-quoted "No impression without expression" indicates a desire for the student to be an active factor in the learning process. He felt that certain reactions or powers to express oneself are unlearned and a part of native endowment. He described the functioning of native capacities not as faculties but as instincts, and his list of these was made with biology in mind—fear, love, curiosity, ambition, pride, imitation, ownership, pugnacity, constructiveness, and the like.

While James did not divorce himself entirely from faculty psychology, his instinct psychology differed from it in the manner in which learning was explained. Made without the aid of laboratory experimentation, the James explanation of instincts anticipated Edward L. Thorndike's subsequent development of learning as "conditioning."

Experimental psychology, just coming into vogue at this time, brought forth studies of heredity and original nature as conducted by Francis Galton (1822–1911), James McKeen Cattell (1860–1944), and Thorndike. The last-named, a student of James, was the outstanding functionalistic psychologist. Especially in the first quarter of the twentieth century did his psychology largely dominate American educational thinking.

Thorndike's initial prominence was gained through experimental studies in animal learning. By observing efforts of animals to escape from a puzzle box, he reached certain notable conclusions about the general nature of the learning process. Fundamentally his theory was that learning the right response is largely accidental, a matter of trial and error. He plotted progress in the form of a learning curve and measured it by reduction in the number of errors and increase in the number of successes. In other words, he claimed, learning is a matter of connecting the right stimulus with the right response. Hence, his earlier educational psychology has sometimes been known as "connectionism," or S-R psychology.

Experiments with animals had a profound influence upon Thorndike's thinking about human learning. Contrary to the then popular belief, he became convinced that in animal behavior-responses the re-action is made directly to the situation sensed. He did not go so far as to deny ideation among animals, ideation being the function or process of the mind whereby it forms or entertains ideas. But he was convinced that the general bulk of learning could be explained by the direct bind-ing of acts to situations, with no idea entering into the mental processes.

After Thorndike began his experimentation with human beings, he compared their learning curves with those of animals. The results led him to believe that essentially those same mechanical phenomena dis-closed in animal learning are also the fundamentals of human learning. He was well aware of the much greater degree of subtleness within that of man, but held that, so far as identification was possible, simpler forms of human learning parallel those of animals.

Despite the many attacks upon it and the rise of several rival schools of psychological thought, Thorndike's S-R connectionism long dom-inated all other learning theories in America. As a principle he had accepted association between sense impressions and impulses to act, which associations came to be known as *connection* or *bond*. These were strengthened or weakened in the making or breaking of habits. Thorndike made use of a new type of experiment in which an animal was placed in problematical situations; then its efforts to reach a goal, such as escape or food, were observed and recorded. An interest in re-wards and punishments growing out of these experiments with animals eventually turned Thorndike's attention to the study of learning as it occurs in schools.

The three-volume *Educational Psychology* (1913–14) represented Thorndike's earlier system of thought covering roughly the period from 1898 to 1930. His position is best understood through the three major laws that form the bases of his famed S-R theory: readiness, exercise, and effect. In the law of readiness, when a tendency toward action is aroused through preparatory adjustments, sets, or attitudes, fulfillment of that tendency in action is satisfying; nonfulfillment is annoying. Strengthening of connections with practice (law of use) and their weakening or forgetting when practice is discontinued (law of disuse) form his earlier law of exercise—the basis for drill work, such as learning multiplication tables and spelling words.

Thorndike's original law of effect refers to the strengthening or weakening of a connection as a result of its consequences. If a child gets a sense of satisfaction from his school activities, the quality of his work will show it; if the work is annoying, the strength of the S-R bond is decreased. In other words, rewards or successes further the learning process; punishments or failures reduce the tendency to repeat the behavior.

After 1930 Thorndike revised his theory by virtually renouncing the law of exercise, holding that only a trivial amount of strengthening of connections results from mere repetition. He expressed belief that a single occurrence followed by a reward strengthens a connection about six times as much as it would be strengthened by merely recurring. Likewise, he repudiated the weakening effects of annoying consequences in his original law of effect, pointing out that difficulties frequently serve as a challenge to the learner.

His later experiments showed that transfer occurs only when the content or method of a school subject is similar to the use to which it is to be put—if students are to be educated to specific ends, they should study those subjects which best contribute to those ends. Such a theory gave great comfort to the new social and scientific studies which were then becoming more insistent in their demands for a proper place in the curriculum. Thus mental discipline received a major setback under the impact of functionalism.*

So, as a result of the influence of laboratory methods, there was evolved a psychological theory that mind, far from being a separate entity or faculty, is really the functioning of the organism in adjusting its behavior more adequately to its environment. Thus in functionalism behavior became more important than consciousness, the essential basic element in structuralism. As William James put it, "Mind is what it does."

Behaviorism and Gestalt Psychology

Behaviorism came about partly as a reaction against Wundt's and Titchener's slow methods of introspection and partly as a result of criticisms of functionalism. Some psychologists had begun to consider it a dubious analogy to predicate human learning to such an extent on animal learning. Certain "diehard" conservatives questioned whether data drawn so largely from the study of physical behavior rather than the field of consciousness could be properly called psychology. This reappearance of mind-body dualism, definitely a threat to scientific investigations of psychological problems, led some functionalists, just before World War I, to magnify the behavioristic approach into a new school of psychology. This movement was initiated by Max Meyer (1873–   ) and popularized by John B. Watson (1878–1958).

The starting point of behaviorism was the conditioned-reflex theory

* For additional discussion of Thorndike and his theories, see pages 77 and 304.

of the Russian scientist, Ivan Pavlov (1849–1936). Under laboratory-controlled conditions, by presenting food to a dog and at the same time ringing a bell, Pavlov soon discovered that simply ringing the bell called out the salivary flow which the food originally had produced. Thus, if two stimuli (food and bell) occur together often enough, and one is strong enough to evoke a reflex (salivary flow), the second or originally inadequate stimulus (bell) will be sufficient to evoke the response.

In 1904, when Pavlov won a Nobel Prize in Physiology and Medicine for his work on the digestive glands, John B. Watson was in his mid-twenties. He was acquainted not only with Pavlov's experiments but also with the work of another Russian, Vladimir M. Bechterev (1857–1927), and the English psychologist, Conwy L. Morgan (1852–1936). And, of course, he had studied Thorndike's conclusions with great interest. Watson followed the paths of these men in trying to arrive at a naturalistic understanding of emotional life. His methods were simple, direct, and effective.

In a series of experiments infants were subjected to such situations as the sight of rats, dogs, rabbits, fire, and assorted sounds. They were dropped through the air and caught safely without being injured; their movements were restrained by holding arms closely to the body. While Watson's trained workers were making careful records of responses, various stimulus situations were used to bring forth a display of emotions. These data were later studied and analyzed to discover if definite patterns of response stood out.

Prior to Watson's studies of emotion, infants and children were generally thought to possess inborn fears of many things. Popular belief had it that babies instinctively fear furry objects. Watson was the first to perform a rigid test of this notion, taking for his subject hospital-reared orphans, four to five months of age, whose complete family histories were known. Such babies had been reared virtually in isolation from the numerous emotional stimuli normally encountered in a home. Thus under laboratory conditions the experimental stimuli were being experienced for the first time.

Superstition had it that the black cat is a naturally fearsome creature, yet the invariable response was for the infant to reach out and touch the animal's fur, eyes, and nose. Responses were essentially the same when a rabbit was presented in a similar manner. Dogs, both large and small, were used with like results. Only in the case of the larger animals were the infants not inclined to reach out and touch.

Thus, finding that children with no previous opportunity to learn fear were not afraid of animals, Watson concluded that the common beliefs that children instinctively fear furry objects were "just old wives' tales." Later experiments showed that babies whose previous emotional life had known no such fear were not afraid of fire—the first response of a child to the flame is to reach for it. Nor were they afraid of the dark or of snakes.

Behavioristic research revealed three types of emotional response in the child: fear, rage, lust. Watson considered these as the bases from which the complex adult emotional structure emerges through the combined action of maturation and learning. He and his followers must be credited for a great impetus given to the study of human emotions. They were keenly aware of possibilities for training children to be emotionally healthy, but were somewhat inclined to neglect maturation in accounting for the growth of emotional complexity.

Critics pointed out that conditioning emotional responses is not quite as simple as behavioristic experimentaton would seem to indicate. Criticisms followed two main channels: there is more than conditioning in the growth of emotional life; and conditioning is much more than a simple process of connecting a previously neutral stimulus to an emotional response through simultaneous presentation of stimulus and response. Behaviorists had given the general impression that emotional growth is a rather simple process to be explained entirely as the conditioning of a few native emotional responses. Other experimenters refuted such claims by showing a number of notable failures to obtain conditioning of emotional responses. Moreover, Watson's position was weakened by his denial of the significance of maternal affection and his underestimation of a child's basic sense of security.

But behaviorists played an important role in discrediting subjective methods of investigation through introspection. Employing the principle that "seeing is believing," they reduced psychological phenomena to instances of overt behavior and hastened the day when educational psychology could be studied as objectively as other sciences. By emphasizing nurture rather than nature, behaviorists held out great hopes to educators, reformers, and politicians for eventually controlling human conduct.

Watson himself went so far in his *Behaviorism* (1925) as to make the claim that, given a healthy normal baby at birth and also control over his subsequent conditioning environment, he could train that child to become a "doctor, lawyer, artist, merchant-chief, and, yes, even a beggarman and thief, regardless of his talents, penchants, tendencies, abilities, vocations, and race of ancestors." Behaviorism thus aspired to predict human behavior with as much certainty as physics predicts physical phenomena.

Gestalt psychology took root in 1912 when a series of experiments in Europe demonstrated transposition, insight, and goal-directed behavior as opposed to blind trial and error. Actually this movement had begun to take form several years before that date. As a reaction against functionalism it was an eruption of dissatisfaction among both European and American psychologists over too strict a dependence upon analytical methods.

Gestaltists protested the use of analysis in psychology though, in fact, they themselves had to use analysis because it is basic to any scientific investigation. They really were objecting to the practice of building up or reconstructing the whole out of analytical elements—and such a process is synthesis, not analysis. The Gestalt quarrel with functionalism was that it made learning appear simply a matter of linking (or associating) bits of experience. This new school of psychology denied that learning is a matter of going from part to whole. Its leaders suggested that in order to learn effectively one should commence with the whole. Teachers can today recognize this particular Gestalt influence in the current emphasis on the "whole child."

Most of the initial Gestalt experimentation took place in Germany. Under the leadership of Wolfgang Köhler (1887–   ) and Kurt Koffka (1886–1941) the Gestaltists began to deny that learning results from the connection between a specific stimulus and a specific response, thus refuting Thorndike's S-R psychology. They held, instead, that the total situation of the learning process and the total activity of the body are involved in learning, not merely the sensory and motor nerves. Gestaltists claimed that the mind is so constituted as to react to the whole pattern, or configuration, of the situation—or, as the Germans called it, to the *Gestalt*.

This word has no exact counterpart in the English language, and even a dictionary definition seems quite obscure. One lexicographer gives this explanation of it: "An undivided, articulated whole which cannot be made up by mere addition of independent elements. For example, a melody may be played in many keys or by many instruments so that the tones heard are totally different; yet the melody remains the same. In the Gestalt each 'part' is not an independent element but a member of the whole whose very nature depends upon its membership in the whole. A tone has a different character when it appears in two different musical settings; it influences and is influenced by the other tones."

Köhler's work with apes is among the best known of psychological experimentation. One chimpanzee, after learning to seize food beyond his reach with the aid of a stick, was given two sticks. Neither of these was long enough to reach the food, but if they were fitted together they could be used to bring the food within reach. After more than an hour of trial-and-error behavior, the solution of fitting the sticks together occurred to the chimpanzee. This action was not caused by random, accidental, motor behavior. Rather, it came so suddenly, resulted in so much apparent satisfaction to the animal, and was remembered so well the next day that Köhler was sure learning had occurred through genuine insight.

Thorndike had emphasized the principle of trial and error in learning. In rebuttal Gestaltists made much of the fact that some solutions come suddenly and in the absence of any observable trial-and-error manipulation of symbols or objects. Frequently, they claimed, there is a period in which no progress toward a solution seems apparent. Then suddenly comes the arrival of the solution, and such a phenomenon is known as insight.

Another investigator used children instead of chimpanzees, and it was found that they did considerably better than the apes. Some of them used trial and error while others seemed to size up the situation, then proceeded to do the proper thing in order to achieve the goal. A toy was placed far enough outside the play pen so that it could not be reached. Some of the subjects wasted considerable time trying vainly to reach the plaything with their hands; others would seize a stick in plain sight and use it to take in the desired object. Suddenness of the correct response, combined with lack of preceding trial-and-error efforts, was labeled by the investigators as definitely the result of insight.

Gestalt psychology holds that learning is the doing of something new. This newness cannot be understood by analyzing the situation alone—it consists of reorganization of the situation so as to bridge the gap between it and the goal. After the gap-bridging is achieved, the situation as a whole is suddenly seen as a pattern including the goal leading to it.

Learning to deal with words always involves some use of the factor of belonging. This is a point that has been greatly emphasized by the Gestaltists. They hold that any element of behavior or experience is integrated with, or incorporated into, a large pattern and has a meaning or significance in terms of past experience or the present conditions of the individual. This means that isolated items, those that do not readily lend themselves to organization into a meaningful whole, are difficult to learn.

To illustrate: in an experiment a boy was asked to memorize a list of nonsense syllables, a list of common words with no relationship to each other, and a list of words that were closely related. Nonsense syllables without logical meaning or pattern took a long time. Ordinary words were learned more quickly, but the words related in meaning required hardly any time at all to memorize. Gestaltists explain that in nonsense syllables there is lacking a background relationship, or a whole.

Older psychologies of learning had long recognized that significant meaning makes for easy learning and permanent retention, but the Gestaltists were the first to give this fact a great deal of emphasis and systematic investigation. Their psychology reached the zenith of its popularity among progressive educators during the period between World Wars. Today it offers a very plausible justification for both the integrated program and activity curriculum.

In presenting the high spots in the development of theories of learning, two other "schools" should be mentioned briefly—purposivism and psychoanalysis.

Purposive (or hormic) psychology is still another protest against the mechanistic explanation of human behavior. Its most enthusiastic spokesman was William McDougall (1871–1938). As a social psychologist he believed that all other theories fail to explain sociological problems, that all human activities are motivated and controlled by inner forces, impulses, and creative drives, and that man's behavior cannot be explained merely on the basis of mechanism and functioning. In short, purposivism claims there is room for some spiritual, nonmaterialistic explanation of human behavior.

Psychoanalysis is associated principally with abnormal psychology, but is mentioned here because of the attention it directs toward the importance of emotional responses. Sigmund Freud (1856–1939) was interested primarily in explaining adult abnormalities. These difficulties he traced in large part to the conflicts between the individual and his social desires that develop in the early years of childhood, principally between the ages of two and five.

Psychoanalysis holds the mind to be dualistic: the conscious mind makes the rational choices; the subconscious does most of the directing of human activities. Freud, a physician, believed that all behavioral abnormalities can be explained in terms of the thwarting of sex impulses which leads to conflicts and complexes. It is unfortunate that popular treatments of this theory have so greatly distorted its real implications.

Individual Differences; Intelligence Tests

Individual differences have been noted here and there throughout the history of education. Plato in the *Republic* sorted out children in order to prepare them to become philosophers, warriors, or artisans, according to whether they possessed gold, silver, or lead talents of mind. Marcus Fabius Quintilian (35–100) not only granted that some Roman boys surpassed others in ability but also claimed that dull and unteachable ones were as rare as those born with monstrous deformities. He recognized that the vast majority are capable of improvement, and stressed the desirability of allowing a choice of studies to provide the greatest possible opportunity for development of special talents. Quintilian sounds almost modern in saying that the good teacher will ascertain the dispositions and abilities of his pupils so as to adapt his methods to each individual.

In the Italian Renaissance the aims of humanistic education were to produce a broadly cultured individual having a well-rounded personality, one capable of assuming leadership in church or state. The educated man was the one with a mastery of classical knowledge; at the same time he was effective in action. The humanists felt that memorizing was most important, but they also advocated that the student should understand the rules as he learned them. In educational literature at that time there was considerable discussion of the importance of individual differences, though it required a stretch of the imagination to apply this principle to the study of Cicero or Virgil.

Juan Luis Vives (1492–1540), a Spaniard who taught Catherine of Aragon (1485–1536) and went to England with her, advocated that the school should adapt instruction to the individual differences and interests of pupils. To achieve this he recommended the use of classics as the foundation for wisdom rather than merely as examples of good literary style. Vives was one of the very few who urged formal schooling for girls. He thought it possible to educate them through letters and moral teaching to become high-principled wives and mothers, intelligent companions and mistresses of the household.

Locke observed that children have such different natures that little or nothing can be done to make the pensive child gay or the sportive one restrained. His *tabula rasa* theory of the working of the mind has been used both to support and to contradict the existence of individual differences. Locke did try to make it clear that impressions made on a mind like wax would not endure as would those made on minds like brass and steel. His French followers, however, missed the significance of this attempt to differentiate, and they proceeded on the false assumption that minds not only are blank at birth but that they all possess the same sensitivity. They held that undeniable differences of individual reactions to learning situations were due to exposure to different sorts of environment and types of education. As a result of this interpretation of Locke's writings, he is held principally responsible for having put into actual classroom practice the extreme viewpoint that there is nothing in the understanding which has not come through the senses.

Jean Jacques Rousseau's (1712–1778) *Émile* proved one of the most influential treatises on education ever written. His main point was that teaching methods should follow the natural stages of development through which children grow to maturity. He presented four of these stages: infancy, childhood, early adolescence, and late adolescence—each with its own physical, intellectual, and social characteristics upon which appropriate educational methods should be based.

Rousseau himself was no educator, nor did his personal life follow the example of his tenets. The four children he was responsible for bringing into the world through a common-law relationship were all turned over to orphan asylums. But Rousseau did a great service in directing the attention of schoolmen to the needs of individual children. His emphasis upon freedom, growth, interest, and activity proved excellent antidotes for overwhelming absolutism in the education of his time.*

With the beginning of experimental psychology it became possible to study individual differences by analysis of the structure of sense perception and consciousness. Sensory, motor, and physiological processes were soon recognized as greatly affecting mental development. This beginning in experimental psychology was supported by studies in heredity and original nature conducted by such men as Galton, Cattell, and Thorndike.

Startling findings as to individual differences led gradually to more emphasis upon the dissimilarity of human capacities and to recognition of the need to take these into account in the instructional process. The notion took hold that each child should receive special attention by means of making the subject fit the pupil rather than vice versa.

* For previous discussion of Rousseau, see pages 62 and 142.

This newer psychology emphasizing individual differences was aided and abetted in America by the self-assertive spirit of a frontier democracy and by the rugged individualism of a capitalistic system. Also, the infiltration of Rousseau's philosophy of naturalism and the humanized teaching methods of the Swiss schoolmaster, Johann Pestalozzi (1746–1827), gave American educators an impetus toward developing the maximum capacities of each individual. The nineteenth century was an incubation period for the idea that the principle aim of education is to enable the child to develop according to his own needs, interests, and capacities. However, it took a long time for the doctrine to crystallize into practice. Among its first effects was the justification of the elective system in high schools, whereby students were given slightly more freedom to choose those studies they themselves considered most valuable.

Individual differences gained the recognition enjoyed today largely because of the development of intelligence testing. Such tests are the tools by which an intelligence quotient (I.Q.) is determined for the purpose of making the education or the job more nearly fit the abilities of the individual. Herbart seems to have been the first to try to achieve precision by casting psychological data in mathematical terms. Since he lacked objective or experimental evidence for his conclusions, Herbart made no headway in the attempt to state a mathematical equation for his doctrine of apperception, such as Sir Isaac Newton (1642–1727) had formed for the gravitation of heavenly bodies toward each other.

The attempt to solve educational problems by application of the statistical method had its more modern origin in the works of Galton, whose studies of heredity and allied subjects developed important statistical principles and suggested the measurement of human traits. In being impressed by the great hereditary differences among human beings Galton was influenced much more by Darwin and biology than by psychology.

Alfred Binet (1857–1911) and his assistant, Théodore Simon (1873–1961), in their work with French mentally deficient children were the first to develop a practical yardstick for measurement of intelligence. After experimenting with a variety of tests they finally evolved a scale (that is, a series of tests arranged in order of their difficulty) made up of questions designed to test common sense and judgment within the child's area of experience. By keeping records, they established norms for children of various chronological ages. From these came the term "mental age."

This Binet-Simon scale was originally published in 1905 and was revised in 1908. The tests achieved startling success; they were soon translated and used in many other countries. First in the United States was H. H. Goddard (1866–1957), in 1911, at the Vineland, New Jersey, institution for the feebleminded. Lewis M. Terman (1877–1956) gave the movement a great boost when he revised the Binet scale (Stanford Revision, 1914) for use with normal children. Further revisions have since been made by Terman and several others.

What Galton had done to point out hereditary biological differences, Cattell began doing by calling attention to psychological differences in reaction time, keenness of eyesight and hearing, and perception of pitch. In 1896, he began to test the students entering Columbia University. Wundt, the so-called father of experimental psychology, had tried to minimize such differences, or to hide them in averages. But Cattell insisted that deviations from the average can be equally as significant as the average itself.

It was Thorndike who really made educators measurement-conscious. As early as 1895, in a course he himself was taking in measurements, he found statistical methods to be quite difficult. Challenged, he mastered this form of mathematics, and by 1902 began to offer the first course ever given on the application of psychological and statistical methods in education. Similar courses soon were organized, and are found today in practically all teacher-training institutions.

The Binet type of test for measuring intelligence usually requires one or two hours for each child. On this basis it was obvious that progress would be definitely limited. So, before World War I, steps had already been taken to develop tests that could be administered to groups. Assisted by Arthur Sinton Otis (1886–   ), Terman, and many others, Thorndike began to develop techniques for finding superior men to be sent to officer training camps. Army Alpha, the first group intelligence test, resulted. As the war-time testing program developed, Army Beta was devised for the many illiterates being drafted into service. Following the war several adaptations of Army Alpha were prepared especially for schools. Probably the most widely used were Terman's *Group Test of Mental Ability* and Otis's *Self-Administering Test of Mental Ability*.

There has been a great deal of discussion concerning the permanence of the I.Q., with most psychologists maintaining that native intelligence as measured by tests is not significantly affected by differences of environment or education. This was denied by George D. Stoddard (1897–   ), whose studies at the State University of Iowa showed that identical twins put into different foster homes developed wide ranges of ability as measured by intelligence tests.

Generally recognized today is the existence of striking differences among individuals in abilities, interests, emotional adjustments, ideals, social development, and health. Each child represents a unique compounding in his own distinctive way. The argument between relative values of heredity and environment is purely academic—the child himself is all-important. Logically, the teacher should bring it about, so far as possible, that each pupil shall find such interests as will best develop his abilities, friends suitable to his social development, and attitudes that will contribute toward making him a worthwhile citizen.

This is a practical and certainly a challenging situation! There is the shy little girl who is "dying" to participate and needs only that extra little push of encouragement to give her an active role in playground activities. Likewise, there is the "rebel" who now keeps the classroom in continuous uproar, but who can be changed into a constructive influence by channeling his energies into more desirable directions. Even in classes that are homogeneously grouped some children are brighter and more talented than others. They all need teachers who are aware not only of the differences among them but also of the causes of their various modes of behavior. Moreover, they need teachers who know just how to reach each individual personality or mind. In this sense alone, teaching is a profession that requires a high degree of ability.

Educational Psychology: Learning

Educational psychology deals primarily with furnishing an experimentally determined basis for methods of teaching. Only incidentally is it concerned with the contents of the subjects to be taught. Economical learning depends first of all upon having suitable aims—the purpose of teaching any particular topic or series of topics must be worthwhile to the class members as well as to the teacher. Thus it seriously handicaps academic work if a teacher begins a course of instruction without definite plans that are based upon clearly determined purposes. In other words, proper guidance of mental growth demands that learning materials be appropriately organized in advance. This is especially true since each pupil possesses a different background of inherited personality traits and training experiences. Logically, identical instructional materials vary in the effect they have upon each class member.

Learning is a process of continuous organization and reorganization in which the pupil makes various types of responses. All too many teachers rely entirely upon memorization. It is an important process, but many other types of responses are involved in the development of new meanings. Frequently procedures already learned must be adapted to slightly changed situations. In fact, one purpose of organizing teaching materials is to provide an orderly background of experience to facilitate the understanding of new situations.

However, as has been constantly indicated in this book, schoolroom procedures have undergone many changes through the centuries. The application of modern psychology to the teacher's daily job hastened those changes, especially in America where experimentation and new ideas were not shunted aside. Therefore, at this point it may be helpful to look very briefly at the contributions of certain men whose discoveries and doctrines have profoundly affected our ideas about the learning process.

Religious tradition had emphasized the importance of the discipline of environment as a means of curbing the individual's nature, presumed to be inherently bad. Rousseau in his development of naturalism as an educational force had taken an opposite stand. He perceived the child's nature to be inherently good; it needed only to be freed from social restraints to permit development into the right kind of adulthood. Herbart's doctrine of apperception directed the attention of teachers to the importance of commencing the learning process at the point where the child's experience had placed him. This led to the idea of learning as being little else than a succession of presentations wherein the pupil constantly passes from familiar to the unfamiliar yet closely associated subject matter.

Apperception not only provided a sensible general theory of learning but was also useful in simplifying a number of other psychological problems in education—for example, the task of enlisting the child's active cooperation. Herbart held that interest is the "hospitality" of old ideas toward similar new ones. His apperceptive psychology seemed to give the teacher the control over the educative process—all that had to be done was to build up the right sequence of ideas and the desired conduct would follow. But it should be remembered that Herbart's doctrines were formed before the time of Darwin's biological evolution; hence, in the light of more recent research, they are now regarded as too mechanical.

One of Darwin's greatest contemporaries was Herbert Spencer (1820–1903). A philosopher with a wide background in science and psychology, Spencer expressed his ideas on the learning process in *Education: Intellectual, Moral, Physical* (1861). This work formed the basis for the new concept of education as a science. It led directly to Watson's behaviorism and indirectly to Gestalt psychology, both of which have been previously discussed in this chapter.

Spencer transcended Herbart's ideas by stating that the mind was an integral part of the total organism. Therefore, he said, it would react along with the rest of the body to environmental influences. From a teacher's point of view this meant that a child's emotional stresses and physical discomforts would affect his ability to spell or learn compound fractions or anything else. No longer could the mind be considered as a separate entity into which knowledge could be poured without regard for the push and pull of other forces. As this idea took hold, it eventually led to progressive education and to the acceptance of the teachings of John Dewey.

Dewey advocated changing school procedures to the end that the child be given opportunities to learn by experience. As he put it, one learns to think by managing experiences. He made a distinct contribution to the enrichment of education in his emphasis on the importance of the interests of the child. These he considered the signs of growing powers in need of careful and constant observation. Extremes, he said, should be avoided; interests should be neither excessively humored nor repressed. Too much humoring results in caprice and whimsy; repression weakens intellectual curiosity and prevents growth of initiative.

The influence of other leaders, like Hall and Thorndike, has already been discussed. Along with the philosophers mentioned in the previous paragraphs, they caused a revolution in American education. No longer did educators plunge blindly ahead with the notion that the child must learn—or else! Instead they asked themselves such questions as: Under what conditions will he learn best? How can we help him acquire good taste and character as well as knowledge? What method will best suit this child or this age group or that class? In short, educational psychology had found its place in the scheme of things.

Another question that educators have constantly asked themselves is: What is learning? In seeking a working definition of learning it is generally agreed that acquiring a vocabulary, memorizing a poem, and operating a typewriter are examples. Then there are the less obvious activities, such as development of prejudices and preferences, social attitudes and ideals. Finally, no less the product of learning are those useless and bizarre acquisitions of the human being like mannerisms, tics, and autistic actions. There are, in fact, many complicating factors that make it extremely difficult to develop an entirely satisfactory verbal definition of learning.

"Improving with practice and profiting from experience" would seemingly serve as an explanation of learning, until we remember that certain learning is neither wholesome nor profitable in its consequences. We learn bad habits which logically do not improve us, and many of these may prove definite liabilities in our efforts to achieve desired goals in life. To describe learning as mere change with practice is to confuse it with growth, fatigue, and other such bodily modifications. However, practice effects are important. Skill usually comes through repetition; but sometimes too much practice brings on fatigue, mental as well as physical. In experimental work, where results are plotted on a so-called work curve, it has been found that efficiency decreases with too much repetition and increases with judiciously placed rest periods. But it is generally recognized that a basic ingredient of efficient instruction is purposeful drill. Carefully directed repetition until the proper habits are formed is one of the keystones of classroom methodology.

Some psychologists define learning as a change in the central nervous system. Here again is reason for noting that a good background in biological sciences is valuable to a teacher. But even without such specialized training the fact cannot be missed that learning of some sort does occur. If adults fail to set up learning situations that are profitable to both the child and the society in which he lives, learning of a less desirable nature is almost certain to take place.

In recent decades much has been made of "maturation," the growth that goes on regardless of formal instruction or its total lack. Behavior is said to develop through maturation if maturity comes via regular stages irrespective of intervening practices. Whenever training procedures seem to have no appreciable effect on the behavior, the process of maturation is at work. The proud parent does not realize it, but his infant talks and walks only when his organisms are ready to permit him to talk and walk. An Indian papoose carried continuously on his mother's back apparently is not handicapped in learning to walk when compared with other children actively encouraged to do so. However, there are relatively few cases of "pure" maturation—most behavior development is an interplay between the natural growth processes and the opportunities for learning.

Child Psychology: Problems of Infancy

Although philosophers and educators have long speculated about the importance of child development in determining the nature of adult behavior, only within comparatively recent years has this subject had scientific investigation. Until the 1890's there was no published information about the sensitivity, emotions, learning abilities, and other psychological processes of children, except in a few scattered biographical accounts written by parents—and most of their stories were less fact than fancy.

When at last experimental investigations with children were undertaken in the twentieth century, the psychologists borrowed many of the methods already being used in experiments with animals. That was logical since very young children, like animals, are unable to report the nature of their experiences. Hence, only their overt behavior can be observed directly.

History reveals many misconceptions concerning the child and his needs in social and intellectual life. In pre-Revolutionary France the upper-class children were dressed as adults, even to the point of wearing corsets and powdering their hair; they were trained in highly ornate manners and courtly practices. But the French of that period were not the only ones to consider children miniature adults. The Puritans frowned upon youthful frivolity and play, and their influence is seen even today in many classrooms where pupils are expected to defy their coltish natures by maintaining absolute quiet over long periods of time.

Another traditional erroneous viewpoint has been that the child is a passive, inactive learner, a sort of a pour-into-the-bottle theory which holds that knowledge, if it can be "got" into the learner, has definite values per se. Experimental psychology brought with it the realization that a normal child is a dynamic being, whose inner urges drive him on to seek new experiences. He does not wait to be acted upon by his immediate environment; he is too busy trying to explore and extend that environment. The wise teacher or parent endeavors to direct the aggressive, self-motivated child into channels where his activities become truly educative. It is, in fact, these activities that provide the adult with the best opportunities to guide effectively the learning process.

Ability to understand children depends upon sensing the relationship and significance of maturation and learning. It must be realized that structure and function develop together, and except for a slight spurt at the beginning of adolescence the rate of physical growth decreases continuously until it finally ceases. Growth in the fetus is from the head downward, and at birth the brain is nearer to full growth than any other part of the body. In fact, development of the brain after birth consists almost entirely of the ripening of the cells and the increase in connections between them. This early rapid development suggests that if there is any checking or interference for even a short period during infancy or childhood, such ill effects are serious and may be carried over into adulthood. Malnutrition, injury, or serious disease in early years likewise may have disastrous effects upon the normal growth of the brain.

Large muscles of the body, especially in the trunk and arms, develop in advance of the smaller muscles of the eyes and the hands; this fact suggests that fine work has little place in the first year or two of elementary schools. The ratio of the child's heart to the rest of the circulatory system and to the length of the body is considerably smaller than it will be when he becomes an adult. Permanent injury from overstrain frequently results because of this smallness and relative weakness of the child's heart. Physiologists now believe that many cardiac ailments among adults originated in childhood; hence they point out the folly of too prolonged or strenuous exercise for pupils in the elementary school.

Both parents and teachers should have a knowledge of human growth from its very beginning—a single fertilized cell smaller than a pin-point that, 40 weeks later, becomes a full-formed baby, averaging about 20 inches in length and a little less than eight pounds in weight. Yet this newborn baby is capable of those processes necessary for maintaining life. He now depends upon his own equipment for respiration as well as for regulation of bodily temperature and elimination of waste. During the prenatal period nourishment had been received from the mother through the umbilical cord, and now he must suck and swallow. His first movements seem aimless and undefined, but developments in behavior come rapidly in those initial few hours of life.

In the rearing of children there arise many problems; the most important are feeding, sleeping, and elimination. When various studies of these problems as reported by parents are analyzed according to grade level, as would be expected it is found that those related to daily routine are more prominent in infancy than in later years. However, even up to the age of twelve, there continues to be a surprisingly high incidence of routine training problems.

Recent research in eating habits indicates that, contrary to generally accepted ideas, a child's own demands can usually be trusted as a guide in determining when, what, and how much he should be fed. Studies of babies during their first year of life, both preceding and following the weaning period, show that spontaneous food demands of young children tend to be unexpectedly wise. It seems logical that the more the diet and eating routines can be based upon natural wants rather than upon rules and formulae the better the habits that may be formed.

In experiments where children were put on a self-demand diet at the infancy level, they seemed well-nourished and gave no evidence of suffering from poor choice of food. At all ages, given a selection of wholesome foods from which to choose, it would seem that a young child can be depended upon to show reasonably good judgment. Apparently a nutritionally balanced diet is not something that needs to be controlled by dishing out every day so much of this and so much of that—a satisfactory balance can be achieved over longer periods of time. Moreover, nagging on the part of parents to get certain foods eaten defeats its purpose; it sets up nervous tensions that can destroy even the healthiest of appetites.

As an infant grows older he spontaneously reduces the number of feedings per day. Likewise, food intake varies from day to day and from feeding to feeding. Definite food preferences are exhibited at an early age. These depend, in part, on taste, texture, appearance of food, and the way it is served. Sometimes there may be organic aversions, that is, allergic conditions. When aversion to food is shown it is wise to discover the cause. One kindergarten teacher found herself in quite serious difficulty when she forced a child to drink free milk that the youngster insisted she did not want. The pupil became ill, and the young woman had considerable explaining to do.

Parental attitudes and idiosyncrasies are also influential in that they set an example observed and imitated by the child as he is growing older. Also, shifts in food preference are quite common. A youngster may dislike a diet item when it is first introduced to him. Efforts to coerce him into eating are likely to beget failure or, at best, sullen compliance. If from time to time this food is made available with no attempt to force its eating, a taste may possibly be acquired spontaneously.

This parental concern so often is useless. For example, at the age of one or two a child may have a voracious appetite, and then at three or four seemingly lose it. Even though they have grown bigger, some four-year-olds apparently require less food than they did at an earlier age. Also, an emotional disturbance can disrupt a youngster's eating habits.

Most of the infant's time is spent in sleep, and even after a child reaches school age he still sleeps about half the 24 hours. Young children show a wide difference in the amounts of sleep they seem to require—in fact, it is difficult to determine natural sleep needs. No problem is presented by the baby in the cradle, left free to sleep whenever he wants to, but as a child grows older there sometimes are complications because the amount of time he spends in bed is governed so largely by conventions.

Also, health is a factor. Whenever a child's equilibrium is disturbed by illness, bodily disorders, malnutrition, and digestive difficulties, such disturbances may keep him wakeful at a time when he is much in need of rest. Likewise, sleep often is affected by fears—in fact, anything in everyday life that excites or relaxes him influences his sleep habits.

Willingness to go to bed is sometimes governed by the extent to which a child is at peace with the other members of the family. A hostile child uses dillydallying at bedtime as an opportunity to give vent to his resistive feelings. But emotions need not necessarily be painful or hostile to make serious inroads into sleep. A child who is alert and happy in his surroundings may be so interested in life that he tries to remain awake as long as he can. Whether or not he falls asleep, it may be advantageous to have a child acquire the habit of taking rest periods during the day. Studies of fatigue show that brief rest periods have more recuperative value than the equivalent amount of time spent in one long rest period. Many primary schools are now recognizing this fact by providing cots for regular rest periods.

In the matter of controlling the eliminative functions, the battle is not always won by the time a child enters school. Even one apparently well on his way to complete control may regress. Frequently such a child resorts to furtiveness and falsehood, disclaiming responsibility, or possibly blaming others. As a symptom of strain or fatigue when first entering school a youngster may resume wetting his bed at night, or he may even lose control of himself in the classroom. Some children exploit the process of elimination as a means to gain adult attention—at least that is one time they are noticed. Here again a teacher sometimes finds it necessary to supplement the training that apparently is deficient at home.

Arnold Gesell is today recognized as the best informed expert on child behavior because of his work in establishing the Clinic of Child Development at Yale University in 1911. There he and his co-workers developed an elaborate method of observing children from behind one-way-vision screens. Among his notable conclusions have been that the first five years of life are the most important in an individual's education, that parent training is fully as important as child training, that children should not be forced to read at six if they are not ready, and that something should be done about those innumerable households where adults still do nothing but scold, threaten, shout at, and beat their children.

In order to compensate for the inadequacies of so many home environments, Gesell believes that public schools should make periodic contacts with two-, three-, and four-year-olds so as to provide wide supervision at an early age. In short, he favors some form of nursery school system.

Physical and Emotional Development

Newborn babies average a little more than 20 inches in length. At the end of the first year this stature is increased by over a third, and by the age of five the child is about twice as tall as when he was born. The infant's head at birth is relatively large, and does not show proportionately the same rapid increase in size as do the other parts of the body. The trunk increases considerably, the arms even more, and, by the time full stature is attained, there is a still greater increase in the length of the legs. Another important fact to remember is that between infancy and maturity the various parts of the body grow at different rates and reach their approximate maximum size at different times. This also holds true for the various internal organs of the body. Furthermore, the pattern of this growth varies somewhat from individual to individual.

It is largely by virtue of his motor development that a child progresses from helplessness of early infancy toward self-help and independence. These motor activities play a large role in intellectual enterprises and social contacts. Of course, individuals vary considerably with respect to timing and sequence, so teachers need to learn to recognize such differences and to take them into consideration when directing pupils into activities. Also, motor activities tend to be rather specific— a child who excels in one performance may not be so good in others, and one who is poor in a certain performance need not necessarily be poor in all other activities.

The practical implication is that opportunities for motor learning should be as varied as possible in order that all children may have a proper chance to come into their own. The wise teacher seeks especially to provide her shy and timid pupils with the thrills of active participation. This is especially important since the motor activities undertaken by adults are influenced to a large degree by what each learned or failed to learn as a child. However, this does not mean that each motor skill learned when young will be used with profit at the adult level, though certainly wise provision of opportunities for motor learning in childhood contributes in important ways to the individual's welfare.

All normal children are born with a disposition to exercise their

limbs and to use their bodies. But a bad tumble, an especially harrow-
ing or humiliating experience, may seriously discourage motor activities. Sometimes children are overprotected by well-meaning parents who
constantly warn against danger and overexertion. Such things influence
a child's habitual use of and attitude toward his physical powers. On the
other hand, successes in earlier motor ventures lead to new ones and
further improvement of ability—motor interests thrive on successful
accomplishment. That is why proper facilities and opportunities, with
judicious instruction when warranted, are so important.

To give him incentive to make full use of his motor capacities a
youngster needs the example and companionship provided by other
children. That is the tragedy of the child left largely to himself or
exclusively in the company of adults. In intermediate and high school
grades especially, if a boy lags far behind his classmates and does not
continue to develop those skills necessary to share in their activities,
he may withdraw entirely from games that are so essential for his motor
development. Thus, when a child for some reason or other does fall
behind his group, there sometimes begins a vicious circle. Embarrassment makes him reluctant to join in the games. The more he shuns
them the greater becomes the difference between his skills and those of
other children who have been continuously getting better from practice.

Motor development is considerably affected by adolescence. During
this period the skeleton, internal organs, and muscles all grow. The
glandular system goes through a period of changes that profoundly affects the chemistry of the body. Growth is especially rapid just before
and during the early years of adolescence.

Physical growth of all types comes earlier to girls than to boys.
This is true throughout childhood. Their pre-adolescent spurt starts
two years earlier and they reach their adult weight nearly four years
sooner. During childhood the average girl is a bit shorter than the
average boy, but between 11 and 14 she is taller. Likewise, in weight
she is slightly lighter until her eleventh year, but heavier from then
on until 14½. Those children of both sexes who grow taller earlier
in life tend to be taller at all ages. Growth in the bones of the legs is
mainly responsible for the rapid increase in height during adolescence,
but increase in weight is due to the growth in muscles as well as in
bones. In childhood, muscles are about 45 per cent of the total weight
but increase to 63 per cent by maturity.

These rapid increases in size not only form a clothing-replacement
problem but are a constant source of embarrassment to the adolescent.
Some gain as much as six inches and 25 pounds within a single year. It

is an awkward age in which the adolescent is overwhelmed by his limitations. The undersized boy may become a "bookworm" because, physically, he cannot compete on equal terms with his stronger companions. A big girl may go in for rough sports as a compensation for her overly generous physical proportions, which serve to limit her popularity as a social date.

During adolescence both boys and girls increase in muscular strength. This holds true especially for boys because they use their muscles more and are greatly concerned about achieving the physical qualities of a "real man." Though longer and heavier than in childhood, the muscles of girls do not show as great a development. After the "tomboy" years are past, the conventions of being a lady serve to discourage them from violent forms of physical exercise. Most of them are prohibited during menstrual periods from doing anything more strenuous than the minimum essentials of daily work. Finally, the characteristic physical proportions of the two sexes favor the boys with more strength because of their wider shoulders, longer arms, and bigger hands.

An emotion has been defined as a "stirred-up state of the entire organism." This is not limited to any single part of the body but spreads over it profusely. Apparently it makes no difference in the external changes what emotion is being experienced. True it is that bodily posture, facial expression, paleness or redness of the body's surfaces vary from one emotion to another, but such changes are superficial. The deep changes within the body seemingly are the same for all emotions, differing only in the intensity of the disturbances.

Under emotional stress the individual has greater strength and endurance than during his normal state of calmness, but lacks normal control over his muscles. These physical changes are produced through action of the autonomic nervous system which has three main divisions: cranial, sympathetic, and sacral. In direct opposition to the sympathetic, the cranial and sacral work together and are known as the parasympathetic branch. Nerves from both sympathetic and parasympathetic run to the vital organs of the body—heart, blood vessels, lungs, stomach, intestines.

The sympathetic branch of the autonomic system has as its functions to inhibit digestion, dilate pupils of eyes, constrict blood vessels, release blood sugar from the liver, and stimulate perspiration. Action of the parasympathetic branch is exactly the opposite, its nerves making the heart beat more slowly, increasing saliva flow, constricting pupils of the eyes. The two divisions are evenly balanced during normal periods, but when an emotion develops, the sympathetic branch is in the ascendancy; as emotion subsides, the parasympathetic becomes stronger until normal balance is restored.

Immediately at the onset of a strong emotion the adrenal glands discharge adrenaline which acts upon the entire body as a drug. It is, in fact, one of the most powerful drugs in existence. Adrenaline is discharged into the blood stream and within a few seconds is carried over the entire body. Its action retards the normal digestive processes of the stomach and causes the heart to beat faster and with greater power. As a result of these and other changes the blood pressure rises for the duration of the emotion. It is significant that violent emotions rarely last more than a few hours, but milder ones may continue for weeks, or even longer, until the person experiencing them actually becomes exhausted.

Emotion cannot be isolated in pure form because it is interwoven with the events of everyday life, such as fears, sorrows, resentments, and joys. An emotion involves an impulse to act in one way or another, frequently to attack in anger or to flee in fear. Nor is there today a universally accepted list of emotions. Some psychologists favor the existence of a single "stirred-up" state that gradually becomes differentiated in response to various stimuli. Others list three, four, or five emotions; still others admit about a dozen, and there are a few who list even more.

At the newborn level the child seemingly is immune to the many conditions that will arouse an emotional response. This changes as he matures. Gesell holds that at the age of one month the infant gives different cries for hunger, pain, and discomfort. But as life progresses it becomes evident that whatever feeling is aroused by a given happening depends, in part, upon what he himself has at stake. Emotions are likely to be aroused by anything that threatens a child's motives and plans, that blocks or facilitates activities which he himself has initiated, and that helps or hinders his hopes and aspirations.

Anger, fear, and love are the three emotions that have been most extensively studied. The angry baby becomes quite rigid; he screams and beats the air with his arms and legs. This is his only reaction since his mental and muscular development is so slight that no other reactions are possible. The preschool child also cries, screams, and becomes rigid; in addition he kicks, bites, jumps up and down, or throws himself upon the floor. By adolescence the response of talking back has become by far the most important, with actual violence being reported in but few cases—the adolescent tends to be generally restless and sometimes shows a degree of subtlety by refusing to speak to those who have made him angry. Finally, even into adulthood there is a persistence of infantile behavior, such as boys' stamping their feet or kicking things and girls' crying. As the normal child grows older the anger responses become progressively less violent.

Fears are both learned and unlearned. Laboratory experiments show the newborn baby to be afraid of two things: loss of support and loud noises. Most of the things of which an individual is afraid he has learned to fear. Reaction to fear at all ages exhibits but little variety, the main behavior being a rigidity of the entire body. However, subtleness in hiding fears accompanies the maturing of the intellectual abilities. In due time experience teaches the child how to avoid situations that may cause anxiety; he learns ways and means of running away before the stimulus appears.

Thus a pupil facing a difficult test finds himself conveniently with a headache. His "pains" are as much an escape as if he had fled the classroom. Fear definitely is a destructive factor in the learning of adjustment processes. It may serve to keep the child from running out on a busy thoroughfare, but ordinarily fear disorganizes the individual whom it assails.

There is a definite development from infancy to adulthood in the stimuli that cause the emotion of love. Affection at first is closely tied up with dependency upon parents for food and protection. Then parents' feelings are sometimes hurt when a child, upon entering school, so readily transfers his affections to a teacher he likes. Later, adolescence brings its problems. A child is affectionate or otherwise in just the way he has been taught from infancy on up to express this emotion.

Intellectual Development: Measurement

Systematic observations of children under controlled laboratory conditions were not begun until the twentieth century, and then the psychologists found it expedient to borrow many of the techniques already in use with animal subjects. A young child is like the other primates in that he is unable to report the nature of his experiences; hence his mental activities must be judged by observing his overt behavior. Nevertheless, these investigations have yielded valuable information concerning sensory functions, emotional reactions, and learning activities. They make possible a reconstruction of origins and development of adult behavior and thus give a better understanding of why we act as we do.

Both parents and educators have gained much reliable information from such experimental work in which psychologists determine with a reasonably high degree of accuracy the level of learning abilities at the various ages and the nature of childish interests. So far as the school is concerned this scientific child study has rapidly been making passé those teachers who traditionally place subject matter, methods, and absolute standards above the personality and social development of the pupil. Theoretically, at least, we are now trying to make the school fit the child after so many centuries of trying to make him fit the school.

Experimental psychology has shown that by the time a child is ready to enter school he is capable of most, if not all, of the intellectual operations that are found in the mental life of an adult. He can use both inductive and deductive reasoning, being limited, of course, by his lack of experience and information. He is capable of imagining, daydreaming, and dealing with problems on the level of ideas. Already he is manipulating symbols without the necessity of having to handle the physical materials or performing the acts such symbols represent. The average six-year-old is, in fact, a highly trained and versatile individual, but one who still has a long way to go to achieve his full intellectual development.

The elementary school increases a child's knowledge, general information, and ability to think in abstract terms. It teaches him to deal with affairs in the world at large that do not directly touch his everyday life—in other words, schooling increases his mental horizon. At the beginning of this formal training period a child's thoughts, plans, and interests are restricted principally to the things that are near him in time and space. But as he moves upward from grade to grade the pupil develops a capacity for intellectual teamwork as well as for understanding and discussing viewpoints of others. How well these lessons of concentrating attention on mental tasks and of dealing with problems of increasing complexity are being learned depends upon both the child's natural talents and the quality of his instruction.

However, the information that a child possesses and the extent to which he grasps the concepts involved in school lessons, radio and TV programs, and other informational contacts, tend to be very spotty. A youngster may seemingly possess a great deal of information and yet, when the adult delves a little deeper, it frequently is evident there is no real understanding. The child knows the right answer without knowing the meanings of his words—he is merely repeating, parrot-like, the phrases he has heard some older person use.

Furthermore, a child's reply to a question may not represent at all what he actually thinks, since bluffing is a habit that starts at a remarkably early age. A youngster is usually reluctant to admit he doesn't know, so he will concoct some answer that comes to mind even though it is inconsistent with his earlier replies. It is quite common for him to go to great lengths in maintaining a position when actually he is in doubt about the matter.

The process of becoming intellectualized does not mean that a child surrenders his individuality—he still is primarily concerned with his own private desires and interests despite an increased capacity for sharing the thoughts of others. Development from infancy to maturity is a gradual evolution from complete self-centeredness to an alert consciousness of community, state, nation, and world. The elementary school pupil, however, is still preponderantly egocentric. He may possess vast stores of information that are peculiarly meaningful to him in his everyday life even though he is seemingly lacking in both logic and consistency when faced with problems beyond his immediate personal interests.

The mere fact of being exposed to a topic that is receiving a good deal of attention from his elders does not necessarily mean that a child is going to form either a clear-cut impression or an opinion. There still is need of "seasoning"—in other words, the accumulation of impressions and experiences distributed over a period of time. Experiments have shown that impressions concentrated within a short time, no matter how dramatic or charged with emotion, as a rule do not produce the same grasp of the subject matter as when impressions and information are accumulated over a longer period of time. Just as in physical growth, intellectual maturation cannot be rushed. Time is an essential element.

Quality of reasoning is likely to vary with different types of mental tasks. Experiments involving children even as low as the kindergarten show at that early age capability to reason that involves the explaining of cause and effect. However, a child may appear quite logical in figuring out one problem and surprisingly inept when confronted by another of no greater difficulty. There seem to be very definite limitations when a youngster goes beyond his understanding, but it must not be overlooked that many adults show similar inability when on unfamiliar ground.

Another factor to be considered is that up to the age of seven or eight reasoning is very likely to be in terms of isolated or particular cases. Ordinarily a child of this age is incapable of genuine argument because he has difficulty in making generalizations and feels no need for verifications or logical justifications.

A few psychologists claim that a young child is unable to reason correctly from someone else's beliefs, or to arrive at pure deductions, until about eleven or twelve. Others deny there are distinct changes in the development of a child's ability to reason. They hold that with age comes improvement in abilities to reorganize experiences and to arrive at generalizations, to formulate answers, and to give reasons. These opponents of the distinct-stage-of-development theories feel that reasoning processes at the age of six are not essentially different from those at the ages of twelve or eighteen. They point to experiments showing that logical or nonlogical thinking is not an either-or phenomenon; the same child may exhibit both varieties.

A pupil who has a difficult time in an intellectual task such as arithmetic may be able to do very well in various practical arts and crafts. A prominent writer failed in every course in mathematics he ever was required to take; yet no one could accuse that man of lacking ability to think. In his case the inability doubtlessly was due to distaste for a specific type of mental process.

If a school neglects to seek out the special talents and abilities of each pupil, it is likely that many of the children will experience failure and humiliation, or at least boredom. Those personal satisfactions and social recognition that can be derived from being able to do something well are important factors in intellectual, emotional, and social adjustment. Intellectual interests thrive upon successful accomplishment!

It has been commonly thought that children have better memories than adolescents or adults. The Binet and certain other tests indicate that growth in memory stops at about twelve, at which time a long plateau begins and lasts through the adult years. However, most of the present evidence favors the view that during adolescence, at least, ability to memorize increases just as other intellectual powers continue to develop during this period. This indicates that children are more willing than adolescents or adults to memorize. But, if the material is so presented as to seem a logical step in gaining a desired end, the adolescent can learn it much more rapidly than a young child.

Little children are generally poor in concentration. If a first-grade pupil walks across the classroom to sharpen his pencil, the intellectual activity of the others is likely to stop for the moment. Concentration is an ability that normally grows with age, but on the surface many adolescents seem quite incapable of exercising this power. Usually the reason is that they are attending to other than the desired stimuli. And yet whenever the interests of the normal adolescent or adult are intense, he pursues them with considerable persistence and resistance to distraction. One of the arts of teaching is to develop the habit of concentration by creating strong motivations to learn.

Motivation is considered an important factor in every classroom lesson today. This does not mean that the child is wheedled into the act of concentrating. Rather, he is aroused through a variety of methods. For example, a primary teacher who wishes the class to read a story involving the adventures of a dog may ask the class to talk about their pets first. Another teacher may motivate the group toward an interest in creative writing by starting a class magazine.

The positive approaches to motivation are numerous indeed in the modern school. In contrast, there were two great negative motivations in the past—fear of physical punishment and fear of failure. The latter is still in effect in some schools today where the emphasis is on examinations. In such institutions the child is given prognostic tests, diagnostic tests, aptitude tests, personality tests, intelligence tests, a battery of achievement tests, teacher-made quizzes, midterm tests, and dreaded final tests.

Of course, testing is a valuable and important educational aid if not overdone. Moreover, the construction of tests has grown into quite an art in recent years. This is especially true of standardized achievement tests—and thereby hangs a tale.

The development of achievement tests paralleled that of intelligence tests. A storm of protest was aroused when this movement began. Joseph M. Rice (1857–1934) tested the spelling abilities of 33,000 school children, and his findings appeared in *The Forum* in 1897. They revealed, among other things, that children who had spent 30 minutes a day on spelling for eight years did not spell any better than those who had spent only half that time on the subject. In the heated discussion that followed educators and the educational press denounced as "foolish, reprehensible, and from every point of view indefensible" the efforts to discover anything about the value of the teaching of spelling by finding out whether or not the children could spell. They claimed that the object of such work was not to teach the children to spell, but to develop their minds.

The NEA Department of Superintendence, in 1912, received a report of Rice's findings in spelling and other investigations, and after considerable acrimonious debate voted by a small majority against indorsing the measurement movement. Two years later, however, that organization reversed itself by accepting a favorable report from its committee on tests and standards. The experimentation of Thorndike was largely responsible for the subsequent development of this movement. Noteworthy milestones were the *Reasoning Test in Arithmetic* (1908) of C. W. Stone (1853–1927) and Thorndike's scale for measuring handwriting (1910).

There followed a rapid growth of testing programs in America. Many schools set up research divisions. It was a very backward provincial school system which did not periodically subject the children to those previously mentioned "batteries" of tests, which annually multiplied in number. For several years tests and measurements had a peculiar fascination for schoolmen and teachers. The superintendent of schools who did not know or neglected to make use of these devices was considered quite out of date. Any teacher or supervisor whose vocabulary lacked such cryptic words or terms as "mean," "median," "mode," "coefficient of correlation," "probable error," "mean deviation," "standard deviation," and "I.Q." was considered a relic of an earlier and unscientific age.

But this almost frenetic passion for measurement did have its good effects. The movement served to give education a certain clarity of purpose and sharpened teachers' thinking on individualization of instruction. Moreover, many school systems set up research divisions which still are in operation. These divisions point up problems, eliminate wild guessing, and help schoolmen to evaluate their progress.

Today the "honeymoon" is over as far as tests are concerned. However, educators have not divorced themselves from the area of measurement. They still consider it a valuable source of information. In brief, testing is now regarded as one factor among many in the educational process.

Social and Personality Development

As a child grows older his strongest motives in life become the desire to be accepted, to belong to the group, and eventually to achieve some measure of recognition and prestige in relationships with others. Such motivation finds its first expression in the longing for security with parents. When a child moves into a larger social world these desires seem to intensify as he finds greater areas to conquer. Sometimes a youngster goes to almost any length to be noticed, and becomes angrier if completely ignored than if crossed or punished. Whether his bid for attention takes the form of extreme timidity or exhibitionism, or somewhere in between, underneath it all is a definite wish to be noticed and appreciated.

Far more important than any specific practices or theories of the parents is the child's underlying sense of security in the home. Actually, many of the modern "rules" for rearing children have done more harm than good, especially when they inhibit natural and sensible reactions, as some of them do. Arthur T. Jersild (1902–   ) holds that the value of any particular technique for disciplining the child depends not so much on the method itself as the attitude of the parent and the total setting in which it is used. Thus there are children who are occasionally spanked, who are more serene and spontaneous in their relationships with parents than those who are never spanked but are rejected and intimidated in more subtle and pervasive ways.

Likewise, the child needs an emotional anchorage in his relationships with adults outside the home. The teacher, in fact, serves as a substitute parent because of the legal authority invested within him. While a problem child's behavior belies the fact, he probably secretly desires the approval and affection of those adults whose life he plagues. That is why the attitude toward the child is so profoundly important. The chances are that the troublesome or delinquent child has convinced himself he is not wanted, leaving in his own mind no alternative but to declare war against his adult world. It is an extremely difficult yet worthwhile task to break through the "crust" of hostile habits and attitudes of such a youth. Thus the teacher needs to be very careful, no matter how spoiled or anti-social the troublemaker, that he does not give an impression he holds a personal grudge against the child. Fair play and a consideration of others are learned best by example.

Desire for status is an important factor in a child's relationships with his playmates. Often he goes to unusual lengths to gain a place for himself. Such outlandish behavior calculated to win esteem of companions frequently is puzzling to adults, but it is part of a youngster's normal development vigorously to seek and eagerly accept those symbols and forms which betoken kinship within the group. That means sharing of secrets, entering into partnerships, and joining clubs that may last years or but a single day.

A child striving for acceptance by others is extremely sensitive to rebuffs and rejections; scorn and ridicule bring about emotions varying from grief to rage. A child heartily dislikes explaining the reasons for such feelings to older people. Even to himself he hates to admit he cannot win the good will of those from whom it means so much to him.

Therefore, he may go to extremes in camouflaging his troubles. Frequently when a girl is telling how much she detests certain other children she, in fact, is admitting how much she wants to be like them. Thus, lacking a proper understanding in such matters, grown-ups often make a situation even more intolerable for a child.

Moreover, in the normal course of social development a reasonable number of rebuffs and slights are part of the training necessary to teach a youngster how to get along with others. A wise adult is always ready and willing to be a friend in need but never tries to live the life for a child even, when so doing, the situation can be made much more pleasant for the moment.

Distinctions based on sex seldom appear when first the youngster is old enough to enter into social relationships with other children. Little girls and boys play together in much the same activities, but even at preschool age some distinctions begin to appear. Boys are usually more active in their play, though differences within each sex group are greater than the differences between the sexes.

Previous to the age of eight, girls show but little embarrassment about physical contacts, posture, clothing, or being alone with a group of boys. While boy-boy and girl-girl relationships are more common than mixed ones, much interplay occurs and it does not seem to disturb a youngster where all other members are of the opposite sex. Naturally this changes whenever older persons begin to tease and thus to put a child on the defensive by making him self-conscious.

Social distance has been noted as early as the age of two, and becomes more pronounced as children advance in the elementary grades. Then as the teens approach there comes the "whispering" period, especially among girls, and this is accompanied by a great show of modesty. As adolescent interests develop, boys and girls begin to pay more attention to each other, with boys lagging somewhat behind in this demonstration of heterosexual interest.

Jersild points out that, generally speaking, boys are more interested in things, and girls in people. However, in adolescence the normal boy begins to take notice of the individuals around him—especially the females. Under wholesome conditions any adolescent's transfer of interest from friends of the same sex to members of the opposite one is easy and natural. For example, in a coeducational high school there are usually many opportunities for social contacts, and a young man is able to find at least a few girls whose personalities suit his own. All that he needs is confidence in himself, a certain amount of know-how, and guidance, but minimum interference from parents and teachers.

Girls at first are not very particular whose attention they attract; any susceptible male may be a temporary target. As they grow older, girls are apt to become more discriminating, sometimes even disdainful of boys their own chronological age. Thus it happens that boys often are inducted into mixed social life before they are emotionally ready for it, then are bewildered when dropped suddenly as the girls find more mature escorts.

Constant falling in and out of "love" is entirely normal during the early and middle years of adolescence. Members of both sexes do a good deal of sampling and experimenting as part of the growing-up process, and the adolescent who through timidity or other reasons avoids these social activities is missing out on some of life's most valuable experiences. What frequently appears as rank inconsistency to adults is proper behavior for adolescents—they are simply acting their age.

An individual's personality is the quality of his total behavior, the organization and integration of his behavior as a whole. Personality constantly changes and grows for better or for worse in harmony with physical, emotional, and mental development. It changes most rapidly during youth when habit patterns are forming and maturing. Some psychologists claim that at a very early age babies show differences in personality traits. These, they say, are exhibited almost from the moment of birth. Certain infants tend to be more or less restless, fussy, irritable; others are placid and serene. Of course, there are many factors which may influence a child's behavior during his first years of life: "age" when born (that is, premature or full-born) and the circumstances surrounding his delivery, whether or not he is wanted or unwanted in the home, and the economic position of the family.

Interaction of hereditary and environmental factors is so complex that it is practically impossible to isolate either in pure form. Complicating the situation are the vast individual differences among parents. The personality of the adult is bound to influence his attitudes toward children and, in one way or another, to be reflected in the specific practices of child care during those extremely important years of early life.

The learning process as the foundation of personality development begins at the moment of birth. Some even claim it starts in the fetus stage of human development—a mother's acts during gestation may have a prenatal influence. However, it can hardly be expected that an infant's behavior soon after birth can furnish a reliable prediction of distinctive personality traits. One investigator made a careful record of babies in a maternity hospital, noting such items as fussiness, restlessness, and frequency of crying. Two years later these same children were scored in terms of a rating scale, and there was discovered very little resemblance between the earlier and later ratings.

Factors underlying human conduct are so numerous and varied that a many-sided approach must be made to a study of personality. In fact, all aspects of behavior development are more or less interrelated; for example, motor ability has an important bearing upon social behavior and thus is a significant factor in behavior as a whole. Other features of personality that meet the eye include almost endless lists of qualities: physical characteristics, bodily size and physique, nature and strength of drives. One's concept of self is strongly influenced by the physical properties of his body. Then there are certain cultural standards to be considered. Age and maturity levels play an important part in the manner in which these social patterns are applied, since behavior that is acceptable to others at one age is considered infantile or immature at a later period in life.

There are other features of personality that cannot be seen—the individual's ideas about himself; conflicts between outward appearance and inner worth; motives, aspirations, and feelings. Varied experiences in life soon teach a child ways of keeping his thoughts and feelings to himself. This means that overt actions are not always trustworthy guides as to how an individual really feels. Laughter is a good example of this. When indulged in by one person it indicates happiness; by another, embarrassment; and sometimes a laugh covers the inner urge to break down and cry.

Also, different forms of behavior are used to express the same feeling or motive. Fear sometimes causes retreat and crying, or passiveness and silence, or even overt aggressiveness intended to cover up the fact that something is dreaded. And again, identical behavior may serve different functions; for example, fighting can be diagnosed as a symptom of poor personality adjustment in one child and as a welcome sign of decided improvement in another.

An interesting example is the case of Maurice, a little refugee boy who came to a New York City school from Germany where both of his parents had died in a Nazi gas chamber. Maurice was subjected to the usual torments that children give strangers—especially meek ones who run or cry when you hit them. The school psychologist recommended that ways be found to make Maurice more outgoing. He was given monitorial jobs, and a special "buddy" was assigned to him. Improvement was slow but sure while all the teachers watched the progress of this timid refugee. Then one day the glorious word spread around the school from the teacher on duty in the playground: "Maurice fought back!"

In progressing through life from infancy to maturity a child has more and more social experiences; his manner of reaction changes and his personality characteristics are increasingly modified in the direction of stability. During adolescence emotional life undergoes considerable change. Social conventionality holds in restraint many drives of a biological or instinctive nature, and these constantly seek an outlet in other less restricted areas of the adolescent's life.

This period of youth experiences intense states of mind; it is passionately fond of excitement. There is also a constant contrast in moods: egocentrism and sociability, selfishness and altruism, radicalism and conservatism, intensified ambition and loss of interest. Habit patterns have not yet fully developed—school work frequently is unsteady, activities in play vary from time to time, and general attitude toward school is easily changed. However, contrary to popular belief, sudden and extreme changes are the exception rather than the rule. Personality is about to leave its formative stages and to become more or less established for life.

Adolescent Psychology: The Problems

To simplify the study of childhood the textbooks make arbitrary divisions; 10 to 12 for pre-adolescence; 13 to 15, early adolescence; 16 to 18, middle adolescence; and 19 to 21, post-adolescence. However, children do not automatically pass from one of these periods to another on a given birthday. A significant factor is individual differences—some mature earlier than others because of inherited traits or environment.

G. Stanley Hall (1846–1924) was far from being the first to recognize the fact of adolescence, but he was the pioneer in describing its characteristics with any degree of scientific accuracy. Hall drew attention to the rapid physiological growth during this period as well as to its psychological counterparts, especially those of sex and maturation. His published studies on children, as begun in the 1880's, reached their grand climax in 1904 with the publication of *Adolescence.**

That book inspired countless teachers and stimulated numerous investigations into the psychological behavior of children at all ages. It opened up the study of many practical questions, some of which continue to receive experimental attention to this very day. And finally, among Americans especially, Hall's pioneering work popularized the

* For previous discussion of Hall and his theories, see pages 287–289.

belief that education to be truly effective must be based on psychology.

Adolescence has been practically unknown in primitive societies, ancient or modern. A short period of puberty, and the child of only yesterday is today's married man or woman with adult responsibilities. One Latin American tribe still assigns all its eleven-year-old girls as "wives" among the older males. It is, in fact, our modern industrial development in America that has made economically necessary an adolescent period of approximately nine years. Older workers definitely do not want competition from younger people when there is a limited number of jobs. Statistics indicate that high school enrollments rise proportionately as gainful employment among adolescents decreases.

The adolescent is said to be impulsive and unstable in nature. It must be remembered that emotional expression is largely a matter of habit—the European adolescent working long hours on a job with few opportunities for social "mixing" logically is likely to be a much more sober individual than the American boy attending a modern high school where informal as well as formal socialization is constantly in progress.

From out of his daily living habits the adolescent develops behavior patterns we classify as extroversion and introversion. Extroversion, or the desire to be noticed, is indicated by pointless giggling, thoughtless impulsiveness, boisterous talking, and other symptoms of instability. It appears far more commonly, or at least is more noticeable, than introversion as revealed by shyness and awkwardness in relation to new situations. Adolescents who are approaching maturity often display both extroverted and introverted characteristics according to the given situation. Sometimes the manifestations in either direction are extreme. However, it is only natural there should be some such disturbances during an age when youth is in the process of developing a new physiological nature and an awakened social consciousness.

There has been a general tendency to stress the severe conflicts and violent reactions of this period because they are so dramatic. The instability of adolescence is especially marked by contrasting personalities, heightened emotional behavior, religious enthusiasm, and juvenile behavior problems. The "problem child" draws our attention, but there are many more adolescents who are socially well adjusted, wholesome in attitude, reasonably courteous in manners, and stable in the exhibition of various habit systems. The tragedy has been that far too many children, after their adolescence, are expected to assume the place of adults with only such training as would enable them to follow authority blindly. Neither parents nor teachers have given them real opportunity to develop habits of initiative and responsibility so essential to those ordinary pursuits of adult life.

Fortunately most adolescents manage to solve their problems by slow degrees. The child enters this period with a dependence upon and attachment to the home. There should now begin the substitution of independence for purely childish relationships. It is so difficult for many parents to realize that this emancipation from home ties is absolutely necessary because the adolescent can never reach adulthood so long as his parents insist on making decisions for him, planning the details of his life, and depriving him of the experiences of winning and losing his own battles.

The typical adolescent usually has made some progress toward self-control, but he still habitually runs away from the disagreeable by camouflaging his problems even to the point of fooling himself. In an inventory of 540 fifth- and sixth-grade New York City public school pupils, it was found that 37 per cent of the girls and 29 per cent of the boys were constant worriers, and that more than half the group worried now and then. A problem of adolescence is to outgrow these anxieties.

Imitation is definitely a characteristic of adolescence. Let a few leaders wear something strange or try a new dance step and there is a good chance this may become the "rage" for a brief period of time. In Denver, Colorado, high school boys and girls keeping company together began to signify that fact by wearing identical sweaters; the idea was publicized by *Life* magazine and quickly caught on in many other cities.

Among adolescents there is, in fact, almost a slavish dependence upon the imitation of friends. Such characteristics are natural and helpful during the early years of this period, but their continuation into adult life is not so desirable. Also, intolerance is more a characteristic of adolescence than of either childhood or adulthood. High school students seemingly enjoy finding fault with their teachers and classmates just for the fun of "picking on" someone. On the other hand, they are quick to rally to support a cause or an individual.

Adolescents normally feel so vigorous and well that they race about constantly in their play, sometimes burning up more vitality than can be rebuilt even by a full night's sleep. Too much exercise, too much social life, or too much work wears them down despite the great vitality of this age. Occasionally there are dizziness, faintness, and chronic fatigue. Such cases should be sent to a physician. Even if an adolescent has overexercised to the extent of straining his heart, it may be but a functional difficulty that can be cured by adequate rest.

Teachers should ever be on the alert for symptoms of overstrain because of this tendency for adolescents to "burn the candle at both ends" in nearly everything they do. Actuarial tables of insurance companies indicate a lower percentage of deaths occurring in junior high schools than in either elementary or senior highs. However, overstraining in early adolescence may prove to be the cause for early fatalities in the adult years to come.

A healthy adolescent always seems hungry. During this period the organs of digestion undergo considerable growth, and more nourishment is needed than formerly. Sometimes an appetite is so voracious that a boy is still hungry even after, in 24 hours, he consumes twice as much food as any adult in the family. The common prevalence of digestive difficulties doubtlessly is due to this overloading of adolescent stomachs as well as to actual deficiencies in calcium and vitamins. Complicating the situation are adolescents' predilections for such delicacies as hot dogs and soda pop.

During adolescence there appear numerous embarrassing skin infections, largely a by-product of this change from child to adult eating habits. Pimples are the source of a great deal of worry, and require tactful handling. In due time most adolescents outgrow their digestive troubles, and their skins become clear. Another embarrassment, especially to girls, is the increase of perspiration during adolescence. Deodorants are used lavishly in the battle against nature's glandular adjustments that accompany this period of accelerated physical growth. Emotional disturbances, as well as warmth and exercise, produce excessive amounts of perspiration. A teacher should remember this, and when he sees an embarrassed youth perspiring excessively, it would be well to relieve him temporarily from whatever academic efforts have him stumped.

The greatest single problem of the adolescent years is the acquisition of a sane, sensible understanding concerning the maturing of the sex glands. There is a wide variation in the arrival of puberty. For girls it can be determined with fair accuracy as being the time of the first menstrual period, although ability to conceive children does not develop until a few months later. It is far more difficult to determine pubescence for boys, and must be estimated from appearance of secondary sexual characteristics, such as change of voice and growth of pubic hair. Arrival of pubescence varies, ordinarily from age nine to eighteen for girls and from ten to eighteen for boys.

Along with these bodily changes the adolescent normally develops an interest in the opposite sex. To the adult with a short memory this stage of life may seem like a joyous time of dates and dances. But for most teenagers it is a period of confusion and conflict. Curiosity, instinct, and glandular changes pull the adolescent one way; previous training, fear, and lack of confidence pull him another way.

American society does not make the situation easier. On the one hand it lays down strict rules, sets up taboos, and tells young people to wait before they get married. On the other hand, adolescents are constantly exposed to movies, tabloids, magazines, TV shows, and other media of communication which are calculated to arouse sexual desires. Moreover, they see so much looseness and cynicism in the adult world that they are often tempted to imitate this way of life. To add to the problem, the tendency has been for the morals and standards of the laxest people in the community to drag down all the others. For example, if the parents of a few high school girls permit them to stay out until the small hours or to give unchaperoned parties, then the parents of the others find themselves accused of being Victorian "squares" who ought to wake up and realize they are living in the twentieth century. To restore peace to the family, some yield to the protestations of their offspring, and the vicious circle grows ever wider. In some communities, incidentally, this circle has become so distended that parents are running dances for fifth graders!

Many teenagers have found a way out of the dilemma by "going steady." This practice has many advantages to high school students. It saves them the trouble of competing in the popularity contest that is always going on among adolescents. For the girl it temporarily lays to rest the specter of possible spinsterhood. For the boy it is easy on the pocketbook—the "one and only" girl does not expect him to splurge on every date. For both it affords a chance to explore the strange new world of romance with a minimum of embarrassment and to be accepted in the crowd without too great a sacrifice of the time needed for studies. But the practice has its dangers, too. It sometimes results in the unwholesome domination of one partner over the other, in early intimacies, and in hasty marriages that founder after a few years.

All in all, it is obvious that adolescents need wise counseling to help them over the hurdles of sexual awakening. The home, the church, and the school need to combine their efforts to find better ways to meet this responsibility.

Finally, the adolescent must face up to his vocational goal. For academic students who can afford to go to college, this decision can be temporarily postponed although it may be a nagging worry for them all through their teen-age years. A number of the others receive intensive vocational training, thereby learning a trade. Except in slack times their chances for job placement are good. Whether they eventually succeed and attain a modicum of happiness is another matter. Too often the square peg gets into the round hole and is uncomfortable forever after.

Even worse is the fate of the so-called general student. This reluctant or slow learner has no talent for the academic course, and he is not wanted in many vocational schools because he lacks the potential to learn an occupational skill. And so he is merely tolerated in most high schools. He usually gets the worst teachers, who compound his problems by their inept pedagogical practices. Even when an occasional superior teacher is assigned to teach these non-academics, he may treat them in an offhand manner and load them with "busy work" merely to keep them out of trouble. Hence, they mark time and drop out as soon as they are of age to get working papers. Some play truant or join gangs to get ego satisfaction; others adopt a defeatist attitude. "I'll never amount to anything," one of these boys told a social worker, "so don't waste your time on me."

Many of the big cities, such as Detroit and New York, are striving to correct this evil. New curricula, geared to the occupational needs of these young people, have been set up; teachers have been carefully chosen to train them; and a system for following them up after they leave school has been inaugurated. But this kind of attack on the problem is still the exception rather than the rule.

Only a few of the difficulties that assail adolescents have been touched upon in these pages. This is indeed a period of turbulence, with one crisis following another. From the point of view of educators, a comprehensive guidance program in every secondary school is an absolute necessity. Otherwise many potentially fine young citizens will continue to be human driftwood, and a burden on society.

Abnormal Psychology: Its Essentials

Although not usually required of a teacher for certification, one of the most interesting and helpful college courses that can be taken is abnormal psychology. There is a continuous demand for professional help in mental institutions even at times when teaching positions are difficult to secure. This work is fascinating to those who are temperamentally suited for it. But abnormal psychology should prove helpful to those in charge of children who are presumed to be perfectly normal. We can only touch the surface of such a broad subject, but to get even a basic understanding it is necessary to know a few of the more important terms.

Roughly speaking, a psychiatrist is a psychologist with a medical degree. A large number of psychiatric patients never require institutional commitment. Their difficulties of adjustment are due to psychoneuroses, now more commonly known as neuroses. These are, relatively speaking, the minor abnormalities, such as hysteria (unconsciously pretending to be physically disabled in order to gain one's ends), neurasthenia (persistent feeling of tiredness despite absence of physical exertion), and psychasthenia (persistent morbid fears, obsessions, doubts, compulsions).

A neurotic patient usually recognizes his nervousness as abnormal. The psychotic lacks such a clear-cut insight and, as a consequence, is apt to injure himself or others; hence he needs institutionalization. Psychosis is the term usually applied to the more serious types of mental illness which ordinarily involve so drastic a personality disturbance as to render hospitalization desirable.

Specialists have sought to discover some bodily disturbance as the basis for abnormal behavior. This has led to a distinction between structural and functional psychoses. Classified as structural are mental symptoms that can be traced to brain injury or damage caused there by syphilitic infection. Functional diseases are those whose presumed underlying bodily causes are so minute or obscure as to defy detection. Although structures may be intact, their dependent functions nevertheless exhibit a loss of efficiency.

A victim of stage fright gives a good example of such emotional difficulty. His pounding heart, trembling knees, and perspiring hands are all symptoms of an abnormal condition. The disturbed muscles and glands behave as if something were damaged. This "as if" character does not mean that functional disturbances are unreal or imaginary. They are as real as the visceral distress of a conscience-stricken person, as real as the loss of appetite experienced during grief, and as real as the sudden muscular weakness of the frightened victim of a hold-up. All these are mild functional disabilities in which the intimate participation of emotional factors is clearly evident.

Some mental disturbances are caused by infections of the central nervous system. Syphilis at times strikes in even the best regulated of schools, and while far more common in high schools it is discovered occasionally as low as the kindergarten. Eventually about 5 per cent of the syphilis cases develop into paresis. The spirochetes responsible for this disease lodge in the tissues of the brain, resulting in disturbances in thought and motor control, and a change in the patient's personality. A paretic is apt to forget his home address, number of children in the family, important appointments, and the like. Generally speaking, he is a confused person. Ordinarily he is exceptionally good-natured and happy-go-lucky, but at times he may harbor some grudge that makes him a dangerous character.

Other infectious invasions of the nervous system are associated with meningitis and encephalitis. Various bacteria may infest the meninges (or membranes) covering the brain. Feeblemindedness sometimes has been a consequence of meningitis in early childhood. It is estimated that approximately 2 per cent of mental deficiency cases in public institutions are there because of this disease. Encephalitis, better known as sleeping sickness, is caused by a virus and not by bacteria. Frequently following this disease are disturbances of muscular coordination, heart action, breathing, and sleeping. Personality changes may result in behavior difficulties of the type that eventually develop into juvenile delinquency.

Alcoholism and drug-taking by their very nature are habits that affect only an insignificantly small minority of the teaching profession—one who indulges does not remain in the profession very long. However, there are occasional scandals involving high school students who seem bent on gaining life experiences in ways not approved by society. Because of their intimate relationship with mental efficiency, alcohol or drugs may produce changes in thinking, feeling, and action.

Disturbances of vision, speech, motor control, ethical judgment, and general intellectual incompetence are associated with alcoholism. One of the better known of these psychoses is delirium tremens, in which confusion is accompanied by hallucinations, predominantly visual, that for some curious reason often take the form of actively moving animals about to attack the patient. There are also structural psychoses due to wounds and injuries, circulatory disturbances, faulty metabolism, brain tumors.

Not all epileptics are psychotic—a few, like Alexander the Great (356–323 B.C.), Julius Caesar (100–44 B.C.), and Guy de Maupassant (1850–1893), have achieved lasting fame. Despite a long and imposing list of eminent victims, the disease does cause mental deterioration.

Grand mal is marked by convulsions preceded by a signal called the aura, such as a slight feeling of nausea, muscular jerk, moodiness. Loss of consciousness occurs as the patient falls, becomes rigid, then is seized by alternate contractions and relaxations of the muscles affected. There may be a loss of sphincter control, and consequently involuntary bladder and bowel action as part of this motor turmoil.

Another type of epilepsy is known as petit mal, in which there is no aura or loss of consciousness. A momentary abstraction sometimes is accompanied by the involuntary jerking of some muscle group. This is all over within a few seconds, and the victim goes on working or playing. In the larger school systems the worst cases of epilepsy are now being sent to separate schools where they may receive medical treatment wherever the attack may occur. This means that but few classroom teachers today must meet the problem of having a child "throw a fit" as sometimes happened in schools of previous generations. But it is well that a teacher should know what to do in the event such circumstances unexpectedly occur in the classroom or on the playground.

There are three functional psychoses: manic-depressive, schizophrenia, and paranoia. Manic-depressives are characterized by extreme shifts of mood ranging from despondency to elation. In the manic type the prevailing emotional trend is toward excitement, which takes the form of either joyous good spirits or bitter vindictiveness. The depressive type exhibits signs of despondency even to the point of attempting suicide. The patient seems to be utterly defeated by his problem. Some victims shift from manic to depressive moods, as if undergoing emotional attacks and retreats. This mental disease is largely a product of frustration, and it definitely is an adult affliction that is found among teachers but seldom, if ever, among students.

About one-half of all patients in psychopathic institutions are diagnosed as suffering from schizophrenia. Formerly known as dementia praecox (Latin for adolescent insanity), this disease frequently appears during adolescence, and mental deterioration occurs quite early. There are, in fact, several types of schizophrenia, a Greek compound meaning "split mind." In general, the patient seems to have divorced himself from effective contact with his physical and social environments—a split between ideational and emotional aspects of mental life.

A schizophrenic is apt to remain unmoved when confronted with situations a normal person would consider exciting or important. This apathy, or lack of interest, is one of the clues for which a psychiatrist looks in seeking the schizophrenic trend. The patient is a "shut-in" personality, one that seemingly prefers to be a spectator rather than a participant. Many schizophrenics do not impress a layman as being mentally disturbed. Those are generally classified as the simple type.

The hebephrenic type is silly, giggles at anything, even funerals. The catatonic type seems to resist outside intrusion, frequently holding fixed queer positions for hours at a time. The paranoid type seems preoccupied with the need of protecting himself from imaginary enemies. Not only is he a victim of delusions of persecution, but also often considers himself a person of great importance, or has what is known as delusions of grandeur. Institutions are full of "Napoleons" and "George Washingtons."

Paranoia is a rare form of functional psychosis. It differs from the paranoid type of schizophrenia where the victim is greatly confused. A true paranoid makes a logical, coherent, plausible elaboration of some misinterpreted actual event about which he continually talks and worries. He is forever the "detective" seeking out plots against himself. His delusions of persecution form a central focus in his mental life. Nevertheless, he keeps in firm touch with all the world and is usually well balanced except with reference to what bears on his personal pet delusion of persecution. The paranoid personality is a fighting personality—he is ready, if necessary, to defend himself by violent means. That is what makes paranoia such a dangerous mental disorder.

Judging from their actions, certain officials of schools and colleges come close to being paranoids. Sometimes they will dismiss individuals for the sheer pleasure of displaying their authority and for the subsequent joy of screening new applicants. Needless to say, the prospective employees have it dinned into them that their interviewer is a man of great importance. Fortunately, this extremely unbalanced type of educational leader seldom lasts. Rare, too, are the true paranoids. They comprise only about 2 per cent of the institutionalized cases.

This has been a very brief review of the high spots in a subject field that has gained a great deal of attention in recent decades. There is, perhaps, as wide a spread of individual differences among what are classified as the abnormal population as among the normal. As a matter of fact each one of us has our own peculiar abnormalities—it is only when they upset the balance of our lives that we become mental cases.

The teacher is in a key position to do much effective preventive work on behalf of his youthful charges, or upon professional colleagues who may be "cracking under the strain," or even upon himself, though self-doctoring is always a risky business. However, there is one caution about the study of abnormal psychology—the reader should be careful not to let it affect him as did, in previous generations, the old-fashioned almanac that so insidiously suggested varied and sundry diseases which, of course, only the patent medicine being advertised could possibly cure. Abnormal psychology is a good study to avoid if everything read is apt to be interpreted into one's own actions or into the conduct of one's associates. Moreover, the teacher must be alert against the temptation to ascribe mental disease to a few pupils who are overly aggressive or defiant, but mentally sound!

Mental Hygiene in Modern Education

Some years ago a census study was made of the inmates of what then were known as insane asylums. The startling fact was indicated that one out of each five persons under confinement, at some time or another, had been a school teacher. Assuming reliability of those figures, such a situation was not really as bad as at first it might seem. Hundreds of thousands of men and women teach school for a year or so, then drift into other occupations. Perhaps they are not temperamentally fitted for the work, or teaching means merely temporary income until some other type of employment is found, or the women teachers get married. Thus the country is full of ex-teachers.

More to the point, several recent investigations have indicated that an alarmingly large percentage of teachers in active service are mentally unfit for the responsibility of helping youth prepare for its place in the adult world. Admittedly, managing a roomful of lively, boisterous children is a nerve-racking business, especially so if the individual takes himself too seriously and fails to enjoy or appreciate the exuberance of youth with its quick flights of interest, its joy of living, and its state of flux in character formation. So it is quite logical that a large percentage of ex-teachers, and some still in service, do suffer from mental illnesses.

More recent and reliable figures indicate that one in five of the adult American population, at one time or another in life, receives treatment for a mental illness (for example, nervous breakdown), and that, at least for brief periods of time, one in twenty becomes an institutionalized case. The ever-increasing tempo of life in an industrial society is largely responsible for these alarming statistics. The adults of today were the school children of a few years ago. Perhaps the American educational system should hang its head in shame because in generations gone by so very little has been done to protect from mental disturbances both the teachers in active service and those children in school who are growing into the adult citizens of tomorrow. The answer to this problem lies partly in what has been called the "mental hygiene" approach. Let us examine how this movement began and developed.

In 1908 Clifford W. Beers (1876–1943) published a startling auto-
biography. *A Mind That Found Itself* was the outgrowth of his own
experiences as a mental-breakdown victim. He related graphically the
events which compelled his family to have him institutionalized after
he had become so depressed he attempted to commit suicide. The strait
jacket was the routine technique used at that time for quieting excited
patients. There was very little real understanding of the psychology of
the mentally sick. Beers called attention to the intensification of inner
excitement produced by such crude methods of restraint, showing that
they merely magnify the patient's emotional distress and make it harder
for him to view the attending physicians as friendly, helpful healers.
This noteworthy book is considered the starting point of the modern
mental hygiene movement.

Beers aroused the interest of William James, the psychologist, and
of Adolf Meyer (1866–1950), a psychiatrist who was the one to suggest
use of the term "mental hygiene." In its beginning the movement was
concerned primarily with improving treatment and status of the mentally ill. Efforts were concentrated on changing the public's attitude
toward the "insane," a word no longer in accepted scientific usage.

The first Society for Mental Health was founded in Connecticut on
May 6, 1908, and in 1909 the National Commission for Mental Health
was established. Thus began the long fight to eliminate superstitions
and misinformation by educating the public to regard abnormal behavior as an illness and not as an invasion by the devil. The practical
problem was to induce people to view mental disease in the light of
twentieth-century science instead of seventeenth-century witchcraft.

Two surveys published in 1928 made strong indictments against
those responsible for rearing and educating children. It was claimed
that but little was being done to safeguard the mental health of our
younger generations. The imperative need for instructing teachers in
the principles of mental hygiene was pointed out. Both investigations
revealed how poorly informed parents and teachers were regarding
symptoms indicative of existing or impending personality distortion.
It was brought out that mental hygienists regarded as serious conditions
what parents and teachers either overlooked entirely or treated lightly;
and what the latter viewed with alarm the former dismissed as negligible. In other words, the mental hygienists were seeking to detect the
troubled child—parents and teachers were concerned with the troublesome one.

Too often in the past teachers have considered behavior of children
a serious problem only when it has violated either conventional mo-

rality or has caused disturbances of classroom routine. Thus until recent years only aggressive behavior was regarded by the average teacher as being serious. Those children displaying recessive traits such as shyness, extreme sensitivity, unsocial personalities, imaginative lying, continuous daydreaming, and the like rarely were reported as problems. Yet from the mental hygiene point of view, the non-interfering, timid, and withdrawing child is perhaps a much graver problem than the overtly socially aggressive youngster. Left to themselves, such children often fail to become happily socialized. If the process of abnormal introversion goes unchecked, there may develop the asocial, the odd, the incongruous, the pre-schizophrenic, and schizophrenic (dementia praecox) types that eventually require hospitalization.

Today, as part of their teacher-training programs, most universities are offering courses in mental hygiene. The idea behind this new addition to the college curriculum is splendid, but at first it did not always work out according to specifications. Just as when many teachers taking their first courses in tests and measurements began thinking of their pupils as "little morons," some even calling them that in more or less endearing tones, so also, at least a few students of mental hygiene began trying to diagnose children in their classes according to types of mental diseases—and the result was not always wholesome. One superintendent of a California school complained: "Ever since some of my teachers took a mental hygiene course at the university, they've been looking at every kid as though he were crazy."

The inexperienced teacher soon discovers there is an individual known as the problem child. Such a youngster never fails to impress himself upon his teachers, and it almost always is an unpleasant impression. Recent research indicates that the delinquent child is retarded in his emotional development—something must be done to bring about better adjustment during the vital school years of rapid growth if we are to stop trouble before it gets too good a start. Those teachers capable of understanding the problems of maladjusted youth have saved countless boys and girls from delinquency. There have been others, however, who doubtlessly have contributed their share in the driving of children into juvenile courts and reform schools, because they were incapable or unwilling to understand them and to do some constructive human salvaging when the time was ripe.

That schools were failing in psychological guidance was the finding of a 1948 survey of 125 cities made by New York City school psychologists. In only 42 of those communities were schools employing psychological staffs, and almost invariably those staffs were small in proportion to the number of pupils. That survey held that the ideal ratio should be one psychologist for every 3000 pupils. In comparison with that, New York City was employing one to every 17,000. Other big cities lagged almost as far behind.

Since 1948, improvements in psychological service have been made. But the problem is still a long way from solution. First, there is a paucity of trained psychologists; secondly, most of them are lured into industry or private practice. The schools find it difficult to pay them as much as they can get elsewhere. One method that has been tried recently is to employ the psychologists on a part-time basis. In this way, they can continue to earn outside the school system. Obviously this is only a patchwork answer since the school psychologists' work calls for continuity and long-range planning.

In 1949, there were announced plans for a mental hygiene program in public schools to be administered jointly by the Office of Education and the United States Public Health Service. Aimed at acquainting teachers at all age levels with principles of preventive psychiatry, the project was also to include study of methods of handling the emotional problems of teachers.

Delaware early gained the reputation of conducting one of the broadest state programs in psychology. Known as the Delaware Plan, it was carried out through human-relations classes aimed to strengthen children emotionally. Those pupils who for one reason or another were considered "socially unacceptable" were helped to develop their personalities by enlisting the cooperation of classmates. Classes were scheduled once a week, either in social studies or English periods; twice a year each group was given sociometric tests to indicate to teachers those pupils most in need of personality guidance. The Delaware State Society for Mental Hygiene reported that this movement was spreading, as indicated by the fact that already patterned at that time were similar statewide programs for Louisiana, Massachusetts, Minnesota, and North Carolina.

PART SIX

Teaching as a Profession

PART SIX

Teaching as a Profession

Teaching as a Professional Career

Recently one of the authors of this book asked several hundred new teachers to state anonymously and frankly just why they had decided to join the profession. The written answers of these beginners provided a startling insight into their motivations. Some gave purely utilitarian reasons; others were completely idealistic. The largest group, by far, indicated that they had chosen the career after considering the practical advantages along with the spiritual and emotional values. And a great number pointed out that they had blundered into the profession partly through accident or expediency.

Typical of the answers on the practical side are those quoted below. Some of them sound almost cynical.

"I chose teaching because it was a fairly well-paying part-time job which would allow me to pursue my other main interest."

"In my previous job in business I found myself at a dead end. Anyway, teaching gives me some respect in the community which I didn't have before."

"As a recently married woman, I plan to raise a family. My present salary will help me meet the financial problems that come with children. Besides, the experience will give me a better perspective as a mother."

"After a liberal arts education with a major in psychology, the economic realities of life caused me to give up hope of getting a Ph.D. and becoming a psychologist. I turned to teaching, influenced by the fact that both my parents are teachers. Security and vacations were other factors in my decision."

"Since my wife was a teacher, this would enable us to have time and interests that coincide."

"I was tired of working seven days a week and 14 hours a day as a nonprofessional."

"For a woman the pay seemed good."

"Frankly, I'd been aware of the teacher shortage, and preparing for teaching seemed like the quickest and easiest way to get a job. I'm not equipped for a trade. What else is there? Labor?"

"I've no head for business. Math is my hardest subject. So I decided to become an English teacher. Besides, after 16 years in school, I was familiar with the environment!"

"The tuition at the state teachers college near my home was much cheaper than the fees charged at private liberal arts colleges. I just couldn't afford to prepare to be an M.D."

The pragmatic responses, such as those given above, can be grouped into a few broad categories: security, prestige of a profession, financial necessity, family adjustment, and the advantages of long vacations and relatively short hours. If these were the only motivations of prospective teachers, then the profession would indeed be in a sorry state. Fortunately the following typical answers, given in just as many instances, serve as an antidote:

"Teaching appeared to be the best way for me to pass on my own knowledge to others."

"As I have always enjoyed being with children, it seemed a natural thing for me to think of teaching."

"I love children and derive a tremendous satisfaction from seeing them progress. They keep you young and alive!"

"Children are uncorrupted by society; luckily I love their ingenuous and refreshing ways. Teaching is perhaps the most creative kind of work. Working with children could never be dull or suffocating—they won't let a creative person become bored."

"Truthfully, as a child I decided I wanted to teach. This was at the age of five years. In public school I helped my teachers and led the class."

"I feel I am helping our future generation become a better one. A job as a junior counselor at camp also helped me make up my mind."

"I had a wonderful history teacher in the ninth grade. This, combined with the fact that I liked the subject, made me decide to become a teacher of social studies."

"I have a fierce pride in American democracy. As one who was brought up in a slum area myself, I wanted to help deprived children get someplace."

"I'm a religious person, but I wasn't sure that I'd make a good clergyman. Teaching is the next best profession, so here I am."

The humanitarian answers can be briefly placed into categories, too: love of children, desire to impart knowledge, interest in democracy and in the next generation, inspiration of a past teacher, childhood ambition fostered by actual experience, and the potentiality of the work for the fulfillment of creative and spiritual leanings.

It is deplorable that all who enter the profession do not have some of the idealistic motivations listed in the preceding paragraph. Frequently, as has been shown, teaching is merely a port in a storm—a temporary haven for the young woman awaiting marriage or children and a stopping-off place for the man who is interested in some more lucrative occupation.

These "marriages of convenience" between individuals and teaching jobs are not conducive to giving education in the United States the stability and respect it enjoys in certain other countries. It is, in fact, this very transiency that keeps teaching from being recognized as a true profession despite the ever-increasing academic standards required for certification. However, American education now seems very definitely on the road toward more stability and greater recognition. There have arisen in recent years many intelligently aggressive leaders who seem intent on gaining for the profession a status on a par with that of medicine or law.

In some European countries the teachers, not only in higher education but also in secondary schools, are well represented in the intellectual cream of the population. In America, however, certain impressive investigations indicate that as a class teachers do not compare so favorably with the membership in other professions. A survey of Pennsylvania colleges by the Carnegie Foundation for the Advancement of Teaching revealed that, in certain subject matter tests, students training for teaching were surpassed by those not expecting to teach. Several other investigations also have shown that students entering normal schools and teachers colleges make scores on scholastic aptitude tests considerably lower than the scores made by those entering the liberal arts colleges and universities with no intention of teaching. It is alleged that the chief reason for this difference is the low salary of the average teacher. Apparently a natural screening takes place at the high school level, especially among young men. The bright student reasons that he can get equivalent job satisfactions outside the teaching profession and at the same time receive excellent monetary rewards. Moreover, because social position in our country is often determined by one's material wealth, the student may feel that there are easier avenues to prestige than through teaching.

In those countries where teachers enjoy positions of the highest respect for their intellectual attainments, the secondary schools and colleges are taught almost entirely by men who, once they are admitted into the profession, devote the rest of their lives to becoming masters of their particular teaching fields. The practice of continually looking around for a better position is almost unthinkable—education to them is a permanent career.

Teaching in America was originally a man's occupation; women worked only with the smaller children. Then came the Industrial Revolution, and the males drifted into fields of manufacturing, trade, and business where the compensation usually promised to be greater. So it came about that schools were largely left to women; at the beginning of the twentieth century the men were far outnumbered in the high schools and rarely seen in the elementary schools. However, the higher administrative and college jobs remained mostly a man's domain.

Ever since World War I more and more men have been entering and remaining permanently in the teaching profession. Today women constitute less than 90 per cent of our elementary school teachers. This figure should continue to decrease as more and more young men realize that the field is especially promising for those anxious to break into administrative work as quickly as possible. In high schools the ratio between the sexes is now almost even, and some principals are already complaining they need fewer men and more women. In normal schools and teachers colleges a little more than half the faculty members are women; in professional schools, colleges, and universities men predominate about three to one. It is interesting to note that in a recent year Great Britain's National Association of Schoolmasters unanimously agreed that teaching is a man's work and demanded that Parliament pass a law to abolish "schoolmarms." Grumbled one schoolmaster: "The avaricious hordes of women have already staked a claim in our field, and the sooner they're smoked out, the better it will be for the boys in this country."

Is teaching in the United States a profession? It has not generally been considered as such in years gone by, yet the years of preparation now being required for certification represent an important step toward full-fledged recognition. The mark of any professional work is the social value of the services rendered; the purpose of training is to insure a high degree of skill and understanding of the scientific principles upon which the profession is based. Thus, to be worthy of the name, a profession must make a genuine contribution to the betterment of society—the services of its workers need to be essential to the improvement of living, actuated only by unselfish idealism for public good.

Of course, medicine has its "quacks" and law its "shysters," but both these professions have long been organized to eliminate their undesirables. Within recent years educators also have been working toward establishing standards, but the fact that in the United States public and private schools employ more than a million teachers makes it extremely difficult to raise teaching to the same satisfactorily high professional level now enjoyed by groups with a far smaller membership.

However, the progress made since World War I is encouraging. Any young person today who chooses teaching as a career is selecting a profession that is rapidly increasing in public esteem. Every state now has its own teachers' association, and the National Education Association is the largest educators' organization in the world. It was organized in 1857 with but 43 gathered in Philadelphia to form the National Teachers' Association. In 1907 the name was changed and it was incorporated under a special act of Congress.

NEA membership now is approximately 700,000. Two kinds of services are rendered. Members are reached directly through publications, including the *Journal* issued nine times a year. There are annual conventions of the entire NEA in June, and of the American Association of School Administrators and other allied organizations in February. These help to promote personal growth and to encourage educational research in building a common mind for the profession. Then there are indirect services, such as continuous campaigns to create a public opinion that demands the following: better schools, a competent, well-educated teacher in every classroom, higher salaries for the expert teachers, tenure for those of proved ability, adequate retirement allowances, sabbatical leave for teachers, an equal opportunity for all children, and greater financial support for public education by both the federal government and the states.

The highly respected profession of medicine has served somewhat as a model for education. The American Medical Association, comprising the great majority of a total of more than 200,000 accredited doctors in the United States, has been ever alert against any invasion of the professional rights of its members, and there are also state and county medical societies.

The AMA boards of medical examiners in the various states have demanded unusually high standards before allowing a doctor to practice; medical schools have limited the number studying medicine to those who can be properly trained with the accommodations available, and the training is long and arduous, ending in a period of internship. Thus, by the simple process of making it extremely difficult to become a physician or surgeon, doctors are so scarce and their services so much in demand that they are reasonably sure of substantial remuneration. An unfortunate by-product, however, is that so many American communities, especially rural districts, are today without adequate medical services—most of the doctors licensed prefer to have their offices in cities rather than villages. Incidentally, the same may be said of certain teachers, who usually swarm to metropolitan school systems in preference to rural schools. There is always the problem of distribution of professional services to the places where they are needed.

The attempt to provide a balance between supply and demand has lately been the chief function of the placement directors at teacher-training institutions. These officials keep an active file of candidates in search of positions and vacancies over a wide area. School superintendents rely on them for leads as to potential administrators, as well as new teachers. However, it must be noted that placement service is usually no better or no worse than the institution from which it stems. This leads us to the very important area of teacher preparation.

Professional Training of Teachers

Whether classed as a job, trade, or profession, every occupation requires at least some training. This apprenticeship usually is quite informal in a factory or shop situation, but as one advances upward in the social scale of vocations there is demanded greater and increasingly more formal preparation. Before certifying a teacher today, all states require a professional training that includes a considerable number of courses in education, psychology, and content subjects. In addition there are periods of observation of the classroom work of experienced teachers and a practice-teaching period in which the trainee discovers under controlled conditions how it feels to be in charge of a classroom full of pupils. In order to gain the proper perspective concerning the type of preparation a teacher gets today, let us examine briefly through the ages why and how professional training has developed.

Knowledge of the subject matter to be taught was the chief qualification for teaching in the ancient world—a teacher's importance depended largely upon how his subject area was regarded. Members of early priesthoods were the only ones capable of reading and writing, and some contrived to make their skills appear to be quite a mystery as they recorded and interpreted sacred and scientific lore. Since ordinarily they were the only teachers, their ability to instruct others represented a mark of personal distinction.

The Brahmans, the highest caste in ancient India, enjoyed exclusively the privileges of being both priests and teachers. The ancient Egyptian priesthood monopolized education to the point where the death penalty was threatened against anyone else who learned to read and write. The ancient Chinese held teachers in respect second only to that paid government officials. The early Jews held teaching as a sacred office and gave the teacher even more honor and respect than they tendered to parents.

With the Greeks there came a change—they revered not priests but poets as their teachers. So long as education had been considered a rare accomplishment it was highly esteemed, but as learning became more common the social status of teachers decreased rapidly in importance, particularly in the case of those who taught the rudiments. A common practice of upper-class Athenians (and later the Romans) was to entrust teaching to slaves. Often these were citizens of another city-state that had been defeated in war, and many were men of cultural background and exceptional ability. Certain outstanding teachers achieved a very high social status and lasting fame; the Athenian schools of philosophy and rhetoric, in fact, continued for some 800 years. There was even some attempt at teacher-training among these higher levels, but in the Graeco-Roman world the status of teachers of fundamentals deteriorated to a point where many were objects of scornful pity.

Aims and purposes of teaching originated largely outside the school, but instruction soon became so routinized that teachers lost not only their touch with the world they supposedly were serving but also the public respect they once had held. The Roman philosopher Seneca (4? B.C.–65 A.D.) criticized teachers as being too prone to teach school instead of life. Quintilian (35–100), Rome's greatest schoolmaster, came nearer than anyone else in the ancient world to writing a manual for teachers, but even he was concerned with describing the educational ideals of the orator and barely touched upon how the individual might be taught to orate.

Throughout educational history great dependence has been placed upon memorizing, and the role of the Roman and medieval teacher was practically that of a taskmaster whose chief responsibility was to punish those who failed to remember. Charlemagne (742–814), who after the fall of the Roman Empire did more than any other man to revive learning, emphasized the necessity of knowing what to do rather than just knowing for the sake of knowing. At that time the ability to teach seems to have been universally regarded as a gift from God. Doubtless it was this belief that postponed so long the study of how to improve the techniques of teaching.

It was the rise of the medieval university that first centered attention upon the professional training of teachers. A reviving interest in learning made it necessary to develop trained teachers—in fact, the university degree conferred upon its recipient the right to teach. The title "doctor" originally meant teacher* when degrees were granted by the faculties of law, medicine, and theology. The arts faculty awarded the title of "master" and thus set an early precedent for making the master of arts distinctively a teaching degree that led eventually to the terms schoolmaster and, later, schoolmistress.

Medieval universities trained teachers in subject matter fields and made no effort to develop techniques for imparting knowledge. The candidate for a degree had to learn to teach by teaching whenever he could create opportunities to do so. His professional training was limited to disputations and an occasional lecture—the two principal methods of instruction at that time.

While the universities of the late medieval and Renaissance periods developed a supply of reasonably competent teachers for higher or professional branches of learning, the schools at the secondary level were not so fortunate. There were a few outstanding humanistic teachers, such as Vittorino de Feltre (1378–1446) in Italy and Johann Sturm (1507–1589) in Germany, but they were the exceptions rather than the rule. Writers of that day frequently satirized teachers for their ignorance, uncouth manners, and general pompousness. Michel de Montaigne (1533–1592) accused teachers of using obsolete language that was quite different from the ordinary way of speaking. He repeated Seneca's indictment that teaching was far removed from life, noting that teachers were often the butt of contemporary humor and saying that no one would ever boast of having a teacher for an ancestor.

From this point on, professional training of teachers as we know it today began to take initial form. Two Catholic teaching orders set up highly effective programs—the Jesuits for secondary education and the Christian Brothers for elementary schools. A great deal of credit must go to Saint Jean Baptiste de la Salle (1651–1719), who not only organized the Christian Brothers but also established the earliest known institution to offer systematic training courses for prospective teachers.

* "Doctor" stems from the Latin verb *docere,* meaning "to teach."

This archetype of the normal schools was founded in 1685 at Rheims, France. Thirteen years later the German educator, August Hermann Francke (1663–1727), also began a famous training school for teachers at Halle.

In 1794 the first government-sponsored normal school was established in France. The interesting feature of this institution was its attempt to apply Rousseau's theories that educators should concentrate more on the mental and physical development of children than on subject matter. This principle was accepted by teacher-training institutions that came on the heels of the French institution. It became so solidly entrenched that child psychology emerged as the basic science of all normal schools.

Prussia, early in the nineteenth century, was the first nation to establish a state-controlled system for the training of teachers, and it was organized with characteristic Prussian thoroughness. The leaders adopted the pedagogical principles of Johann Pestalozzi (1746–1827), who based his instructional methods upon knowing child nature and observing how pupils react to certain learning situations. Teaching had been a fairly simple matter when it was only necessary to know the subject matter. It increased tremendously in technical complexity when the teacher also had to know the child. Prussia added much to the dignity of teaching by making teachers public officials; those who faithfully sought self-improvement were promoted and later pensioned. All of this—especially the provision of schools specializing in training teachers—represented a great contribution toward professionalizing education.

In their teacher-training programs the Prussian seminaries eventually put great emphasis on the theories of Johann Herbart (1776–1841). This gave added impetus to the movement that made psychology so important in the normal schools. For Herbart had advocated the study of the psychology of learning and the careful presentation of knowledge through specific steps from the known to the unknown. The Herbartian method was later adopted, a basic principle in all European and American normal schools.

In American colonial history, oddly enough, teachers were recruited from all classes of society. Many clergymen combined the teaching of Latin and Greek with their other duties. However, at the elementary levels, indentured servants and even slaves were often used as teachers. The emphasis was almost entirely upon subject matter, with little attention paid to the techniques of instruction or to those being taught.

Teachers in the common schools ordinarily lacked even a secondary school education themselves, a situation so unsatisfactory that it demanded action.

The first action came from the teachers themselves. A group in New York City formed in 1794 the Society of Associated Teachers. One of their goals was to establish qualifications for the occupation. Mayor De Witt Clinton took up the cause in 1805 by establishing a Free School Society to educate the poor children. This society organized a two-month course of study specifically to train teachers. The idea received much attention in the Northeast, and in 1818 Philadelphia opened the first model school for the training of teachers. But it remained for a Congregational minister named Samuel Read Hall (1795–1877) to bring the movement to complete fruition. In 1823 he established the first full-time normal school in America—a three-year seminary at Concord, Vermont. Eleven years later the legislature of New York began subsidizing private academies to train teachers for the state's common school system. The public school teacher had gained status at last.

It was Massachusetts, in 1839, that instituted a state-supported teacher-training program patterned on the Prussian model. The idea met with strenuous opposition and was successful only because of a last-minute donation contingent upon the state's matching it with an equal amount. Even then the state normal school was launched for an experimental period of only three years, and met stiff opposition to continue on a reduced budget when it was time to refinance the venture. Many still thought the academies were competent to train all the teachers the state might need, and there was also some opposition from religious groups.

Considerable objection was voiced against the normal school because of its Prussian origin. The fact that the Prussian seminary served to inculate prospective teachers with a willing obedience to their superiors or masters was pointed out. Actually, normal schools founded before the Civil War were more like the American academy than the Prussian Lehrer-seminar. The curriculum was almost the same as the so-called English course of the academy.

In its beginnings the normal school movement progressed rather slowly. Enrollments were small at first, and many who matriculated failed to stay throughout the three-year course. During the great expansion of free public education after the Civil War, the staffing of the common schools came to depend almost entirely upon women; and normal schools gained rapidly in popularity, especially in the midwestern states. Even before the Civil War the larger cities had been establishing training classes operated in connection with their own schools as a means of meeting the increasing demands for teachers. Some of these (the classes in Boston, for example) developed into normal schools. Throughout this period the Catholic Church and other denominations also organized teacher-training institutions for supplying personnel to their own schools.

By the beginning of the twentieth century the normal school had become a well-established part of the American educational system. Training facilities had been expanded to include preparation for high school, as well as elementary, teachers. This created two problems. It became necessary to improve the quality of instruction and to lengthen the training period to meet the requirements of accrediting associations demanding that high school teachers hold college degrees.

Of those entering normal schools in 1890, only 20 per cent had high school diplomas and an astounding 65 per cent had attended only the grammar grades. Normal school training lasted anywhere from one to four years, depending largely upon the amount of high school work being offered. This meant that practically no normal school extended more than two years beyond high school. Then, in 1890, New York reorganized its first normal school at Albany into the New York State Normal College, and in 1903 Michigan constituted its normal school at Ypsilanti as the first state teachers college in the United States. Four-year teachers colleges, granting regular college degrees, gradually supplanted normal schools thereafter in many states.

The rise of teachers colleges caused a hue and cry in academic circles. Liberal arts colleges had voiced no particular complaints about the degrees in pedagogy awarded by normal schools, but they raised grave objections when the teachers colleges began to hand out A.B. degrees. Their contention was that the teachers college graduates had not acquired enough points in subject matter because they were taking so many courses in pedagogy.

The work of John Dewey (1859–1952) helped to resolve this controversy. Led by that distinguished philosopher, educators were able to convince many doubting Thomases that the study of teaching methods was a science on the same level as sociology. Also, the careful work of Edward Thorndike (1874–1949) in the field of educational psychology helped to give status to courses in teacher preparation.

As the years went on, the professional schools gradually put more emphasis on the academic studies and pared the courses in pedagogy. Simultaneously the universities began to establish departments of education. Today, in some of the universities, the students who matriculate in the departments of education far outnumber those enrolled in any other department. Consequently, some academicians are grumbling that the tail is wagging the dog.

The above phenomenon coupled with the increasing clamor for better academic preparation of teachers has brought a halt in the rise of teachers colleges. Some states have renamed those institutions and have designated them liberal arts colleges. For example, Montclair State Teachers College in New Jersey is now officially Montclair State College. Indeed, some educators are of the opinion that the teachers college will eventually fade from the scene altogether.

Despite the tremendous advances in the field of teacher preparation in this century, professors of education have been constantly under fire. They have sarcastically been called "educationists" who feather their own nests with a multiplicity of useless courses and who grant higher degrees to students for sloppy dissertations on trivial subjects. Furthermore, the critics have claimed that these professors have overvalued the "how" (methodology) at the expense of the "what" (subject matter), that their courses are ridiculed by students as "snaps" or soporifics, and that they use unnecessary jargon in their books and lectures.

A great deal of this criticism has stemmed from reactionaries and anti-Deweyites who in their search for a scapegoat have centered on progressive education as the cause of all of society's ailments and faults. The education professors give credence to Dewey's findings; therefore, they must be villains and nincompoops. Such is their logic.

But some of the indictments have come from sober, fair-minded people who have recognized the need for an overhauling of education courses and an upgrading of standards. In many instances, their criticism has been warranted. As a result, many changes are taking place. Teacher-training institutions are now actively seeking personnel who have had valuable experience in the elementary and secondary schools. Courses have been reduced in number and revised in terms of practicality. Students are carefully screened and some are advised not to continue; their dissertations are being scrutinized for depth and significance. Finally, professors who write are making a real attempt to descend from esoteric and clouded ivory towers.

This movement to improve standards has proceeded in spite of an ever-present shortage of qualified teachers. If the shortage problem should ever be overcome, it can be assumed that requirements for certification of teachers from kindergarten through college will become very stringent. Even now the trend is upward. For example, New York State plans to require five years of preparation for all students who wish to become elementary school teachers, as well as for would-be secondary school teachers.

To sum up, it is obvious that the teaching profession in America has made remarkable gains since colonial days. Not only are the standards for certification more exacting, but the preparation itself is recognized as an important science. "Anyone can teach" is no longer recognized as a valid statement. However, there are still some knotty problems to be unraveled if the profession is to attract its share of the best young adults in each new generation. Most of the questions center around the fact that teaching is controlled by the public. Does the public have a right, therefore, to control the private life of a teacher? Is the public unwilling to pay for teachers of high caliber? On the other hand, do teachers have the right to force the public into action through the weapon of strikes? These are some of the areas that we will consider in the pages that follow.

Taboos of the Teaching Profession

The dictionary definition of a "taboo" calls it something set apart, made sacred or untouchable by religious custom—or more specifically, when considered in connection with the teaching profession, that which is prohibited by social law, custom, or prejudice. Practically all people are subject to taboos, many of which have come down from time immemorial. The price one pays for being in the public eye in a position such as teaching is to be placed upon the proverbial pedestal and looked up to as an example of decorum and good taste—the penalty for falling off that pedestal is to discover that no one is so much despised as a "fallen idol."

A typical example of this occurred in the 1920's in Pasadena, California, when a well-liked teacher was accused by several boy students of contributing to their delinquency. Later that teacher, who incidentally was also a minister, proved his innocence; but his professional life was ruined beyond repair. A significant feature about this particular case was the part that suggestion played in creating a rank injustice. The principal of the local vocational school had been sentenced to prison for a similar crime against society shortly before, and the publicity accompanying that case had suggested to the boys that they make the same charge against a completely innocent man. In fact, for months thereafter a segment of the general public let its imagination run wild, and all other men teachers were constantly being suspected of betraying their public trust by taking vicious advantage of their close contacts with youth.

Parents frequently take such personal interest in the teachers of their children that the social activities of the instructional staff are closely scrutinized and sometimes very narrowly circumscribed. Thus it is that common sense would dictate that educational work—except possibly in some of the large cities—is not the vocational field for anyone unwilling to submerge himself and his activities into the public interest and become an accepted member of the community. It is true that some localities make unreasonable demands upon their teachers—they treat them as personal property, chattel slaves, or at least as some strange race set apart and not expected to live normal lives.

One teacher, recalling her earlier experiences in a Louisiana school, has told the authors that she had to sign a contract agreeing not to bob her hair or wear slacks. But those local parish board members were quite proud of their liberalism. In a nearby community the situation was even worse; women teachers had to agree not to have dates with any man, to remain in town on weekends, and to retire before 10 P.M. Fortunately Americans everywhere are gradually beginning to accept teachers as normal people and to expect that in their personal and social activities they behave no differently from any other respectable local citizen.

However, anyone who becomes a teacher must realize, the sooner the better, that no longer is he a private citizen—rather he is a public servant and as such is constantly under more or less critical surveillance. Teachers are the perennial subject of family conversation at the dinner table. Their appearance, their mannerisms and idiosyncrasies, their opinions and actions—everything about them is discussed at one time or another during the year. This is true even in the large cities, but there the teachers do have the advantage of seldom encountering the pupils and their parents in out-of-school hours. In the smaller community the teacher must expect to rub elbows constantly with his fellow citizens. This is not as bad as it may sound. The teacher in the suburban or rural school often develops many personal friendships and gets a chance to exert leadership in neighborhood projects. If balanced and personable, he feels a certain camaraderie and warmth; he is liked and wanted by the friendly people whose children he teaches. Often he is a guest at their homes, or they at his. Unlike his colleague in the big city, he is not someone who is merely talked *about* through the year —he is talked *to*. Thus, the gregarious and upstanding teacher may consider personal involvement with the community an asset, not a liability.

Actually every private citizen, no matter what his vocational calling, has many limitations on his personal conduct. The lawyer or plumber who becomes involved in a neighborhood scandal may not be fired, as doubtless would the school teacher, but he would be certain in one way or another to feel the resentment of the community. A teacher occupies a strategic position where, consciously or otherwise, he is being imitated by growing youth. Certainly he deserves to lose his position if he persists in making himself a poor example. Teachers supposedly are mature individuals whose business it is to bring the best possible out of their students. Logically there is no room in this profession today for immature or immoral teachers.

In contrast, history records the fact that some of the men teachers in early colonial times were rather rough characters—getting inebriated, being placed in pillories, and sometimes causing the people to label them as "good for nothing else but teaching." Even now throughout the United States at least a hundred teachers a year are discharged for making improper advances to children. Occasionally one is sent to prison, but most school boards take the easy way out of a public scandal by demanding an immediate resignation and departure from the community.

The worst offenders, of course, are men. But sometimes a young woman just out of college, not realizing that officially she has come of age and is no longer a carefree girl trying to outwit the college dormitory matron, gains the reputation of being "wild" by going out to road-houses with questionable local characters, driving home in the early morning hours, and naturally looking bleary-eyed in the classroom the next morning. Of course she soon becomes the topic of conversation, and perhaps she may enjoy this brief sojourn in the spotlight of public attention, shrugging her shoulders and saying, "So what!" But her teaching career is slated for a quick ending; her dismissal notice is just around the corner.

It sometimes happens that a teacher who fails in one town may make a creditable success in another. This may occur because the teacher has learned a bitter but profitable lesson from the failure. More often it is because communities differ from each other in the personal stand-ards they expect from public officials. In Williamson County, Texas, for example, under the state local option law one of the two important cities is dry—any teacher observed drinking beer would immediately lose his effectiveness and possibly his position. In the other city, how-ever, where there are several wholesale beer-distributing warehouses, no eyebrows are raised when a male teacher enters or leaves a tavern, provided, of course, his private drinking does not interfere with his public teaching responsibilities. Another factor is the teacher's earlier training and background. There are "prayer meeting" towns and there are cities with wide-open gambling and other forms of vice. A teacher reared as a child in one type of community may have considerable difficulty in getting adjusted to the other type of environment.

As a teacher advances in his profession and holds more important positions, he still remains a slave governed by public opinion. Take for example the recent case of the college president in Ohio. An ordinary citizen might divorce his wife, and only close friends and neighbors would pay more than passing attention to the affair. But not so this college president who began courting his dean of women. Someone, presumably a student, gave unwelcome publicity to the courtship by printing on the wall outside his home: "Dottie loves Willie—Willie loves Dottie." Despite this petty persecution the president married his dean of women, and almost immediately was asked by the board of trustees to resign, although they gave him credit for being an exceptionally good administrator. It made no difference that the faculty teaching in the summer session when the blow fell almost unanimously backed him, that he had served long and honorably as an educator, and had earned a national reputation. The trustees felt that the man's usefulness had ended. Like Caesar's wife, anyone in the teaching profession must be above suspicion.

To sum up, there is no doubt that any educator is always in the public eye. Sometimes the sanctions imposed upon him are narrow and unfair. But in this century there has been a considerable decrease in the number and degree of taboos. Although the eccentric and unconventional teachers are still courting trouble, their mature and sensible colleagues are usually given friendship and respect. In exercising good judgment in or out of the classroom, they bring credit not only to themselves but also to the schools in which they serve.

Ethics of the Teaching Profession

A profession is distinguished from an occupation by its adherence to a set of principles governing the behavior of its members. In 1846, the American Medical Association adopted a code of ethics which had its roots in the Hippocratic oath. Although the American Bar Association did not formally adopt a code of ethics until 1908, many of its provisions had taken form 70 years before.

Apparently the first state teachers' association to adopt a code of ethics was that of Georgia in 1896, followed by California in 1904, and Alabama in 1908; today only a handful have failed to follow suit. There is a great variety among these various codes: the Pennsylvania statement, for instance, sets forth principles to be observed by the teacher in practically every aspect of his professional conduct, while certain other codes are brief and quite general. The code of the Pennsylvania State Education Association provides for a commission on professional ethics to make interpretations and to investigate violations. Only a few other state codes make any provision for enforcement, wherein lies the great weakness in the present organized effort to make of teaching a true profession. Some effective method of enforcement is definitely needed to control the behavior of the small minority whose actions reflect so poorly on the entire profession.

The NEA research bulletin, in 1931, examined carefully the provisions of 32 state codes, the attitudes of teachers toward certain practices, and their conceptions of what constitutes violation of professional ethics. Those violations dealing with the relationships of the teacher and his associates were reported most frequently. Typical cases involved the spreading of rumors and gossip about fellow faculty members, selfishness in sharing equipment and materials, and interference with the management and control of pupils in the classes of other teachers. Ranking second in point of frequency were violations of the standards relating to the public and pupils, such as revealing confidential information concerning pupils to persons whose main interest is in spreading the story. Ranked third was questionable conduct with respect to obtaining a position and terminating a contract, such as underbidding another candidate and leaving a position without sufficient notice to the school authorities.

For many years the NEA had shown an interest in a national code of ethics, and in 1924 a committee had been appointed to draft a set of ethical principles to serve, nationwide, as standards for professional conduct. This code was officially adopted at the annual NEA meeting in 1929. Thereafter many critics contended that it was not sufficiently specific to give adequate guidance, particularly to the inexperienced teacher—also they complained that no provision was made for its enforcement. Such criticisms led to a revision of the code that was finally adopted in 1941.

After the preamble this NEA code of 1941 is divided into four articles, the first of which deals with relations to pupils and the home. A teacher is to be just, courteous, professional, and to consider the individual differences, needs, interests, temperaments, aptitudes, and environments of his pupils. Those in a teacher's own class are not to be tutored for pay or to be referred to any member of his immediate family for tutoring. The professional relations of a teacher with his pupils demands the same scrupulous care that is required in the confidential relations of one teacher with another. A teacher, therefore, should not disclose any information obtained confidentially from a pupil unless it is for the best interest of the child and the public.

A teacher should seek to establish friendly and intelligent cooperation between home and school, ever keeping in mind the dignity of his profession and the welfare of the pupils. He should do or say nothing that would undermine the confidence or respect of his pupils for their parents, and it is his responsibility to inform the pupils and parents regarding the importance, purposes, accomplishments, and needs of the school.

The article pertaining to relations to civic affairs states that it is the obligation of each teacher to inculcate in his pupils an appreciation of the principles of democracy, directing full and free discussion of appropriate controversial issues with the expectation that comparisons, contrasts, and interpretations will lead to an understanding, appreciation, acceptance, and practice of the principles of democracy. A teacher should refrain from using his classroom privileges and prestige to promote partisan politics, sectarian religious views, or selfish propaganda of any kind. He should recognize and perform all the duties of citizenship, subordinating his personal desires to the best interests of the public good.

A teacher should be loyal to the school system, the state, the nation, but should exercise his right to give constructive criticism. The life of the teacher should show that education makes people better citizens and better neighbors—a teacher's personal conduct should not needlessly offend the accepted pattern of behavior of the community in which he serves.

The third article dealing with relations to the profession calls for proper personal dignity and the encouragement of able and sincere individuals to enter the teaching profession, and the discouragement of others who plan to use teaching as a steppingstone to some other vocation. It is the duty of the teacher to maintain his own efficiency by study, by travel, and by other means which keep him abreast of the trends in education and the world in which he lives. Every teacher should have membership in his local, state, and national professional organizations, and should participate actively and unselfishly in them. Professional growth and personality development are the natural products of such professional activity. Teachers, however, should avoid the promotion of organizational rivalry and divisive competition which weaken the cause of education.

While not limiting their services by reason of small salary, teachers should insist upon a salary scale commensurate with the social demands laid upon them by society. They should not knowingly underbid a rival or agree to accept a salary lower than that provided by a recognized schedule. They should not apply for positions for the sole purpose of forcing an increase in salary in their present positions; correspondingly, school officials should not refuse to give deserved salary increases to efficient employees until offers from other school authorities have forced them to do so.

Since qualification should be the sole determining factor in appointment and promotion, it is unethical to use pressure on school officials to secure a position or to obtain other favors. Testimonials regarding teachers should be truthful and confidential, and be treated as confidential information by the school authorities receiving them. A contract once signed should be faithfully adhered to until it is dissolved by mutual consent. Ample notification needs to be given by both the school officials and teacher in case a change in position is to be made.

All teachers should observe the professional courtesy of transacting business with the properly designated authority. Thus, unless the rules of a school system otherwise prescribe, a candidate should file his application with the chief executive officer. School officials should encourage and nurture the professional growth of all teachers by promotion or by other appropriate methods of recognition. School authorities are acting unethically when, because they do not desire to lose his services, they fail to recommend a worthy teacher for a better position outside their school system.

A teacher should avoid unfavorable criticism of other teachers except that which is formally presented to a proper school official for the welfare of the school. It is unethical to fail to report to the duly constituted authority any matters which are detrimental to the welfare of the school. Except when called upon for counsel or other assistance, a teacher should not interfere in any matter between another teacher and a pupil. Finally, a teacher should not act as an agent, or accept a commission, royalty, or other compensation, for endorsing books or other school materials in the selection or purchase of which he can exert influence, or concerning which he can exercise the right of decision. Nor should he accept a commission or other compensation for helping another teacher secure a position.

The fourth and final article of the NEA code of ethics provides for a commission on professional ethics. This standing committee consists of five members appointed by the NEA president, which studies and takes appropriate action on the cases of code violation that are reported to it. Whenever a reported case comes from a state which has an ethics committee, it is immediately referred to the state committee for investigation and action. When violations are reported from the states that have neither a code nor an ethics committee, the NEA commission on professional ethics takes such action as seems wise and reasonable—the thought is to impress members with the importance of respect for proper professional conduct. Whatever action is taken is reported to the chief school officers of the community and state from which the violation is reported. The committee is further vested with the authority to expel a member from the NEA for flagrant violations of the code.

Despite these praiseworthy efforts of the NEA and the various state teachers' associations, American teachers have not yet reached the point where a professional code is as effective as, let us say, that of the AMA. The test of the effectiveness of any code depends upon its enforcement. So, with more than a million teachers in active service—a large percentage of them still novices in the classroom—it can be seen how colossal is this problem. Compare in any community the number of doctors with the number of teachers, and one can understand why the AMA does so much better with its relatively small, compact membership than can the NEA with less than half our American teachers voluntarily within its membership.

Strikes in the Teaching Profession

The first major strike in American history occurred in 1877, when a labor organization known by the high-sounding name of "The Noble and Holy Order of Knights of Labor" called a walkout to protest a reduction of wages by the eastern railroads. Eventually it spread over 17 states and demonstrated dramatically how powerful this new weapon could be.

Until World War II there had never been an important teacher strike. A few smaller communities, notably in the mining districts of Pennsylvania, did cause school stoppages in the 1920's; but no large city had ever found reason to worry about its schools being closed and its teachers going on the picket line.

The NEA and other large organizations of teachers oppose strikes as a general principle. However, they insist that conditions be improved so that teachers will not want to resort to strikes. In fact, in 1947, at the height of the strike fever, the NEA convention adopted a resolution stating that "the strike is an unsatisfactory method of solving professional problems," and deploring "the existence of conditions which have caused teachers to strike." The resolution then advocated removal of these conditions.

Doubtlessly stimulated by the wartime strikes, teachers and other school employees became belligerent in demanding their rights in face of the rising living costs and the relative smallness of their salaries when compared with what other groups were receiving. Let us look at a few typical instances of this unrest.

In Grand Rapids, Michigan, in 1944, AFL and CIO labor leaders threw their support behind striking public school maintenance workers in an attempt to force the school board to meet their wage demands and to insure reinstatement of all the strikers. They volunteered to supply a hundred pickets to help keep pupils from entering the schools. After principals reported warm classrooms in virtually all the buildings, even after four days of the strike, union leaders halted coal deliveries to the schools. The strikers were urged, however, to withdraw temporarily their appeal to parents who were union members to keep their children out of school, and also to make no attempt to persuade school firemen to leave their boilers unattended.

Similar strikes occurred in Pontiac and other Michigan industrial cities. Usually it was not the fault of school boards; they were unable to raise salaries because the state constitution limited municipal expenditures to the money raised by a 15-mill tax.

By August 31, 1946, only nine of its 236 public school teachers had signed contracts for the ensuing school term in Norwalk, Connecticut. Nevertheless, the school board hopefully voted to begin classes the day following Labor Day. Just eight teachers reported at the city's 16 schools. The rest, including the daughter of the mayor and the wife of a board member, stayed home. Issues were clear. The Norwalk Teachers' Association insisted upon recognition as sole bargaining agency in negotiating contracts and demanded a 15 per cent general hike in pay. That increase, if granted, would have added $90,000 more to the school budget. The board of education, though it sympathized with the teachers' needs, rejected the demand on the ground that only the board of estimates and taxation could appropriate the extra money.

Because of confusion in the city charter, the two boards became involved in the popular sport of "passing the buck." While townspeople howled at the possibility of higher taxes, the teachers were adamant and schools remained closed. The state commissioner of education then stepped in to break the deadlock. Negotiations were carried to the governor's office and, after the state had threatened to take over the running of Norwalk's schools, a compromise was reached. All the teachers, including the nine previously under contract, received a 10 per cent raise; the association was recognized as their bargaining agency; and class work started 12 days late.

Proportionally speaking, the biggest teachers' strike so far in American history took place in Buffalo, New York, during February, 1947, when 2400 of the 2968 teachers walked out. Strange to say, it was a local union and not the more aggressive AFL or CIO organizations that initiated the strike demanding more adequate salaries, but the two national unions quickly joined in enthusiastic support. Approximately 500 teachers refused to join the strike and walked past the picket lines amidst catcalls. Roving bands of boys invaded those schools that still remained open, creating general disorder and chalking the word "scab" on blackboards. Many other pupils were on the picket lines with placards, such as: "We want OUR OWN teachers back." Bitter accusations were hurled by strikers against those who had decided to carry on.

After three days those remaining on duty petitioned the school board to close the few buildings that had remained open, claiming that education in Buffalo had become a farce. Acting on this request, the board then closed the schools. One repercussion was the passing in New York State of a stringent no-strike law that prohibits teachers and other governmental employees, under pain of severe penalties, from engaging in strikes. However, a partial answer to the problem came from a committee appointed by the governor; this group recommended higher salaries based upon general schedules according to the size of the cities.

America's largest twin cities both caught the fever. Teachers in St. Paul went on strike for a full month. Neighboring Minneapolis, in 1948, then became the scene of the nation's second biggest teachers' strike, a protest by union teachers in a strongly unionized community against a state tax-ceiling law that left Minneapolis schools $2,000,000 short of paying for its annual educational needs.

This strike movement carried through the latter part of World War II and the years immediately following. It did not involve so many cities, but the very fact that it was teachers who were striking made newspaper headlines. Most of those strikes were relatively insignificant. In Bunn, North Carolina, a stubborn little schoolmarm who had dared to discipline the principal's son and had thereby incurred that administrator's wrath stopped school for a complete day, to the delight of 489 pupils. At a mass meeting that same night irate school patrons shouted for the principal to "leave her alone" and to resign at the end of the year.

Children are ready imitators, especially when dramatic elements are involved. And so, in some cities during the mid-forties, students started going out on strike at the least provocation. The most alarming revolt occurred in the fall of 1945 and involved intense racial prejudices. At a Gary, Indiana, high school where Negroes had attended for 30 years, 500 white boys and girls struck for a "Jim Crow" school. After 10 days their number had swelled to over 800. The school board ordered legal action against parents of all strikers and the dismissal of any striker 16 or over. Said the Gary PTA: "We feel ashamed. . . . This strike is the work of some unknown organizers of racial hatred."

At a nearby Chicago high school, where attendance was some 60 per cent Negro, a race-strike idea was taken up by 800 more. At another Chicago high school a Methodist minister broke in on a strike rally at a vacant lot, told the students they would be striking against the United States Constitution, and talked most of them out of the notion. Chicago's mayor at that time termed the strikes "prank stuff." Certain local civic groups hurriedly put on a city-wide youth rally, starring Negro and white entertainers, in the effort to get the children back to their classes by making them realize that under the skin all men are the same.

In New York City several thousand students stayed out; some tangled freely with policemen in a strike that long before had completely lost its point. Originally they had cut classes in sympathy with the teacher-coaches, who had struck to get extra pay for their athletic work. But long after the coaches had been satisfied and returned to work, their pupils were not. The strikers simply changed their slogan from "No sports—no school" to a call to arms with more appeal: "Shorter hours, more sports, less homework."

In 1947 students at the high school in Willits, California, "tore the community wide open" by going on strike against a veteran principal who had taken a firm stand against "petting," and in so doing allegedly had called many of the parents and students "morons, agitators, hoodlums." After that, all but two of his 15-teacher staff joined the strike. Reputedly an excellent administrator and an old-fashioned disciplinarian, the principal is said to have attributed the strike to the wartime change in local population. Still backed by a sizable segment of the community, he handed in his resignation to the newly elected board before its members could get around to investigate the charges that "he had beaten and maltreated students."

Quite different was the half-day student strike in Irving, Texas, to protest against a school board decision not to reappoint two principals. In Cokes, Texas, another student walkout took place because school authorities had ordered a soft-drink machine removed after a small boy stuck his arm up the chute, an act that resulted in a painful injury. Students demanded their machine back. They also had a few other grievances—they were not permitted to go home for lunch or to play on the school grounds after hours.

In Rogersville, Tennessee, the school gong rang unexpectedly. Teachers assumed it to be the signal for a fire drill, but instead it was part of the students' plan. And so, all 260 of them filed out of the building and refused to return. That was the beginning of a strike for something students are not reputed to care much about—they wanted more and better teachers. The principal had sought his personnel from all over the state, but had found few candidates for jobs which required four years of college and five years of teaching experience, yet paid only $149 a month. What had really worried the students was the danger that the state educational officials would refuse to grant them credits in subjects for which qualified teachers were unavailable. For two days the school was picketed with signs: "We want teachers" and "Seniors want to graduate." Students, parents, and faculty met to arbitrate; subsequently a telegram to the state capitol brought the assurance that graduating students would not be penalized for their shortcomings in teacher-shy subjects.

However, we were not the only country that had post-war strike troubles. Students at National University in Mexico City held their rector a prisoner in his office until he agreed to present his resignation. About 3000 of them, seeking less study and more time off, struck classes and occupied university buildings.

Also, in post-war Japan under American control, high school girls struck and demanded the resignation of their principal. This act alarmed occupational authorities who were not sure how far such "democratic" ideas might travel. Nevertheless, those Japanese students seemed to have far more substantial grounds than the strikers running rampant about the same time in several American schools; at least they were not protesting such minor grievances as curtailed recess time. The girls complained that their principal mobilized them to work in wartime gardens, and then appropriated the beans and tomatoes to sell for big profits in the black market.

Strikes on the part of teachers and students subsided in the 1950's except for areas in the South where efforts to enforce the Supreme Court's decision of 1954 against segregated schools were bitterly resisted.* The earlier strikes had come partly as a result of the tension and upheaval of wartime. During the next decade the economy boomed and the public began listening to the pleas of teachers. Furthermore, stories about the progress of the Russians had a sobering effect on Americans. Students, again reflecting the mood of adults, paid more attention to their books and less attention to grievances and pranks.

Attitudes of students in the 1950's were also affected by the stiff competition for entrance to college. The overall expansion in population and the advance of mass education on the high school level, along with the increasing earnings of millions of families, had created this competition. Also, facilities for higher education had not kept pace with the burgeoning demand. As a result, many colleges found themselves with far more applicants than they could accept. The word soon got around that high school grades, service to the school, and scores on College Board examinations were all-important. Admonished by their teachers and parents, many students turned away from carefree pursuits to the serious business of school.

The comparative calm in the teachers' ranks was broken on November 7, 1960, when an estimated 4600 members of the United Federation of Teachers (AFL-CIO) stayed out in New York City. From a numerical standpoint this was the largest teachers' strike in history, even though almost 90 per cent of the New York City staff crossed the picket lines and kept the schools running.

The UFT launched the strike on the grounds that the Board of Education had failed to keep its promise to grant sick pay to long-term substitutes, duty-free lunch hours for teachers, and salary adjustments. They also wanted a collective bargaining election and a dues check-off system. School officials and other observers claimed that the real reason for the strike was a bid for power on the part of UFT leaders. There are approximately 40 teachers' organizations in New York City, all competing to gain a dominant role.

This strike, the first in the city's history, collapsed after one day largely because the great majority of teachers could see no reason for such drastic action. Newspapers reported that the only gain salvaged

* For aspects of that story, see Part Seven.

by the UFT was a promise that a panel of outstanding labor leaders would "evaluate the circumstances" of the dispute. Also, the Board of Education agreed not to punish the strikers through enforcement of the state law that had been passed after the Buffalo walkout. The teachers who had stayed out lost a day's pay—not their jobs.

On the debit side, the strike left the various teachers' organizations more bitterly divided than ever before. Worse yet was the enmity that arose at individual schools. Crossers of picket lines had been jeered and reviled; in many cases they had found punctured tires when they returned to their cars in the afternoon. The months that followed were marked either by fiery faculty arguments or by icy stares from colleague to colleague. In such an atmosphere new teachers and neutral teachers considered seriously whether they should leave the profession altogether. Some did.

Labor has proved that the strike is an effective weapon. It is dramatic and forceful; it often serves to bring things to a head. But most teachers agree that strikes have no place in schools. They note that just as it would be inconceivable for a group of hospital physicians to stage a walkout, so it is wrong for professional educators to go out on strike. Nor must it be forgotten that the greatest argument against school strikes is that the children are the ones who suffer most.

This means that the public and its elected officials must do everything possible to avoid giving teachers the awful temptation to strike. School authorities are the key figures in this situation. It is their duty to keep the public keenly aware of the effect of current salaries and working conditions on the morale of the teachers. Finally, the officers of teachers' organizations must make every effort to arbitrate and to publicize their grievances rather than impatiently push the strike button.

Salary Status of the Teaching Profession

Anyone ambitious to get rich should shun the teaching profession, although a few teachers have been highly successful in business ventures as a sideline—for example, the California schoolmen in the early 1900's who planted citrus fruit orchards and prospered with the industry. Naturally the question of salaries is of vital importance to the young person contemplating education as a career; more important, however, is what the money actually buys. Furnished houses in a small Texas town can be rented for $40 a month, but the same accommodations in the nearby state capital would cost at least three times as much. A further consideration is that the amount of income must be judged against the standard of living the position or job requires. To present a reasonably neat appearance, a teacher needs to invest a good portion of his salary in clothes; a garage mechanic drawing an identical paycheck does not need so extensive a wardrobe.

Salaries for American teachers started as mere pittances. A recent Russell Sage Foundation study showed that in 1841 the average weekly salaries for men and women were, respectively, $4.15 and $2.51 in rural schools—and $11.93 and $4.44 in city schools. Texas teachers had their salary troubles in 1850, according to a 1950 study. The 341 persons then teaching in that state had monthly stipends ranging from $4 to $15, and they were often paid in corn instead of cash. When parents of students could not pay tuition fees in money, they presented the teacher with farm products.

To compensate for such inadequate salaries teachers worked at additional jobs, including preaching, surveying, and mending shoes—thus following the example of their colonial predecessors who had made extra money by digging graves and ringing the town church bell. Housing was a problem of the 1850 teacher, too. Part of his salary was usually paid in board and room at the home of one pupil or another. A big disadvantage of this arrangement was that, as combination guest-boarder, a teacher was in no position to complain about such annoyances as cold bedrooms, poor food, and noisy children.

A study in 1937 indicated that the average annual income of public school teachers, which at that time was $1350, ranked twelfth among the incomes of 16 occupations. From top to bottom those making more money than teachers were physicians, lawyers, engineers, dentists, architects, college professors, journalists, librarians, ministers, social workers, and skilled laborers. Those who earned less than teachers were nurses, unskilled laborers, farmers, and farm laborers. Other studies of that time confirmed the general impression that incomes of teachers were low.

However, it must be remembered that the teaching population of more than a million men and women has always been an unusually heterogeneous group in ability, education, and experience, when compared with others in the professions of medicine, dentistry, law, and engineering. Nor should it be forgotten that doctors, dentists, and lawyers must use much of their income for office rentals, equipment, and secretarial help—all of which somewhat minimizes the strikingly apparent differences in the range of financial return whenever teaching is compared with other professions.

In the past the usual way for a teacher to be employed was on the individual bargaining basis—services were bought for as little as a teacher agreed to accept. Since such a method proved so one-sided and unsatisfactory there has since been developed the idea of a salary schedule to encourage experienced teachers to remain in service and new ones to enter. This involves small annual increments which, over a period of years, reward those who have remained faithfully on the job. The trouble with such schedules based merely on years of service has been that the good, bad, and indifferent among teachers all receive the same salary increments, no matter what the quality of the individual's work or his value to the school system.

It is not unusual to find a few overworked teachers who, willingly or otherwise, take on extra assignments requiring them to toil day and night for the benefit of the administrative officers and pupils. These "workhorses" receive the same salary increases as those given to others who habitually rush out of classrooms at dismissal time even faster than the children—or still others who do a very indifferent job when given extra assignments, or even the ones who prove themselves experts in evading such duties! Yet, under an ordinary salary schedule, there seem to be no satisfactory ways of rewarding the willing and efficient "live wire" and penalizing the lazy and indifferent "slacker."

This situation has led to a few attempts to give promotions on a merit basis. Theoretically such an idea is splendid. But teaching, unfortunately, so frequently has been dominated by petty politics, or at least by charges of politics, that few merit systems have ever worked out in practice. At the 1948 annual convention of the American Federation of Teachers (AFL) these efforts to base salaries on merit drew hot comments. Merit rating scales were declared to be tools which politicians use to deprive teachers of their professional freedom as well as handy devices of ambitious administrators and supervisors who want teachers to bow to their whims. It was further charged that plans for merit pay usually emanate from taxpayers' organizations or from industrial groups which are continuously waging campaigns against adequate support of schools.

Previously the NEA had qualifiedly favored merit systems, but in 1948 its representatives meeting in Cleveland voted to fight merit pay. They bitterly condemned the system as then operating in New York State and warned localities considering adoption of similar plans that they usually become unfair and vicious.

Prior to 1921 a few school systems had experimented with what is now known as single salary schedules. The principles involved are not only the equality of the sexes but also that elementary instruction is fully as important as that of high schools, which traditionally had been paying higher salaries and thus attracting better teachers. That year the NEA went on record as favoring the same salaries for all teachers having approximately similar professional preparation and years of teaching experience, regardless of sex or grade level taught.

Twenty years later, in 1940–41, only 31.3 per cent of the cities reporting in the NEA biennial salary study had adopted single-salary schedules. But six years after that the proportion had doubled, and the momentum of the movement has continued to the present day. Typical of statewide adoptions was Texas where there developed an immediate rush of non-degree teachers into college classrooms because accredited schools were given a few years' grace before being penalized by loss of state support. Included among the teacher-students were many who had received no additional formal training, or contacts with newer ideas in education, since they had first started to teach. For many, then, it was an eye-opening experience!

The distinguishing characteristic of the single-salary schedule is that the salary step to which a teacher is entitled when being employed, or reassigned after securing additional professional preparation, depends upon the combination of schooling and teaching experience. The usual practice is to give some credit for previous service outside the school system. An inexperienced teacher usually begins at the very bottom, unless he has obtained a higher degree. From then on there is usually a salary increment every year until the teacher reaches the maximum that has been determined within each classification of professional preparation.

With but few exceptions the general pattern of these classifications is: Class A, teachers without degrees; Class B, teachers with bachelor's degrees; Class C, teachers with master's degrees; Class D, teachers with master's degrees and one additional year of graduate study; and sometimes Class E, teachers with doctorates.

Prior to 1939 teachers were exempt from federal income taxes. This meant that the take-home pay of a teacher during the era of the Depression was a sizable amount even though salary scales were low in comparison with those of today. But Hitler was on the move, and our national defense had to be bolstered. Legislation was passed to insure that teachers, along with other groups, would make their annual patriotic contribution to the government. As it turned out, salaried employees like teachers soon were hardest hit by the income tax. The loopholes and tax dodges resorted to by businessmen were not for them!

But World War II was an ill wind that eventually blew some good things in the direction of education. Largely because of the shortage of personnel, teachers began to win the greatest financial gains in their history. In a survey conducted by the *New York Times,* it was shown that the average increase in a teacher's salary throughout the country during 1947–48 was $400. The biggest boost had been given in Indiana—a jump in average pay from $2011 to $3000. Mississippi, the lowest paying state, had raised its average salary from $875 to $1195. Sabbatical leaves, scholarships for teachers, and other attractions came into favor, too.

The gains continued through the 1950's as Mr. John Q. Citizen realized that he "never had it so good" and that it was about time he took an interest in education. The facts were published and broadcast everywhere: truck drivers were making more money than teachers; some teachers were forced to hold down two or three jobs to make a decent living—many were working at night as bartenders and garage mechanics, for example. These stories affected the public conscience. Furthermore, people saw that their children were receiving an inferior education in double-session situations because there were not enough teachers or classrooms. In town after town, the voters approved of higher school budgets; and some states adopted laws setting a minimum salary for teachers. By 1960, the total of such states had reached 34, and for teachers with bachelor's degrees the median prescribed salary for beginning teachers was $3390.

All of this was still not enough to stem the shortage, but it did make the picture brighter for teachers. The above-quoted figures for 1947–48 now look almost ridiculous. For example, according to the Research Division of the NEA, the average salary of teachers in 1959 was $5013. But it is pointed out that this is no great cause for rejoicing. *In the 1939–1959 period the average annual earnings of all persons working for salaries and wages increased more than the average annual salaries of teachers.* Moreover, the average annual earnings of teachers in 1958 were less than half of the average earnings of a combined group of 17 other professions, including both high-income and low-income groups requiring college graduation.

From the standpoint of more immediate trends, however, there is reason for hope. Gains in average salaries of teachers have exceeded increases in the cost of living each year since 1951. This is reflected in a comparison of the 1958–59 salary schedules of the states cited in the 1947–48 survey. Indiana raised its average salary from $3000 to $4980. Mississippi, still the lowest in rank, moved from $1195 to

$3070. Alaska headed the list with a $6400 average salary, but it must be remembered that the cost of living there has always been extremely high. Otherwise, the leading states in the salary race were as follows for 1958–59:

State	Average Salary— All Teachers*
New York	$6,200
California	$6,050
Delaware	$5,650
New Jersey	$5,530
Connecticut	$5,350

Investigations have shown that the chief reason given by college graduates for *not* entering the teaching profession is salary. And when asked to give an estimate of the salary scale of teachers, these same people usually quote a much lower figure than the actual one. Apparently the publicity about poorly paid teachers has had its detrimental effects, too, but the profession no longer deserves a reputation as one for paupers.

Legal Aspects of Teacher Contracts

Common sense dictates that not only teachers but also patrons should be familiar with school laws and the interpretations the courts have made of them. Teachers are, in fact, "legal creatures of the state." They hold their positions, receive salaries, enjoy certain rights, and have definite limitations in what they may and may not do, all because the state by enactment of statutes has so decreed. That is the reason many states do not issue teaching certificates until applicants successfully pass a course in school law.

Each commonwealth has its own laws governing certification. Such a certificate is in the nature of a commission or license; it is not a contract between state and teacher. Some states retain full power to revoke a certificate at pleasure; others specify definite causes for revocation, and in such cases most courts hold that no other reasons are valid. Local authorities have the power to set criteria higher than those of the state, but it definitely remains in the power of the state to prescribe such minimal standards for issuance of certificates as it deems necessary and advisable.

The purpose of certification is to safeguard the schools against incompetent teaching. Thus anyone who teaches in public school without

* Figures taken from "Teaching Opportunities" (1959 Edition); U.S. Office of Education.

a certificate is legally considered a volunteer, and such a person cannot be paid for his services from state funds. Even the fact that the board was willing to accept those services does not alter the matter, nor can the uncertificated person who has thus illegally given his teaching services hold the members of the board personally responsible.

The courts are not agreed as to the time when a teacher must possess a certificate to be qualified to sign a contract to teach. It has been held that a teacher must have a certificate at the time the contract is signed, but other court decisions hold that contract is valid if certificate is granted before actual teaching begins. In making such decisions the courts usually inquire into the wording of existing statutes to discover the apparent intent of the lawmakers. In all cases courts recognize the possession of a certificate as the final evidence of qualification to teach; hence a board wishing to get rid of a teacher cannot get the courts to inquire into the validity of the credentials that were submitted in order to obtain certification.

The law recognizes that the right to "hire" implies the right to "fire," but this depends largely upon the status of the employment. A board must show good legal cause for severing a contract that has been made for a definite period of time. Most courts reason that a contract for an indefinite length of time implies the intent to teach for an entire school year. Wherever statutes grant express authority to dismiss teachers without cause, notice of charges against the teacher facing dismissal is not required and no hearing can be demanded. But whenever statutes enumerate the causes for discharge, those alone may be offered as sufficient reason for termination of services.

In those states where school boards are permitted to dismiss teachers for "reasonable and just causes," the courts are agreed that a hearing is necessary before a cause can be said to exist. Should a teacher desire to contest discharge by a board, trial does not have to be held before a court of law unless, of course, the teacher demands it. As a further protection, any board member prejudiced against a teacher may be barred from acting as a member of the group before which the teacher stands trial. Courts have also restrained anyone who has publicly proclaimed his ill will against a teacher from serving on a committee to hear charges against him as a defendant.

The general trend has been that a teacher may be dismissed for any cause that makes his removal serve the best interests of the school—for example, immorality, inefficiency, incompetence, unprofessional conduct, negligence, insubordination, and violation of reasonable rules and regulations of the school board. Courts have held invalid for dismissal such reasons as refusal to be transferred, anticipated incompetency, and popular dissatisfaction.

A teacher's dismissal is mandatory when his position is abolished, when an inadequate statutory quota of pupils enroll, or when his salary causes the district to exceed its statutory debt limit—and for teachers this is an important point to watch when signing a contract, as some districts have been notoriously inefficient in the way they handle their finances. However, a teacher cannot be dismissed for lack of funds to pay his salary if there are any legal means by which those funds can be raised. Nor is consolidation or abolition of a district after the term starts or tenure has been established considered grounds for dismissal. In such cases the teacher usually must be paid for the period of the contract. One woman in Colorado sat an entire year in the empty classroom to fulfill the terms of her contract after school had opened without a single pupil enrolling. In cases of tenure where consolidation takes place, the teacher enjoying permanent status must be transferred to the consolidated school.

A number of cases have been brought into court because boards have attempted to circumvent the tenure law in order to dismiss unwanted teachers. Some have been reassigned to other positions, perhaps in the guise of a promotion, in such a manner that they lose their tenure status and are eventually dismissed; but courts have declared such reassignments illegal and have ordered reinstatement. When wrongfully dismissed, the teacher who has secured permanent status under a tenure law may ask the court to compel the board to reinstate him and to compensate him for the time lost. In non-tenure cases of wrongful dismissal, certain recourses have likewise been established by the courts.

Reinstatement to a position cannot be compelled by a teacher employed for a definite period of time and then wrongfully dismissed—the only recourse lies in being awarded damages, usually the unearned salary for the period of the contract less any money earned elsewhere while the contract was in force. Furthermore, a teacher who has been wrongfully dismissed cannot be compelled to accept work of a kind for which he is not prepared—one board offered a teacher under contract a janitorship at the same salary. However, boards of education acting in good faith cannot be held liable for mistakes in judgment beyond the remedies of salary awards and reinstatement, even when it is clearly shown that a teacher's personal reputation and professional standing have suffered through faulty judgment.

During depression years especially—in fact, any time there are more applicants than positions available—the sentiment arises not to employ as teachers women who are already married and to dismiss those who marry during the school year. The theory: one breadwinner is enough for a family, so public money should be distributed as widely as possible and where it will do the most good. But it is significant that marriage does not constitute a legal barrier in any state to the issuing of teachers' certificates. Frequently, however, on the legal principle that the right to contract is the right to choose, the courts have upheld boards in the right to discriminate by refusing to employ married women when they are eligible for the existing vacancies.

Mosts courts have held that boards may not include in their contracts provisions that a woman teacher is to be dismissed if, and when, she marries. This follows an accepted principle of law: restraint of marriage is against public policy. The general court practice is to hold that marriage is a mere incident to the contract to teach and, therefore, may be disregarded. In those few scattered decisions stating that a woman may be discharged before the end of her contract for reason of marriage, the evidence has shown that the marital status was misrepresented, thereby constituting fraud. Thus, if a married woman secures a position by representing herself as single, dismissal is legally in order.

Should a school building be destroyed by fire or an epidemic close a school, the teacher is entitled to salary for the time lost, unless that right has been specifically denied by statute or has been signed away by contract. With but few exceptions it has been held that when a teacher has a contract, he must be paid for the time, even if for some extraordinary reason school cannot be held.

Sometimes the question of making up lost time hinges on the technical point whether the school board or the board of health orders the closing. If the school is closed by health authorities, the time does not have to be made up, as would be the case when school officials assume responsibility for the closing. Whenever there is any way not in conflict with the statutory restrictions by which funds may be raised, a board's failure to collect monies with which to pay salaries does not permit it to shorten the school term and to reduce salaries proportionately. In cases of illness the board may allow full pay for a reasonable length of time, provided the teacher furnishes a substitute; but it has the optional right to deduct salaries for time lost without proper leave of absence.

Sometimes teachers are employed without written contract; employment offer and acceptance for the school year are made through correspondence. This, in fact, is called an implied contract and is good in the eyes of the law, although in those cases that come to court the burden of proof of the existence of a contract rests upon the teacher. In this connection, the law does not permit by implication any contract which could not have been legally made in written form. Also, whenever statutes demand a written contract, no implied contract can exist. Further, even for services rendered in good faith on an implied contract, salary payments that cause the statutory debt limit to be exceeded cannot be recovered.

Most contracts today specify that the rules and regulations of the school board constitute a part of the contract. In those cases that have been brought to court, ignorance of the rules and regulations has not been accepted as a defense—this is so even when such policies are adopted by the board after the teacher's contractual status has begun. However, whenever rules can be proved arbitrary, unreasonable, or illegal, the courts will not enforce compliance. Courts have considered as unreasonable any rules in opposition to statutory law, those made in bad faith or with malice, regulations on matters that are outside the powers of the board, and any that are clearly irrelevant to the purpose of education. Court decisions have declared it reasonable that a teacher be required to reside in the community where the school is located, that he readmit a child who has been expelled from classes against the wishes of the board, and that the Bible must not be read in school.

There remain in effect today many absurd "blue laws" simply because no one has had the courage to challenge them. Sometimes when brought to court these are sustained by "local justice," but when carried into higher courts they invariably are declared void. Typical of such unreasonableness were the stipulations in one Louisiana contract forbidding women teachers to have dates or to leave the community on weekends, and requiring both men and women to teach Sunday school. Needless to say, the professionally minded teacher is showing sound judgment when he keeps up-to-date on school laws, and is well-informed on his legal rights and privileges as well as limitations.

Teacher Tenure and Retirement Plans

Because of its large annual turnover, teaching has been called facetiously a "procession" rather than a profession. This situation is improving, but until recently about two out of every five teachers changed positions or left teaching entirely at the end of each school year. This has been due partly to the fact that the profession is "feminized" and most women are matrimonially minded. Also, teaching so frequently has been used as a steppingstone to some other professional or business career—money earned in the classroom is invested in further training needed to qualify for some other type of employment.

Another important reason for this highly demoralizing large annual turnover in teaching positions has been the uncertainty of reemployment. For reasons sometimes incredibly petty, many teachers have been released by school boards whose members take a selfish rather than an impersonal viewpoint in discharging their important responsibilities. Thus teachers frequently need legal protection against troublemaking parents; religious, political, economic, and social pressure groups; and unfair administrators. It is true that uniformity within a school system may be brought about by making teachers fearful of losing their means of livelihood, but such a policy seldom inspires them to perform exceptional services, inasmuch as uncertainty and lack of security always handicap effective teaching.

On the other hand, compared with workers in many occupations, teachers have greater assurance of tenure—and sometimes even too much. Should an inefficient instructor be hired for the school year, during the term of his contract pupils must suffer from poor instruction. In many other lines of work, when for any reason at all the boss considers an employee unsatisfactory, services are terminated with at best two weeks' notice, unless there is a strong union agreement to protect the workers.

In 1883 civil service superseded the "spoils system" in government work, but it was not until 1906 that the first teacher tenure law was passed. The NEA had begun its fight for tenure in the 1880's, and ever since its origin in 1916 the American Federation of Teachers (AFL) had supported this cause. The question is indeed controversial, so much so that some states have passed tenure legislation and then, a few years later, have repealed it. A report by the NEA in 1944 indicated that 44 states had some type of tenure law at that time, but at least six of those were tenure in name rather than in fact.

Broadly speaking, there are several types of contractual relationships at the present time. These include annual agreements, permissive contracts for more than one year, permanent tenure, and most recently what is known as indefinite tenure (or continuing contracts) assuring teachers of reemployment unless they are notified to the contrary before a certain specified date that is sufficiently early to permit them to seek employment elsewhere. In some of the states, tenure provisions vary—California, for example, gives tenure protection to teachers in the larger school districts while others are given only annual contracts.

Although a good teacher ordinarily enjoys tenure without the aid of the law, experience has shown that the additional protection of statutory provisions is needed to guarantee teachers their positions (except for stated reasons) and to provide that services be terminated in an orderly way according to specified procedures.*

Under tenure the three most common legal reasons for dismissal have been immorality, inefficiency, and insubordination. Teachers, after serving a probationary period (usually three years), are thereafter employed indefinitely, so long as their services and conduct are satisfactory. When services or conduct are in question, the usual procedure is for the school board to charge the teacher in writing with the alleged deficiencies or acts and to give a proper hearing in which the defendant has the privileges of legal counsel and of calling witnesses. In most states, if the board is satisfied that the charges have been sustained, the teacher facing dismissal has the right to appeal to the state educational department, or its head, and sometimes directly to the courts.

Educational authorities are quite generally agreed that tenure laws operate in the interest of society and its children as well as in that of the teachers. Nevertheless, there has been considerable bitter opposition—and some with good reason. Tenure laws have often worked to put the school board on trial as much as the teacher being charged —newspapers have sensationally exploited tenure cases to the serious detriment of public education. Adducing this kind of unpleasantness as a reason, some boards have denied tenure to many deserving teachers.

The situation that existed for several years in two California cities was notoriously unfair. At the end of the three-year probationary period all teachers who would automatically attain tenure by starting their fourth year were given legal notices of dismissal, regardless of the degree of their value to their respective school systems. Previous unsuccessful attempts to get rid of poor teachers caused those two boards to devise a "gentlemen's agreement" to circumvent legally the tenure law by a mass exchange each year of all their teachers ending the probationary period. For the teachers, such a transfer involved the cost and inconvenience of establishing new homes every three years, and required them to begin anew a probationary period that had no chance of ever leading to permanent tenure. Of course, none of those teachers were "forced" to move between the two cities, but to many of them it apparently was a case of considering any position

* For previous discussion of the legal aspects of tenure, see pages 214-216.

as better than no position at all. Incidentally, the case that has been cited was by no means the exception in the 1930's and 1940's. Fortunately, the practice was abandoned by most boards when the shortage of teachers became acute.

As noted above, one of the chief complaints against tenure laws has been that it is practically impossible to remove inefficient teachers once they have attained tenure. Critics stress that the important group to be protected is the children, not the teachers. Newspapers several years ago carried a story out of New York City about a violent-tempered teacher who had the habit of throwing books and other objects at pupils when they annoyed her. Apparently in her youth she had been a pretty fair ballplayer as her percentage of direct hits was high, although occasionally she did miss the child and knock out a window light. Naturally such actions brought protests from parents, and official investigation showed that she was unbalanced to the point where she had no place in a classroom. However, the state commissioner of education was forced to rule that under the existing tenure act there was no legal way to dismiss her.

The publicity concerning that woman led to further investigations of teachers in the service of our nation's largest city. These uncovered data showing that about a hundred New York City teachers should be considered unfit for teaching because of extremely serious mental conditions. Unfortunately for the children, tenure had made it difficult to relieve any of these from active duty.

While tenure is a controversial issue, it has many more good points than bad. The more recent and better laws seek to protect the children from poor teachers as well as to safeguard the proper professional rights of those in educational work. Tenure has served to give more freedom in class discussions of controversial subjects, which seems a highly desirable procedure in a democracy where children presumably are being taught to think for themselves. In many school systems where tenure does not exist, academic freedom is severely limited because of domination of the schools by prejudiced parents and community leaders, or the fear of administrators that such discussions may stir up trouble.

On the whole, the steady growth of the tenure movement has been attracting better teachers into the profession, because they know that their positions and personal liberties are safeguarded. In states where good tenure laws are now in operation the superior students do not hesitate to adopt teaching as a lifetime career. What is most unfortunate is that there are still a goodly number of new teachers who do not inquire about tenure rights before signing a contract. It would seem that teacher-training institutions must assume more responsibility for giving students guidance in this important area. Sometimes a wrong choice made by a "young innocent" just out of college can adversely affect that teacher's entire career.

Another area in which prospective young teachers need guidance is the consideration of *retirement plans*. Bubbling with youth, they tend to forget that people grow old in service or that some develop handicaps which may make it impossible for them to continue working.

Retirement plans are now being operated in all but one state and in more than 50 cities. In the majority of these the state (or city) and the teachers contribute to the operating costs. However, two states (Delaware and Rhode Island) provide the retirement benefits without deducting from the teacher's monthly salary checks—New Mexico has recently found it necessary to change from this plan to one where the teachers pay part of the costs.

Unfortunately, many of the present plans, both state and local, pay the retired employees benefits that prove too small for their necessities even on a mere subsistence level. One state pays less than $400 a year. Some of the plans are not financially sound—they need more generous support or some modification in the basic legislation on which they rest.

Many communities give larger monthly retirement checks to men than to women. The reason is that mortality tables show that the average woman will live longer than her male counterpart. In other communities the benefits to men and women are the same, but the women are required to pay in more money each year while they are serving.

The above is just one aspect of the many variations in retirement plans. Some systems are more generous than others in allotting retirement money for disability. Some permit actively serving teachers to borrow from the retirement funds at a low rate of interest. In many cases, the heirs of teachers who had been eligible to retire but have died in service lose thousands of dollars.* Moreover, systems differ widely as to the amount of money to be paid in, the minimum retirement age, and the age for compulsory retirement. Altogether, evaluation of retirement plans is no easy task—especially for a new teacher. Therefore, it must be emphasized by placement directors and

---

* This "deathbed gamble" was in effect in New York City until 1961 when the state passed legislation insuring full benefits to the heirs.

others that the young teacher seeking to establish a permanent position in a school system should make careful inquiry about the retirement systems, state and local, and seek expert help in assessing their worth. The wise and farsighted individual seeks to find out what is at the end of the trail as well as at the beginning.

Opportunities and Conditions in the Teaching Profession

As in all other businesses and professions the economic law of supply and demand largely governs employment, but never at any time in American history have there been nearly enough fully qualified teachers to fill the positions. The early years of the Depression in the 1930's may seem to be an exception because 200,000 teachers could not find jobs. But this phenomenon was caused by a variety of factors. Old-timers who were no longer fully qualified remained in service; class sizes zoomed, thus putting teachers out of work; and when many administrative and special services were eliminated as economy measures, the supervisors went back into the classrooms and edged out the newcomers fresh from teacher-training institutions. Finally, the industrial collapse caused many former teachers to return after failing in the business world.

At that time there arose the demand that the standards for entrance into teaching be placed so high that only a small percentage of those applying would be admitted. New Jersey, through the close control exercised by the state educational department over its six teachers colleges, put such a plan into action. However, the New Jersey plan bumped into the problem of what to do with those teachers trained in other states who legally qualified for its teaching certificates. If New Jersey refused to recognize the college degrees and professional credits earned elsewhere, other states would be certain to retaliate by penalizing New Jersey college graduates seeking positions within their borders.

Montana, on the other hand, made no such effort to curtail teacher-training candidates. Throughout the Depression years its State Normal College located in one corner of that vast commonwealth offered in its catalogue to pay the railroad fares of those from distant points as an inducement for their enrollment. In our western, sparsely populated states there never have been sufficient teachers to supply the widely scattered rural schools.

Then to this nation came the prewar business boom and the World War II manpower shortage, which made it necessary for many of our schools to bring back to the classroom many teachers who had not taught for years and to employ others with virtually no training, who should never have been allowed to teach at all. During the war American public schools employed 125,000 teachers on emergency or substandard licenses. At that time one out of every seven teachers could not meet the minimum requirements of his respective state. Those minimum requirements then ranged from a high school diploma in one state to a master's degree in another.

Whenever a state educational department finds it cannot get sufficient teachers able to meet the minimum legal requirements for certification, the practice has been to waive existing standards by declaring that an emergency exists—hence the term "emergency certificate." Immediately after the end of World War II and the Korean conflict these substandard teachers were largely replaced by better qualified personnel. Some of the emergency teachers qualified themselves by seeking further professional training in institutions of higher learning; others resigned rather than do so.

But the unraveling of confusion and chaos in the profession was of short duration. History has shown that each war brings a rise in the birth rate. Therefore, in postwar periods the elementary schools soon feel the pinch. There are not enough qualified teachers to take care of the increased enrollment of pupils. And less than a decade later the secondary schools are affected.

And so in the 1950's the shortage of teachers again became acute, just as had occurred in the 1920's after World War I. But this time the problem was compounded by another factor—the decrease in the birth rate during the depression years. Thus, in the 1950's there were fewer young adults to fill vacancies in any occupation whatever. The teaching profession had to compete with a booming industrial market and with other professions not governed by the public purse strings. The fortunate "depression babies" who had obtained a college education were wooed with all kinds of lucrative offers. Many who normally would have taken teaching positions turned elsewhere. In addition, veteran teachers were lured away by business firms.

The areas that were hardest hit were mathematics and science. New electronic firms, engineering companies, and a host of other big corporations needed mathematicians and physicists in large numbers. Not only were they willing to pay fabulous salaries but they also offered "fringe benefits" that were calculated to turn the head of any young man.

These companies set up elaborate recruiting programs headed by high-salaried administrators. Following the example of the scouts employed by professional athletic organizations, these recruiters would visit the campuses and pay court to the prospective *magna cum laude* graduates. They went to almost fantastic lengths to outbid each other. In some cases the objects of their attentions were offered completely furnished homes, new cars, and lavish expense accounts.

Of course, the teaching profession could not compete in such a market. Meanwhile the "war babies" kept pouring into the schools and the resignations kept increasing. Soon the emergency certificates crept back into the picture. In the late 1950's the state of New York, for example, allowed provisional certificates to be issued any college graduate requested by a community that could not get a fully qualified teacher to fill a vacancy. The stipulation was that the provisional appointee obtain a minimal number of educational credits while serving. The certificate would be reissued after a period of satisfactory service under this "earn while you learn" plan.

As has been indicated previously, salaries of teachers have been considerably increased in the last decade—partly as a result of the shortage of personnel and partly because of the general rise in the standard of living. Salaries are still not high enough for a profession of such importance to humanity, but it is a fact that they run second in the list of complaints currently given by teachers. The chief source of discontent is working conditions, except perhaps in the case of the man who is the sole support of his family.

Working conditions vary, of course, in different school systems, and they may even change drastically in the same school system from one year to another. But, generally speaking, teachers have been complaining with some justice about such problems as oversized classes, clerical work, severe discipline problems, lack of proper facilities and equipment, unsympathetic or inept administrators, and compulsory attendance at evening meetings.

These grievances of teachers not only lead to resignations but also snag recruitment efforts. The young woman who has just acquired her A.B. degree may be doubtful about teaching because of the salary situation but when she hears from the lips of experienced teachers how "awful" things are at school, she decides that such a bedraggled profession is not for her.

Spurred on by teachers' organizations and by the example of industry, school authorities have effected many improvements in the last decade. In this process of amelioration, the shortage of teachers has also been a compelling force. Necessity is often the mother of attention, as well as invention.

Today an astute college graduate with a brand-new certificate to teach does not merely look for an attractive salary scale but he carefully scrutinizes the "fringe benefits" that the school system offers. Pension plans, leaves of absence, in-service training, opportunities for advancement, tenure policy, and the like are important considerations.

New York City is a typical example of the way in which large school systems have moved on the improvement of working conditions in recent years. Following are listed some of the "fringe benefits" now available to teachers in that city:

Pension: For every dollar that a teacher puts into his annuity fund, the city adds another dollar. Within certain limits the teacher may choose his own rate of payment. The higher the rate, the greater the returns at retirement. Thus, a teacher earning $8000 can draw an annual pension of $6400 on retirement. All kinds of options are given the retiree, and he is offered professional counsel as to which option to choose. During service he may borrow money from the Retirement Board at a low rate of interest.

Leaves of Absence: As in most other cities and towns, all kinds of leaves of absence are granted. Among them are sabbatical leaves, given every seven years for study or travel or other reasons; military leaves, maternity leaves, and child-care leaves. The latter are extended from year to year if the teacher so requests.

Sick Leave: Regular teachers are allowed to take ten days off each year for sickness. They do not lose pay for these days. They may accumulate unused days up to a total of 200. Thus, if a healthy teacher has "banked" 100 days and is suddenly hospitalized for three months, he does not lose a penny. This same benefit is given to substitutes, but on a more limited basis.

"Terminal Leave": A retirement leave of absence with full pay is granted on the basis of one half of the accumulated unused sick leave up to a maximum of one school term. Thus, in effect, the teacher is given the opportunity to retire several months earlier without penalty and he is simultaneously rewarded for faithful and continuous service.

Early Retirement: Teachers are compelled to retire at 70. But they may retire earlier if they wish. For example, a 55-year-old teacher who has served for 30 years may retire and draw a pension. Retirement for disability is also permitted.

Health Insurance Plan: All regular teachers living in the city are permitted to join H.I.P. Thus, for a relatively small fee they are entitled to medical services given by a pool of cooperating physicians.

Social Security: Teachers in New York City are now entitled to social security benefits. It should be noted that teachers in 36 states are now covered by social security.

Tenure: After serving satisfactorily for a three-year probationary period, a teacher receives tenure. He cannot be dismissed except for some extreme cause like immorality or gross insubordination. Even then, the charges must be thoroughly documented and proved. The cases of teachers who lose tenure are rare indeed. This is also true in most other big cities throughout the country.

In-service Training: More than 500 free professional courses are arranged each year by the Director of In-service Training. These courses are voluntarily given by supervisors and master teachers. At certain stages in his career a teacher must take an in-service course to make himself eligible for a salary increment.

Salary Differentials: Teachers holding an M.A. or the equivalent are given a $400 differential. Those who have obtained at least 30 points beyond the M.A. degree are given another $400.

Benefits such as those listed above continue to increase in almost every large school system year after year. But this movement has received its principal impetus from the growth of rich suburbs that have recently been draining off the cream of the teaching crop. Whereas in the 1930's the great cities occupied a preeminent position in salary schedules, they now find it difficult to keep up with the "dormitory towns" around them. Suburbs often offer the best salaries and excellent working conditions. Moreover, the exodus of the middle class to the land of lawns has transplanted thousands of prospective teachers from the cities. In other words, an important factor governing the new teacher's choice of a school is proximity to home.

This competition for the services of qualified teachers has caused a remarkable rise in recruitment activities. Many school systems now prepare attractive brochures and send them to teacher-training institutions. A number of cities and states have set up recruitment offices. These officials send out literature, give talks at colleges, and attend teachers' conventions in the hope of persuading likely young men and women to accept positions. In small towns this task is still left largely in the hands of the superintendent of schools, but he usually has the advantage of being able to make an on-the-spot commitment. Also, he can often adjust monetary offerings to meet the expectations of the particular person he interviews.

Another outgrowth of the shortage of personnel has been the movement to give adolescents in secondary schools a behind-the-scenes view of the profession. Under the aegis of the NEA, many Future Teachers of America clubs have been operating throughout the country. These groups are officially chartered after paying for membership in the organization. They receive all kinds of literature about teaching and ideas for club activities. In addition, several cities have formed their own Future Teachers clubs on the senior and junior high school level. The purpose is essentially to give information and inspiration to youngsters who have expressed interest in the vocation. However, a few high schools have gone one step further and have formed Teacher Cadet, or Teacher Apprentice groups. Under this plan the students receive credit for helping out in elementary school classes near the high school. In short, they receive a taste of actual teaching so that they can decide whether they will really enjoy the work. College officials attest that this early experience gives the students more confidence when they become student teachers four years later.

PART SEVEN

Current Trends and Issues

PART SEVEN

Current Trends and Issues

Throughout the history of American schools, change and experimentation have been the key words. This is as it should be. A dynamic and democratic society is never complacent but is always conducting a restless search for something better. This desire to explore untraveled territory is linked with the pioneering heritage of the American people, their relative freedom from restraint, and their penchant for self-criticism. Educators in the United States have always reflected the questing spirit of their land. Indeed, they have often been in the vanguard in finding new avenues of approach or rising to meet the challenge of the day.

In recent years, however, there has been an unprecedented upsurge in new departures at every level from the elementary school through college. This phenomenon can be attributed to a whole host of factors. First and foremost, technological advances came with breath-taking speed in the 1950's. Willy-nilly, school administrators had to recognize that the field of electronics alone was exerting a vast influence on our culture and might have tremendous implications for school programs. Thus, the use of educational television, teaching machines, and language laboratories became increasingly popular.

Another cause for soul-searching and experimentation was the severe shortage of both teachers and classrooms. As personnel and space dwindled both in quantity and in quality, schoolmen were forced to look around for new ways to meet the problem. Those who never before had questioned their existing setups now discovered that even under the best conditions the old ways left much to be desired. Officials at teachers' colleges and graduate schools of education were also moved into action by the paucity of students training to be teachers. One result of all the above efforts was that new ideas like team teaching and the use of teacher aides evolved in various sections of the country.

Russian scientific advances, especially in the race for space, caused a rash of criticism of American schools. The storm entered around our educational programs and facilities for gifted children. Almost simultaneously, Dr. James B. Conant (1893–   ) was investigating American secondary schools and finding most of them inadequate. The opinions of so distinguished an educator attracted a wide audience and served as an added catalyst. In some cases, new approaches were tried; in others, more attention was paid to experiments already in existence. And in a few instances, the "innovations" represented a return to the pre-Progressive era. For example, the concern about Johnny's ostensible lack of reading ability led to a strong revival of the teaching of phonetics and a renewed interest in departmentalized reading programs such as the one used in Joplin, Missouri, on the elementary school level.

But the greatest interest centered on the bright students. Acceleration, enrichment, and the downward flow of difficult subjects into the grades became topics for debate. Summer schools, traditionally reserved for slow or reluctant learners making up their failures, were now opened to the gifted for advanced studies. Likewise, Saturday classes were started—often with the cooperation of local colleges. Teachers in some communities received bonuses to meet superior students one hour before school or to stay with them after the final bell. Serious discussion arose as to the possibility of running schools on a twelve-month basis.

Aside from the three R's, science and foreign languages seized the limelight in the 1950's. Sections of the National Defense Education Act of 1958 gave special stimulus to those subjects—and simultaneously provided an ironical touch: Congress had been moved to support educational progress not out of concern for the nation's culture and enlightenment, but for purposes of defense. Naturally, the interest in science stemmed from fear of hydrogen bombs and the achievements of the USSR, but it came also from the realization that well-trained persons were needed by rapidly growing industries specializing in electronics and chemical research. In fact, Americans discovered that science had practically taken over the domination of their lives, whether they liked it or not.

Enthusiasm for the study of foreign languages was stimulated by amazing advances in the Jet Age. The 70-day journey of Columbus now took only about six hours. The world had shrunk to such proportions that the necessity arose to speak and understand the languages of other nations, whether friendly or hostile. Consequently, many school administrators scrapped traditional language programs that had emphasized grammatical forms and, at best, had taught students merely to read a foreign language. Instead, they instituted the aural-oral, or conversational, method. Also, publicity given to the fact that European children began foreign-language training at an early age gave impetus to a movement to introduce the subject in the elementary schools of the United States.

Another phenomenon of the era that followed World War II was the influence of foundations upon education. The Ford Foundation became especially active in encouraging experimentation and the construction of new buildings. Some educators applauded these efforts and gratefully accepted the millions of dollars allotted to them. But others complained of "education by foundation" and urged that the government stop this "tax-dodging farce" and step into the picture itself. Specifically, the cry was raised for federal aid to reduce the load on the local property owner and to equalize educational opportunities throughout the country. This plea, it should be added, fitted neatly with the growing extension of power upward—as exemplified by the trend toward the welfare state.

On the world-wide scene, certain occurrences affected Americans' concepts of the role of public schools, with particular reference to social studies. The decline of colonialism and the upsurge of nationalism had special meaning for all educators in a democratic nation. These movements, together with the ever-present threat of Communism, caused a considerable reappraisal of the teaching of geography, history, civics, and the like.

Events in Africa alone compelled white people in the entire Western world to face up to the hard fact that the paternalism of the past, benevolent or otherwise, was no longer acceptable. People of color all over the globe were asserting their rights and striving for cultural and economic advancement. Opportunistic Communists were attempting to lure millions into the Red fold as "fellow workers."

This situation spilled over into American life when Negroes in the North and the South began to fight for their rights through the medium of the courts. A mighty challenge confronted American schools, especially in the South where segregation had become an ingrained practice. At first, shameful riots led by rabble-rousers made democracy look like a mockery. But the moderates finally prevailed, and progress toward eventual integration of schools continued slowly but inexorably.

But most educators agreed that the advance of desegregation only pointed up the more difficult problem that lay ahead; namely, in-culcating in all students the attitude that brotherhood is not merely a high-sounding word but is necessary for their survival in the world of tomorrow. The white man, after all, is part of a minority group. He is destined to be further outnumbered in the years to come. In short, the white adult of the future will be a misfit and a menace to his own society if he allows prejudice to dominate his thoughts and actions.

The above is a brief outline of some of the more important areas of concern in education today. What follows is a discussion of major experiments, developments, and problems that have arisen in recent years.

Educational Television

The development of a new medium of communication often causes enthusiasts to hail it as a panacea for classroom ills and alarmists to decry it as a threat to the teacher. In the past, such extreme optimism or pessimism has proved to be ridiculous. The phonograph and its offshoots, the record player and the tape recorder, have not revolutionized education. The same can be said of motion pictures, filmstrips, slides, and radio. All have become valuable in-structional aids; they have not solved the complex problems involved in the learning process nor have they usurped the role of the teacher.

Nevertheless, many people jumped to emotional conclusions when television came on the scene. Here was an amazing medium that far surpassed all the others. It combined pictures and sound with immediacy. Surely, it would shake the foundations of the school and make the classroom teacher as outmoded as the horse and carriage! At the least, it would put an end to all worries about the shortage of teaching personnel. Now hundreds of children would assemble in an auditorium and learn from a master teacher while a few discipli-narians hovered over them with arms folded. Even more startling, so much educational information would pour forth into the homes that the schools would play a secondary role. Children might even become smarter than their teachers!

To a certain extent this viewpoint is justifiable. Television cer-tainly has immense possibilities, some of which have not been given a fair chance to materialize. To begin with, let us consider the kind of "education" that television has brought into the American home. In 1961, a congressional committee was moved to investigate this matter because of the prevalence of violence and sex on television and the relative dearth of cultural and educational programs. The reasons are not difficult to ferret out. In a country committed to the concept of free enterprise, private industries are often encouraged to develop a new medium. Naturally, their motive is to make profits. And it does not take long for an astute TV executive or sponsor to realize that a shocking program will get a higher "rating" than an instructional one. For every listener who tunes in to "The Development of Incan Culture," there will be thousands drinking up "The Pistol Packers" or some other hypothetical program that promises excitement and escape.

In short, television has taken the same general path as its predecessor, the radio. We are prone to make each new medium into a vehicle for entertainment before the pangs of conscience and the yawns of boredom and satiety force us into a second look. Actually, that reappraisal is now being undertaken. Not only are the legislators bestirring themselves, as noted above, but also, under new leadership, the Federal Communications Commission is cracking down on TV networks. The warning has gone out that licenses will no longer be renewed automatically; the retailers of passion and perdition must show evidence to the FCC that they have produced more than a "vast wasteland."

Parents, psychologists, and educators have added their voices to the crescendo of protest. With good reason, they fear that children will suffer from hardening of their emotional arteries if raised on a steady diet of malice and murder. The rise of juvenile delinquency, they claim, has been abetted by television. Worse yet, they point out that the medium has not fulfilled its early promise as an uplifter of culture. Sometimes the sins of omission are more heinous than those of commission.

The potential impact of commercial television on the lives of Americans, young or old, can be underscored by bald statistics. In 1959, there were 52 million TV sets in use in the United States. About 44 million homes had at least one receiver. And a recent survey showed that youngsters from the age of 3 to 16 spend just as many hours in front of those TV sets as they do in school. A great deal of their watching time falls in the "prime" hours between 7 P.M. and 10 P.M. when the call of the Wild West lures them away from their homework.

But, if legislators and ordinary citizens continue to beat the drums for improvement, the outlook for television is bright. Even now, the situation is not so bad as most people believe. Quietly, but efficiently, more than a thousand school systems have been moving ahead to make television an aid to *education,* in the better sense of that word. Instructional broadcasts have been emanating from various stations since 1952, when the FCC reserved 242 channels for education. (The total has since been raised to 274.) At this writing, 62 of those stations have been activated, and ETV can boast of approximately 2,500 program hours each week. In contrast, only 340 hours per week were devoted to education in 1955.

Even more significant, Congress has just passed legislation providing a fund of $25 million to build educational television facilities. This new allocation of money will insure a continuation of the gains already realized.

Cooperation with the ETV movement has often been obtained from commercial stations that have rented their facilities at reasonable rates. Station WTVW (Channel 7) at Evansville, Indiana, is a good example. Since 1958, programs for almost 25,000 school children in the southwestern part of the state have been sent out from that station. The instruction is under the supervision of the Southwest Indiana Television Council, an organization created by the superintendents of 16 school districts. Parochial schools have participated as well as public schools. Backed by the Ford Foundation, the project has brought such subjects as science and conversational Spanish to elementary school pupils who never before had received that kind of enriched program. Since the channel is open to all viewers, parents have been tuning in and learning along with their children. They have also learned something else—that television can be a wonderful instrument for advancement if properly used.*

Prompted partly by the success of the experiment in the Evansville area, another council of educators in the Midwest has gone a step further. With the support of the Purdue Research Foundation, early in 1961 they sent up an airplane equipped with video-taped lessons in subjects ranging from elementary science to college English. Circling about 23,000 feet overhead, this "flying classroom" is now beaming out instruction over two UHF channels to 500,000 students in six states. The project is subsidized by the Ford Foundation.

Whether airborne TV is the final answer is yet to be known, because this method of instruction is still in its infancy. A less glamorous but a tried-and-true approach is closed-circuit television.† Under this

* Alabama has the largest state-wide open-circuit system. A network of three states transmits 67 hours of lessons each week to schools in most parts of the state. The project has been especially beneficial to children in rural areas.

† In 1961 there were 350 closed-circuit ETV systems in operation. Only 77 existed in 1956.

system, only those receivers that are connected by cable with the studio may be tuned in on the programs, but the advantage is that more than one studio can be used at a given time. This kind of hookup was worked out successfully in the Chelsea section of New York City, beginning in 1957. It has proved to be especially valuable on approximately 120 college campuses where the lectures of eminent professors are witnessed and heard by large numbers of students assembled in front of TV sets. Hunter College, among others, uses the system as an aid to the preparation of new teachers. Students in various campus classrooms tune in on lessons given at Hunter's demonstration high school. Under the guidance of their professors, they then discuss what they have observed. Some lessons are kine-scoped for future presentation to other classes.

South Carolina has established the country's first state-wide, co-ordinated, closed-circuit TV project for school instruction. In a few years the state administrators hope to reach 413 white and Negro high schools via three channels offering 36 TV classes a day—each class to run for 25 minutes. The cost per pupil is less than $13 per annum.

The South Carolina project started with just 30 schools and is adding others gradually. Algebra, geometry, and state history were among the subjects featured when the program was undertaken. The lessons are produced on video tape two weeks before the broadcast, and classroom teachers receive summaries of the lessons in advance. After each broadcast they conduct follow-up activities.

But the most widely heralded use of closed-circuit television for educational purposes has been the setup at Hagerstown, Maryland. More than 16,000 students in 37 elementary and secondary schools of Washington County benefit from live programs put out by a net-work of five studios. As in the case of other stunning but costly experiments of this sort, a large part of the bill has been paid by foundation money. But a lion's share of the credit must go to the school administrators and teachers there. They prepared the way carefully so that the curriculum would not be placed in a Procrustean bed of television. Since its inception in 1956, the experiment has been under tight control and constant evaluation. Students see the programs for an average of no more than an hour a day. Tests have been administered to gauge their achievement vis-à-vis the progress of students in control groups who do not watch the TV lessons. Teachers, students, and parents have been polled regarding their reactions. The results on all counts have been so remarkable that the administrators plan to continue the arrangement long after the foundation funds are exhausted.

No matter what form of broadcast is used—closed-circuit or otherwise—there seems to be no doubt that educational television is here to stay. Its values for students in rural schools alone can justify its perpetuation—and it must be remembered that many thousands of our schools fall into that category. Denied the equipment and variety of teaching specialists that urban youngsters receive, these students can now be trained via television. They can benefit from a complete and well-rounded program, thus enhancing their chances for a college education.

Colleges, in turn, have recognized the immense possibilities that TV offers for extending the opportunity for higher education to those Americans who might otherwise be prevented from advancing their level of learning. The "Continental Classroom" is an excellent example. More than 250 institutions have cooperated with over 150 stations throughout the country in presenting this unique form of instruction. Students enroll in the TV classes, watch the programs religiously, take notes, read the assigned books, and finally tackle an examination. If they pass, they are given full credit just as if they had been on campus. This method has proved to be a boon to shut-ins, students with transportation problems, and people working at full-time jobs. Above all others, it has attracted housewives whose education had been interrupted by marital responsibilities.

Obviously, television can play a vital role in the education of gifted people, whether children or adults. Through the miracle of electronics they can sit at the feet of great scientists, musicians, writers, statesmen, and industrialists. Top teachers can present them with challenges befitting their intelligence. For instance, in the Washington County experiment, approximately 50 high school seniors voluntarily assembled at 8 A.M. each day for an advanced TV class called "Math for Mathematicians." Their interest in analytics and calculus brought them to school an hour before the start of regular classes. Another example of high motivation is the fact that a physics course given at 6:30 A.M. recently attracted a daily audience of 300,000 adults!

Certain subjects lend themselves better to television than others. Foreign languages, commercial subjects, science, arithmetic, art, and even social studies have been taught successfully in this way. But, regardless of the subject, the best results are obtained when a systematic plan is followed. The ingredients of the formula might be described as follows:

1. Convince the taxpayers, the teachers, the students, etc., that educational television is worth trying. To do this, involve them in the responsibility for planning and carrying out the program. One way is to set up an advisory council.

2. Educational television is expensive. Therefore, try to get federal or state aid. Look also for help from foundations and other philanthropic groups.

3. Choose the form of TV best suited to your needs (closed-circuit or open-circuit) and select the subjects that apparently would be best suited for TV in your particular situation. Of course, this means that you must also decide on the level and the number of children who shall receive the instruction.

4. Make a decision as to whether you will need "live" programs or films or kinescopes and video-tape recordings which can be used over and over again. You may want to use a combination of all of these.

5. If your plan calls for "live" lessons, carefully screen the best teachers to find the ones whose personalities and backgrounds seem likely to beget success. Then get experts to train them as TV "actors."

6. Give each TV teacher a full day to prepare a lesson that lasts less than an hour. Let him have access to the best equipment and materials you can find. See that his staff of aides is properly trained.

7. Be sure that each classroom teacher knows about a program long in advance. Provide him early with a guide-sheet that will tell him what to look for, how the TV lesson is intended to fit in with the subject matter in that curriculum area, and how he can follow up.

8. Provide some kind of feedback system through which individual teachers and students can write in their questions, criticisms, and suggestions. Let the TV teacher be guided by these reactions.

9. Measure the achievement of your TV viewers versus your non-TV classes. Try to measure their attitudes, too, as well as the attitudes of the community.

10. Don't overdo a good thing. The greatest mistake is the use of

television as a *substitute* for face-to-face classroom instruction by good teachers. The medium has its values for presenting information and motivating children, but it also has its limitations. When overused, it can become a bore. Children learn a great deal through discussions. They need on-the-spot answers to their questions. This the TV set cannot give them.

The above is merely a suggested list of some of the chief attributes to be found in a good educational television project. Actually, if a school system were to embark on such an adventure, the best advice would be to consult officials in the areas that have already pioneered in this field.

But the question might be asked: Is educational television worth all the trouble? Isn't it merely a glamorized gimmick? The answer is that the returns are not all in. Some districts claim amazing results and can document their statements with the scores of achievement tests given either on a before-and-after basis or in a control group plan. But other impartial studies report no significant differences in either the learning or the retention of subject matter. However, many of those surveys have centered on school systems that jumped on the bandwagon immediately after educational television had received its first trial in 1953. Several of the early experiments were marked by more enthusiasm than good sense. With no preparation or follow-up, children were packed into auditoriums to learn from the fascinating box that would make scholars out of dullards. When such chimerical thinking was replaced by sound and careful use of television, the academic achievement scores went up. The moral is: good planning makes for good results in this field as in most others.

As educators have gained experience with television, new potentialities for the medium have been discovered. In recent years, its value for the in-service training of teachers has been realized. Often this training is a happy offshoot of the TV lessons that are beamed into ordinary classrooms. Weak and inexperienced teachers who watch the master teachers learn how a subject should be presented and do some critical self-evaluation.

But sometimes the in-service training through television is formally planned. One illustration comes from New York City, where teachers must take "refresher" courses at certain points in their careers in order to receive increments. Noting that elementary schoolteachers were weak in science methodology, in 1961 the administration set up an open-circuit TV course in that subject for one afternoon each week after school. Approximately 9,000 teachers gathered in various classrooms scattered throughout the city and witnessed the program. Each viewing was followed by discussion and activities supervised by master teachers and principals in the individual schools. It is reasonable to assume that the science lessons of some 300,000 pupils improved after their teachers had gone through 15 such sessions.

Another intriguing by-product of television is its use in the drive for the recruitment of qualified teachers. Let us say that a certain state discovers that among its citizens are thousands of liberal arts graduates who lack credits in pedagogy. Perhaps they need courses in the history of education, child psychology, and methodology. The authorities then enlist the cooperation of one or more colleges that offer such subjects, and "telecourses" are arranged on an open circuit. College graduates who enroll and pass the final examinations are then certified as teachers.

A word should be said about the use of television for "remote monitoring." Under this system, cameras are placed strategically in such places as the lunchroom, the auditorium, and the halls. A receiving set is located in one of the offices, and the activities of the students are viewed. Obviously, the wiseacres and the pranksters will think twice about cutting capers when they realize that an unseen eye is watching somewhere in the building. Those who are inclined to cheat on tests will also be deterred by the realization that the hidden proctor may be looking right at them. Some educators believe that "remote monitoring" smacks too much of Gestapo methods; others feel that it is presently too expensive. But its adherents claim that its value in releasing teachers from distasteful jobs as overseers of large groups outweighs the negative factors.

From all that has been said so far in this section, the reader may be led to gather that educational television has been greeted with almost universal enthusiasm and stung by only a few minor objections. This is definitely not the case. Among its critics are legions of classroom teachers who complain that the medium has robbed them of the most exciting part of their work—presenting new material to eager youngsters. They resent their new roles as a mop-up squad, reviewing what the "master teacher" has taught. They say that the TV programs are showy intrusions which distract the children from the business at hand.

Some superintendents and principals are opposed to TV, too. New Jersey, which tried an ETV experiment as early as 1950, dropped it from the state budget in 1954. The criticisms there, as in many other places, centered on the fact that the tail was wagging the dog. Even today, when an attempt is made to avoid the mistakes of the past, complaints about regimentation and disruption of schedules are heard. In addition, educators note that many a bright child is bored and many a slow child is puzzled by even the best ETV "lecture." They state that the medium promotes mass education but lessens attention to individual differences. Moreover, they are concerned lest it lead to an overemphasis on the passive acquisition of knowledges and skills at the expense of the active give-and-take of classroom discussion.

In view of the high cost of television, some administrators ask: What can the medium do that films cannot do? Great artists and statesmen can be seen on commercially prepared films just as easily as on TV. Kinescoped lessons are really just another form of motion pictures. Furthermore, a film can be shown at the discretion of the classroom teacher—not in accordance with a prearranged TV schedule. True, it has been said that it is now technically possible for a teacher who wants to show a film or set of slides to check a guidebook for the title, dial a code number, and in a few seconds have the material on a TV screen in front of the room. But where are such closed-circuit libraries functioning now?

So runs the list of criticisms. But in spite of its detractors, educational television can be expected to play an increasingly important role in American schools during the next decade. Today, approximately two million students in schools and colleges get direct TV instruction, yet educators have only scratched the surface. New teachers, trained in colleges to accept the medium as a valuable aid, will help to swing the tide in its favor. Administrators who had expected miracles from it in the past will use it more judiciously. School systems that formerly held back from installing TV sets because of hostility, parsimony, or natural caution will probably recognize that television, like radio before it, can be a valuable educational tool.*

Teaching Machines

During and after World War II, automation revolutionized the handling of clerical and menial tasks in businesses, industries, and governmental agencies. Now it has invaded the classrooms. Educators

---

* UNESCO has published "Television Teaching Today," a description of the uses of ETV in countries throughout the world. It is printed by the Columbia University Press.

and parents everywhere are talking about teaching machines and wondering what their effect will be on the organization and curriculum of schools.

So far, the revolution has been mild, indeed. Most superintendents and boards of education are warily refusing to invest in the new-fangled gadgets until their worth has been established. Meanwhile, the manufacturers of the machines and those school administrators who have purchased them are in pious agreement that the teacher need not worry. Nothing can adequately substitute for her face-to-face contact with children. Her role may eventually be a bit different, but her job is secure. As in the case of instructional television, a machine is an additional tool that a teacher may use to improve the rate and the quality of learning.

Broadly speaking, there have always been "teaching machines"—from flash cards and abacuses to laboratory equipment, radio, television, and other audio-visual aids; but currently, the term is employed for any device that presents a question to a student and then tells him whether or not his answer is right. Although some of the devices are simple punchboards or tutorial workbooks, the most popular type is a mechanically operated contrivance.

Most teaching machines are based on the principle of self-instruction. They break down the informational material into sequential steps, usually called frames. The question-and-answer technique, or Socratic method, is used. Bit by bit, the student progresses from the simple to the complex. His rate depends on his ability. If he has given the right answer to a question, the machine will allow him to go on to the next one; otherwise, he must try again until he succeeds. Review tests are provided at regular intervals to serve as a check on progress.

One of the most popular machines is the device constructed by Dr. B. Frederic Skinner (1904–   ) at Harvard. About the size of a portable typewriter, it contains a hidden paper disc from which a cycle of 30 questions is rolled out. The questions appear one by one under a little window at the top of the machine. Alongside is another opening that reveals part of a roll of blank paper. Here the student writes his answer to the question. Then he pulls a lever on the side of the machine. Presto, the correct answer appears; but simultaneously his own answer is moved up under a plastic cover. He can see it but no longer change it. If he is right, he flicks the lever again and reads the next question.

Some of the mechanized instructors do not require the student to write his answer. Instead, he is confronted with a row of buttons. Above each button is a suggested answer to the question. The student makes his selection after reading each answer. Proponents of this multiple-choice type of machine claim that it permits faster reinforcement of learning. Professor Skinner, however, feels that it rewards recognition rather than recall. He claims that the act of writing the answer strengthens the learning bond. He also says that a student who is exposed to a plausible but erroneous answer may run the risk of remembering it later.

Regardless of the kinds of machines, all the people behind them agree that the material should be presented so simply and clearly that students rarely make errors. The step-by-step arrangement of a topic for use in a machine is called a program, and this sequential material is the real key to the value of the device. Ideally, a programmer should have a thorough knowledge of the subject matter, familiarity with auto-instructional machines, and a deep understanding of the learning process. This combination is hard to find in one person. Therefore, teams are often organized to set up programs. Today, in addition to the experts employed commercially, professors and advanced students at a dozen colleges throughout the country are systematically preparing programs for machines. Foundations and college research grants are supplying most of the funds for this work. The U.S. Office of Education has thrown its weight behind the project.

Obviously, the term "teaching machines" is a misnomer. The machines do not actually teach; they merely provide the student with material arranged in such a manner that he can teach himself. Their great advantage is that they tell a student immediately whether he is right or wrong. The teacher often does this, too. But just as often the student must wait several days until his homework paper is checked or his examination is marked. Meanwhile, the misconceptions, like thick cement, have a chance to set.

Another asset of machines is that they allow the student to progress at his own rate. Thus, the age-old problem of individual differences in ability is handled. The bright youngster need not sit idly staring out the window while his teacher patiently explains the algebra problem to his slower classmates. Instead of developing poor work habits, he is actively moving ahead from one plateau of questions to the next. It should be added that some of the programmers have cleverly tackled the problem of accelerating the pace for young geniuses. They have occasionally thrown in a very difficult question.

Students who surmount that hurdle are permitted to advance several steps. Of course, even without such a feature, the machine enables the intelligent student to finish a program faster than others. His quick selection of correct responses carries him forward.

Some educators predict that extended use of machines may cause new problems to emerge for the teacher. Students learning by machine will be at so many different levels that the present concepts of group teaching will not work. Moreover, the class "quiz kid" may advance so far that he will know much more than his instructor.

Such eventualities can be handled when and if the time ever comes. A much deeper concern is voiced by psychologists who fear that the isolation factor might have serious consequences. Most children are by nature gregarious creatures. To closet each of them with a machine in the pursuit of facts and skills, they say, would be to produce a monstrous generation of antisocial egomaniacs.

But it is extremely doubtful that such a danger will ever materialize in America. The students themselves would rebel. In an experiment conducted in 1961 at Roanoke, Virginia, a group of eighth graders used machines to study ninth-grade algebra. They had no textbooks or homework; above all, they had no math teachers. When the experiment was over, more than half of them said they would prefer a combination of the machine and the teacher. This preference was expressed despite the fact that 41 per cent of them had scored higher on the average than ninth-grade students who had been taught in the conventional way.

Other experiments like the one in Roanoke seem to indicate that in some areas the machines may do a better job than the teachers. The freshman logics course at Hamilton College in New York State is a good example. Using "programmed sheets," the students raised their average grade from 68 per cent to 86 per cent. Earlham College in Richmond, Indiana, has had similar success in a statistics class. Other colleges and schools have used machines for the study of languages, with stress on vocabulary and grammar, and for introductory psychology. One group of students finished Dr. Skinner's psychology program in an average of 13 hours!

Although these results are encouraging, it must be emphasized that the use of teaching machines is still in the experimental stage. If their early promise materializes, the possibilities are immense. For example, mathematics, the very area in which teaching machines seem to do the best job, is currently suffering from an acute shortage of qualified teachers. Machines may provide part of the answer to that problem. The population explosion and the increasing demands for education in remote parts of the world suggest another way in which machines may be put to use. Certainly, when enough teachers are not available to cover the needs, then aids to self-instruction become very important. In rural sections of America alone, machines may someday prove to be a boon to students, along with educational television. Their cost is certainly not prohibitive. Smaller types can be bought for $20, and mass production may reduce even that price.

At present, however, the demonstrated value of auto-instructional devices is that they free the teacher from a great part of the chore of transmitting rote material to students. Repetitious drill can be handled mainly by the machine, thus giving teachers the time to concentrate on the more creative aspects of their work, on personal guidance of students, and on discussions and activities relating to large projects and units.

In areas such as philosophy, art, and English literature, where generalizations and attitudes and individual talents are so important, teaching machines are obviously less suitable than in the drill-and-skill fields of mathematics and spelling. Also, they seem to be better adapted to high school students than to pupils in primary schools. Nevertheless, instances have been cited in which tots have learned how to read through the use of machines.

In fact, Dr. Skinner and Dr. James G. Holland (1927–   ) have recently been conducting an experiment in the use of simple teaching machines by mentally retarded children with I.Q.'s of 50. They have not reached any definite conclusions as yet, except to say that the machines keep the children actively interested for long periods of time.

It was Dr. Skinner who popularized teaching machines in 1954. Actually, the prototypes of current devices appeared more than 35 years ago, but they did not catch the public fancy. Professor Sidney L. Pressey (1888–   ) developed a machine back in 1926 at the Ohio State University. Though originally conceived as a testing device, it had the same potentiality for instructional purposes as present-day machines.

Perhaps Dr. Skinner's dramatic flare was what turned the tide of interest toward teaching machines. In another experiment he taught pigeons how to play table tennis through the use of the reward-and-punishment method. This same principle, he claims, is at the root of teaching machines. The difference is that, instead of getting a

kernel of corn for the correct movement, the student gets the satisfaction of knowing that his answer is correct.

But at the University of Indiana Medical School, Dr. Charles
Ferster (1922–   ) does use food as one incentive for schizophrenic
children. When they push the proper button on his vending machines,
they get a bar of candy or a sandwich. Elsewhere in the room a toy
starts running when a button is pressed. Dr. Ferster's purpose is to
make the children see that the same simple action causes the same
pleasant result each time.

Dr. Norman A. Crowder (1921–   ) is another exponent of teaching machines. He has developed sets of "programmatic" workbooks
called *Tutor Texts;* their purpose is fundamentally the same as that
of the mechanical devices. Dr. Crowder anticipates that the self-teaching machine will eventually produce quite a change in the role of
teachers. One of the teacher's chief tasks will be to help individual
students to understand the explanations given by the machines; they
will also clear up general difficulties not anticipated by programmers.
He even suggests that housewives with college training may some
day be brought into the classroom as noncertified teachers to supervise a roomful of students using machines.

This leads to the concept of the electronic classroom. In 1960,
the New York Institute of Technology gave a demonstration of its
new electronic testing laboratory to several hundred amazed spec-
tators. Each student's desk is equipped with a record player and a
two-way communication system for private conversation with the
teacher. Individual TV screens, tape recorders, and other accessory
devices may be plugged into each desk when necessary. Students are
also equipped with earphones and specially treated paper. They
listen to the programmed information given by the recording device
and then answer the questions, which are spaced at five-minute intervals or less. A telemetering device on the teacher's desk immediately
records their responses. Moreover, each student can be supplied with
material suited to his own level of achievement, just as in the case of
the other teaching machines described earlier.

The new lab is designed for use in all kinds of school systems and
at all levels from elementary grades to college postgraduate courses.
Its proponents state that it will permit schools to free themselves of
conventional semesters and will allow more flexible scheduling of
classes.

The above may sound fantastic, but it is only the beginning.

Manufacturers of electronic computers have recently taken an interest in the movement and have already developed machines that can carry on a "discussion" with Johnny while tutoring him in history, and can tell him what lifework he should choose. What lies ahead, therefore, is very difficult to predict. It is possible that the interest in this whole field, from simple, self-teaching devices to complicated electronic systems, may die down when the novelty wears off. On the other hand, it is conceivable that the school of the future may be staffed with more technicians than teachers. The probability is that the acceptance of machines will fall somewhere between the two extremes. It seems likely that they will have a place in the educational picture. What or whom they displace and replace will be interesting to observe.

In the meantime, the thing to remember is that a machine is only as good as its program—and there is still a great need for research on the value of most programs.

Language Laboratories

A language laboratory may be defined as a set of teaching machines designed to help students who are learning to speak and listen to a foreign language. But these machines are quite different from the type discussed in the previous section of this chapter. Their roots can be traced to the use of phonograph records for language study—a well-known feature of the Berlitz System. That method was expanded by the Army Specialized Training Program, and the idea of a laboratory emerged. Before long, it was tried commercially and eventually adopted by the schools.

Late in the 1950's, language laboratories became increasingly popular among educators. Today, approximately 30 companies manufacture them and have a hard time keeping up with the demand. Plans for more than one-fourth of the new high schools built in 1961 called for the installation of the laboratories. Even on the junior high school level the idea has taken hold. Reports show that at least 15 of every 100 new junior high schools were linguistically mechanized in 1961. Moreover, more than 2,000 older secondary schools have been equipped with the machines in the last five years.

The reasons for this sudden interest are numerous. First, it stems from the realization that the language barrier must be broken down in a world where no nation is isolated from another, even if it wishes to be. Second, the laboratories are admirably suited to the aural-oral method of teaching—an approach which many modern instructors espouse because its purpose is to train the student to understand and to speak a foreign language. Then, too, the installation of the machines offers no great problem; they can be easily placed in an ordinary classroom. Finally, they appeal to the gadget-conscious American or to administrators suffering from a shortage of competent teachers.

The last of the above points is the weakest. Here, as in the case of ETV and the self-instructional machines described earlier, the agreement is that the new facilities are meant to supplement—not supplant —the work of the teacher. School systems that have provided for maximum independence in students' use of the laboratories have experienced less success than those that have furnished the equipment only as an aid to skilled and enthusiastic teachers. For example, it has been found that students often do not hear correctly. The recorded voice may be saying "amigo, amigo"; but the student may hear "amico, amico." He may even compare his own pronunciation with the correct one and not notice the difference. In short, he needs a teacher's on-the-spot guidance and correction. He also needs to see how the words are formed on the lips as well as to *hear* them.

This leads to the question of how the laboratories work. There are many varieties, and their uses depend on the purposes of the learner and his classroom teacher. They can help with everything from phonetic drills to skill in conversation, from practice in the use of grammatical forms and idioms to aural comprehension or the memorization of songs and poetry.

In the most elaborate setups, students go into booths and listen to a warm and pleasant voice speaking correctly in the foreign language via a tape recorder or disc. Sometimes the students use headphones, sometimes they listen directly either as a group or on an individual basis. Following the instruction given on the recording, each student then talks through a microphone. Afterward he may listen to the playback of his own voice and compare it with the one he has heard. When tape is used, the student's voice may be erased later, but the recording of the instructor's voice will remain intact.

The classroom teacher, meanwhile, is seated at a control panel, called a console, which is connected with each student's booth. Like the students, the teacher has earphones and a mike. If he wishes to talk privately with any student—perhaps make an immediate speech correction or clear up an aural difficulty—he flicks the proper switch. A master switch allows him to talk with all the students at once whenever necessary. Some companies even provide motion pictures and other audio-visual materials to enrich the language instruction.

In its simplest form the laboratory is used merely for listening, with or without earphones. In other cases, the emphasis is on listening and responding; but students cannot readily compare their intonations, pronunciations, and inflections with what they have heard. Also, some schools prefer to have the teacher move from student to student rather than to station himself at the console.

In some areas, the economical but efficient "traveling lab" has been put to use. Arlington, Massachusetts, has such an arrangement for 350 sixth graders studying French at several schools. A 36-foot trailer visits each building once a week and is enjoyed by 18 students at a time. The van was developed under the leadership of Professor I. A. Richards (1893–   ).

Cost is a factor that boards of education always weigh before deciding on laboratories. Naturally, the most complex systems are the most expensive; they run to as much as $500 per student. Simple laboratories can be set up for limited purposes at a cost of approximately $30 per student.

But even more important considerations are the goals of the school and the motivations of the teachers. If the purpose of the instruction is to inculcate the ability to read a foreign language, rather than to understand and speak it, then labs are not the answer. And if the teachers do not desire laboratories or comprehend their benefits, then it is useless to install them. In some schools today the labs are lying idle because zealous but hasty administrators purchased them before orienting the teachers.

Sometimes instructors shy away from the new facilities because their own accents are so poor, or because they are used to teaching foreign languages by the "old-school" methods. One teacher in a high school in Virginia stated flatly: "I don't want to use the laboratory. It will show me up." When such teachers have tenure, the administrators have a hard row to hoe. Re-training is a glib answer, but in many instances it will not work: the old dog refuses to learn the new tricks. Often a school system is forced to wait until that kind of teacher retires; then the new apparatus is brought in along with the freshly trained teacher.

Often, however, a teacher's aversion to a language laboratory may stem from her fear of anything that smacks of science. In such cases, wise administrators have used the technique of gradually getting the teacher accustomed to the idea through visits to other schools where teachers are known to be having happy and successful experiences with the new equipment. One big-city principal even played the role of the "reluctant dragon" and, by a process of reverse psychology, his foreign language staff finally convinced him that a laboratory was just what they had always wanted. What they did not know was that he had been a year ahead of them in that desire.

Like the other startling devices that have appeared on the educational scene in recent years, language laboratories must be tested in the crucible of time. Thus far, when the way has been carefully planned for their use, they seem to be effective. Teachers report that the students look forward to the lab work and get far more practice in conversation than in a non-lab situation. Also, the teachers say that the active participation of so many students makes it easier to detect and correct general errors, to give individual guidance, and to gauge each student's progress. But it must be remembered that language laboratories are still a novelty. The true test of these facilities will come when the sheen has worn off. Certainly they should be given a fair chance and not misused, as happened in the case of the teacher who announced in the faculty lunchroom: "My language lab broke down. Now I'll have to teach!"

Finally, it should be noted that some schools are now using laboratories for other subjects besides foreign languages. Speech, literature, and business education are areas in which the idea has proved to be useful.

Foreign Language in Elementary Schools

A Joe Miller story tells of an American tourist who returned from Paris full of admiration for the cultural advancement of the people there. "Those foreigners are really smart," he observed. "Why, even the little urchins in the streets speak better French than I do!"

No one can deny that the best "laboratory" for learning a language is the natural setting in which that tongue is spoken. Failing that, many experts maintain, the next best thing is to be taught to use and hear the language at an early age. For centuries, that philosophy has permeated the European schools. It has had its ups and downs in America.

One motivation for the introduction of a foreign language in a public school in the United States has been the desire of the people to perpetuate the culture of the "old country." For example, many people of German background settled in Milwaukee. Naturally, they wanted their children to speak and understand—and even love—the language in which they themselves had been reared. And so, in the latter half of the nineteenth century, German was a subject in the elementary schools in that city. The same is true of Cincinnati, St. Louis, and Buffalo.

Similarly, Spanish emerged alongside the three R's as part of the basic curriculum of many elementary schools in the Southwest where the descendants of the conquistadors had settled. French was offered to young children in several New England cities in post-Civil War days and was taught in elementary schools as far west as San Francisco.

But there were forces in America that militated against the popularity of foreign language teaching in the early grades. Nature study, which eventually was broadened to cover all elementary science, had its advocates in the 1900's. History and geography, health and hygiene, music, literature, and art—all these subjects had their champions ready to challenge anyone who would deny them to children. The Industrial Revolution caused even shop and commercial subjects to move into the grammar schools. What room was there for such an impractical subject as French or Spanish?

The greatest of all the weapons of the anti-linguists was America's location, far across the Atlantic from Europe. Also, some of the immigrants were eager to be assimilated into American life and reluctant to look back toward the lands of their birth. They reasoned: Let my children learn to speak English, and let no study of another language interfere; let them be 100 per cent Americans.

This new nationalism devolved into outright jingoism in some parts of the country. The outbreak of World War I proved to be the climax of such anti-foreign feeling. In the aftermath of that holocaust, Americans reacted emotionally against anything that suggested entanglement with Europe. But foreign language teaching proved to be hard to kill. Although German was anathema, French still had its outspoken adherents. Had not France been our gallant ally in 1918? And so, the "language of Lafayette and Foch" was allowed into the curriculum for superior children in Cleveland's elementary schools as early as 1921. Several other school systems soon followed suit.

World War II had a different effect altogether. Although isolationists roared and raved, they were in the minority. Most Americans realized that any event in any area of this planet could affect them. Then, too, there were other facts to be faced: the Communists and the Cold War, the emerging importance of the United Nations, the NATO pact, the Truman Doctrine, the Marshall Plan, the Jet Age. Whether we liked it or not, our destiny was linked with Europe's.

Simultaneously, Americans fretted about their own inability to speak anything but English, as contrasted with the bilingual proclivities of Europeans. Soldiers and postwar tourists discovered that three years of studying a foreign language in high school had done them no good whatsoever. They were unable to converse on the simplest terms with the natives. Surely something was wrong with the schools. Perhaps the method was to blame. All that grammar, and so little practice in speaking! Perhaps, too, the Europeans had the right idea. Begin the training early, when a child is impressionable; high school is too late. The knowledge just doesn't stick when you begin so late.

Such arguments led to an increased interest in the possibilities of conversational French or Spanish on an informal basis in the early grades. Private schools and a few public schools began to try out the idea. These disparate efforts finally received official blessing, and the rush was on.

The encouragement came in 1952 from Earl J. McGrath (1902–), at that time U.S. Commissioner of Education. He spoke out in favor of teaching foreign languages in the elementary schools. Consequently, in 1953 the movement that became known as FLES really got into high gear. A total of 145 communities adopted the idea. A few years later, more than 300,000 children were receiving foreign language instruction in grades one through six. Over 75 per cent of them were taking Spanish; about 20 per cent were studying French; the others concentrated on German and other languages. College professors spurred the advance by producing materials that could be used by classroom teachers. Professor Theodore Anderson (1918–) of Columbia and Dr. Kenneth Mildenberger (1921–) made notable contributions to the field.

Smaller communities are often the first to try new ideas; big cities usually wait until the first experiments have proved to be reasonably successful. This is what happened in the FLES movement. Throughout the country, little suburban towns with flexible curricula and eager, articulate parents adopted the program immediately. Some tried it as early as the kindergarten; others postponed the instruction until the fourth grade or later. New York City, on the other hand, held off until 1958 before taking official action, although it must be said that as far back as 1934 a few elementary schools in that metropolis had been teaching foreign languages.

FLES has still a long way to go before gaining general acceptance. In fact, it has stirred up a major controversy among educators. In

New Jersey, to give one illustration, Commissioner of Education Frederick Raubinger (1908–   ) takes a dim view of the whole idea. But scores of school superintendents in his state regard FLES as a must for their elementary schools.*

Critics like Raubinger point out that there is little dependable research to prove that preadolescents have greater linguistic potential than teen-agers, as some FLES advocates have claimed. They also raise the "something's gotta give" objection, meaning that the introduction of a foreign language will crowd some other area out of the curriculum, or cause teachers to stint on the basic subjects. Drop the frills, they say, or else add a few hours to the school day.

To the argument that early study of a foreign language will imbue children with respect for other cultures and promote tolerance, the anti-FLES educators respond that such attitudes can be instilled in a good social studies program. They add that the only way to master a language is to be constantly motivated to use it, now and in the future. As an example, they cite the fact that a bright Swiss child whose father owns a château frequented by tourists from all parts of the world soon becomes a polyglot without much formal training. Finally, they observe that, if world peace is the goal, then Russian and Chinese would be more appropriate subjects than French and Spanish.

The FLES proponents counter that preadolescents can learn a foreign language without self-consciousness and that a child who begins early will be able to saturate himself in the language when he reaches high school. They contend, too, that the program will cause more adolescents to elect a foreign language because of their familiarity with the basic vocabulary and pronunciation.

In the above argument, the FLES men received a fortuitous boost from the Modern Language Association. That organization recently estimated that less than 9 per cent of America's high school students are studying a modern foreign language, and that in the junior high schools the figure is only 4 per cent. Furthermore, four out of every ten public high schools in the United States do not teach *any* foreign languages.

But, in the final analysis, the success or failure of FLES must depend on the teacher. Opponents of the movement state with good

* According to the U.S. Office of Education, a total of 20,488 public elementary school children in New Jersey were studying foreign languages in 1959—the seventh largest state-wide enrollment in the nation.

reason that very few teachers on the elementary school level have the proper background to teach even the simplest lessons in a foreign language. Their pronunciation, in some cases, would be so bad that the pupils would be linguistically scarred for life.

True, say the FLES enthusiasts, but this argument is currently being met in four ways: colleges are behind the movement and are training new elementary schoolteachers in modern foreign languages; ETV is saving the day because the classroom teachers, as well as the children, learn to follow and imitate the "master" on the screen; record players, tape recorders, and simple language laboratories are being used as aids; and lastly, competent specialists are being employed to move from class to class or school to school.

Regardless of the worth of the arguments pro and con, at the present moment the FLES side is winning. The U.S. Office of Education recently published a study which showed that 1,227,006 elementary school pupils were studying foreign languages in 1959, as contrasted with only 145,643 in 1953.* The state with by far the largest FLES enrollment was California (293,554 pupils). Ohio with 40,293 was second, and New York was third.

Spanish was still running strongly. According to the above report, about 70 per cent of the FLES pupils were taking that subject. French, German, Russian, and Italian trailed in that order. The range of difference can be seen by contrasting the following figures:

Pupils studying Spanish 485,825
Pupils studying Italian 1,188

Other languages being studied in the elementary school included Latin, Japanese, Hawaiian, Chinese, Norwegian, Greek, and Swedish. Minnesota reported one child studying Serbian!

But the decriers of FLES are not worried by the above figures. They note that 96 per cent of more than 30 million children enrolled in America's public and non-public elementary schools do not study foreign languages. The movement, they declare, is still a fad. Even the FLES supporters are cautious about predictions. They admit that the idea is still experimental. Whether or not it will really sweep the country remains to be seen. It is to be hoped that the decisions for or against it will be based on its merits or faults, not on blind emotionalism.

* These figures include non-public schools. In public elementary schools alone the total was 1,030,097 pupils in 1959. Of these, 337,381 were studying languages over ETV.

Team Teaching

The spectrum of differences among individuals in any given school is always a difficult challenge. Not only are there bright, average, and slow pupils; but teachers, too, are seldom cut from the same cloth. They range from the new and weak to the experienced and talented, with all varieties in between. Moreover, in a school organized along conventional patterns they rarely get a chance to work together. A veteran teacher may be assigned as a "buddy" to a neophyte, but the help he can give often consists of a few kind words in the hall while each is hurrying toward his self-contained classroom.

The problem, then, is triple-barreled. Ideally, a school should arrange for each child to fulfill his unique potential under the tutelage of the very best teachers, who at the same time are giving in-service training to their less gifted or less experienced colleagues. But how? A group of educators at Harvard University believe that they have come up with a possible answer—team teaching. Their idea has been tried out in an elementary school in Lexington, Massachusetts, and it seems to work. Indeed, it has captured so much interest that scores of schools, from New York to San Diego, are adopting the idea in whole or in part.

Team teaching departs in two essential ways from the ordinary organization of an elementary school. To begin with, no single teacher is responsible for all the instruction that a class receives; instead, he is part of a team. Actually, this is not a radical innovation. Supervising teachers and other specialists have often taken over instruction in areas like music, art, and remedial reading. Also, departmentalization is not a total stranger to the elementary school. In that respect, team teaching is merely a variation of the old concept that each subject should be taught by an expert in the field.

But the second difference is more startling. Class size is not fixed but varies with the activity. A group of as many as 200 pupils may assemble to hear a lecture from a team teacher or to see an educational film. They may then break down into smaller groups ranging from fewer than 10 to clusters of 50. Often while the majority of the pupils are assembled, smaller groups may be receiving advanced instruction or doing remedial work. Flexibility is the key to the program. Kaleidoscopic combinations are possible in the arrangement of groups not only in terms of numbers but also in the organization of schedules, if the building facilities permit.

The Franklin School at Lexington has three teams—Alpha, Beta, and Omega. Each group has a team leader and aides to do the clerical work. In addition, the composition of each group is as follows:

Alpha	*Beta*	*Omega*
Three teachers	One senior teacher	Two senior teachers
	Five teachers	Five teachers
75 pupils (Grade 1)	187 pupils (Grades 2–3)	230 pupils (Grades 4–5–6)

Each team leader receives $1,000 beyond the regular salary. The job entails supervision of others on the team, as well as teaching. Senior teachers, who are experienced specialists, are paid $500 beyond the regular salary.

The idea has caught on in Connecticut. Four schools in Norwalk have had their own version of team teaching since 1958. All teams there are composed of three teachers—a leader, a regular teacher, and an aide who is not a fully certified instructor. In Greenwich, the new Dundee Elementary School is among the most recent to join the team-teaching ranks. In fact, that school was designed specifically for such a setup.

Many secondary schools have been converted to the plan. An excellent illustration is the Rich Township High School in Park Forest, Illinois. In that school several teams teach mathematics, typing, American history, and a combined ninth-year social studies and English program. One interesting feature of the plan is that the small groups, or buzz sessions, are conducted by student leaders immediately after the introductory lecture has been given at the large meeting. As many as 11 separate groups, each having eight or nine students, meet in one room. They pool their information at the end of the session.

The Rich Township High School was not built for team teaching. Consequently, at first the cafeteria had to be used for the large groups. Although this makeshift arrangement involved many difficulties, the experiment showed enough potential value to stimulate school authorities to build a new wing with expansible classrooms designed for team teaching. More significant, brand-new Olympia Fields High School in the same district has been designed particularly for team teaching. Large classrooms can be divided into two, three, or four smaller areas by means of soundproof, movable partitions. If the school decides to drop team teaching, this flexible design permits easy conversion.

One of the most widely advertised team-teaching programs is conducted at the Evanston Township High School, also in Illinois. Approximately 350 eleventh-grade English students are taught by a team of four teachers, each responsible for one aspect of the work. Another team conducts a course in the humanities for almost the same number of seniors.

Evanston, incidentally, is also renowned for its school-within-a-school idea. Confronted with an enrollment of more than 3,500 students, the administrators divided the school into four equal groups, each headed by a principal with four assistants. The groups cross grade lines and are heterogeneous. The students in each group are selected at random from the total enrollment in each grade.

A prominent exponent of new ideas such as those being tried at Evanston is J. Lloyd Trump (1908–   ). A former professor of education at the University of Illinois, Dr. Trump is associate secretary of the National Association of Secondary School Principals—a group that has been encouraging experimentation. In his book, *Images of the Future,* Dr. Trump makes a good case for team teaching. He even suggests a plan for division of students' time in the schools of tomorrow: large group instruction (40 per cent), individual study (40 per cent), and small group meetings (20 per cent). He conceives of the staff as a mélange of teacher specialists, general teachers, instruction assistants, clerks, aides, and community consultants.

But Dr. Trump and others have not convinced everybody that team teaching is the answer to an educator's prayer. Aside from the fact that most school plants do not permit the fluid arrangement of large and small groups, the main objection is that team teaching features the outmoded lecture method. The same criticisms that are leveled at instructional television are applied here. The lecture may be too elementary for the bright children or too deep for the slow. They must then be retaught in the small groups.

The argument that team teaching has the virtue of flexibility comes in for some sharp criticism, too. Advocates of the self-contained classroom wonder if team teaching actually militates against flexibility. They point out that it is easier for one teacher to change her plans in accordance with a sudden lively interest of the pupils than it is for a whole team. They add that moving from room to room and group to group each day is possibly a deterrent to concentration and creativity. In the case of elementary children, they maintain, team teaching has all the faults of departmentalization: inner confusion caused by many changes, the problem of adjusting to several teachers and groups instead of one, a tendency to emphasize subject matter rather than individual guidance, and subservience to a clock indicating that it is now time to move on to another group.

There are other questions about team teaching. Is it more an expedient than an experiment because of a shortage of teachers in the face of rising pupil enrollments? Is it, as some people declare, a subtle way of introducing the "merit salary scales" that teachers' groups have opposed for so long? Do the pupils learn more or less? Do they develop the right attitudes and work habits, or are these lost in the shuffle?

Adherents of team teaching have some good answers. A partial list of their claims might read as follows:

1. Teachers on teams share their knowledge of individual children with each other; thus, snap judgments and misguidance are nipped in the bud.
2. When large groups assemble, some teachers are freed to give individual help to pupils or to plan and consult.
3. Team teaching permits each teacher to use his talents to the best advantage for the maximum number of children.
4. Pupils develop a greater sense of responsibility; they learn to think for themselves, to adjust to all kinds of situations and groups, to make decisions, to participate actively in discussions, and to understand all the facets of a subject area.
5. The work load is eased for teachers because they are part of a team. Salary benefits are commensurate with the type of work and training. Professional growth is fostered by daily contact with other team members. New teachers improve faster.

Like many other experiments described in this chapter, team teaching cannot be truly evaluated as yet. In time, the decision as to whether it is valid or vapid may boil down to a choice between two old sayings: do too many cooks spoil the broth, or are two heads better than one?

The Non-Graded Elementary School

The traditional way of doing things is not always the best. Sometimes its popularity is due to accidental circumstances. Often it becomes outdated. New discoveries are made; customs and mores change; one invention alters the face of the world. Yesterday's coffee grinder becomes tomorrow's antique.

Today there is a growing belief among educators that the division of an elementary school into grades should have died with Victoria. They see no reason for the first six rungs on the educational ladder, and they are busily chopping away. Already 18 per cent of the elementary schools in the United States have instituted a non-graded system.

This theory of continuous progress grew out of dissatisfaction with the grade-to-grade lockstep. The old plan had too many faults. It caused slow children either to fail in their work and repeat a year, or to be pushed onward and upward to realms beyond their ken. In the first case, they would feel frustrated and stigmatized; in the other, confused and oppressed. Meanwhile, the bright pupils alongside them were suffering from narrow interest and wide yawns. Grouping children according to their ability at each grade level might be a partial answer in schools with tremendous enrollments, but it was no solution for small schools with only 30 or 40 children in any given age bracket.

Besides, psychologists had been saying over and over that generalizations could not be made on the basis of age. A certain seven-year-old might be far more mature than his nine-year-old cousins. Or he might be ahead in one area and behind in another. Date of birth was just a statistic for record cards, license agencies, and tombstone carvers—it had little or no relevancy in the classroom.

Another objection to grade lines came from the curriculum makers. The system tended to freeze everything into compartments. A bright second-grader interested in Eskimos might be told: "Wait a year or two; right now we're studying our community." And a fourth-grade teacher might have conniptions if she learned that down in the primary grades a few little geniuses were learning fractions. What would be left for her to teach them?

In that connection, the numbered grades received many a critical salvo from administrative quarters. Too often, they complained, teachers came to regard a given grade as their own little province. They became specialists, for instance, in second-year or fifth-year teaching, and repeated the same old lesson plans year after year. Attempts to budge them upward or downward resulted in tantrums and tears.

And so in the 1950's the ungraded school gained favor, especially in suburban and rural areas. In the latter case, it was only a short step away from the program carried out by some one-room-school-teachers.

The non-graded system has many variations. In a great number of schools it is used only at the primary level. Grades 1–2–3 are lumped; the ladder starts in the fourth year. Others have reorganized entirely, but keep the children in self-contained classrooms. Thus, a class of 30 might have 13 average eight-year-olds; ten bright seven-year-olds; and the rest, slow nine-year-olds. In such cases, reading achievement is often the keystone for grouping.

A few schools have carried the idea through to its logical extreme. Grouping is done in every skill subject. A child who is advanced in reading but poor in arithmetic may find himself sitting with older children in the one case and younger children in the other. This system, of course, is the twin brother of the departmentalized program—a phrase that is anathema to many elementary school leaders because they fear the disintegration of both the topics and the tots.

Appleton, Wisconsin, is leaning toward the mixed groups described above. All the elementary schools in that city of 50,000 people are non-graded, and some of the classes cross age lines. Appleton features four-page folders called skill cards that are profiles of the children's progress. The cards are handed on from teacher to teacher. The progress, incidentally, is good. Under the non-graded system the young Appletonians are doing better work than their older brothers and sisters who had attended graded schools there. Whether this is because the youngsters were motivated by being "part of an experiment" remains to be seen.

In a few cases, the non-graded schools are also trying out team teaching. The two ideas fit together well because both give much attention to ability grouping. The little village of Carson City in Michigan is trying this double-edged experiment. The elementary school there has no individual classrooms. Instead, there are clusters of open space, each about the size of four conventional classrooms. The team teachers often improvise the instructional program. Every three weeks they decide on how the children will be grouped, what the team-teaching assignments are, and what the schedule will be.

Along with promotions and retardations, conventional report cards have been discarded by most schools using the non-graded plan. Instead, written descriptions of each pupil's progress are sent home or parent-teacher conferences are held from time to time.

There are still some unanswered questions about non-graded schools. How many of them are really following the old system under a new title? In other words, how many have merely dropped grade nomenclature, old-time report cards, and the task of deciding each year whether a child has passed or failed? If they have kept everything else, it is asked, what is all the shouting about?

At the other extreme, is it not logical under the non-graded system for a very bright child to advance to the junior high school in four years and for a very slow one to take as many as eight years? Further, what is the effect on a child when he goes through a non-graded elementary school and then enters a conventional junior high school?

The pioneers who have been trying out the new idea do not as yet have all the answers to such questions. Perhaps solutions will be reached in the present decade. Meanwhile, to confuse the issue a little more, the Dual Progress Plan has come to the foreground.

Dual Progress is the brainchild of Dr. George D. Stoddard (1897–), Chancellor of New York University. The plan is designed to provide individualized learning for the third to the eighth grade under the guidance of specialists. Dr. Stoddard suggests that each teacher who is hired should be a specialist in one of seven curriculum areas: language arts, social studies, science, math, physical education, arts and crafts, and music.

The pupil's progress, according to Stoddard, is "dual" because he is given *cultural imperatives* (language arts and social studies) and *cultural electives* (science, math, and the arts). All must master the former for social living; achievement in the latter depends on interests and abilities.

Stoddard would have the schools work out grade placements, courses of study, and promotions only in *cultural imperatives*. Non-graded grouping would be permitted for math, science, and the arts. Non-gifted children would spend the same time in those three areas as talented pupils, but their rate of progress would differ.

Experiments in the plan have been directed by Stoddard at Long Beach and Ossining, New York, with the support of the Ford Foundation's Fund for the Advancement of Education. Mixed reactions have come from educators.

In a sharply worded booklet entitled *The Self-Contained Classroom,* the Association for Curriculum and Development* recently took up the cudgels against Stoddard's plan and other similar "reforms." Such ideas, they declared, are merely the old hat called "departmentalized programs" with new trimmings to brighten it up. Mincing no words, the A.S.C.D. went on to say that a number of the innovations had been generated by "sincere but uninformed pressure groups." They took a firm stand in favor of the self-contained classroom.

* The A.S.C.D. is a branch of the National Education Association. It is located at 1201 16th St., N.W., Washington, D.C.

The Year-Round School

A newspaper headline in 1960 asked: "Is vacation obsolete?" Aspects of that question have been debated wherever educators have gathered in the past few years. Slowly but surely, it seems, the tide is turning toward an extension of the school year. For example, the NEA Research Division reports that 26 per cent of the urban school systems with populations of 2,500 or more have longer terms than they had 10 years ago. It is even being predicted that the average school program in the next decade will run for 200 days, about 25 more than the average throughout the nation today. Furthermore, the pupils' day may be increased to eight hours.*

One of the chief reasons for growing interest in the longer school year is the sharp reappraisal of education that has taken place in the post-Sputnik period. Americans have awakened to the fact that, although European children spend fewer years in school than ours, most of them are getting more educational hours per year; in Germany and Russia, for instance, schools are in session on Saturdays, and the average little Muscovite attends classes 230 days each year.

Schoolmen have also noted the gradual proliferation of subjects in the curriculum during the past century. For years, teachers were complaining that they could not give enough time to basic areas or cover the topics completely. The last few chapters in many a textbook were left unread when June rolled around. Meanwhile, Johnny's reading and writing needed improvement. Drastic action was obviously needed.

Three Pennsylvania educators gave impetus to the movement in 1960. Under the auspices of the Association for Supervision and Curriculum Development, they wrote a 60-page booklet entitled *Extending the School Year.* Reminding teachers that the nine-month plan is a vestige of the days when children of an agrarian nation were needed to take care of the crops, they urged that summer courses become an integral, though non-compulsory, part of the year-round curriculum under a 12-month budget. "In the near future," they prophesied, "teaching will attain the status of a year-round profession and opportunities for organized study during the summer will be provided increasingly for children."

The present low state of teachers' salaries gives rise to another argument in favor of the extended school year. It is propounded that

---

* Strangely enough, according to the NEA Research Division, both elementary and junior high school pupils are enjoying a *shorter* median school day than did their predecessors of 20 years ago. The school day has been slightly lengthened for senior high school students.

taxpayers often use the nine-month year as a plausible reason for underpaying teachers. The year-round plan allegedly would knock the props from under such an excuse.

Here are some of the other opinions expressed by advocates of shorter vacations for teachers and pupils:

1. Billions of dollars invested in school buildings all over the nation would not be wasted during the summer.
2. Teachers would be actively engaged in improving their techniques and their knowledge of the profession, rather than working in some other field.
3. Juvenile delinquency, which now runs rampant in August, would be reduced.
4. Taking away the long vacation would prepare students for life; business firms do not give three-month vacations.
5. The plan may enable some students to finish school earlier; it would be especially helpful for future physicians and others whose training takes many years to complete. Slow students, on the other hand, would have a chance to catch up on the work.
6. Under a staggered system, the idea may eliminate the double-session plan that is now used because the number of new buildings in many areas has not kept up with the rise in pupil enrollment.
7. Money presently needed for additional buildings and equipment might be allocated instead to teachers' salaries.

Opposition to the year-round school has mounted in proportion to the publicity in favor of the idea. Parents who fear the disruption of family life during the summer are objecting. Teachers who regard the long vacation as a much-needed chance to restore their frazzled nerves or to take courses for advancement are protesting. Some of the other arguments in favor of the *status quo* are as follows:

1. Summer courses and night schools are already available for the slow or disadvantaged students and for bright youngsters who want to finish four years of school in three.
2. Recruitment of teachers is a severe problem now. To extend the school year would mean an increase in the shortage of new personnel.
3. Older students would be deprived of the opportunity to earn money as a nest egg for college tuition or as an aid to their struggling families.

4. Compulsory attendance during the summer would cause an outbreak of truancy.

5. In many sections of the country, summer heat would be too oppressive for teachers and pupils. The expense of supplying air conditioners would have to be undertaken. Also, renovation of buildings would be interfered with.

6. During vacations children often develop new interests, gain many broadening experiences, and build up their health through exercise and sunshine. Summer school would stifle such gains.

7. If the longer school year permits youngsters to take full-time jobs at an earlier age, the labor market will be flooded and unemployment will climb. Many high school graduates are too immature, as it is.

The American Association of School Administrators published a study called *Year-Round School* (1960), which set forth four possible approaches to the extension of the school year. They are as follows:

Plan I.   Under a four-quarter system schools would be open for 48 weeks. Students would attend for three quarters. Their vacations would still last three months, but a different group would be out during each quarter. Communities would employ teachers for three or all four quarters; teachers would get one month's vacation.

Plan II.   This is also a 48-week plan divided into four quarters of 12 weeks' duration. Four weeks of vacation for students and teachers would be distributed so as to fall at Christmas time, Easter, etc.

Plan III.   A summer program of from 4 to 12 weeks would supplement the regular program. Stress would be on enrichment courses, vocational education, and the like.

Plan IV.   The school year for children would be the same as it is now, but teachers would be employed on a 12-month basis. They would work in such areas as instructional improvement and curriculum planning.

At present, variations of the arrangement suggested in Plan III are most popular. The aforementioned A.S.C.D. booklet cites several examples. In the Neshaminy School District in Pennsylvania, summer courses are given in subjects ranging from quantitative analysis and electronics to oil painting. Seattle's elementary-school children may take up any of five different foreign languages, including Japanese.

"Interest Centers" have been set up in Winnetka, Illinois, for mathematics, science, dramatics, and language study. Newton, Massachusetts, allows prospective teachers from Harvard to serve as interns in the summer program.

In some cases, day camps have been established on a learn-and-play basis. One example is the program set up at Darien, Connecticut, in cooperation with a nonprofit group called Science and Arts Camps, Inc. Recently 160 gifted children in grades five to seven were carefully selected for this experience. They developed such enthusiasm that they continued to meet on evenings and weekends during the next school term. Their interests ranged from the study of Russian and chemistry to medical science.

Colleges, too, have been offering summer programs for gifted high school youngsters. At the University of Vermont, for instance, hundreds of the top high school musicians (mostly from eastern schools) assemble every year and study the subject for four weeks. The program culminates in two concerts which are enjoyed by the professors and advanced college students on campus.

Thus, the trend has been toward expansion of summer schools in one form or another. Whereas remedial and make-up work had once predominated, programs in recent years have been geared to the interests of the bright as well. Students are no longer embarrassed to admit that they are going back to high school for summer work. In all the states except two, enrichment programs are offered sometime between mid-June and mid-September. Some of the most popular courses are: driver education, study skills, music, typing, commercial law, arts and crafts, creative writing, and psychology. In New York State alone, enrollment in such classes has leaped to more than 130,000 from a total slightly below 50,000 in 1950.

A word should be said here about the use of educational television for summer learning. The public schools of Oklahoma City have pioneered in this phase of holiday instruction. As early as 1958, the local educational station, KETA-TV, offered courses in conversational French, Spanish, and Russian, and in reading skill improvement—all for the benefit of third and fourth graders. The program took up two hours of TV time every weekday morning, and lasted for six weeks.

Perhaps the above experiment is one answer to those who insist that the school year should be extended. Perhaps, too, sentiment will swing toward a lengthening of the school day or to classes on Saturday mornings. At any rate, the country is still not sold on the year-round school.

The "What America Thinks" poll recently took a nationwide sampling and discovered that only five people out of nine favor shorter vacations for children and teachers. It will be interesting to note what changes take place in the near future. The movement is definitely under way. Whether it will gather steam, or be derailed, or move suddenly onto a different track—all this remains to be seen.

Reporting to Parents

Once upon a time, reporting to parents was a simple process conducted a few times each year. On a stiff white card Junior's teacher put down, in numerical or alphabetical form, the marks that he had earned in each subject and in the all-important area of "Deportment." Junior took the card home, received a lecture or a quarter, and brought back a parental signature. Neither the school nor the home conducted any correspondence in the matter. In relation to the standards for his grade, he had passed or failed, and that was that. Seldom was there any other interchange except on the occasions when the principal summoned Junior's parents prior to his possible expulsion, or when the truant officer paid a call.

All is different now, and rightly so. Essentially, the old process was so simple that it was superficial. It failed to recognize the obligations of the school and the home in an adult-controlled world. Junior's chances for success, psychologists pointed out, would be enhanced if his parents and teachers met more often and shared their ideas concerning his unique problems and talents. Mothers who had weaned their infants on Dr. Spock started speaking up at PTA meetings and popping up uninvited at the school. They wanted to know more about the curriculum, the methods, the classification of pupils, and the criterion for those marks on the report cards.

Simultaneously, educators were becoming dissatisfied with the traditional ways of doing things. Progressive education put the emphasis on the child rather than the subjects to be learned. Attention to individual differences, as has been noted earlier in this book, became an important aspect of a teacher's job. Obviously, under this new philosophy the school felt compelled to set up a two-way communication system with the home. Thus, the two groups of adults who supervised most of Junior's activities began to work together for his benefit. Gradually the gulf was crossed, and one of the first bridges was the establishment of a new method for reporting to parents.

The elementary schools took the lead, as they have often done in other areas. The initial attack centered on the numerical system of reporting. Progressive educators claimed that it was splitting hairs to give Mary an 85 and John an 84. They argued that the "numbers game" encouraged guesswork on the part of teachers and invidious comparisons by pupils and parents. The broader base of letters like A-B-C-D, or simpler numbers like 1-2-3-4-5, soon gained acceptance.

But once the wall of tradition had been cracked from the inside, the schools moved farther and farther away from the old report card. A logical extension of the new system was the P-F idea—Passed or Failed. This evolved into S and U—Satisfactory or Unsatisfactory. One possible reason for the demise of the P-F notations is that the two letters look so much alike. A myopic parent might think Junior had passed when he had failed. Indeed, the boy might be tempted to do a little creative writing to transform every F into a P! But the ascendancy of S and U can be better traced to educators' leanings toward euphemisms. Somehow a U sounded less harsh than an F. Besides, it was reasoned that a child could be marked Unsatisfactory and still not be an outright failure.

In the 1930's and 1940's, when the S-U ratings were gaining popularity, another earthquake was taking place in the schools. It, too, stemmed from interest in child psychology and individual differences. The new philosophy was that a child should be encouraged to compete with himself, not with others. Teachers were told to rate each pupil in terms of his I.Q., Reading Index, and the like. If Mary had an I.Q. of 120 and a reading achievement score of 4.3, she was expected to do more and better work than John with his I.Q. of 85 and his second-grade reading ability. It was deemed ridiculous, and even criminal, to expect John to compete on the same track with a highly gifted classmate. Hurdles for him would be set at a different height. If he then made no effort to jump them, he would receive an Unsatisfactory rating.

Naturally, under the self-competitive system, failures were reduced. If a child received a U from a teacher, the parents and the principal might ask: "Weren't your standards too high for him? Was it really his fault? Is his lack of effort possibly the result of your failure to motivate and interest him?" Such questions often put teachers on the defensive. They tended to give Satisfactory ratings on a wholesale basis, partly because they were actually adjusting their methods and materials to the individual pupils. The era of "continous progress" set in. Retardations reached a proportional all-time low in those days. The counterreaction came in the late 1950's, and the entire subject is presently being hotly debated throughout the nation.*

One outgrowth of the mark-him-for-effort epoch was the use of an exponent under the rating on the report card. For example, if a child in the third grade happened to be reading on a second-grade level and was plugging along as well as could be expected, his mark in that subject would be S_2. The only trouble was that some schools failed to communicate to the parents what the little exponent meant. One mother, on seeing the above notation, is said to have exclaimed: "My boy is second in his class!"

Teachers and parents fretted under the S-U yoke. It was so broad that it allowed for no nuances at all. Consequently, what has been facetiously called the IOUS System arrived on the scene. The I stood for Improvement Needed and the O was reserved for pupils who were Outstanding. Thus the old A-B-C-D system appeared in a new guise: O-S-I-U. Educators, in keeping with the trend of the times since the days of Franklin D. Roosevelt, were cooking up an "alphabet soup." Another concoction that evolved featured the use of NI for Needs Improvement. To compound the confusion, under that plan the I rating stood for Improved.

But marks for proficiency in subjects were not the only areas of change. The old Deportment category was expanded and expounded in keeping with psychologists' emphasis on personality development and human relations. Long lists of headings burgeoned on the report card. Parents found out how well their children worked and played with others. Health habits, use of leisure time, and a score of other subdivisions soon received ratings. The schools went hog-wild in their eagerness to communicate.

The proliferation of areas affected both the shape and the size of the report card. It became a two-page affair in many school systems; others developed it into a small booklet of four to six pages. Room

---

* In 1960, the U.S. Office of Education published the results of a nationwide survey on promotional policies. Fewer than 1 per cent of all urban schools were promoting pupils "solely on the basis of group progress." Nine out of ten public elementary schools were using academic achievement either as the major or only factor in deciding whether to move a child up to the next grade. Automatic promotion was definitely on the wane—a fact borne out by an NEA survey during the same year. The NEA research men discovered, however, that 80 per cent of all districts with elementary grades were basing promotions on social and emotional factors, as well as academic achievement.

was allowed for teachers' brief comments in addition to ratings. Since some parents felt the urge to respond, a space for their comments soon appeared. In that connection, many superintendents and principals set up parent-teacher committees to draw up new report cards suitable for their communities. The home-and-school partnership grew ever stronger.

In the 1950's, a reaction against the plethora of items on the report cards caused the rating system to be superseded by teachers' descriptive comments. It was felt that parents were more perplexed than enlightened by the morass of headings. Aside from talking to them directly, the best method of informing them about their children's progress seemed to be a series of statements in sentence form. Marks were regarded as old-fashioned instruments, dependent on the whims of individual teachers and subject to misinterpretation.

Troubles, however, cropped up in the use of the progress reports. In New York City, for example, the elementary-schoolteachers complained that they were spending inordinate amounts of time composing essays four times a year. They also noted that even carefully prepared paragraphs were misconstrued or resented by parents. Another by-product of the written report was the problem of circumlocution. Teachers were given scrupulous instructions on how to inform a parent that his child might be a kleptomaniac or an incipient schizophrenic, without using abstruse language on the one hand or making blunt accusations on the other. Many a principal conducted several faculty meetings on the how-to-say-it topic and then personally read each report before it was released to the parents.

It should be added that in cities like New York the progress reports ran into another snag—the Spanish-speaking parent. Thousands of teachers and principals struggled with the problem of how to tell a *madre* that the work of her *muchacho* could not exactly be classified as *muy bien*. A manual for Spanish expressions helped considerably, but a great deal of the burden fell on the shoulders of bilingual teachers.

Cursive reports obviously could not provide the final answer. Although they originally had the virtue of giving the parents a thoughtful review of their children's talents and problems, they soon deteriorated into exercises in intricate or banal phraseology, or they smacked too much of psychoanalysis. Therefore, a few schoolmen decided to take the alternate step of dropping all written reports and ratings in favor of face-to-face interviews with parents.

Today the parent-teacher conference is regarded as the best

method of reporting on pupils' progress. It is not the only method, nor will it ever be, because there is always a core of parents who are either unable or unwilling to come to school or converse on the phone. In a recent bulletin* the NEA Research Division notes that the trend at all school levels is toward the practice of supplementing report cards with conferences. A parallel tendency is to increase the number of reports per year. Only 0.5 per cent of senior high schools send home reports as infrequently as two or three times a year. The figure for junior high schools is 1.2 per cent, and for elementary schools it is 2.4 per cent.

In many elementary schools, the practice is to employ one system for reporting the progress of kindergarten children and another for pupils in the grades. Naturally, there is less formality and more dependence on oral reports in communicating with mothers of kindergarteners. It should also be observed that many of the changes discussed above were originally tried out at the kindergarten level. In some instances, those changes were then brought up only as far as the first three grades. In other cases, they were effected up to and beyond the sixth grade.

To summarize, the present theory is that parents should be informed as often and as completely as possible about *what* and *how* their children are doing at school. American Education Week, or Open School Week, has become a nation-wide institution. Personal talks with parents are supplementing written rating and descriptions. The rigid, unfriendly report of the past has been transformed or discarded. Junior may still do poorly in school, but his failure is not likely to be the result of adult apathy at home or in school.

Gifted Children

When the Russians put that initial satellite into the sky on October 4, 1957, they unwittingly brought to a head all the criticisms of our schools that had been seething slightly below the surface for a few decades. It was a rude shock to most Americans to realize that we were not first in everything. Where were our scientists and mathematicians? What was wrong with our teachers that they had let such a terrible thing happen? Were they neglecting our gifted youngsters?

Immediately, a host of educators rushed to their own defense. Russian superiority in the space race had nothing to do with our school system, they claimed. We had many well-trained scientists to

* The bulletin referred to is called *Reports on Pupil Progress and Elementary School Promotion Policies:* December, 1960.

do the job. The real trouble was that the government had not allotted enough money to get our satellite program off the ground.

Regardless of who was right, the fact remains that the American people were afraid for the first time that we had a "gifted student program lag" as well as a "missile lag." Nobody had paid much attention, in 1948, when a U.S. Office of Education survey noted that only a handful of schools were providing special education for the gifted and that the number of classes for them ranked far behind those for the crippled and mentally retarded. Now, however, citizens rubbed their eyes and started to point fingers as schoolmen immediately went into action to take up the slack.

The Conant Report on the American High Schools drove the point home. Talented teenagers were electing snap courses; hundreds of high schools were conducting substandard programs that gave young people inadequate preparation for college; we were putting far too much emphasis on sports and too little on scholarship.

Critics of the Progressives had a field day. Whether they beclouded the issue is a moot question. One of the most resounding blows came from Teachers College at Columbia University, of all places! President John H. Fischer (1910–   ) threw his weight against the child-centered school and urged educators to "give priority to intellectual competence." Another shot was fired in 1960 by a group of professors who had made a survey of the San Francisco schools. They stressed that the "purpose of education is to inform the mind and develop intelligence." Simultaneously, they insinuated that the schools were downgrading standards in order to accommodate subnormal children. This raised a hue and cry from the Commission of Educational Policy of the California Teachers Association. Chiding the professors for weakening democracy by attempting to freeze educational goals, that group supported "multiple-purpose" schools set up to prepare youngsters for college, to help them to hold a job, or "even to drive an automobile safely."

On the national front, Vice-Admiral H. G. Rickover (1900–   ) recommended early segregation of the talented child from the average, and a much "tougher" curriculum. Deriding the schools for their courses in "cooking and canasta," he warned that Russia's real threat to the United States would come "through their educational and not through their military processes." In his attacks on the "educationists" he was supported by the Council for Basic Education, a group with headquarters at Washington, D.C. Our schools were too soft, the C.B.

E. claimed; life adjustment programs and "frills and fads" should be eliminated.

As the controversy raged through the nation, certain facts emerged. Only one of every seven high school students was studying a modern language. Worse yet, about 40 per cent of those who entered college never finished. On the latter subject, Professor George Weigand (1917–) of the University of Maryland reiterated an old charge. "Study skills should be taught in the high school," he said, "but they aren't. Some private prep schools have courses in how to study, but you will find them in only a handful of public schools." Professor Weigand noted that half the college drop-outs possessed the tools—intelligence and ambition—but had never been taught how to use them.

Meanwhile, the schools were making a concerted drive to atone for their sins. At first, the rush was toward bigger and better programs in science and mathematics, but the proponents of the humanities protested immediately that a well-rounded person needed to be versed in literature, languages, and the like. Early in the 1960's the Ford Foundation backed their cause by awarding a ten-year grant of $5,670,000 to aid scholars working in nonscientific fields. Eventually most schoolmen agreed that it was not an either-or situation; training in both the sciences and the humanities was essential for the gifted.

The new emphasis produced a flood of literature. In addition to many textbooks and articles on the subject, reports were issued by various groups. The Rockefeller Brothers Fund came out with "The Pursuit of Excellence," and President Eisenhower's Commission on National Goals published its findings in 1960. Both groups were led by John W. Gardner (1912–), president of the Carnegie Corporation of New York. "Education," said Mr. Gardner, "has become a centrally important activity in our national life." He recommended "either a separate Department of Education at Cabinet level or a National Education Foundation."

Gardner's reports are still being discussed enthusiastically. Administrators approve his ideas on upgrading professional standards; teachers acclaim his plea for higher salaries; and laymen cheer his emphasis on minimum goals, high priority for the subject of reading, and intensive reappraisal of the entire curriculum. All agree with his statement that the greatest problem is not to recommend goals but to get action.

In the interests of action the NEA has been conducting a project on the *Academically Talented Student,* financed by Gardner's Carnegie Corporation. Since 1958, at least twelve publications have emanated from that group. Several of them deal with specific programs in such subject areas as science, foreign languages, social studies, mathematics, and English—all aimed at the education of the bright child.

Action has been taken, too, by boards of education. At present more than 75 per cent of the city school systems have special classes for talented secondary school students, and almost 70 per cent of the urban elementary schools have programs for the gifted. In the latter case, however, it should be pointed out that many of the programs are merely experiments with conversational approaches to modern languages. Akron, Ohio, is one of the exceptions. In that city a well-organized foreign language program begins at the fifth-year level and continues through high school.

It is also true that in the rush to provide special instruction for the gifted, some schools have not bothered to make certain necessary distinctions. Actually, there are all types of "gifted" children. Roughly speaking, their talents fall into three categories: academic aptitudes, creativity, and leadership. Although some fortunate youngsters excel in all three areas, a great number are outstanding in only one. It is a halfway measure, therefore, to set up one program for all talented children. The budding musician who has no proclivity whatsoever toward science needs a different type of handling from the mathematical genius with a high I.Q. And the well-liked boy who is running for president of the student council, but is not particularly brilliant or creative, needs another kind of program to suit his talents.

To underscore this point, many business executives confess that they hated school and some even proudly declare that they never finished high school. A study by Dr. Victor H. Goertzel (1914–   ), president of the National Association for Gifted Children, bears this out. With the assistance of his wife, Dr. Goertzel has been looking into the childhood adjustments of 500 celebrities. He notes that such gifted people as Mark Twain, Grover Cleveland, Winston Churchill, and scores of others disliked school and misbehaved in the classroom. Obviously there has always been a problem in meeting the peculiar needs of the talented nonconformist. But many believe that the schools can do so, if they overhaul their conventional programs and set up challenges for creative thinkers. It is claimed, for instance, that educators put too much store on I.Q. tests, thus depreciating the truly creative child who becomes so bored by these examinations that he does poorly in them.

Johnson O'Connor (1891–   ), the well-known specialist in aptitude testing, has some interesting observations on the "brilliant failure." In studies conducted at the Massachusetts Institute of Technology, he and his aides discovered that students' success increased as the number of strong aptitudes went up, until a maximum of four or five was reached. After that, they had increasing difficulty. "The nine-aptitude man almost never graduates," O'Connor declares. His theory is that the seeds of later failure are planted early in school when "the child who succeeds easily at everything is highly praised and never learns to work." Perhaps, too, the difficulty is due to the pull of so many interests in so many different directions on the proverbial jack-of-all-trades.

Thus, the problem of providing special education for the gifted is most complicated. Very few public school systems have ever met this challenge adequately. At best, they have settled for either of two broad answers—acceleration or enrichment. In actual practice neither method has ever been completely satisfactory.

Skipping a bright child to the next grade does have some obvious advantages, but the practice is often dangerous. Not only does it create gaps in a child's learning, but it also puts a premium on speed and superficiality rather than on depth of scholarship. Another defect of this system is that the child who is skipped two or three times finds himself in a classroom with older pupils whose interests and social attitudes are far different from his, thus steering him toward pseudo-sophistication or super-shyness. For this reason, some school systems permit a child to skip no more than one grade in his school career.

One variation of the acceleration plan has become popular at the college level. The program known as Advanced Placement is operated by the College Entrance Examination Board. More than 400 colleges and universities are offering gifted students the chance to skip college work that they have already covered in high school, or at summer school, or on their own initiative. Examinations are given by the Education Testing Service in this project which was originally piloted by the Ford Foundation. In 1960–61 approximately 13,000 students from 1,200 high schools took 17,500 tests. Some universities have granted some students as much as a full year of credit.

The alternate, as noted above, is enrichment. Under this system the gifted child presumably plunges deeply into each subject at his grade level, or he receives instruction in areas above and beyond the regular curriculum for his age group. However, there are some schools that glibly talk about "enrichment" when they are merely piling on more homework or giving talented pupils extra arithmetic problems to solve at their desks. In small communities, genuine enrichment programs are difficult to work out because low enrollments do not permit flexibility in grouping. Also, in some cities the program is set up for clusters of academic scholars rather than for creative students or young leaders.

Another danger has sprung up from enrichment programs that provide young children with instruction in areas usually reserved for older students. For example, some talented eighth graders are now studying calculus and epistemology. When such a step is taken, articulation with the higher grades is needed. Otherwise, the child merely repeats what he has already learned. Such articulation can possibly be worked out in a single school system, but one wonders how it can extend to the various colleges that the gifted students will eventually attend.

Perhaps teaching machines and the new laboratories will supply some of the answers to the question of how to provide for the gifted. Perhaps, too, some of the recent curricular experiments will furnish clues. For example, the project started by the American Institute of Biological Sciences may lead indirectly to discoveries of better ways to teach talented students. The education committee of that important organization in 1959 established the Biological Sciences Curriculum Study, with the purpose of improving education in that subject and raising students' comprehension of science in general. Three new versions of secondary school courses were prepared by a group of 60 experts led by professors, editors, and high school teachers of biology. The materials were pre-tested on students from Boulder High School in Colorado. At present the courses are being given to 14,000 students in 107 schools.

The important point about the above experiment is that it presumes nothing. Its director, Dr. Arnold B. Grobman (1918–   ), states: "No one knows today what will be the best general approach at the high school level." He also observes: "It remains to be seen how different students—the average, the slow, and the gifted—can best be taught." In this spirit of inquiry, three different approaches are being tried (the biochemical, the genetic, and the ecological), and fifteen testing centers have been established throughout the nation. An incidental but significant outcome of the entire project is that it unites university professors, high school teachers, and research men in a common endeavor—a rarity in these days of sniping back and forth from one level or discipline to another.

But no program for any type of student, gifted or otherwise, will ever succeed unless it is placed in the hands of a good teacher. From this point of view, the outlook is not bright. One-fourth of the nation's elementary schoolteachers are not college graduates. Moreover, approximately half of the secondary schoolteachers are giving instruction "out of license"; that is, they are teaching subjects for which they have not been certified or which had not been their majors in college. Finally, despite the recent increase of students in teacher-training institutions, the number of new teachers has not kept pace with zooming enrollments of pupils.

Even if all of our teachers were fully qualified, only a small percentage of them would have the superlative personal characteristics, high intelligence, and wide background needed to help gifted children fulfill their potential. Some reputed reasons for this situation are the low salaries of teachers and the American public's lack of esteem for the profession. Although teachers' salaries have risen almost 50 per cent since 1949, it is commonly known that the cream of the college crop still goes out into other fields.

A suburb of Los Angeles furnishes a good illustration of how gifted children are being cheated because their instructors are not superior people. Recently, the school district board of that community heard testimony from a dozen talented high school graduates who complained that their training had not properly equipped them for college. One boy, a former A-student, asked: "Of what use is it to have a teacher not prepared for the course—who is one chapter ahead of us in the book? We read two chapters and we're one ahead of the teacher who is supposed to teach us." A girl, whose grades in high school had also been outstanding, complained: "In my three years I had only three instructors whom I considered to be real teachers who challenged me, made me want to learn, increased my intellectual curiosity."

That girl's experience is duplicated in schools all over the country. In fact, some would say that she was fortunate to have had as many as three top teachers. Sometimes, however, the problem is attributable more to mass education than to the alleged inferiority of teachers. Even the best teacher has a difficult time challenging each of 30 bright youngsters and providing for their individual talents. To compound the difficulty, administrators often boost the registers of their "fast" classes to the vicinity of 40 so that the teachers of the slow children in the same grade will have fewer problems to deal with. The theory is that bright children are not so emotionally distressed or potentially obstreperous as their dull compeers. Principals have an easy time getting staff members to volunteer to teach children with high I.Q.'s, but only a few teachers ask for the retarded pupils. Hence the compensation of smaller enrollments is offered to those who eventually take the subnormal classes.

The intrinsic handicaps under which mass education is laboring were recently brought to the attention of the public by a celebrated court case in New Jersey. The West Windsor Township Board of Education had brought suit against a local doctor and his wife because the couple had refused to send their children to school. Instead, they were educating the youngsters at home by means of courses from a correspondence school. The defense proved that the three children were marvelously gifted, especially in music, and three years ahead of their age level in scholastic achievement. The couple claimed that public schools cannot help but place a ceiling on the academic growth of pupils, but their chief plea was that they had provided at least the "equivalent" of a classroom education for their prodigies. In a decision that may yet have many repercussions, the court upheld their defense.

The above-mentioned children are of elementary school age, but in regard to the instruction of high school students the U.S. Office of Education has focused on another hindrance to teachers, namely, teenage mores. A study made recently by that Office indicates that teenagers are avid status seekers in their own society. Boys consider success in studies as less important than proficiency in athletics. Girls put the greatest store in attractiveness to boys and in student activities. The brightest girls deliberately shy away from academic excellence because it may lower their popularity ratings with the boys. To put it succinctly, members of both sexes prefer to be known as "good eggs" rather than as "eggheads." Moreover, they are less interested in parental approbation than in the approval of their classmates.

The study, entitled *Social Climates in High School*, further discovered that the tendency of teenagers to revolt against the reward-and-punishment controls of adults is more prevalent in upper middle-class suburbs than in rural towns or lower income city neighborhoods. Hence it is likely that anti-intellectual pressures will increase because of the continuing build-up of suburban areas.

Questions for educators and parents are raised by this report.

Are coeducational high schools detrimental rather than beneficial? Should the present rating system be abolished or modified so that it is controlled more by the adolescents themselves than by the adults whose authority they resist? Should there be more academic competition on a team basis, just as in athletics? Should interscholastic rivalry be developed among the "brains" as well as the "brawns"? Finally, should teachers make use of more games in classroom instruction?

Some educators maintain that we overemphasize the development of gifted teenagers at the expense of concentration on talented children in the lower grades. Their theory is that early identification and development of top pupils will provide such momentum that they will be carried over the high school hurdle with relative ease. Much of this latent talent is overlooked, they claim, because the children come from underprivileged homes. But if a real effort were made in the primary grades, or even earlier, to seek out these "diamonds in the rough," then a great mine of previously untapped giftedness would enrich our nation.*

The NEA ties up the early-identification idea with the movement toward guidance counseling at the elementary school level. Their recent 144-page report, entitled *Guidance for the Academically Talented Student,* recommends a program built around a strong guidance system in the entire school. Among the chief goals of the program are the development of good work habits, the inculcation of self-esteem, and the raising of levels of aspiration. In this connection the report adds that some schools may have to overcome poor social attitudes toward the role of women in order to enable talented girls to set proper objectives for themselves.

One of the many elementary schools attempting to carry out the kind of program that will bring out the best in children at an early stage is the much discussed Amidon School at Washington, D.C. There a real effort is being made to give the children a basic education and yet retain the best features of the progressive schools. Reading starts with phonics in the first grade; writing is stressed throughout; formal grammar is introduced in the fourth grade; geography deals with specific places; and history is taught in chronological order. The "progressive" side of the program is found mainly in an emphasis on problem-solving in all areas rather than on rote learning. Whether the Amidon School program is merely a return to the traditional

* For further details on this topic, see "Higher Horizons," the section that immediately follows this one.

methods of the past or whether it will really provide a new blueprint, especially for those interested in the education of bright children, will take many years to discover. Results, it must be remembered, are not measured in scholastic achievement alone—good or bad—but in social and emotional adjustment and in eventual competency as an adult.

Generally speaking, the tendency today is to toughen up the educational process and to begin instruction earlier. Bright three-year-olds, we are told, should be taught how to read. Conversational foreign language, as has been previously noted, has been added to the curriculum in many elementary schools. And a recent experiment conducted in four Massachusetts school districts under the leadership of Boston University's Center for Economic Education is alleged to have proved that elementary school pupils, even first graders, can learn economics!

But there are many educators who still believe that the presentation of more difficult subject matter is only a small part of the program needed by gifted children. They maintain that the teacher's most important function is to instill in the pupils an avid desire to learn *away from school* as well as in the classroom. They warn that in seizing on "new" ideas we may really be clutching at old straws that were proved worthless in the past, or that we may be discarding an essentially good program which has not been given a fair chance to live up to its actual potential.

In truth, the whole issue may boil down to a question of goals. Naturally, everyone would like to see the academically talented child fulfill his potential in terms of knowledge and social adjustment. But a school may not be able to achieve the first goal to the maximum if it also tries for the second. Should it, therefore, reduce its efforts in the area of life adjustment or cast this goal out entirely? If so, will the parents be willing and able to fill in the resulting vacuum? Will democratic ideals be sacrificed in the effort to produce millions of highly skilled and cultured scholars? These are some of the quandaries that confront educators as they look for new and better ways to teach talented children.

Finally, to put the problem in its true perspective, it should be recalled that gifted children are part of one large category known as *exceptional children*. Under this heading come the blind, the deaf, the mentally retarded, the orthopedically handicapped, and the like. Public school figures released in 1958 by the U.S. Office of Education showed that for every mentally gifted child enrolled in a special class or school, there were four mentally retarded children (with I.Q.'s below 75) who had been so placed. Of course, a great number of schools have been assigning their talented children to high sections of regular grades, but this kind of grouping is much less drastic than the establishment of a program of special education for them. In other words, the philosophy in the past has been to siphon off the mentally retarded much more than the mentally gifted. If the new trend in educational practices continues, this discrepancy will eventually disappear.

Higher Horizons

The dream of Thomas Jefferson and other early patriots has materialized in the country they founded. Theoretically, every child in the United States is now entitled to twelve years of free education, largely supported by revenue from taxes collected in his community and state. In September, 1961, public school enrollment climbed to an all-time high of more than 38,000,000 children, and enrollment in non-public schools leaped to almost 7,000,000—a new record.*

Those Americans who realize that our nation's strength and freedom will depend on the skills and knowledge of its future adults are delighted by the above figures. Simultaneously, however, they have awakened to the fact that underneath the mass of rosy statistics is a layer of grim truths. In an era when a college education is considered so important, only half of our high school graduates go on to some form of higher learning. No less disturbing, 20 per cent of those in the upper quarter of their class drop out of high school, and 40 per cent of those who do go on to college fail to graduate.

This appalling waste of talent has several causes, but one of the chief factors is environment. In a predominantly urban civilization, children from "culturally disadvantaged" homes often fail to fulfill their true potential. Their uneducated parents struggle along only a notch or two above the subsistence level. Homes are barren of books, and travel beyond the fringes of the slum-jungle is rare. Legions of these youngsters come from broken homes or live with aunts and grandmothers. Lacking security and affection, they sometimes become so emotionally upset that they cannot concentrate on classwork. Caught in a vicious circle, they leave school to take menial jobs as early as the law allows. A high school diploma is a prize indeed, and college is out of the question. They have neither the money nor the

* All but 6 per cent of the nation's school-age youth were enrolled in schools in 1961.

desire for such a luxury, regardless of how inherently gifted they may be.

In various cities throughout the country, special programs for such children have been established. Educators are no longer content to point to vocational courses and watered-down versions of the academic curriculum as the only solutions. Results of non-verbal I.Q. tests have proved to them that thousands of students previously regarded as intrinsically slow really have the brains to succeed in high school and even in college. Therefore, a movement to do something more for these young people is sweeping the nation. In part, it has been spurred by Negro leaders because that group, along with the Puerto Ricans, has suffered from so much deprivation. Their arguments make good sense: the schools have the moral obligation to make up for the gap created by society as a whole; furthermore, since tragic and costly juvenile delinquency goes hand in hand with failure at school, lives and money will be saved by "success programs," and simultaneously the nation's professional manpower pools will be considerably enlarged.

The project that has won the most kudos is New York City's Higher Horizons program, directed until recently by Daniel Schreiber (1909–   ). This experiment now serves about 12,500 pupils in 52 elementary schools and 13 junior high schools. Its aim is to raise the educational and vocational sights of all students—bright, average, or slow—so that each can achieve at a level commensurate with his native ability.

In the 1959–60 school year, Higher Horizons concentrated on children in the third and seventh grades. Extra guidance counselors and special teachers were supplied to the schools in the project. The counselors worked with individual children and groups; they set up hundreds of interviews with parents and various kinds of workshops; they contacted dozens of outside agencies for help. The special teachers gave remedial instruction to pupils and demonstration lessons to teachers; they arranged for extra trips, drew up helpful materials, conducted testing programs, and made available audio-visual aids.

Has Higher Horizons succeeded? The results, in terms of academic achievement, are still incomplete. But the outlook is very promising. Schreiber has this to say: "The children's attitude toward learning has become more positive. For both parents and children, education has apparently become more important. Principals and teachers report that discipline in the halls and classrooms has improved, and vandalism has decreased. The change in pupil attitude has diminished tensions for the teacher. Since less time must be devoted to discipline, more time and energy are available for instruction."

Schreiber also notes that attendance of parents at meetings has skyrocketed. One school, with a third grade register of 250, drew 150 parents to an afternoon meeting. In addition to a corps of teacher aides furnished by the Public Education Association, individual parents have volunteered to take small groups of children on trips on Saturdays and Sundays.

Higher Horizons is an outgrowth of a six-year pilot project started in 1956 at Junior High School 43, Manhattan, when Schreiber was the principal there. Called the Demonstration Guidance Project, its original aim was to identify able students, build their self-esteem, arouse their interest in schoolwork, and guide them into college channels. The Board of Education's Committee on Integration gave impetus to the idea, with some financial support from the National Scholarship Service and Fund for Negro Students (called Nessfeness), and the College Entrance Examination Board.

Junior High School 43 was an excellent choice for the experiment. Not only was it headed by an able and experienced principal; it also had a pupil population suited to the purpose of the project's originators. Located on West 129th Street and Amsterdam Avenue, the school was attended by many culturally deprived children whose normal procedure was to seek employment at age 16 regardless of their talents. Of the 1400 students, 48 per cent were Negroes and 40 per cent were of Spanish-speaking background. With the exception of a few Orientals, the rest were whites stemming from a wide variety of European nationalities.

When the project began, three guidance counselors and four teachers of remedial reading and arithmetic were added to the staff. In addition, a psychologist and a social worker were hired on a part-time basis. A battery of tests was administered, and teachers were asked to rate students in terms of their college potential. Approximately one half of the student body was judged to have sufficient academic potentiality to be included in the experiment. It was discovered, incidentally, through non-verbal tests, that the median I.Q. of the school was 100—not 80, as previously administered group verbal tests had indicated. This new knowledge gave the teachers good reason to expect more from their pupils and encouraged them to make an all-out effort from the very start.

To raise the cultural level of the students, teachers escorted them to places like the Metropolitan Opera House, Carnegie Hall, college campuses, art galleries, and atomic laboratories. Money supplied by the supporting agencies was used to help defray the cost of these trips.

As the project gathered momentum, the attack proceeded on many fronts. Teachers were given special courses in reading methods and in techniques for improving speech patterns of children. Daytime and evening meetings kept parents informed and roused their enthusiasm. Those who could not attend were visited by the social worker or a guidance counselor. Voluntary classes for extra help to students weak in mathematics were set up before and after school. Every class received information about various careers, especially the professions. Through photographs and charts, students were shown how distinguished men and women from different ethnic groups had achieved success and had contributed to social progress. In short, every effort was made to keep the goals of the project constantly before the faculty, the students, and the community.

Most of the graduates of Junior High School 43 attend George Washington High School. Therefore, that school was included in the project, and a continuation of the intensive drive toward higher aspirations and achievement levels was effected there. Double periods in English were organized; registers in mathematics and foreign languages were limited to 15; class size was restricted to 25, and tutoring was given to small groups after school. The program of trips was expanded, and special guidance facilities were set up for the graduates of Junior High School 43.

So great was the progress that in two and one-half years the project students gained four years in reading growth, and the drop-out rate was cut in half. Moreover, five times as many of Schreiber's graduates passed all their subjects at the high school as had their older brothers and sisters in pre-project days. Finally, the students reversed the usual I.Q. pattern of children from culturally deprived backgrounds. Instead of losing ground over a period of four years, from 1955 to 1959, they actually showed an increase on the Otis Mental Ability Tests.

Perhaps the best criterion for such a project is the change in the attitudes of the students. On this subject, Henry T. Hillson (1908–), principal of George Washington High School, offers some interesting testimony.

"In the past, the students from '43' were our worst behaved. More teacher and administrative time was spent on them than on any other group. Since we had the project group this has changed. Not a single student in the project group has been reported to the dean's office for discipline. All are attentive in class, even in those cases where the subject matter seems to be too difficult for them. Today, they are our best behaved."

The success of the Demonstration Guidance Project prompted New York City school authorities to expand the program in 1959, and Higher Horizons was born. The Ford Foundation recently donated a million dollars to begin similar programs in Chicago, Philadelphia, Detroit, Pittsburgh, St. Louis, and Milwaukee. The NEA has also thrown its support to the idea, and in 1961 Schreiber left New York City to conduct a nationwide program. His place was taken by another outstanding principal, Jacob Landers (1912–   ).

If Higher Horizons proves nothing else, it does show that a number of "culturally disadvantaged" students can overcome most of their handicaps through special emphasis on guidance, remedial work, trips, and the like. The program also reveals the importance of early identification of talented pupils and the need to enlist the cooperation of their families. It has been estimated that the project costs an extra $50 per student each year, a sum that seems small in relation to the rewards it brings.

Some educators maintain that any well-run school, given the same help as those in Higher Horizons, can come up with similar results. This may be true, but it cannot be denied that the program has served to point the way toward a reappraisal of the role of the school in society. In an age when critics clamor that teachers are trying to do too much, the people behind Higher Horizons seem to answer that *far too little* has been done in the recent past.

Dean John Monro (1897–   ) of Harvard College is one of the ardent champions of programs like Higher Horizons. But he chides the colleges for not doing enough at their end. He suggests that they scour the "submerged" schools for academic talent with the same fervor as football coaches.* Scholarships, he thinks, should be given only to poor but brainy students, and not to the offspring of the affluent.

Dean Monro puts his finger on a problem that may grow more intense as the Higher Horizons idea develops and expands. At present, approximately 50,000 potential college graduates drop out of high school each year. It is argued that if these students were given

* There are about 26,500 high schools in the United States. Of these, approximately 5,000 produce 82 per cent of all our college students.

the inspiration and enlightenment necessary for them to go on to higher education, they might still be frustrated because of financial considerations.

If such were the case, then the proverbial half a loaf might be worse than none. But some educators hold that the National Defense Education Act of 1958 provides a partial answer to the problem. They note that loans up to $1,000 a year are available to needy but able students for science, mathematics, or language study. They also point out that pessimistic predictions about the acceptance of such loans have not proved true. For example, in 1960 a total of 115,450 students borrowed an average amount of $437 each.

The counter argument is that the N.D.E.A. does not go far enough and that we should do more than ask a struggling student to mortgage his future. Certainly, in the years to come, the whole area of scholarships and loans for the indigent (whether they come through a Higher Horizons program or not) will be a topic for consideration in all countries devoted to democratic ideals. This point is underscored by the fact that 43 per cent of our high school graduates in 1961 enrolled in college courses leading to a degree—an increase of 6 per cent over the number in 1960. The movement toward higher aspirational levels in this nation is apparently gathering tremendous momentum.

Teacher Aides

Any principal will attest that faculty morale is the most important key to the success of a school program. If morale is low, then instruction suffers because teachers put out only a minimum of effort. Further, the greatest reason for low morale is not a poor salary schedule but an overload of clerical work. Teachers resent nothing more than the dozens of tedious chores that assail them every day. Countless jobs like collecting milk money, checking attendance sheets, and setting up equipment drain their energy and take away valuable time that could be used for the improvement of learning.

One way to solve the problem can possibly be traced to the old monitorial schools discussed earlier in this book. It is certainly evident in the time-honored use of laboratory assistants for teachers of science. Essentially the idea is to hire an intelligent but non-certified person to act as the teacher's aide. Throughout the year this person, usually working on a part-time basis, performs a thousand and one services, ranging from menial tasks to reviews of skills and facts already learned by the pupils.

Probably the most publicized project in the use of teacher aides is the one conducted at Bay City, Michigan. The Ford Foundation's Fund for the Advancement of Education supported this experiment, which began in 1953 and has since spread to scores of other communities in Michigan and elsewhere. The original thought behind the plan was to find a solution to the problem of the increasing enrollment of pupils and the decreasing supply of teachers. But non-teaching duties came in for consideration, too, when school authorities discovered that at least 26 per cent of a teacher's time was being consumed by those chores.

In the beginning, Bay City hired only eight aides from a list of 64 names suggested by PTA officers and other leading citizens. A high school diploma and an enthusiastic attitude toward children were high on the list of criteria set up by the officials. As it happened, some of the candidates for the $45-per-week jobs turned out to be talented in such areas as music and art. This extra dividend paid off as the program developed.

Bay City increased its class size from 30 to 45 when the teacher-aide program was introduced. Thus, the Board of Education spent approximately the same amount of money as in the pre-aide days. Reports from that community indicate that both pupils and teachers are happy with the new system.

One of the values of the teacher-aide program is that it provides a wholesome outlet for educated housewives who are bored by the wash-dust-and-cook routine. Most of them are unable to take full-time positions but welcome the chance to spend a few hours each day away from their homes. In an era when we hear about our nation's terrible waste of womanpower, the use of teacher aides can supply a partial answer. In fact, some of the present aides have been encouraged to continue their interrupted education and receive certification as full-fledged teachers.

But the aide idea has not yet been accepted on a wide scale. Some teachers and parents have worried lest the use of noncertified persons might jeopardize professional standards or cause penny-pinching authorities to raise the size of classes and keep salaries at low levels. Also, the argument has been advanced that the employment of an aide separates the teacher from her pupils. The reasoning is that she can develop better relationships with individual pupils by helping them with routine tasks.

The use of aides to supervise pupils in school lunchrooms, however, has been welcomed by teachers. These workers are called noon mothers, dining-room aides, lunch matrons, and the like. Housewives, parents, and college students are employed for this job in various communities. In a few cases, they are in complete charge of the lunchroom. Their pay, according to the Research Division of the NEA, varies from $1.05 to $3 an hour, and sometimes includes free lunches.*

Less than 3 per cent of the school districts reporting to the NEA said that they used such aides in 1958–59, but the idea continues to catch on because of the protests of elementary school teachers who are given little or no chance to eat lunch. Five states—California, Illinois, Ohio, Massachusetts, and Pennsylvania—have laws which enable classroom teachers to get a duty-free minimum lunch period. In 1961, New York City adopted a plan to provide aides who would relieve elementary schoolteachers of the burden of supervising lunchrooms.

A number of the school districts that employ lunchroom aides give them manuals prescribing the type of dress they will wear, the safety rules they must follow, and the duties they are expected to perform. In some cases, candidates are asked to sign a loyalty oath and receive a chest X-ray. A few districts require the lunchroom worker to have had leadership experience, especially with children.

Another use of aides that most teachers have applauded relates to the correction of homework papers. The Conant Report showed that the problem was particularly acute for English teachers. Burdened with large pupil loads, most of them were assigning and correcting very few themes. There were not enough hours in the week for them to fulfill this aspect of their jobs. The solution was either to hire more English teachers, or to employ aides. The first solution becomes ridiculous if the facts are reviewed. About one-third of the English teachers in the nation are "emergency" people who do not meet minimum requirements. Also, approximately half of our English teachers did not major in that subject while at college. Moreover, the situation promises to be twice as bad before 1965 because of the large increase in high school enrollments. Apparently the better way to face the problem, at present, is to hire people to read and rate the students' essays.

Here again the Ford Foundation has stepped into the picture. After trying out the "reader" idea in two cities in the 1957–58 school year, the Ford people extended their grants to 16 cities in 1961. The experiments included six high schools in Chicago and four in Detroit. Also by 1961, more than 100 other communities had adopted the plan.

* These figures are taken from the NEA Research Bulletin: Dec., 1960

In all cases, the response from applicants has been enthusiastic and overwhelming. Dr. Paul Diederich (1906–   ), one of the leaders of the movement, states: "Even when schools have been able to pay them only fifty or sixty dollars a month, there have always been at least five times as many qualified applicants as jobs in every community I have studied."

Among the qualifications that Dr. Diederich lists are: a college degree, a good background in English, and the ability to pass four different exams—verbal intelligence, paper-grading, paper-correcting, and an essay test of writing ability. He looks forward to the day when these aides will also be employed to supervise students' readings, to give weekly tests on self-correcting exercises (a variation of the teaching-machine idea), and to discuss the items missed by the students.

All in all, there seems to be a place for teacher aides in the future of our public schools. It is difficult to predict the various roles they will play and the extent to which their services will be used. But at present it is reasonable to expect that the idea will eventually be accepted in one form or other throughout the land.

School Buildings Today

"A school," said Oscar Wilde, "should be the most beautiful place in every town and village—so beautiful that the punishment for undutiful children should be that they should be debarred from going to school the following day."

Anyone who has traveled through the United States since World War II will attest that Oscar Wilde's dream is materializing. On every side the forbidding "egg-crate" structures of the past are being replaced by attractive modern buildings of various shapes and sizes. Local communities have been approving bond issues and consenting to higher taxes to build better and more beautiful school plants. Approximately half of the nation's children are now being taught in postwar buildings, and the prospect for a continuation of the boom in school construction is great.

But the era of lavish allotments for individual school buildings is at an end. Taxed beyond reasonable expectations, the public has recently reacted against "palaces" for children. Citizens are inquiring whether certain construction is necessary, whether a gymnasium or large auditorium is really required, and whether unnecessary frills can be omitted. Boards of education are comparing the cost per square foot of a proposed new plant with the national median of $16. In this connection a recent survey by the United States Bureau of Labor Statistics has revealed that the average elementary school costs $370,000 and has 15 classrooms costing $24,800 each. The average high school is much more expensive; its cost is $1,433,000 for 32 classrooms, each of which is built for $44,300. Approximately 56 per cent of the construction contract goes into materials.

It should be pointed out, however, that there is a wide variation in costs depending on the location of a community and the year in which a building is constructed. The only valid comparisons are those made with costs of schools built in the same year in nearby localities. Even then, technical problems and other hidden factors may cause great differences in outlay. For example, three similar elementary schools recently constructed in adjoining communities in New Jersey had a spread of several hundred thousand dollars. One was built on rocky soil that necessitated the blasting of boulders; the second was erected on swampland that had to be filled in; the third, and cheapest, was constructed on good farmland.

As a result of the growing concern about costs, school officials presently are stressing economy in construction. This has given rise to much greater use of standardized parts, laminated wood, aluminum, plastics, prefabricated materials, "demountable" buildings, and even portable classrooms. Los Angeles, for example, has more than 3,000 portable units that ease the pressure on overcrowded schools or temporarily solve the problem of sudden shifts of population. Such standard-size classrooms cost $3000–$6000 apiece, with electrical heating and cooling. The expense of moving them is almost negligible.

Another outcome of the economy trend is the renewed interest in the multi-purpose room. Under this plan, a gymnasium may also serve as a cafeteria or an auditorium; any other combination that is desirable and feasible may be employed. New terms like "cafenasium" or "cafetorium" have been coined to describe such rooms. Certainly they cut down on costs, but they can cause serious difficulties for the professional and janitorial staff of a school. One New York City principal whose new school contained a multi-purpose room complained of the constant moving of equipment in and out. "All we do," she said, "is play not-so-musical chairs!"

One answer to the cafeteria problem in elementary schools is to eliminate this costly space altogether. Instead, food carts carry hot lunches to the children in their classrooms. On the high school level, the enormous, noisy cafeteria of the past seems to be on the way out.

Many new schools divide this area into several different sections for small groups. The long tables have been supplanted by smaller ones of normal size.

The trend, in fact, has been away from bigness in the construction of schools, especially at the elementary level. Smaller buildings, it is reasoned, do not frighten the children and can be more smoothly run. Also, because the fire risk is lessened, the insurance rates are decreased.

Sometimes, for the sake of economy, auditoriums and gymnasiums are not included in the plans for new schools. Instead, field houses are often erected to serve a double purpose. In a number of new schools the auditorium is so constructed that it may be divided into smaller spaces for lectures to medium-sized groups, for audio-visual work, or for other purposes. Thus a costly area that ordinarily stands idle most of the time is put to use throughout the day.

A nonprofit corporation called Educational Facilities Laboratories, Inc. has been aiding school districts in their attempt to erect economical but superior plants. Established by the Ford Foundation in 1956, E.F.L. has stated that its main purpose is "to help American schools and colleges with their physical problems by the encouragement of research and experimentation and the dissemination of knowledge regarding educational facilities." Headed by Dr. Harold B. Gores (1909–   ), this agency has discovered some remarkable facts about school construction.

In Montgomery County, Maryland, for example, the Board of Education was torn between the construction of a conventional box gymnasium and a field house with a geodesic dome. Thereupon, E.F.L. made two grants to finance a thorough study of comparative costs. The upshot was that the domed structure proved to be a better investment. It offered greater adaptability, freedom from obstructions, and more space for activities. Furthermore, it was shown to be far cheaper in the long run.

Another illustration comes from San Angelo, Texas, a community located in a warm, dry, dusty area. There, with the aid of an E.F.L. grant, school officials in 1956 opened the first circular, air-conditioned school in the world at a cost of only $8.96 per square foot.

Technically speaking, the Belaire School at San Angelo is not circular but decagonal. It consists of ten wedge-shaped rooms, eight of which are classrooms, built around an all-purpose area in the center. This geometrical arrangement is in keeping with the modern trend toward getting more use out of every square inch. Pentagonal and hexagonal schools and classrooms have become quite popular of late.

Another trend has been toward the construction of one-story plants. Contrary to general opinion, these are no more expensive than schoolhouses with two or more floors. The outlay for the land is small in comparison with construction costs—and the erection of stairways in multistory buildings runs to a considerable cost.

Several kinds of one-story school buildings have been evolved. In the campus plan, classrooms are grouped into small clusters. Among the chief values of this arrangement are the separation of younger children from older ones and the possibility of orderly, inexpensive expansion. One variation of this type of school is found in Scarsdale, New York. There the Heathcote Elementary School (opened in 1953) is set on 22 acres of rolling, sylvan land. Its decentralized hexagonal clusters are connected by enclosed corridors with a "core" which contains the administration offices, the gymnasium, the auditorium, and all kinds of special rooms.

Another variation of the campus plan is found in the new high school at Wayland, Massachusetts. This building, opened in 1960, is divided into six separate centers—arts, math and sciences, languages, social studies and business, administration, and physical education. The last is a domed field house similar to the one in Montgomery County, Maryland. Separated from the main building, it is designed to handle as many as 1,200 students; it serves as an auditorium as well as a place for athletics.

The purpose of the centers at Wayland is to enable a student to concentrate on the subject that interests him most. One of the problems in such a setup is rigid separation of subjects, but the entire faculty is trying to overcome this danger through interdepartmental meetings stressing correlation and teamwork.

In fact, team teaching is the new mode of instruction at Wayland. The building was designed specifically for such an approach. Rooms for large, medium, and small groups were built; also, places for individual study were provided since the chief aim of the program is to establish self-reliance.

Like Wayland, many other school systems are erecting new buildings in accordance with a predetermined instructional plan—one that seems best suited to the needs of the children in the particular community. In many districts where the team-teaching method has been decided upon, the new buildings feature removable partitions and operable walls that can be opened for large groups or closed for small groups. This may remind some readers of the rolling-door rooms that were built many decades ago as an economy measure to avoid the construction of an expensive auditorium. In most cases, however, the movable walls in the new buildings are reasonably soundproof. Although this feature may considerably increase the initial investment, it is claimed that its adaptability makes it economical in the end. Communities that wish to turn from team teaching to another method are not forced to build another new school—they merely adjust the size of the rooms by moving the walls.

The well-known doctrine that "form follows function" is not always easy to put into practice today, because school programs are in a state of flux. Educators and architects are carefully surveying the host of new experiments to see which will survive the test of time. They are also aware that technological advances may cause a new school to be educationally obsolete in a short time. Flexibility, therefore, is the chief objective. This covers everything from operable walls and zone-controlled heating systems to the installation of hundreds of outlets ready for the day when machines are to be used extensively. Some school systems, with an eye to the future, have even included television studios in their plans for new schools. In several cases, the studio space is now used as an additional office or visual-aids room, but is available for conversion if and when the administration wishes to institute ETV programs.

Long-run economy, as noted before, is the principal argument for making a new school versatile and adaptable. Once a building has gone up, alteration can be very expensive. Most school buildings last about 60 years before they deteriorate to a point where they are abandoned, but they can become educationally obsolete in less than a decade unless foresight has gone into their planning.

Economy, too, is the basis for a new idea that New York City is considering. High real estate costs on that tight little island are always a problem when building a new school. Consequently, a plan has been devised to combine a new office building and commercial high school. Thus, a great part of the bill for the site and construction would be paid by private interests. The design calls for separate entrances, floors, and elevators for office employees and students so that one group would not interfere with the other. However, if desired, a program to give some students vocational training in the business offices could easily be worked out.

New York City has also drawn up plans to include elementary schools on the first two floors of some new housing projects. These schools can easily be converted for residential or commercial use if necessary. This approach not only adheres to the concept of the neighborhood school but also attacks the potential problem of a shifting population. In the past, for example, schools have been built in areas teeming with children, only to have them become almost emptied because the age patterns of the residents have changed.

In California, Illinois, and elsewhere, windowless schools have been built by some communities. Again, economy is a factor because as much as one-fifth of construction costs can be saved. From the educational viewpoint, it is argued that pupils are able to concentrate better on their work when no outside noise or glare from the sun distracts them. Advocates of windowless, air-conditioned school buildings also claim that they are necessary in the coming era of year-round education. On the other hand, it is maintained that such schools may be psychologically bad because children need to look out the window once in a while as a release from tensions. There is also the aesthetic angle to be considered; schools without windows could easily take on a cold, institutional look.

New ideas abound everywhere in a country where the value of school buildings has soared to about $30 billion. There are new schools with landscaped courts, schools within schools, house plan schools, and even schools on stilts. In most cases they are the result of many conferences among boards of education, superintendents, principals, teachers, architects, parent leaders, and officials in various agencies of the city or town. Often they are regional schools built by two or more communities. Always they represent current and local ideas as to the best and safest framework for education.

Yet it must be remembered that there are still thousands of unsatisfactory school buildings throughout the country in communities that are unable or unwilling to provide the proper educational environment for their children. Many have wooden stairways and other potential fire hazards; others are structurally unsafe. There are schools without artificial light and with no central heating. Some have no flush toilets and no hand-washing facilities. Moreover, in many districts there are not enough schools, old or new. Classes are taught in firehouses, basements, old warehouses, private dwellings, and other unlikely places.

Until these conditions are corrected, Americans cannot look upon their schools with unmitigated pride. Presently we need more than 100,000 classrooms to keep up with the rising enrollment and to take the place of structures that have outlived their usefulness. Moreover, in the foreseeable future we will need an average of 60,000 new classrooms each year. Along with the recruitment and retention of teachers, this problem must be placed high on the priority list of every citizen who understands the importance of education.

Federal Aid to Education

Since colonial times, local responsibility for education has been jealously guarded by the American people. Initially this democratic concept was simple to execute. At a general meeting, natives of a village would decide to build a schoolhouse and hire a teacher. Each family then paid its share of the expenses; and any villager theoretically had a right to voice his opinions as to the content of the curriculum, the administration of the school, or any other matter affecting the education of the youngsters. But as the country grew, the problems became more complex. Villages overlapped and developed into towns; towns burgeoned into cities. Many families moved from one community to another and mingled with people of different backgrounds. Agreements and concerted action were increasingly harder to obtain.

As knotty situations needed unraveling, the state and the county were gradually given more power in school affairs. Taxes were levied at those levels, and funds were set aside for education. Soon a shuttle system evolved. The state derived its income largely through the taxation of citizens within its borders and then provided aid to local communities. In recent history, this system has usually benefited small towns and rural areas far more than the big cities.

And so purely local control of education lasted for only a relatively short period in the United States. As time went on, the individual communities still retained a most important role, but state legislation and county supervision began directing from the wings. Minimal qualifications and salaries for teachers were set; standards for buildings were fixed; curriculum was prescribed; and laws relating to pupils' attendance were adopted in state capitals.

But as some states grew richer than others, differences in educational opportunities in various parts of the country became more pronounced. The income of New York, for instance, grew to four times that of Mississippi. This problem was aggravated by the increasing mobility of the people. Families traveling from a wealthier state to a less fortunate one began to raise protests about the inferior schools in their new neighborhoods. The feeling arose that the federal government ought to correct such inequalities through financial aid.

Meanwhile Congress was enacting laws to increase federal revenue by means of taxation. And then in 1913 the Sixteenth Amendment enabled the government to levy a tax on personal income. After that, more and more money poured into the U.S. Treasury while the plight of the states grew worse each year. In the postwar period, from 1946 to 1959, state and local debts increased by more the 300 per cent, whereas the federal debt increased by only six per cent. Moreover, federal tax dollars increased 85 per cent during the same era while the annual cost of public education in the states was leaping from $284 per child to $496.

Behind these statistics is the startling fact that the burden still falls on the local property owner, a citizen who, in most cases, is already saddled with a long-term mortgage. Most of the tax money that is turned over to his community is for the school budget. Variations, of course, occur from state to state. Nebraska leans most heavily on the local property tax. There, 87 per cent of the money for school support is derived from that source. At the other end of the scale, the figure for Hawaii is only 7 per cent. More typical is New York, where 54 per cent of the revenue for schools comes from local property taxes and 43 per cent from the state. The remainder is from the federal government and the counties.

In recent years, local taxes have soared because boards of education have found it necessary to erect new buildings and raise teachers' salaries to an unprecedented degree. Some communities, as mentioned in our section "School Buildings Today," have reacted against this trend by rejecting the school budget in the voting booths. Increasingly, citizens have asked why the federal government, with all its vast resources, has not channeled money to the states for distribution to local schools. In this connection, it should be noted that in 1959 only four per cent of local and state costs of education were paid for by the federal government, as compared to 12 per cent for highways and 46 per cent for public welfare.

Heeding the demands of their constituents, legislators at Washington have been debating the question of federal aid ever since World War II. As a matter of fact, such support was recommended by the President's Advisory Committee as early as 1938. The committee suggested grants to the states ranging from $70 million in 1939–40 to $190 million five years later. But the advent of the war prevented Congress from taking any action relating to aid to schools.

After the war, however, Capitol Hill blazed with oratory on the subject. Three principal pieces of legislation emerged. The G.I. Bill helped thousands of veterans to get an education through federal funds. In 1950, Public Laws 815 and 874 provided funds for school districts affected by an influx of people connected with a federal project. In 1958, the National Defense Education Act authorized more than a billion dollars for loans to college students, grants for graduate study, and several other forms of assistance to schools and students.

None of these laws, however, provided for direct grants to the states, as had been recommended in 1938. Although school construction bills came up for consideration by the 84th and 85th Congresses, they were defeated. Arguments advanced against federal aid to states centered chiefly on the fear that such assistance would lead to indirect, and eventually direct, control over the administration and curriculum of local schools. Some people also contended that there was no real crisis in education. The states, they said, were dealing with their problems adequately. To extend federal assistance would be to encourage local communities to relax their own efforts to improve their school systems and would simultaneously bankrupt the federal government.

Powerful forces lined up against federal aid to education. Lobbies were led by the National Association of Manufacturers, the Farm Bureau Federation, and the Chamber of Commerce. Even the National School Boards Association opposed the idea on the ground that it was a threat to local autonomy. On the other side, the NEA kept up the attack in favor of the legislation. In this fight they were joined by unions like the AFL-CIO and by many liberals.

The post-Sputnik awakening of the American public, together with the devastating indictment in the Conant report on senior high schools, seemed to swing the tide in favor of federal aid to education. In 1957 the Gallup poll asked: "Do you favor or oppose federal aid to help build new public schools?" The results were: Yes—76 per cent; No—19 per cent; No opinion—5 per cent. It was further learned that "every major group in the population" approved of the federal aid proposal. The array in favor of the idea looked like this: Catholics —78 per cent; Protestants—75 per cent; Democrats—79 per cent; Republicans—74 per cent.

But the legislation ran into a new snag in the House of Representatives. Congressman Adam Clayton Powell (1908–   ), a Democrat from New York, insisted that no federal aid should go to segregated schools. Southern opposition to the "Powell rider" helped defeat bills offered during the late 1950's. The only important legislation that passed was the aforementioned N.D.E.A.

Then a wave of new hope buoyed up the advocates of national support to education when President John F. Kennedy (1917–   ) took office in 1961. In his campaign Kennedy had spoken unequivocally in favor of federal aid to public schools. True to his word, the new President outlined a plan in a message to Congress on February 20, 1961.

The Kennedy Bill, as it was later called, proposed appropriations amounting to $5.6 billion. Of this sum, $2.3 billion would go to public schools for building construction or teachers' salaries, at the option of the states. President Kennedy stipulated that each state would use 10 per cent of its allotment to help overcome problems in "areas of special educational need." This included slums and rapidly growing suburbs, as well as attention to the needs of exceptional children. He also recommended a sliding scale for the allotments. States like New York would receive a minimum of $15 per pupil, but poorer states like Mississippi would get as high as $29.67 per pupil.

Secondly, the Kennedy Bill recommended that another $1.25 billion be used for the expansion of the existing federal loan program for college dormitories. To start a new federal loan program for the construction of college classrooms and other academic buildings, $1.5 billion would also be allotted. Finally, Kennedy proposed that $577,-500,000 be set aside over a five-year period to be used for awards for more than two hundred thousand college scholarships based on need and ability. The average annual award would be $700, and the college of the student's choice would get an extra $350.

President Kennedy called the program a modest one. Some might have termed it provocative because of the heat of the debates that ensued. Some Catholic leaders took exception to the provision that the money allocated to the states was to go only to public schools. The President gave his opinion that aid to sectarian schools would violate the constitutional principle of separation of church and state.

The opposition that came from some sections of Catholic opinion was reminiscent of the resistance against the Barden Bill in 1949, in which $314,500,000 had been proposed for aid to public schools. Some of the Catholic press had protested against that measure, and it was defeated. Now the arguments for and against aid to sectarian schools were revived, and the issue was hotly debated in every part of the nation.

Whether President Kennedy was right in calling aid to parochial schools unconstitutional is a moot question. The problem rests upon interpretation of a clause in the First Amendment: "Congress shall make no law respecting an establishment of religion." The intent behind these words is not clear. Thomas Jefferson said that the purpose was to erect a wall of separation between church and state. But according to some historians, other early patriots thought that the words would merely convey the idea that no single church, like the Anglican Church of England, should be supported on a national basis.

It is also debatable whether the Supreme Court has contributed more light than confusion to the issue. In the Everson case in 1947, the justices held it to be constitutional for a state to provide public bus service for parochial school students. However, they added: "Neither a state nor the federal government can pass laws which aid one religion, aid all religions, or prefer one religion over another . . . no tax, in any amount, large or small, can be levied to support any religious activities or institutions, whatever they may be called, or whatever form they may adopt to teach or practice religion."

Then, in the Zorach case in 1952 the Supreme Court held that public schools may cooperate with churches in providing released time for religious classes so long as the instruction is not given on public property. In elucidating this decision, the justices made a statement that has since been cited by Catholics in support of their plea that federal loans be given to parochial schools. This *obiter dictum* reads in part:

"When the state encourages religious instruction and cooperates with religious authorities by adjusting the schedule of public events to sectarian needs, it follows the best of our traditions. For it then respects the religious nature of our people and accommodates the public service to their spiritual needs.

"To hold that it may not would be to find in the Constitution a requirement that the government show a callous indifference to religious groups. That would be preferring those who believe in no religion over those who do believe."

In the Cochran case, which emanated from Louisiana, the Supreme Court held that states may supply textbooks free to parochial school pupils on the grounds that the children, not the schools, were the beneficiaries, and that the books were not bought specifically for sectarian education. Eight states, incidentally, follow this procedure. Moreover, in 27 states parochial schools and other private institutions receive direct aid through the federal lunch and milk program; and about a dozen states provide additional health and safety services to parochial schoolchildren.

Some have maintained that President Kennedy also beclouded the issue when, in his bill, he drew no distinction between public and sectarian colleges eligible for federal grants of $350 per scholarship student. They say it is inconsistent to allow a church-related college to receive money and to deny allotments to church-related elementary and high schools. But precedent for this feature of the Kennedy Bill is found in the G.I. Bill of Rights, the college housing loan program, and the National Defense Education Act, all of which give federal aid to private and sectarian institutions of higher learning as well as to public ones.

The reasoning behind such aid is that higher education is voluntary and that tuition fees are charged, even at most public institutions. To this argument, Catholic leaders reply that their opponents are straining at gnats. Even elementary education, they claim, is not free; it is paid for by taxes. They add that Catholics are doubly taxed— once to send their neighbors' children to public schools, and again to send their own children to parochial schools.

There are more than five million pupils in schools operated by the Roman Catholic Church. They represent 12.5 per cent of our total school population. Their education is financed entirely by private funds—tuition fees, contributions, and endowments. Catholic spokesmen point out that if these children were enrolled in public schools, the present overcrowded condition in those institutions would be severely aggravated. Thus, they hold, it is unfair and discriminatory to withhold federal aid from state-approved parochial schools that are performing a public service and are simultaneously saving the taxpayers nearly two billion dollars a year.

Those who oppose the Catholic point of view argue that, as far as the state is concerned, the Catholic parents are free to send their children to public schools if they desire.* Therefore, they are entitled

* At present more than four million Catholic children attend public schools in the United States.

to no more consideration than those who elect to have their children educated in private, nonsectarian schools. Discrimination, they maintain, is a valid accusation only when the state deliberately routes the child into a different educational pattern, as in the case of Negroes in some southern states.

The National Council of Churches, with almost 40 million church members of Protestant and Eastern Orthodox background, contends that if private schools get public tax funds "full-scale parochial or private education with reliance on public tax support" would be undertaken. The Council further argues that "fragmentation of general education" would destroy or weaken the public school system.

The Protestant Episcopal Church, with about two million communicants, plans expansion of its 400 schools but is not in favor of federal aid. The same stand has been taken by Lutheran and Jewish groups operating their own school systems. These religious organizations fear that government interference and control, or favoritism at the least, will develop if the principle of separation of church and state is violated.

Those who would like to see the controversy settled offer a compromise: Let the individual states decide whether and how to aid non-public schools. This solution, however, is fraught with difficulties. The constitutions of 38 states expressly prohibit the use of public funds for sectarian schools, and 14 states deny assistance to any type of private school.

In such a maelstrom of pressures and counter-pressures, President Kennedy's proposals naturally ran onto reefs during the summer of 1961. Supporters of the Catholic viewpoint asked for an ironclad guarantee that another bill, enlarging the scope of aid for non-public schools, would get equal treatment on the floor of the House of Representatives. It was thought for a time that these provisions could be tacked onto the National Defense Education Act. But agreement could not be reached, and three bills incorporating the Kennedy recommendations died in the House Rules Committee—victims of religious and economic forces. Congress voted only to extend aid for two years to federally impacted school districts and to extend the N.D.E.A. to 1962.

In a bitter editorial on the above actions, *The New York Times* stated in September of 1961: "This session's shameful disregard of the nation's school needs and educational future will saddle Congress with a heavy burden of responsibility for years to come. The time wasted in strengthening the country's education is irreparably lost."

Desegregation of Schools

It is generally believed that desegregation is a new movement in southern schools. But in actuality it has had a long and tortured history. Before the Civil War there were a few mixed schools on plantations where owners simply included the Negro children along with their own. A few free Negroes got education along with white youngsters in the cities.

Reconstruction governments gave a great impetus to public education and legalized mixed schools. Ex-slaves were then developing a great enthusiasm for education and all that it seemed to promise for the renascence of the race. Negro workers were reported to be tilling the soil with a book attached to the plow so that every possible moment to study might be utilized. Not only children but also adults were active seekers of formal education.

When the military control of the South was withdrawn as part of the settlement of the disputed Tilden-Hayes presidential election, southern whites once more were in full control. They were virtually unanimous in their opposition to mixed schools forced upon them in some areas by the northern carpetbaggers. Negroes at that time had no effective leadership for the fight to retain what had been gained under the Reconstruction governments. There were, in fact, several instances in which they themselves opposed mixed schools. In both Alabama and South Carolina, Negro delegations told state legislators in no uncertain terms that there should be no such mixing of the races.

Throughout the remainder of the nineteenth century the educational position of the Negro deteriorated. Postwar interest in Negro education, as fostered by the Freedman's Bureau and private philanthropic groups of the North, had nearly died out. The historic Plessy vs. Ferguson Supreme Court Decision (in 1896) established, in effect, the principle that states may segregate the races if the two races are provided substantially equal facilities. Thus it became legal as well as traditional to keep Negroes and whites apart in such places as trains, waiting rooms, and schools. More than a half-century was to pass before the Supreme Court was to render any decision contrary to that theory.

The Negroes' situation in the last two decades of the nineteenth century became so desperate that many of them began to regard their struggle for equality as unrealistic. Consequently, they advocated a policy of conciliation, so that gains might eventually accrue through appeasement of the whites. The most famous Negro to uphold this attitude was Booker T. Washington (1856–1915). Born a slave, Washington had worked his way as a janitor through Hampton Institute. After teaching and studying for a number of years, he founded in 1881 the Tuskegee Institute in Alabama—a school for practical training of Negroes. It was Washington's idea that his people should cultivate the soil and gain economic stability by acquiring ownership of land. Stating that agitation for social equality was "folly," he urged Negroes to secure the good will of white persons and accept their philanthropy.

Some Negroes accepted Booker T. Washington's counsel, but when economic and social forces caused thousands of them to migrate to cities in the North and South, a more militant spirit emerged. It was typified by the establishment (in 1909) of the National Association for the Advancement of Colored People. Conciliation was denounced as an "Uncle Tom" attitude that would keep the Negro in semi-bondage for centuries to come. The NAACP organized a plan to gain for the Negroes what the Fourteenth Amendment had long promised them—"equal protection of the laws." In 1917 an educational program was launched to obtain as its initial objective decent elementary schooling for Negro children in the rural South. And in New York City the Committee on National Aid to Education was formed for the purpose of influencing the nation's lawmakers to take an active, sympathetic interest in the Negro's aspirations for true equality as an American citizen.

The early NAACP strategy in regard to public schools was to bring into the courts cases of unequal educational facilities being furnished for Negro children. A concentrated attack was made in border states, since it was realized that the principle of segregation would be harder to crack in the Deep South.

As a result of these efforts, changes came about. What happened in Virginia is an apt illustration. King George County floated a bond issue to build a modern Negro school. A federal court went so far as to fine the Gloucester County superintendent and the three men on his board of education for failing to comply promptly with its order for full equality.

Emboldened by success and spurred on by the growing demands of its membership, the NAACP enlarged its goals. No longer would Negroes be satisfied with equal facilities; hereafter their children were to be admitted to previously all-white schools. Five cases with varying backgrounds were brought through the courts. They originated in

Delaware, Kansas, South Carolina, Virginia, and Washington, D.C. Finally they reached the highest tribunal in the land.

It was on May 17, 1954, that Chief Justice Earl Warren (1891–   ) read the decision outlawing racial segregation in American tax-supported public schools. What confounded the legal prophets was not the principle laid down: the Supreme Court had been approaching that position for many years. The greatest surprise was that the decision was unanimous. Not one of the associate justices dissented from Warren's announcement: "We conclude that in the field of public education the doctrine of 'separate but equal' has no place. Separate educational facilities are inherently unequal."

This decision created a storm in the District of Columbia and the 17 states that were directly affected. The members of the court were described as leftists, destroyers of states' rights, and usurpers of legislative functions. It was also argued that the decision contradicted the findings of the Court in 1896 and hence was unconstitutional. On the last point, defenders of the justices noted that the Supreme Court is not bound by precedent, and that decisions of the past are not necessarily correct today. Times change, and the Court must change with them. There are numerous other instances in which the Court has reversed the decisions of another era.

Regardless of the arguments, either the Court had to be defied or action had to be taken in the South. In 1955 the Supreme Court, referring to the School Segregation cases, directed the lower federal courts to take whatever steps would be necessary "to admit to schools on a racially non-discriminatory basis, with all deliberate speed, the parties to these cases."

Three states—Alabama, Mississippi, and South Carolina—resisted the decision completely. By 1961 not a single school district in those states had been desegregated. At the other extreme, a flurry of immediate action took place in the border states. In Delaware and Kentucky this early response soon gave way to a counter-reaction which caused little more to be done. But in the District of Columbia, Maryland, Missouri, Oklahoma, and West Virginia every one of the school districts was desegregated, by policy at least, over a seven-year period.

Baltimore led the way in 1954. That city adopted a policy that gave every child the opportunity to attend the school of his choice on a first-come, first-served basis. At first the plan was resisted by some white extremists, but it soon resulted in widespread desegregation. Eventually it was copied in whole or in part by several cities in the North where residential segregation had separated Negro pupils from whites.

But in a few other places in the South, desegregation did not come so easily or quickly. Instead, the fears of the moderates were tragically realized; hate and violence erupted. Little Rock, Arkansas, is the prime example. In September, 1957, a screaming mob was held back by 1,000 federal troops with fixed bayonets while nine Negro students became the first of their race to enter Central High School. All the emotional turmoil that had been seething beneath the surface since 1954 seemed to come to a head at Little Rock, and the scars remained for a long time. A gubernatorial proclamation closed all four of the city's high schools in 1958, and they were not opened for the rest of that school year. But it must be noted that three years later 48 Negroes entered Central High, two other high schools, and four junior high schools without the slightest hint of violence—an indication that the people of Little Rock are basically as peace-loving as those in any other city. Though the majority still favored segregation in 1961, the consensus was that the law should be obeyed.

Clinton, Tennessee, came in for its share of ugly headlines. In the 1956–57 school year the high school there was desegregated. Mob riots followed; 600 National Guardsmen were called out; and the school was closed. Tensions mounted during the next year, although only eight Negro students were enrolled, as opposed to 12 in the previous term. White students continued to transfer elsewhere, and unpleasant incidents recurred. Then in October of 1959, just when it seemed that the community had adjusted to the change, the school was destroyed by dynamite. But here again the story has a happy ending. Contributions poured in from all over the world, and a new school, with better facilities than the old one, was soon erected. Peaceful desegregation became the accepted procedure at Clinton.

In 1960, New Orleans felt the brunt of the tension when four little Negro girls entered two formerly all-white elementary schools by order of a federal judge. Typifying extremists' resentment of this disruption of Deep South mores, jeering mobs of mothers lined the streets and precipitated riotous outbreaks. White parents who sent their children to desegregated schools were harassed and intimidated.

But a year later the continuation of the grade-a-year token desegregation plan at New Orleans was greeted without incident, even though it was expanded to include four additional schools. Part of the credit for this nonviolent reaction was attributed to Save Our Schools, Inc., an organization that had been working throughout the year to promote peaceful compliance with the law. In addition to S.O.S., the mayor, school officials, and the police cooperated in an all-out effort to keep things peaceful. As an illustration, the Mardi Gras slogan was rephrased from "The City that Care Forgot" to "The City that Forgot to Care."

But the absence of howling hordes in 1961 did not mean that New Orleans had accepted desegregation. Officials of the Citizens' Council, an anti-integration group, urged continuation of the white boycott which had practically emptied the desegregated schools in the previous year. Furthermore, legislators at the state capitol in Baton Rouge issued a resolution calling on parents opposed to desegregation to apply to the New Orleans school board for transfers to all-white schools.

Perhaps the most tragic result of the desegregation impasse is not the temporary flaring up of tempers but the loss of schooling. It has been estimated that from 1955 to 1960 more than a billion class-room hours were lost by children in the South while adults on both sides refused to yield.

The situation that developed in Virginia is an example of how children can become innocent victims of disagreements among their elders. Under the leadership of their governor, Virginians adopted a policy of "massive resistance" shortly after the Supreme Court's decision. In 1959, all the public schools of Prince Edward County were closed, and they remained shut through the following year. The county had been one of the original defendants in the School Segregation cases and it had received a direct order from the Federal District Court in Richmond to desegregate in 1959. Instead, white leaders established a privately subscribed fund of $200,000 and opened makeshift classes in vacant stores and church basements. The next year tuition grants from state and county funds supported the plan. The rates were $225 each for children in elementary grades, and $245 for high school students. These new "private schools" were fully accredited by the state and almost unanimously supported by the whites. In fact, a new modern secondary school was erected later through money collected by the Prince Edward School Foundation.

Meanwhile, Negro children throughout the county received virtually no education. Some attempts were made to establish training centers for them in churches and private homes but these efforts amounted to little more than "keeping them out of the rain." Their parents did not apply for the tuition grants since such an action would have defeated the very goals they sought.

In August of 1961, a federal court ruled that Prince Edward County could not use public funds to maintain private segregated schools as long as the public schools remained closed. The whites then attempted to raise $300,000 in "private funds" to keep their schools going, but some admitted that they could not hold out much longer.

Prince Edward County typifies the problem in rural areas in the South where Negroes outnumber whites. Prior to 1959 its 1,700 Negro children attended 13 schools, and its 1,450 white children were enrolled at seven other schools. There are 137 counties in the South with similar racial distributions or with an even greater percentage of Negroes. This situation, combined with the conservative viewpoints of the rural people, indicates that the road toward integration will be much rockier in the outlying districts than in the cities.

Virginia itself is typical of two main trends in the segregation issue: first, the concerted effort to use nonviolent means to thwart or delay desegregation; and second, grudging acceptance of the inevitable. From the beginning, Virginia's "massive resistance" policy caused the legislators to enact a tangled web of laws protecting their system of segregation. The compulsory attendance law was abolished; the state school system was placed under control of the governor, and the authority of local boards was removed; a pupil-placement board was established at Richmond to regulate transfers of all pupils throughout the state; and the aforementioned tuition grants were given to children electing to attend private schools.

But as fast as the lawmakers thought up new ideas, the courts knocked them down. By 1961 the resistance seemed to have lost its "massive" quality. In September of that year, 547 Negro pupils were accepted for enrollment in desegregated schools. They entered 75 formerly all-white schools in 19 communities. This figure represented an increase of more than 100 per cent over the 211 Negro youngsters who had been admitted on a desegregated basis in the previous year.

In fact, the month of September in 1961 appeared to mark a turning point in the South's fight against desegregation. Not only did 22 school districts move toward integration for the first time,* but

* In September of 1961, some degree of desegregation had been effected in 801 of the 2,813 bi-racial school districts in 17 southern states and the District of Columbia.

18 of them acted without direct court orders, and all the changes were accomplished without incident. The hard lessons learned at Little Rock and New Orleans had apparently been effective.

Dallas, Texas, and Atlanta, Georgia, are striking illustrations, even though some observers point out that in both cases only token integration was adopted. Elaborate preparations were made for the event. Church sermons, radio-TV coverage, newspaper campaigns, meetings of community leaders, orientation of teachers and students, and announcements at movies were some of the devices used to break down the resistance of bitter-enders. The citizens were reminded that the good name of the city would suffer, that business would be hurt, and that lives might possibly be lost if calm acceptance of the change did not prevail. Above all, obedience to the law of the land was stressed.

The desegregation process in Dallas had been preceded by five years of litigation. In 1960, Dallas had been the largest city in the country still resisting the Supreme Court ruling, and some of its citizens had loudly proclaimed their intention to continue outright defiance indefinitely. But months of careful planning under the leadership of Superintendent Warren T. White (1896–   ) and other officials permitted 18 Negro children to enter the first grade unchallenged and unmolested in September, 1961.* Thus, eight of the 124 elementary schools in Dallas were no longer completely segregated as the grade-a-year plan for admission of Negroes was inaugurated.

Similarly, the acceptance of nine Negroes by four white schools in Atlanta was a milestone in the history of desegregation. Until September, 1961, no school in all of Georgia had acceded to the Supreme Court's directive. It should be noted that Atlanta, like Dallas, adopted the "stair-step" policy of desegregating one grade each year, beginning with the first grade. Perhaps this factor, along with careful planning, was responsible for the calm acceptance of the change. In Little Rock, by contrast, the first steps toward integration had been taken at the high school level, while the elementary schools were scheduled to remain segregated until 1963. It is claimed that most white Southerners are less ready to accept desegregation for teenagers because they fear the mingling of Negro boys with white girls and

---

* In September, 1961, Dallas admitted 3,100 Negro children to the first grade. The number of Negroes who entered white schools was less than 1 per cent of the total enrollment of Negro pupils.

eventual miscegenation. Therefore, the Little Rock plan was almost sure to cause trouble.

Nashville, Tennessee, was one of the first southern cities to work out the grade-a-year plan. Acting under a court order in 1956, the school board made a child's place of residence the only criterion for his assignment to a school. An "escape valve" in the Nashville plan is that a child who has been assigned to a school in which he is a member of a racial minority may apply for a transfer to a school of his own race. This ruling not only stills the protests of whites living on the fringes of Negro neighborhoods, but also prevents a white majority from transferring to other schools just because a few Negroes have enrolled. Such an incident occurred at the Orchard Villa School in Dade County, Florida (1959). Originally all-white, the school became almost all-Negro one year after officials had adopted a policy of voluntary desegregation.

But the commonest device in southern communities where the whites desire little or no desegregation is the pupil-placement plan used in Alabama and at least nine other states. Under this arrangement, a Negro child is initially placed in an all-Negro school, but he may then seek a transfer to a white school. The theory behind the plan is that most Negroes either will be reluctant to "stir up trouble" or will succumb indifferently to the placement.

When a Negro parent attempts to fight this system, the application for a transfer is subjected to rather arbitrary standards. These criteria vary in different states, but some of them are as follows: emotional adjustment, home background, morals and health, scholastic aptitude, and adequacy of the child's former training. Other factors are the available space at the school to which a transfer is desired, the number of teachers, transportation, the effect of the admission on the educational program and on the other pupils, and the possibility that the transfer may cause disturbances.

Those who have devised the pupil-placement plan declare that it is nondiscriminatory since whites who wish to transfer to Negro schools are held to the same criteria. However, in actual practice, no whites ever apply for transfers to Negro schools. Thus, the policy holds down desegregation but is difficult to challenge legally. Furthermore, it puts federal judges in the position of placing Negro pupils in white schools one at a time after reviewing the facts in each case.

At first, the federal courts patiently tolerated such devices as long as the machinery for desegregation had been set up. But after several years the judges began to deal more firmly with the school districts. It was ruled, for example, that hostility of the community toward desegregation was no excuse. Also, several courts noted that the criteria were used differently for Negro and white pupils. When school authorities were ordered to apply their standards uniformly, the foundations of the pupil-placement plan were shaken.

Nevertheless, desegregation proceeded more deliberately than speedily. Six years after the history-making decision of 1954, a total of 213,532 of the South's three million Negro school children were attending classes with whites. In other words, segregation was the lot of approximately 93 per cent of the Negroes enrolled in southern schools, including the border states and the District of Columbia. In the eleven Old South states, segregation prevailed for more than 99 per cent of Negro children. A year later, in 1961, Texas was the only one of these eleven states to bring desegregation above the one per cent level.

Some observers have stated that inertia on the part of the legislative and executive branches of the federal government has contributed to the above situation. Too much was being left to the judicial branch. Although platforms of both major parties contained declarations in support of civil rights, neither Congress nor the President took much action beyond calling on troops to preserve order at Little Rock.

But these criticisms, mostly from Northerners, were partially answered in the fall of 1961 when the Civil Rights Commission unanimously exhorted Congress to require that every segregated district submit plans, within one year, for a first step toward desegregation. The six-man panel further proposed that federal educational grants to any state be cut as much as 50 per cent in proportion to the number of segregated schools. Among ten other recommendations made by the Commission was the suggestion that it be authorized to serve as a clearinghouse for information and counsel on procedures and problems in desegregating.

Many reasons are given for the reluctance of white Southerners to capitulate to the ruling of the Supreme Court. Scores of articles have been written on the economic basis for the resistance to change. Some attribute the attitude to fear, with deep emotional roots and sexual overtones. Historians note the feudalistic tradition of the old plantations, the resulting paternalism of the whites, and the Negroes' long-standing acceptance of southern ways—including separate but equal facilities. Others point out that even the most liberal white parents worry lest their children's education will suffer if they are mixed with Negroes having higher delinquency rates and lower academic achievement. In the rural areas, it is observed, this anxiety is compounded by the fact that the whites are often outnumbered.

Most white Southerners are shocked by the sudden demand that they forsake cherished traditions which, in their eyes, have worked for the best interests of both races. They resent the prodding of Northerners and they remind their Yankee critics that integration is far from a reality above the Mason-Dixon Line. They are especially bitter toward the National Association for the Advancement of Colored People for its unrelenting assertion of Negroes' rights by carrying case after case into the courts. In some quarters of the South they have sardonically substituted "Agitation" for "Advancement." Their contention is that the white man in the South, ever since the humiliating Reconstruction Period, has worked along with Negroes to help the entire group raise themselves higher and higher. They take special pride in sturdy, bright buildings newly erected for Negro children, and they note that in states like South Carolina teachers' salaries and requirements are the same for Negroes as for whites.*

Goaded by the NAACP, the white Southerners declare, the government is trying to compel people of different races to mingle against their will in schools and other places. Therefore, violence and hatred must erupt where harmony had once prevailed. "Give us time," they ask, "and greater gains for the Negro will evolve."

But the Negro leaders want no part of slow, haphazard evolution. They claim that advances can be accelerated and controlled, and that the Negro has been patient long enough. The NAACP admits its role as a gadfly but insists that the organization could not have achieved any success if the time had not been ripe for a change. In other words, the "new Negro" would have risen up against extremist whites with or without the NAACP—and perhaps the revolution would have been tinged with bloodshed if the organization, along with Negro ministers, had not steered the people into legal and peaceful channels.

As for the low scholastic level of Negro children in the South, spokesmen for the race argue that this situation stems from a vicious circle originated and nourished by the whites. They note the findings of psychologists that nature draws no color line in bestowing mental ability. But the heritage of servitude and illiteracy, together with

* It should be noted, however, that such gains for Negroes often came about as a result of the pressure of the NAACP.

"separate but unequal" schools, is a stone around the neck of the brown child. In brief, the Negroes' position is that poor environmental conditions have kept their children from realizing their true potential. They maintain that Negro schools, no matter how well equipped they may be, serve to perpetuate an evil, partly because many Negro teachers are themselves victims of culturally impoverished backgrounds.

In answer to the allegation that desegregation brings down the pillars of learning in white schools, the Negroes cite the cases of Washington, D.C. and other localities where school officials have produced figures showing that scholastic achievement has not been hurt by placing bright children of several races in the same class. Even if the results were discouraging, they contend, the step must be taken for the sake of democracy, because it is essentially unwholesome for children of one background to be shielded from daily contact with those of another ethnic origin. In fact, their argument goes, the mingling of races at school is good for each group of children since all will have a realistic opportunity to respect one another's rights and to shed prejudices born of ignorance.

Interestingly enough, the original battle for mixed schools was not fought in the grades but on the graduate school level. In its 1935 Murray vs. Pearson decision, the Supreme Court had ordered Maryland to admit a Negro applicant to its previously all-white law school because equal facilities had not been furnished for him elsewhere in the state. Maryland complied, and student Murray subsequently graduated, thereby setting a precedent in his state. But to forestall further applications, Maryland proceeded to purchase a private institution, renaming it Morgan State College, and setting it aside for Negroes.

The following year (1936), the Supreme Court gave similar orders to Missouri in the Gaines vs. Canada decision. Instead of capitulating immediately as Maryland had done, Missouri created Lincoln University and went through the motions of establishing graduate instruction in every field where Negroes applied for admittance at the all-white University of Missouri. Similar strategy was used in Oklahoma, Texas, and Arkansas.

The first frontal assault to break down segregation of higher learning in the Deep South came in 1956 at the University of Alabama. A long legal fight to compel the board of regents to admit a Negro girl named Autherine Lucy (1930–   ) resulted in riots of dangerous proportions, Miss Lucy's suspension as a matter of personal safety, and her final defeat because of a careless legal slip—the impugning of the personal integrity of regents members.

In January, 1961, two young Negroes of both sexes were finally enrolled at the University of Georgia. Again the pattern of student rioting and police indifference drove the pair off the campus temporarily. This time the NAACP made no errors, and the Negro students were restored to their classes. In the following summer session still another Negro enrolled for special class work, and in September history was made at Georgia School of Technology by the admission of Negro students.

All this pressure and resistance on various educational levels in the South has resulted in a deepening of bitterness between whites and Negroes. Optimists feel that an era of peaceful integration will arrive after the smoke of the transitional battle has dissipated. But others believe that the public school system in the South is doomed. They note the recent use of private schools for whites, and they argue that the only recourse left to segregationists is to abolish the public schools altogether. Judicial decisions as to the legality of this move may eventually determine the course that education will take in the South.

Certainly the Negro children and young adults who were the first to enter desegregated classes displayed great courage. As pioneers, they had to face a daily gamut of abuse and vilification, and the ever-present threat of bodily harm. Most of them met this challenge with dignity and good sense. The fact that only a few cracked under the social and academic pressures that had suddenly been thrust upon them is truly a tribute to their fortitude.

On the other hand, the effects of desegregation on white students have ranged from an intensification of hatred and contempt to a development of compassion and understanding. In some cases, the movement has caused quiet acceptance or casual indifference. Commenting on the enrollment of 48 Negroes in Little Rock schools in 1961, a white girl said: "We couldn't care less."

But the upheaval caused by desegregation has not been confined to the South. In many northern cities, after 1954, Negro leaders took issue with *de facto* segregation caused by discrimination in real estate practices and by the natural tendency of minority groups to cluster in separate communities. Before World War II, most educators in the North had shrugged their shoulders at all-Negro and all-white schools in big cities and suburbs. It was not their fault, they argued, but the result of residential patterns beyond their control. The concept of the neighborhood school was regarded as sacred, and the idea of allowing any choice whatsoever to elementary school pupils was considered akin to anarchy.

In some cases the we-can't-help-it claim proved to be an outright lie. Delving into the facts, Negroes discovered that some school districts in several large cities were being deliberately gerrymandered so that there would be no mixing of the races in fringe areas. Moreover, they discovered that some all-Negro schools were running on a double-session basis because of overcrowding, while nearby all-white schools were under-utilized. One group of Negro parents took an unexpected tour through a white school and found large classrooms turned over to guidance counselors as "offices," or entire floors vacant and unused.

Negro protests about segregation in northern schools brought a host of other factors into play. Some authorities were assailed by guilt and fear; in other cases, conservative leaders retired and were replaced by more liberal individuals. Finally, as in the South, federal judges ordered reluctant boards of education to bestir themselves immediately.

From 1954 to 1961, many varieties of the Baltimore plan for desegregating its schools cropped up in northern states. In September of 1960, the tremendous weight of New York City was thrown behind the movement when its Open Enrollment Program was adopted. Under the plan, pupils in schools with 90 per cent Negro or Puerto Rican registers are permitted to transfer from their home schools to others that are under-utilized by ten per cent or more.

The New York City leaders put Open Enrollment into effect with some trepidation. At the time there were approximately 600 elementary schools in the city, and 248 of them had Negro enrollments above 90 per cent. It was feared that wholesale applications for transfers would disrupt the entire system. But such worries proved to be unwarranted. In the first year only 397 children applied, a figure that represented merely three per cent of those eligible. In the second year the number rose to 2,831; yet this was still only a handful in comparison with the tens of thousands who might legally have applied. Apparently Negro parents wanted the right to send their children to nonsegregated schools but were still reluctant to dispatch them out of their neighborhoods. It was, in brief, the "principle of the thing" that counted most.

In the fall of 1961, the NAACP turned the spotlight on Chicago, claiming that at least 103 of that city's 462 elementary schools were virtually all-Negro and that too many of them were overcrowded. Chicago's superintendent defended the existing community school plan, but observers agreed that the Windy City would be forced to yield sooner or later to the hurricane of pressure for integration. As a comparable example, they pointed to the eventual capitulation (in 1961) of the Board of Education in New Rochelle, New York, where 267 Negro pupils transferred from the Lincoln Elementary School to eleven other schools after several years of litigation. In the New Rochelle case, the school board had thought itself to be beyond reproach because the Lincoln School was not all-Negro. "You can't desegregate a bi-racial school," the board president declared, but the courts turned a deaf ear to this plea.

Thus, the integrationists—whether Negro or white—have seen the tide turn slowly in their favor on southern and northern fronts. As more Negroes win and exercise voting privileges, this tide is likely to inundate segregationists. True integration, in which children work and play together in classrooms and on school playgrounds, is a long way off. But desegregation of schools is a fact of life. And just as the Freedom Riders and the sit-in demonstrators have been waging war on discrimination in buses and lunchrooms, so Negro youth will continue to storm the walls of all-white schools until segregation is conquered completely.

A Look Ahead: Some Hopes and Recommendations

Anyone who has read the preceding pages cannot help but realize the vast scope and complexity of the activities and problems that engage the attention of education today. From the simple methods of tribal training in primitive times we have developed a formal network of techniques and curricula for youths and adults having a wide variety of interests and needs. In the United States alone the cost of this program has gone beyond the $15-billion mark and will probably be doubled in less than a decade. All of this serves to underline the fact that the story of education is the story of the advance of civilization itself, from the fundamental struggle for survival to the many-sided cultural and social aspirations of the human brain and spirit. President Kennedy expressed this idea conversely for Americans when he stated: "Our progress as a nation can be no swifter than our progress in education."

How can we progress faster? And if we do, how can we be sure that progress is not retrogression in disguise? The answers to these questions are difficult to arrive at, but certain clues are obtainable from the experiences of the past and from an objective look at the present. Though we have only a vague idea of the kind of world that awaits tomorrow's adults, there are guidelines to follow and touchstones to apply as we try to plan an educational program that will continue to reach toward democratic ideals.

A primary principle in education, or any other field, is that goals should determine actions. But this is not as simple as it sounds because of the many conflicting forces crying for attention and priority. For example, a decision must be reached as to whether the school should relegate social objectives into the background and concentrate on academic achievement. In other words, is the acquisition of facts and skills more important than the development of attitudes and values? If both goals are important, how can the school accomplish one without cutting down the time and effort devoted to the other? Similarly, how can the sciences be stressed without neglecting the arts? It is understandable, therefore, that leading educators are seriously advocating the longer school year.

Even when goals are agreed upon, there seldom is unanimity as to the methods to achieve them. Two schools may agree that children must be taught how to read as early and as efficiently as possible. But one school may stress phonics and begin the training in kindergarten, while the other uses a contextual approach and delays the instruction until the child has reached a mental age of six or above. Although it often happens that several avenues to the same objective are equally good, still the problem points up the need for research and further experimentation. It also indicates that an expansion of services on the national level may be required. As noted before, some Americans believe that a body of distinguished citizens should be appointed in Washington to set minimal standards for local districts and to suggest distinctions between necessary subjects and merely desirable ones.

The chief objection to such a council is that local control may give way to federal dictation. It is akin to the fear that assails some people when discussions of federal funds for education arise.

But Americans must soon decide whether the system of local control is obsolete in theory and in fact. As one example, the establishment of a coast-to-coast network of educational television is a definite possibility. Already children in large areas are being instructed through television programs concocted by a small group of people. To give another illustration, teaching machines and electronic laboratories are now gaining popularity in the schools. As the use of these aids increases, it is conceivable that the course of education may be enormously influenced by programmers, studio experts, and writers. A board of education might find itself in the dilemma of either buying a curricular package of recognized efficiency or lagging behind with its homemade, but democratically evolved, program of learning.

A related problem, then, is the role that agencies outside the school should play in the training of tomorrow's youth. Certainly school leaders must be flexible enough to adjust their goals and programs to technological developments. But the day may come when local boards and superintendents find that their control has been taken away by a *troika* of technical industries, Madison Avenue men, and government on the state and federal level. It is not claimed here that such an eventuality is necessarily detrimental to education. A case could be made, for instance, against thousands of politically orientated, semiliterate, and openly hostile boards of education that do the children more harm than good. However, the essential point is that if the transfer of control is made at all it should come from a clear assessment of the pros and cons—not from blind and gradual abrogation of local powers.

Consequently, it is incumbent upon educators to double their efforts to involve the community in school matters. Despite much progress in this area in recent decades, there are many localities where the average citizen knows little or nothing about the schools. Boards of education need to advertise their open meetings widely, and to use other methods to increase attendance. Newsletters, questionnaires, and other forms of communication should be sent to the homes so that the public will know the problems and decisions of their board. This assumes, of course, that board members of the future will be capable and confident people with the best interests of public schools at heart. Otherwise local control will—and probably should—continue to drift away into the hands of state and federal authorities.*

Simultaneously, parent-teacher groups should make an effort to attract more fathers, to conduct provocative and informative meetings, and to involve themselves in activities above the level of mere fund-raising. One job that must be done—and is not done by most PTA's—is to conduct hard-driving campaigns arousing the public to elect the best people to the board of education, and whipping up support of school budgets. Another PTA function might be to show

* In 1960, local governments in the United States were footing 52 per cent of the bill for education; state governments were paying 42 per cent; and federal and county governments were contributing 6 per cent to the total.

alertness, candor, and creativity about matters relating to school policy. Downright interference with administrative actions is not recommended, but the PTA of tomorrow must be a force that the superintendent and his board will respect, not a rubber stamp subservient to the will of the men at the top.

Finally, superintendents and principals need to extend a hand of welcome to parents and give them a greater share in educational planning. The axiom that responsibility generates interest is important to remember; parents who participate actively in school affairs usually become enthusiastic supporters of the program and help to interpret it to others. And in the years to come, educators are going to need all the assistance and support they can get from the community.

It is generally agreed that no single area calls for more extensive community understanding than the status of teachers. Citizens ought to know more about teachers' salaries and the conditions under which they work. The professional standards for teachers in a particular locality or state must be measured objectively in the light of standards elsewhere. Throughout the nation a concerted effort is required to attract and retain highly qualified teachers, since they will continue to be the heart and soul of any school program.

Any student of the history and progress of education will also concur that the quality of the schools greatly depends on the quality of their leadership. Movements are already under way to choose principals and superintendents with care, to demand that their qualifications be superior, and to pay them well for the tremendous responsibilites they assume. In many communities, boards of education have been appointing advisory councils of outstanding citizens to recruit and screen applicants for supervisory positions. Placement offices of graduate schools of education have also been playing an increasingly important role in the selection process. Whatever is done, objective analysis of all candidates seems to be of the greatest importance. Since the supervisors of the future will be confronted with problems even more complex and technical than those faced by their counterparts of today, it would be a betrayal of the children's interests if boards of education were to select candidates on the basis of *whom* rather than *what* they may know.

One thing the administrators will have to come to grips with is the drop-out rate of high school students, especially those who are retarded or underprivileged. Today American schools are making an effort to combat the charge that they are primarily for the "rich and ready," but giant steps must be taken in this direction so that the movement will not be swallowed up by the growing demand for harder and more stimulating courses for gifted children. The recent surge of community colleges and junior colleges is one hopeful sign. As a corollary, the interest in programs like Higher Horizons is encouraging, too. Developing the latent talents of children from low-income families will not only soothe Americans' consciences but, more important, will substantially aid the cause of democracy.

In the final analysis, the greatest task of American education in the near and distant future will be to insure the survival of democracy and to defeat Moscow-Peking Communism, not through war but through a many-sided effort to promote culture, prosperity, and good will. The United States and the USSR are not necessarily on a "collision course" that will lead to Armageddon, as many defeatists claim. Communism can be stifled and eventually asphyxiated by the peaceful advance of democratic achievements. The air it breathes has several known elements: ignorance, illiteracy, hunger, weaknesses of rival ideologies and nations, distrust of capitalism, and blind prejudice. The positive approach to survival, then, is to reduce those elements to an ineffectual state.

Aside from our efforts to prevent war by building our national defenses, the United States has moved along other lines to choke off the threat of Communism. The Peace Corps, the exchange program for teachers and students, the extension of international education, the movement toward desegregation of schools, the revival of the study of world geography in the curriculum, and the new scope and emphasis of our foreign aid program—all these are fingers around the throat of totalitarian tyranny, whether it comes in the form of Communism or Fascism. We cannot afford to let up in any one of these areas; in fact, we are compelled to expand them even if this calls for great personal sacrifice.

From kindergarten up through graduate school, a concerted effort is required to build in American children a social and civic awareness that transcends nationalistic boundaries. Leaders of the future will have to be well-informed and well-balanced individuals who have been trained to see the world as a place where destinies are interlocked. It follows, therefore, that the citizenry must be educated enough to choose leaders through criteria of skill, poise, and vision— not through an appreciation of the candidate's pleasant smile or his empty eloquence.

How can this be done? Immediately, one thinks of geography, history, and civics as the key subjects along with a foundation in reading. But the need extends into every area of the curriculum, including the guidance program. It involves a deep plunge into the fields of human relations, ethics, and morality—all of which have been neglected to some extent in a "things-centered" and science-minded society. Concepts of service, sacrifice, and sensitivity to others must be given utmost importance. The adult of the next generation must be inculcated with the idea that he is indeed his brother's keeper and that rugged individualism, whether on a personal or national basis, cannot lead to anything but the destruction of democracy—just as it did in ancient Athens.

Nor can the schools afford to waste time in this effort. Lost moments today may be paid for bitterly tomorrow. Although it may seem melodramatic to state the case so urgently, the facts cannot be controverted. An anxious world looks toward the United States for leadership in the discovery of peaceful solutions to problems that are literally and figuratively explosive. The future of this leadership lies largely in the classroom, and the success or failure of the schools will forever affect the destiny of mankind.

Index

Abelard, Peter, 150
Abnormal psychology, 332–337
Absence from school, causes of, 238–239
Academic freedom in America, 150–154
Academies, American, 100, 117
Acceleration classes, 242, 435
Accounting procedures, 235–240
Achaeans, 15
Achievement tests, 321–322
Administration of schools, 190–193
Administrative officers, 216–219
Adolescent psychology, 327–332, 438
Adult education, 129–134
Advanced placement, 435
Adventure schools, 111
Aegean civilization, 15
Aesop, 21, 111
Agriculture, teaching of, 75, 109, 123, 133
Aides for teachers, 446–449
Alabama, University of, 472
Alcuin, 38
Alexander the Great, 24, 334
Alexandria, library in, 24, 120
Alfred the Great, 38
Allen, James E., 198
Allgemeine Landrecht, 68
American Association of School Administrators, 84, 425
American Education, 93–158
   academic freedom in, 150–154
   adult and part-time, 129–134
   economic influences on, 154–158 (*see also* Economic influences on education; Industrial Revolution)
   elementary, 110–115
   in eighteenth century, 97–102
   of handicapped children, 78, 107, 134–139, 440–441
   higher education, 120–125
   morality as aim in, 139–145

American Education—(*Continued*)
   in nineteenth century, 102–105
   preschool, 125–129
   religion in, 145–150
   scientific, 75
   secondary, 115–120
   seventeenth-century, 93–97
   social realism in, 56
   training of teachers in, 351–355
   in twentieth century, 106–110
   universities in, 45
American Education Fellowship, 83
American Education Week, 271, 431
American Federation of Teachers, 370, 378
American Foundation for the Blind, 135
American Library Association, 251
American Revolution, 100, 113, 123, 146
American School Board Journal, 213
Amidon School, 439
Ancestral tradition, authority of, 7
Anderson, Theodore, 413
Anglo-Saxon Chronicle, 38
Antioch College, 105
Antisthenes, 26, 27
Apostles, 7
Apperceptive psychology, 306
Aptitude testing, 435
Aquinas, Saint Thomas, 42, 141, 283
Architectural planning, 232, 449–455
Aristocracy of learning, 10, 12, 17, 28, 39, 94, 99
Aristotle, 24, 25, 26, 33, 41, 42, 49, 54, 70, 74, 120, 121, 139, 155, 276–277, 283, 285, 286, 288
Arithmetic, teaching of, 21, 24, 30, 38, 40, 51, 53, 97, 99, 113
Army Alpha and Beta Tests, 304
Art, teaching of, 29, 46, 60
Asia Minor, 22, 24

481